Beyond micro-cred

Beyond micro-credit

Putting development back into micro-finance

Thomas Fisher and M.S. Sriram

With contributions from:

Malcolm Harper
Ajit Kanitkar
Frances Sinha
Sanjay Sinha
Mathew Titus

Vistaar Publications
New Delhi

Oxfam
Oxford, UK
Published in association with

New Economics Foundation, London

Distributed exclusively in South Asia (India, Pakistan, Bangladesh, Nepal, Bhutan, the Maldives, and Sri Lanka) by Vistaar Publications (A division of Sage Publications India Pvt Ltd), 32 M-block Market, Greater Kailash-I, New Delhi 110 048.

Distributed exclusively outside South Asia by Oxfam Publishing, 274 Banbury Road, Oxford OX2 7DZ, UK. Tel.: +44 1 865 311 311; Fax: +44 1 865 312 600; E-mail: publish@oxfam.org.uk; Website: www.oxfam.org.uk/publications.

Distributed exclusively in the USA for Oxfam GB by Stylus Publishing LLC, PO Box 605, Herdon, VA 20172-0605, USA. Tel.: +1 703 661 1581; Fax: +1 703 661 1547; E-mail: styluspub@aol.com; Website: www.styluspub.com.

First published in 2002 by Vistaar Publications, 32 M-block Market, Greater Kailash-I, New Delhi 110 048.

Oxfam GB is co-publishing and distributing *Beyond Micro-credit: Putting Development Back into Micro-finance* with Vistaar Publications as part of its work in disseminating interesting and challenging contributions to development practice and learning.
Oxfam GB is a registered charity, no. 202918

A CIP catalogue record for this book is available from the British Library.

ISBN: 085598-488-0 (PB)

Table of contents

List of tables   9
List of figures   10
List of boxes   11
List of abbreviations   12
Acknowledgements   16

1. Introduction   19
2. Introduction to the financial sector in India   33

Part One: Micro-finance and development

3. Micro-finance and social and economic security   49
4. Micro-finance and livelihoods:
   The challenge of BASIX   73
5. Micro-finance and people's organisations   104
6. Micro-finance and system-wide change   137

Part Two: Micro-finance: Organisations and institutions

7. Self-help groups and Grameen Bank groups:
   What are the differences?   169
   Malcolm Harper
8. Costs in micro-finance: What do urban
   self-help groups tell us?   199
   Mathew Titus
9. Exploring empowerment and leadership at
   the grassroots: Social entrepreneurship
   in the SHG movement in India   234
   Ajit Kanitkar
10. Sustainability and development: Evaluating
    the performance of Indian micro-finance   263
    Sanjay Sinha and Frances Sinha

11. Rising to the challenge of scale in India:
Growing the micro-finance sector   300
Mathew Titus

12. Emerging lessons and challenges   325
Thomas Fisher

Appendix: Capacity-building and organisational
learning project for development finance in India   361

Glossary   370
Bibliography   372
Index   380
About the authors and contributors   389

List of tables

Table 2.1: Present rural financial system in India   44

Table 3.1: Incidence and cost of economic
stress events   58

Table 4.1: BASIX' seven I's of new generation
development finance   78

Table 4.2: Comparing financial indicators for
BASIX and fully sustainable micro-finance
organisations reported in the *Microbanking
Bulletin* (as on 31 March 2000)   81

Table 4.3: BASIX clientele by type and sector   84

Table 5.1: SHGs, their clusters and federations,
promoted by the DHAN Foundation   117

Table 6.1: BASIX' characterisation of existing and
new generation financial intermediaries   146

Table 7.1: Summary of the pros and cons of
the SHG and Grameen systems   170

Table 8.1: Areas and financials of Sharan's
SHG programme (March 1996)   206

Table 9.1: The life-cycle of an SHG
(as set out by PRADAN)   239

Table 10.1: MFOs rated by M-CRIL up to
November 2000   269

Table 10.2: M-CRIL sample totals   270

Table 10.3: Different approaches to
impact assessment   285

Table 10.4: Summary of impact assessment
studies of micro-finance in India   286

Table 11.1: The role of stakeholders in
developing the micro-finance sector   314

List of figures

Figure 1.1: Combining outreach and sustainability   20

Figure 2.1: Hierarchy of credit needs and credit
availability from formal sources, leading
to 'adverse usage'   40

Figure 3.1: Moving out of the vicious cycle of poverty   63

Figure 4.1: The pyramid of rural producers
and BASIX clientele   83

Figure 8.1: Three functions that contribute to
the costs of promoting SHGs   201

Figure 8.2: Structure of SHGs and federations
promoted by Sharan   206

Figure 10.1: MFOs' sources of funds   274

Figure 10.2: Utilisation of funds by MFOs   276

Figure 10.3: Relationship between portfolio
size and efficiency   278

Figure 12.1: The organisational pyramid   341

List of boxes

Box 2.1: Chronological summary of development
initiatives with the Indian financial system   34

Box 3.1: SEWA Bank and the SEWA movement   51

Box 3.2: Insurance services provided by SEWA
Bank in 2001   59

Box 4.1: Summary of technical assistance and
support services provided by BASIX   87

Box 6.1: Policy work by BASIX   145

Box 6.2: Sa-Dhan, the association of Indian MFOs   151

Box 6.3: SEWA campaigns   155

Box 10.1: Micro-Credit Ratings International Limited
(M-CRIL): An innovative organisational
mechanism for Asian micro-finance   264

Box 10.2: Clients have diverse credit needs   291

List of abbreviations

AIMS	Assessing the Impact of Micro-enterprise Services (programme of USAID)
AKRSP	Aga Khan Rural Support Programme
APDDCF	Andhra Pradesh Dairy Development Cooperative Federation
APMAS	Andhra Pradesh Mahila Abhivruddhi Society (capacity-building organisation for savings and credit groups)
ASA	Activists for Social Alternatives (NGO in Tamil Nadu)
ASA	Association for Social Advancement (MFO in Bangladesh)
ASSEFA	Association for Sarva Seva Farms (NGO based in Chennai)
AWID	Association for Women's Rights in Development (based in Toronto, Canada)
BAAC	Bank for Agriculture and Agricultural Cooperatives, Thailand
BASICS	Bhartiya Samruddhi Investments and Consulting Services Ltd, Hyderabad
BASIX	Name of the group of companies of which BASICS is the holding company (see Chapter 4, note 2)
BRAC	Bangladesh Rural Action Committee (MFO)
BRI	Bank Rakyat Indonesia
CBGP	Community-based Group Promoters (of SHGs supported by PRADAN)
CDF	Cooperative Development Foundation (NGO based in Hyderabad)
CDRA	Community Development Resource Association (NGO in South Africa)
CEO	Chief Executive Officer
CGAP	Consultative Group to Assist the Poorest (consortium of donors on micro-finance, based at the World Bank)

CSA	Customer Service Agent (of BASIX, Hyderabad)
DflD	Department for International Development (British aid agency)
DID	Desjardins International Development, Canada
DHAN	Development of Human Action (Foundation) (NGO in Tamil Nadu)
DOW	Development Organisation for Women (NGO in Tamil Nadu)
DWCRA	Development of Women and Children in Rural Areas (Indian government programme)
FAMIS	Financial Accounting and Management Information System (of BASIX)
FWWB	Friends of Women's World Banking, India (based in Ahmedabad)
GB	General Body or federation of SHGs in Barhi block of Hazaribag district, Jharkhand
GIC	General Insurance Corporation, India
GTB	Global Trust Bank, India
GTZ	German technical assistance agency (Deutsche Gesellschaft für Technische Zusammenarbeit)
HDFC	Housing Development Finance Corporation, India
HUDCO	Housing and Urban Development Corporation, India
IBP	Individual-banking Programmes (category used by the rating agency M-CRIL)
ICICI	Industrial Credit and Investment Corporation of India Ltd
IDPM	Institute for Development Policy and Management, University of Manchester, UK
IDS	Institute of Development Studies, University of Sussex, UK
IFAD	International Fund for Agricultural Development (United Nations agency)
IFC	International Finance Corporation (World Bank affiliate)
IGS	Indian Grameen Services (part of the BASIX group, Hyderabad)
IIM-A	Indian Institute of Management, Ahmedabad
ILO	International Labour Organisation (United Nations agency)
IRDP	Integrated Rural Development Programme (Indian government programme)

KfW	German development bank (Kreditanstalt für Wiederaufbau)
LAB	Local Area Bank (operating in up to three contiguous districts in India)
LIC	Life Insurance Corporation of India
LINK	Livelihood Initiatives in Northern Karnataka
Ltd	Limited (company)
MACS	Mutually-aided Cooperative Society (a new form of cooperative autonomous of government control)
MBB	*Microbanking Bulletin*
M-CRIL	Micro-Credit Ratings International Limited (based in Gurgaon outside New Delhi)
MD	Managing Director
MFI	Micro-finance institution
MFO	Micro-finance organisation
MIS	Management information system
MYRADA	Mysore Resettlement and Development Agency (NGO based in Bangalore)
NABARD	National Bank for Agriculture and Rural Development, India
NBFC	Non-banking finance company
NCL	National Centre for Labour, India
NEF	New Economics Foundation
NGO	Non-governmental organisation
NORAD	Norwegian Agency for Development Cooperation
OBC	Oriental Bank of Commerce, India
OBC	Other Backward Castes (formal categorisation in India)
ODI	Overseas Development Institute, London
OSS	Operational self-sufficiency (financial measure)
PAR	Portfolio at risk (financial measure)
PCO	Public call office
PKSF	Palli Karma Sahayak Foundation, Bangladesh
PRADAN	Professional Assistance for Development Action (NGO based in New Delhi)
Pvt. Ltd	Private limited (company)
RBI	Reserve Bank of India (India's central bank)
Re	Indian Rupee
RGVN	Rashtriya Gramin Vikas Nidhi (foundation for the north-eastern states in India)

RMK	Rashtriya Mahila Kosh (National Credit Fund for Women, India)
RNBC	Residuary non-banking companies (NBFCs that can raise unlimited deposits but must place 80 per cent of them in government or bank deposits)
ROSCA	Rotating savings and credit association
RRB	Regional Rural Bank, India
Rs	Indian Rupees
SANASA	Sinhala acronym for the movement of thrift and credit cooperative societies in Sri Lanka
SDC	The Swiss Agency for Development and Cooperation (bilateral aid agency)
SDI	Subsidy Dependence Index (financial measure)
SEWA	Self-employed Women's Association (union based in Ahmedabad)
SFMC	SIDBI Foundation for Micro-credit, India
SHARE	Society for Helping, Awakening Rural Poor through Education (NGO based in Hyderabad)
SHG	Self-help group (savings and credit group in India)
SIDBI	Small Industries Development Bank of India
SJSY	Swarna Jayanti Swarozgar Yojana (Indian government programme that succeeded the IRDP and other programmes for supporting poor self-employed people)
UK	United Kingdom
UNDP	United Nations Development Programme
USA	United States of America
USAID	United States Agency for International Development
UT	Union Territory in India
WWB	Women's World Banking

Acknowledgements

In addition to those to whom this book is dedicated, who have provided us so much friendship, insight and inspiration, both as individuals and through their organisations, we would like to thank the five experts who have contributed so much to Part Two of this volume: Malcolm Harper, Ajit Kanitkar, Frances and Sanjay Sinha and Mathew Titus. Titus has also helped facilitate this book within the Indian micro-finance sector. We would also like to thank Jenny Chapman and Dave Harding who wrote informative background papers on social enterprises and on capacity-building.

This book would not have been possible without the generous support of the Ford Foundation, New Delhi for the long-term project that enabled the New Economics Foundation to engage in the micro-finance sector in India. This book concludes the project. Special thanks to Jane Rosser who helped design the project and supported it through its early years with such enthusiasm and determination, and to Rekha Mehra who ably saw it to its completion.

At the New Economics Foundation, Thomas would like to thank Genevieve Matthews for providing vital support, Sarah McGeehan who managed the team so well while I was in India and Ed Mayo for his encouragement and inspiration. Dave Harding, my mentor, also provided much food for thought during the project which led to this book.

Thanks also to Bharti, Sushil and Divi who provided such hospitality when finishing the manuscript in Delhi, to Mum and Dad while doing the proofs, and to Julie who was so supportive and loving throughout the process of bringing this book into reality.

For Thomas this book marks the end of 12 years of work on livelihoods in India—thanks to all the organisations I worked with, especially BASIX, CDF, PRADAN and SEWA Bank, and above all to my many friends and colleagues, especially Vijay and Savita, for such generosity and inspiration, which has made my experience of India so profound. I am particularly indebted to Vijay for all his support over 12 years and his deep experience which has informed so much in this book.

At the Indian Institute of Management, Ahmedabad, Sriram would like to thank Professor Gopal Naik for his encouragement. Thanks also to appa and amma for understanding the pressures of work, and to Gowri and Arjun for being a source of strength, as always.

We hope that the book will contribute in its own small way to the development of micro-finance in India, and make the richness of Indian micro-finance practice better known and understood.

Delhi and Ahmedabad
March 2002

Thomas Fisher
M.S. Sriram

Chapter 1

Introduction

Micro-credit has become a major tool of development, and is fast developing as an international industry, with its own trade associations, dedicated finance, training and other support organisations, research and journals. In a phase in the international development endeavour in which ideology is out of fashion, the search is on for practical, workable solutions to the deep-seated challenges of poverty. Micro-credit seems to provide just such a solution.

By delivering financial services at a scale, and by mechanisms appropriate to them, micro-credit can reach poor people. By providing poor people with credit for micro-enterprise it can help them work their own way out of poverty. And by providing loans rather than grants the micro-credit provider can become sustainable by recycling resources over and over again. In other words, micro-credit appears to deliver the 'holy trinity' of outreach, impact and sustainability. No wonder the development sector has become so excited.

International debate has been dominated by two schools of thought, which we call the finance school and the poverty school. Sometimes these schools have been in conflict with each other. The former celebrates the mainstreaming of micro-credit as a financial service (BancoSol, a micro-finance bank in Bolivia, has sold certificates of deposit on Wall Street), the latter emphasises the need to reach poor people and may be suspicious of financial sustainability, believing it is likely to lead a micro-finance provider away from its focus on poorer clients.

The micro-credit industry has sought to resolve the tensions between a focus on poverty and a commitment to sustainability by integrating them within a matrix defined by two axes, of outreach (or access) and financial sustainability.

Figure 1.1: Combining outreach and sustainability

High sustainability

2. Sustainable financial services with low access by target clients	1. Sustainable financial services reach target clients
3. Highly subsidised financial services with low access by target clients	4. Highly subsidised financial services reach target clients

Low access   **High access**

Low sustainability

Source: Mahajan and Ramola (1996).

The formal financial sector may achieve financial sustainability, but has little outreach to poor clients (quadrant 2 in Figure 1.1). Traditional efforts by non-governmental organisations (NGOs) may reach poor clients, but are often unsustainable (quadrant 4). Good micro-finance practice, on the other hand, combines both outreach and sustainability in the virtuous quadrant 1. Such practice is perhaps most clearly embodied in the micro-finance bank, which marries the best of the formal financial sector in terms of sustainability with the outreach to poor clients of the development NGO.

This book argues that if such a framework is allowed to dominate debate and practice, as it often has, it will severely limit the potential developmental ends to which micro-finance, as a means or instrument, can be put. The industry has become dominated by a techno-managerial perspective, with a large number of technical manuals and courses on how to manage micro-financial services and financial sustainability, and how to achieve outreach.[1] In the process, the development impetus which first gave rise to micro-finance is often lost (except in the narrowest sense of outreach to poor people).

It is time to put development back into the provision of micro-financial services, and for this we need to go beyond micro-credit. Going beyond micro-credit has usually been framed in terms of including micro-financial services other than credit for micro-enterprise: savings, consumption loans and insurance in particular (Rutherford, 2000). In other words, micro-finance can embrace a range of financial services that seek to meet the needs of poor people, both protecting them from fluctuating incomes and other shocks, and helping to promote their incomes and livelihoods (Rogaly et al., 1999).

In this book we seek to explore developmental purposes to which micro-finance can be put that go well beyond integrating a range of micro-financial services for poverty alleviation. We include livelihood promotion, developing the local economy, empowerment, building democratic people's organisations, and changing wider systems or institutions within society. We elaborate on the practice of using micro-finance to address these developmental objectives in the first part of the book.

Putting development back into micro-finance presents challenges to all those involved in micro-finance. Technical experts in micro-finance need to see that there is more to the provision of micro-financial services than technical and managerial inputs to enhance performance and efficiency. Micro-finance organisations (MFOs) may be well managed financial organisations, but are they developmental? Indeed, if micro-finance is to achieve any developmental outcomes, the nature of these inputs must be shaped and guided by a clear understanding of the developmental outcomes sought.

The same applies to those who have apparently resolved the tension between the demands of development on the one hand and of managing financial services on the other by combining outreach with sustainability. With millions of poor people in developing countries still unbanked, there is clearly a need for the provision of micro-financial intermediation at a mass scale, and this can often only be achieved through sustainability. In this sense, the combination of outreach and sustainability is developmental. However, there is much more to development than the provision of financial services. Micro-financial services on their own are clearly not going to solve poverty, but can only serve as a complementary tool within a broader strategy to reduce poverty.

Putting development back into micro-finance also presents challenges to the poverty school. Too often, debates on poverty and micro-finance have been limited to the number of clients reached, to income and the gendered control of resources within the household, and to impacts on different categories of poor people, from the destitute to those just below the poverty line. The poorest people have been a particular focus of attention, even though many others also have valid and developmental financial needs.

A narrow focus on micro-financial services for poor people has therefore often hidden the range of development purposes to which micro-finance as an instrument can be used. As just two examples, we illustrate micro-finance practice that suggests the need to lend to the non-poor to generate wage-employment for poor people (Chapter 4), and that an exclusive focus on poor people may work against the development of effective local democratic organisations (Chapter 5).

Research on outreach and impact on poor people has also not contributed significantly to better product development (Rutherford, 2000: 109) or to strategies on how to combine micro-finance provision with developmental outcomes for poor people that go beyond access to financial intermediation (however necessary the latter is).

Finally, putting development back into micro-finance presents a challenge to the growing number of critics of micro-finance. Development is concerned, on the one hand, with ideology and processes that underlie current economic structures, and, on the other, with practical solutions to address either the immediate needs of poor people or to change the underlying structures. Ideological critiques are only helpful if they contribute to the process of finding such practical solutions.

This book explores practical initiatives to use micro-finance instrumentally to address a range of developmental needs. This is the key challenge for the micro-finance industry: to find how micro-finance as an instrument can be combined *in practice* with appropriate developmental objectives to achieve positive change.

This challenge can only be met by organisations that seek to combine micro-financial services with clear development missions. Such organisations fall into a category that is sometimes referred to as 'development enterprises' and increasingly (at least in the industrialised world) as 'social enterprises'.

The organisation of micro-finance is therefore at the heart of this book, both in Part One and then in Part Two, from small local savings and credit groups to developing the whole micro-finance sector in India. The organisational challenges of combining often broadly conceived developmental goals with the technical delivery of micro-financial services are a key theme of the analysis. Organisational sustainability, including sustaining a focus on development mission, is as challenging as achieving financial sustainability!

While the micro-finance industry generates many manuals on how to manage the technical delivery of micro-financial services, genuine analysis either of MFOs, which goes beyond managing a board of directors or staff, for example, or of development entrepreneurs who are by and large responsible for founding and leading MFOs, remains very weak. This applies in particular to analysis that can help practitioners when they confront, often on a daily basis, the tension between their developmental objectives and the demands of micro-finance as a technical tool.

Fortunately, micro-finance practice in India has much to offer on these dilemmas. Indian practice is extraordinary in its diversity, not least in terms of the development missions with which micro-finance is combined. As suggested above, these include poverty alleviation, livelihood promotion, developing the local economy, empowerment, building people's organisations, and changing wider systems and institutions within society.

India is also fast becoming one of the largest micro-finance markets in the world, especially with the growth of women's savings and credit groups (known in India as 'self-help groups' [SHGs]) which are set to reach 17 million women by 2008 at the latest and which we explore in depth, and from a range of different perspectives, in this book.

In India, an exclusive focus on micro-credit for micro-enterprise is the exception rather than the norm. It is no surprise that Ela Bhatt, India's micro-finance pioneer who founded the Self-employed Women's Association (SEWA) Bank in 1974, chaired a working group that produced a paper for the first Micro-credit Summit entitled 'Beyond micro-credit: Structures that increase the economic power of the poor'

(Bhatt, 1996). Indian practice, therefore, makes much clearer the diversity of potential developmental agendas for micro-finance, that go well beyond a financial tool.

At the same time, most Indian practitioners have always worked on the assumption that developmental objectives need to be combined with financial sustainability. Take the example of SEWA Bank again, the oldest MFO in India. The bank has been sustainable throughout its history, because it is based on savings, while its mission is clearly focused on the empowerment of women slum-dwellers.

The Cooperative Development Foundation (CDF) provides another example of integrating some of the polarities and tensions we have drawn attention to. Its primary purpose is to promote cooperatives as local democratic organisations, and it has discovered that micro-financial services are a particularly good activity around which to organise cooperatives. In this way micro-financial services have been used as an instrument for democratic organisation. At the same time CDF is passionate about the smallest technical detail for co-operatives to manage micro-financial services. Without effective management by local people there can be little empowerment.

India therefore has much to offer, not only in terms of current international debates on micro-finance, but also in terms of combining micro-finance with development, and how organisations can achieve this in practice. In the process, for over 25 years Indian MFOs have developed a range of innovative products and services: insurance services; linking savings and credit groups to banks; integrating micro-finance into agendas for women's empowerment and local democratic organisation; using moneylenders as intermediaries to change market prices; etc. In spite of all this, Indian practice is little known beyond the circles of Indian practitioners and those who have worked alongside them.

To those who are familiar with India, the diversity, flexibility and integration of its micro-finance practice will come as no surprise, and for three reasons. First, India itself is as diverse as many continents. Second, its integrationist culture has often led practitioners, from Gandhi to humble village workers, to integrate new ideas and methods and make them their own, rather than see them as irreconcilable polarities. Third, India remains the largest democracy in the world, and democratic issues have been at the heart of many developmental initiatives, including micro-finance.

At the same time, India has a long tradition of attention to entrepreneurial and organisational development. Indeed, India has been a major home of the growth of these professional disciplines.[2] This makes it appropriate that this book reviews some of the organisational challenges that face MFOs, from an organisational development perspective rather than from a technical perspective that sees them purely as functional financial intermediaries.

This book in fact arises out of a four-year organisational development project, managed by the New Economics Foundation (NEF) in London, for four major MFOs in India (see the Appendix). It would be presumptuous to suggest that either the project or this book have provided simple guidelines to manage these organisational challenges, but at least they place them at the heart of practice rather than burying them under a heap of technical manuals.

The project also provided the insights that underpin the analysis in this book, an encompassing and integrating analysis that ranges from the diverse developmental motives of development entrepreneurs to hard analysis of costs in promoting micro-financial services at the community level; from detailed attention to the dynamics of individual savings and credit groups to developing the whole micro-finance sector to meet the challenge of scale that India always presents; from the need to achieve financial sustainability in order to serve and empower poor people to a diverse range of potential impacts that micro-finance can have on them, for example in terms of their security and democratic voice.

In many chapters in this book we challenge a narrow focus on the technical 'solutions' that micro-finance seems to offer. At the same time we challenge weak performance by taking a hard look at sustainability and impact issues (Chapter 10). We challenge the dominant understanding of efficiency as a highly unsophisticated measure (Chapter 8). We also challenge some of the ideals of local democratic organisation by looking at the hard realities of how small savings and credit groups within poor communities work (Chapters 8 and 9).

Indian practice of micro-finance has taught us not to see irreconcilable differences but to recognise the value of different perspectives and to seek to integrate them into a more coherent rather than compartmentalised whole. The point is not to decide, for example, between pursuing financial sustainability or developmental impact, between offering credit or savings and insurance, between addressing poverty or building democratic organisations. All of these may be needed in a given developmental context or a given community.

The point is to recognise and understand the complexity of the developmental challenges within that context or community, to see how a range of appropriate strategies can be combined in practice to meet those challenges, and how the tensions likely to arise within an organisation (or a group of organisations) embracing different strategies may be managed effectively. This is more in tune with the complex daily realities poor people face, and with the complex daily realities of most micro-finance practitioners we know.

Beyond micro-credit:
An outline of the book

Some issues

The link between micro-credit and poverty reduction has not been proven. Among the range of possible micro-financial services, micro-credit has predominated, on the assumption that it will deliver higher incomes and increased assets to the poor through micro-enterprise. Far less attention has been paid to the need to reduce risk, perhaps the most pressing need especially for the poorest households. Indeed, injecting capital into existing micro-enterprises, or creating new ones, may enhance the risk that their poor owners face. There is indeed evidence that, as a result, a proportion of micro-credit clients have become worse off after accessing micro-loans (Hulme and Mosley, 1996). The need to reduce risk is why many poor people would prefer regular wage labour than managing their own micro-enterprise, if only such opportunities were available (Mahajan, 1997).

Micro-credit providers cannot of course take their poor borrowers for a ride. While most providers emphasise investments of working or fixed capital in micro-enterprises, the reality is that many clients use the credit for consumption-smoothing, especially as most funds are fungible within a household. Such consumption-smoothing can allow households to cope more effectively, but it also runs the risk of pushing them further into debt if they cannot repay the loan out of enhanced income streams. More appropriate financial products for this purpose are savings, insurance and loans to allow poor people to repay their high-interest loans to moneylenders and to meet emergency expenditure. And yet these have received far less attention than micro-credit for micro-enterprise. At the same time, while such products to enable consumption-smoothing can stabilise a poor household's condition, they cannot propel them out of poverty.

With such a strong focus on micro-credit for micro-enterprise, it is perhaps surprising that less attention has also been paid to linking poor people to growing market opportunities and to enhancing the control they can exercise over their economic environment.

Enterprise promotion was a focus of development activity until the early 1990s. Many involved in those endeavours feel that the growth of minimalist micro-credit has diverted attention from the on-going challenges of creating or strengthening enterprise. An important conclusion of initiatives to promote enterprises had in fact been that finance is often not the ruling constraint, and yet thinking and practice on the wider needs of enterprises has progressed little since the early 1990s. It is gradually resurfacing under the name of 'business development services'.

Another important conclusion was that assisting individual enterprises was often not effective, whether through minimalist micro-credit or wider business services. A more systematic approach, often encompassing a sub-sectoral focus, was needed to impact a wider range of enterprises or local or regional economies as a whole (Dichter and Mahajan, 1990; USAID, 1987).

In terms of greater control within the economic environment, the ownership of assets in particular can significantly reduce risk to households in the face of fluctuating incomes or expenditure demands. However, as individual micro-entrepreneurs, most micro-credit clients remain as vulnerable to economic circumstances as they were before taking any micro-loans. Economic development is therefore as much about empowerment, of individuals and groups, as about incomes and individual assets.

For many poor people the only route to empowerment is through collective endeavours that can overcome the severe limitations imposed by individual isolation. This immediately brings in issues of collective ownership, including of the organisation delivering micro-financial services. This is such a fundamental issue in a development context, where unequal access to and ownership of assets often underpins the unequal distribution of power, that it is surprising that debate on the ownership and governance of MFOs has so often ignored it.

Outline of the book

These are some of the issues that lead into the first part of this book (Chapters 3 to 6). After a short introduction to the Indian financial sector (Chapter 2), for those unfamiliar with the context of practice analysed in this book, we take the first step beyond micro-credit to embrace a range of micro-financial services (savings, credit and insurance) to provide social and economic security to poor people (Chapter 3). We illustrate this through the case of SEWA Bank, as well as other MFOs innovating micro-financial products, from savings to credit for housing and education to insurance for women to cover a broad range of diseases, including gynaecological disorders and occupational health, and provide maternity benefits, and for farmers against crop failure.

In Chapter 4, we analyse the work of BASIX in promoting rural livelihoods. BASIX goes beyond minimalist micro-credit by integrating the provision of micro-credit with a wide range of technical assistance and support services, including in highly cost-effective ways. However, BASIX also seeks to go beyond such integration of financial and non-financial services by developing them as instruments within wider strategies for livelihood promotion, which also involve, for example, supporting small enterprises to generate wage employment, intervening in promising sub-sectors and engaging a range of relevant market actors, and reviving moribund rural infrastructure and organisations.

In Chapter 5, we go beyond micro-credit to look at the democratic functioning of groups providing micro-financial services. We go beyond the concept of 'social intermediation' as a process to prepare potential clients to access micro-financial services and turn the argument on its head. Micro-financial services are a tool or instrument around which to build social capital through democratic people's groups and organisations. We illustrate this through the savings and credit operations of SHGs, and through detailed analysis of savings and credit cooperatives promoted by CDF.

With its focus on democratic organisations, this chapter tackles the issue of who owns the assets and profits that arise from the provision of micro-financial services. The analysis therefore takes us beyond the efficient delivery of micro-financial services to embrace issues of accountability, ownership and control.

In exploring women's empowerment through micro-finance, we also go beyond an exclusive focus on poor people to recognise the broader (village) community and its democratic organisations. We also go beyond the traditional focus on who controls loans within the household to look at opportunities for women emerging out of savings and credit groups to engage in informal and formal democratic processes.

Finally, in Part One, we look at how MFOs have sought to bring about wider system-level or institutional change (Chapter 6), taking us beyond a focus on individual MFOs to their role in wider systems. We briefly review the impacts that micro-finance can have on the local economy as a whole, beyond financial services or individual clients. We look in detail at the practical strategies of BASIX and the Indian association of MFOs, Sa-Dhan, in influencing the policy and regulatory environment for micro-finance; at the integration of micro-financial services within the trade union SEWA's broad strategy to promote the recognition and rights of poor self-employed women; and at

CDF in changing the legal environment for cooperatives throughout India, for which CDF is putting its savings and credit cooperatives to good instrumental use.

It is in Chapter 6, as well as Chapter 8, that we introduce the only technical language in this book, drawing on economic theory to distinguish carefully between institutions and organisations. Institutions are not formal organisations of some significance, but the rules of the game that shape human interaction by providing the structure for transactions and incentives. Because of this distinction we refer throughout this book to micro-finance organisations rather than micro-finance institutions (MFIs). Few MFOs could claim to be institutions even as commonly understood as formal organisations of some significance beyond their immediate operations, although Chapter 6 shows how those who aspire to such a role strive to do so in practice.

Part Two of the book then focuses in greater depth on the organisational and institutional issues confronting micro-finance. The first three chapters (7 to 9) analyse SHGs in detail.

Chapter 7 compares Grameen Bank groups with the SHGs emerging in large numbers in India, contrasting the greater 'regimentation' of Grameen-style operations to the more autonomous and democratic groups in India, placing each within their institutional context and investigating how the differences may influence costs, sustainability and empowerment outcomes. This chapter makes a significant contribution in analysing the diversity in group mechanisms in practice that are often lumped together as one micro-finance tool.

Chapter 8 looks at SHGs operating in urban slums, which takes us beyond the traditional reliance on community and kinship ties, which are often regarded as critical to any group mechanisms, to see how groups fare when such ties may not exist. The chapter places SHGs within the context of other financial services available to slum-dwellers, and shows how fragile groups can be.

Above all this chapter challenges a prevalent but simplistic approach that assumes costs simply reflect organisational efficiency, demonstrating that many factors contribute to the costs of promoting SHGs, only some of which are under the control of the promoting organisation. These different costs have to be recognised if more efficient and appropriate micro-finance practice is to develop.

The analysis also challenges negative attitudes towards NGO ideology, which often regard such ideology as incompatible with the efficient delivery of micro-financial services, to show how it can in fact enhance efficiency by significantly reducing transaction costs.

Chapter 9, on the other hand, goes beyond the use of groups as channels for financial services to analyse the development stages of SHGs, their tasks and processes, and in particular, leadership and social entrepreneurship within them. Like Chapter 8, this chapter demonstrates the wide variations in performance of SHGs, even when promoted by the same organisation. This is perhaps inevitable given that SHGs are autonomous organisations which determine their own policies and processes within widely different contexts. For such groups, leadership is clearly vital, and the chapter explores entrepreneurial traits and qualities among women leaders, and the costs and rewards of such leadership.

In Chapter 10, we then go beyond financial sustainability and outreach, first by incorporating organisational as well as financial parameters into a sophisticated rating mechanism for micro-finance, and second, by looking at evidence of wider developmental impacts, as well as reviewing evolving methods in India for measuring such impact. Thus this chapter both takes a hard look at the financial and organisational performance of micro-finance, and pays detailed attention to developmental outcomes.

Drawing on all this analysis, we shift focus in Chapter 11 to the sectoral level, looking at measures that are needed to promote the micro-finance sector in India to address the vast demand for micro-financial services at an appropriate scale. For this, all the different stakeholders in the sector have to play clear and distinctive roles.

To conclude, Chapter 12 first draws out five emerging lessons and challenges, on micro-financial services as an instrument of development; on the adaptation of those services to their context; on the distinct role of NGOs; on dealing with systems; and especially on how the fast emerging movement of savings and credit groups in India urgently requires system-wide attention. Finally this chapter draws on the insights developed in the book to take up five additional challenges of capacity-building, a topic that has often failed to attract sufficient reflective analysis, and provides a framework for capacity-building that places development at the heart of micro-finance practice.

Notes

1. For examples, see especially www.cgap.org, as well as the *Microbanking Bulletin*, Ledgerwood (1999) and those cited in Rutherford (2000: 121).
2. See, for example, McClelland and Winter (1969), Lynton and Pareek (1992) and Lynton (1998: 159–60).

Chapter 2

Introduction to the financial sector in India

The financial sector in India as a vehicle for development: Three phases

This chapter provides a brief introduction to the financial sector in India, for those who are unfamiliar with the context in which micro-finance organisations (MFOs) in India operate. The chapter focuses in particular on efforts to achieve developmental goals through the financial sector, which have a long history in India, going back almost a century (see Box 2.1).

Box 2.1 suggests three broad chronological phases. During the first phase until the 1960s, pursuing developmental objectives through the financial sector focused primarily on delivering agricultural credit through cooperatives.

With increasing frustration at the outcomes of these endeavours, attention shifted in the second phase to the commercial banks, 14 of which were nationalised in 1969, while a network of Regional Rural Banks (RRBs) was established in the 1970s. This had a major impact. India still has one of the largest banking networks in the world: there is a bank branch for every 15,000 rural households and a cooperative in almost every village.

The impact on rural credit supply was also significant as the proportion of rural credit from the formal financial sector

Box 2.1: Chronological summary of development initiatives with the Indian financial system

- 1891 – The earliest cooperative societies established.
- 1904 – The first cooperative societies act passed by the state.
- 1915 – Maclagan Committee advocates one-village one-coop concept.
- 1928 – Royal Commission on Agriculture advocates expansion of rural credit with state patronage.
- 1931 – Central Banking Enquiry Committee suggests linking agricultural finance with central banking functions.
- 1934 – Committee headed by Malcolm Darling examines if the operations of commercial banks could be coordinated to the advantage of agriculturists.
- 1935 – Agricultural Credit Department established in the Reserve Bank of India (RBI) to promote cooperative credit.
- 1945 – The agricultural finance sub-committee submits its report, recommending liquidation of non-performing assets of members by adjusting the claims of the cooperative to the capacity of members to repay. This marks the first blow to credit discipline.
- 1945 – The Cooperative Planning Committee advocates that the cooperative sector receive state protection from private competition.
- 1949 – The Rural Banking Enquiry Committee finds that cooperative infrastructure is satisfactory but commercial banks have not shown any significant interest in agricultural and rural credit.
- 1954 – All India Rural Credit Survey submits report. Advocates majority participation by the state (51 per cent share capital) in cooperatives at all levels; recommends a common cadre for employees of cooperatives and suggests a three-tier cooperative structure. Share of informal sources in total rural credit usage is 70 per cent, compared to cooperatives (6.4 per cent) and commercial banks (0.9 per cent).
- 1960 – The Committee on Cooperative Credit proposes a strong and stable institutional framework for cooperatives.
- 1969 – Nariman Committee introduces 'Lead Bank Scheme', thereby starting a process of district credit plans and coordination among various formal financial intermediaries.
- 1969 – Nationalisation of 14 commercial banks.
- 1971 – All India Debt and Investment Survey shows that share of the formal financial sector in total rural credit usage is 29.2 per cent compared to 70.8 per cent from informal sources.

- 1975 – The concept of Regional Rural Banks (RRBs) advocated to overcome the failure of cooperatives. Agricultural Refinance and Development Corporation set up.
- 1975 – Hazari Committee advocates the integration of short- and long-term credit structure.
- 1976 – National Commission on Agriculture experiments with a new form of cooperative, the Farmers' Service Cooperative, with active collaboration from the commercial banks.
- 1980–81 – The government sets up the Integrated Rural Development Programme (IRDP) to direct subsidised loans to poor self-employed people through the banking sector. Over almost two decades IRDP extended assistance to about 55 million families.
- 1981 – All India Debt and Investment Survey shows that share of the formal financial sector in total rural credit usage is now 61.2 per cent, while informal sources have fallen to 38.8 per cent.
- 1982 – The National Bank for Agriculture and Rural Development (NABARD) is set up.
- 1982 – The government establishes Development of Women and Children in Rural Areas (DWCRA) as a sub-scheme of the IRDP to enable poor women to take up income-generating activities by giving groups of 15 to 20 women a revolving fund.
- mid-1980s – Savings and credit groups (self-help groups or SHGs) begin emerging all over the country, most catalysed by non-governmental organisations (NGOs) without the involvement of the state.
- 1989 – The first formal loan waiver announced, seriously impacting credit discipline.
- 1989 – Khusro Committee recommends a more market-oriented approach for cooperatives.
- 1991 – Economic liberalisation takes off.
- 1991 – All India Debt and Investment Survey shows that share of the formal financial sector in total rural credit usage is 56.6 per cent, compared to informal finance (39.6 per cent) and unspecified (3.8 per cent).
- 1991 – Brahm Prakash Committee comes out with a model cooperative societies act, with less state involvement.
- 1991 – Narasimham Committee's *Report on the Financial System* suggests, among other things, phasing out concessional rates of interest.
- 1992 – NABARD starts its 'linkage' programme of refinancing and encouraging bank lending to SHGs.

(Contd)

(Box 2.1 Contd)

- 1993 – Rashtriya Mahila Kosh (RMK or the National Credit Fund for Women) established to accelerate the flow of credit through NGOs to self-employed women in the unorganised sector. (Until March 2001, RMK had supported close to 1,100 NGOs with disbursements of Rs 72.6 crore [726 million] to benefit 393,000 women.)
- 1995 – The Government of Andhra Pradesh passes the new Mutually-aided Cooperative Societies (MACS) Act, granting autonomy to cooperatives.
- Several states follow suit and pass the new act.
- Several savings and credit cooperatives in Andhra Pradesh register under the new cooperative act.
- 1996 – RBI deregulates interest rates for small loans (below Rs 200,000) by Cooperative and Regional Rural Banks.
- 1996 – RBI introduces a new form of bank, the Local Area Bank, to operate in three contiguous districts, modelled on similar banks in Indonesia.
- 1998 – R.V. Gupta Committee submits report on the flow of rural credit from commercial banks and suggests freeing interest rates and introducing substantial changes in appraisal methodologies.
- 1998 – Sa-Dhan ('The Association of Community Development Finance Institutions') set up by micro-finance organisations (MFOs) in India.
- 1998 – The Small Industries Development Bank of India (SIDBI) sets up a Foundation for Micro-Credit with initial capital of Rs 100 crore (1,000 million).
- 1999 – Taskforce on Supportive Policy and Regulatory Framework for Micro-finance submits report, signifying a major step towards mainstreaming micro-finance.
- 2000 – RBI declares bank lending to MFOs as part of the priority sector.
- 2001 – By April 2001, 285,000 SHGs have taken loans from 41 commercial banks, 166 RRBs and 111 cooperative banks (average loan per group about Rs 18,000). During the year 2000–2001, 171,000 SHGs take loans, of which 149,000 are first-time borrowers.
- 2001 – The Andhra Pradesh Mahila Abhivruddhi Society (APMAS) is established to provide capacity-building inputs to the vast movement of SHGs and MACS providing savings and credit facilities to women in the state.
- 2001 – A Working Group to review the legislation and regulatory framework for RRBs is established.

(banks and cooperatives) rose from 29.2 per cent in 1971 to 61.2 per cent in 1981, although this fell back to 56.6 per cent by 1991.

During this phase, the government also established the Integrated Rural Development Programme (IRDP) in 1980–81 to direct subsidised loans to poor self-employed people through the banking sector. Over almost two decades IRDP extended assistance to about 55 million families.

The second phase culminated in 1989 with the first official loan waiver which severely undermined what was left of any credit discipline.

The third phase was started by the financial crisis of the early 1990s leading to the first significant economic liberalisation measures, including reforms in the financial sector. These included the slow restructuring of the commercial and regional rural banks, the freeing of some interest rates, the consolidation of the government's self-employment schemes (into Swarna Jayanti Swarozgar Yojana [SJSY]), the introduction of Local Area Banks, the introduction of mutually-aided cooperative societies (MACS) autonomous of government control, and other such measures. This process of restructuring continues to date.

As the 1990s progressed, a fast growing number of savings and credit groups (known in India as self-help groups or SHGs), predominantly with women members, also emerged, as well as a range of specialised MFOs. By the end of the century significant support structures for SHGs and MFOs had been put in place, including active promotion by the public National Bank for Agriculture and Rural Development (NABARD) of bank lending to SHGs and a Foundation for micro-credit set up by the Small Industries Development Bank of India (SIDBI).

The impact has been significant. For example, by April 2001, 285,000 SHGs had taken loans from 41 commercial banks, 166 RRBs and 111 cooperative banks, with an average loan per group of Rs 18,000. During the year 2000–2001 alone, 171,000 SHGs took loans from banks, of which 149,000 were first-time borrowers, suggesting a rapid acceleration of this process towards NABARD's target of ensuring bank loans are extended to 1 million SHGs by 2008. With an average membership of 17, this would mean banks reach out to some 17 million members, the vast majority of whom will be women (see Chapter 7 below).

In 2000, specialist MFOs in India (including the new mutually-aided cooperatives) had over a half-a-million clients. The MFO SHARE, in the state of Andhra Pradesh, projects that it alone will be reaching over 1.7 million women by early 2006.

Many of these new mechanisms, especially the SHGs and MACS, are essentially addressing financial services on the basis of mutuality, sorting out local demand–supply gaps locally, while looking beyond the local context to meet incremental or residual capital needs from the formal sector.

The consequences for the formal financial sector

The context in which micro-finance initiatives emerged in India is not dissimilar from many other countries in the South. The financial sector developed in India by the end of the 1980s was largely supply- and target-driven, characterised by:

- a hugely expanded bank branch and cooperative network, and new organisational forms like RRBs;
- a greater focus on credit rather than other financial services like savings and insurance, although the banks and cooperatives did provide deposit facilities;
- lending targets directed at a range of 'priority sectors' such as agriculture, 'weaker sections' of the population, and so on;
- interest-rate ceilings;
- significant government subsidies channelled through the banks and cooperatives, as well as through related government programmes;
- a dominant perspective that finance for rural and poor people was a social obligation, not a potential business opportunity.

The outcomes were not entirely surprising:

- high default rates. For example, the IRDP programme experienced repayment rates of less than a third and created 40 million defaulters. An official loan-waiver in 1989 undermined what was left of a repayment culture;
- corruption and a high-degree of cynicism among bankers about the credit-worthiness of poor people;
- significant government intervention and control, badly eroding the autonomy of the financial sector, making it highly dependent on subsidies even though it had access to a huge base of savings, and creating groups with large vested interests.

All of this might have been acceptable had the measures been able to extend effective financial services to poor people. Unfortunately, this was far from the case. Savings products were inflexible and inappropriately designed, and appropriate insurance products few and far between. On the credit side, while the share in rural borrowing supplied by informal sources fell to 40 per cent in 1991, households with the least assets were far more dependent on informal sources.[1] Borrowers faced high transaction costs to secure subsidised loans, making their real cost around 22 to 33 per cent (Mahajan and Ramola, 1996). There were very few repeat loans available, and defaulters were excluded from further loans.

Worse still, the formal financial sector failed to recognise the mismatch between the hierarchy of credit needs and credit availability, resulting in 'adverse usage' of credit (see Figure 2.1). Credit needs start with consumption purposes, which are only being met through informal sources at high cost. Higher needs come into play only when the lower needs are satisfied. However, credit (often at subsidised rates) is usually available for new enterprises (i.e., for diversification). Since money is fungible, loans are therefore taken for diversification but used in lower rungs of the hierarchy. This means that any appraisal of the loan is not honoured, resulting in adverse usage and hence adverse repayment performance.

*Figure 2.1: Hierarchy of credit needs and credit availability
from formal sources, leading to 'adverse usage'*

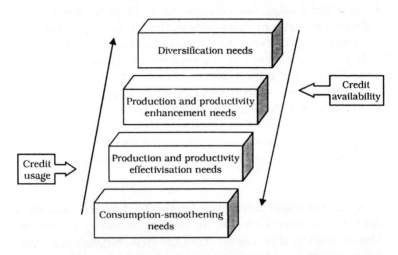

Note: Effectivisation means small improvements to an existing livelihood activity to increase the return from existing resources (e.g., improved feed for cattle instead of traditional fodder). Enhancement means increasing the asset base (e.g., more cattle). Diversification involves the introduction of new livelihoods.

The immediate impact of the reforms to the financial sector that became necessary by the 1990s have in many ways made things worse for poor people. There has been a drastic fall in the share of cooperatives in rural credit (Karmakar, 1999: 108–9). The share of rural credit in the total credit disbursed by commercial banks, which grew from 3.5 to 15 per cent from 1971 to 1991, has now declined again, to 11 per cent in 1998 (Sa-Dhan, 2001). During the 1990s the banks could not in fact meet their agricultural credit target of 18 per cent of net bank credit. This was also a decade when the RRBs went through a restructuring programme. All these developments have resulted in a fall in the availability of credit from the formal financial system, leaving informal sources as well as SHGs and MFOs to fill the gaps.

Demand for micro-financial services[2]

Given the context described above, it is not surprising that there is large demand for micro-financial services (savings, credit and insurance). Indeed, such demand is apparently insatiable, and India is perhaps the largest emerging market for micro-financial services in the world.

In the case of savings, while banks have provided access to a large number of small depositors, demand is nowhere near being met, particularly for small, frequent, 'recurring' deposits. Transaction costs of savings in formal financial intermediaries such as banks can be as high as 10 per cent for poor rural households. Poor people therefore turn to other means such as informal chit-funds and *bishis*, and to savings mobilisation companies.

The large non-banking finance companies like Peerless, Sanchayani and Sahara raise thousands of crores of rural deposits. In fact there is so much demand for savings that people are willing to pay for savings services, in the form of lower than inflation interest rates on deposits and high transaction costs, apart from the risk of losing their deposits altogether, when saving with numerous private 'finance companies'. There has been much malpractice among such private companies, and many poor people have lost their money as a result.[3]

In the emerging micro-finance sector, SHGs and mutually-aided cooperatives in the state of Andhra Pradesh alone have already collected more than Rs 500 crore (5,000 million) in micro-savings.

In terms of micro-credit, India has nearly 400 million people living below or just above an austerely defined poverty line. Approximately 75 million households therefore need micro-finance. Of these, nearly 60 million households are in rural India and the remaining 15 million are urban slum-dwellers. The current annual credit usage by these households was estimated in 1998 to be Rs 465,000 million or US$10 billion. This represents usage and not unmet demand.

Compare this with the supply of small loans by banks. It is estimated that the number of small loan accounts from banks covered some 40 million households in 2000. The remaining 35 million households are perhaps meeting their credit needs from the informal sector. Micro-finance organisations have of course arisen because of this gap between demand and the formal sector's limited supply.

One million SHGs, NABARD's target for 2008, will absorb at least Rs 50,000 million worth of funds, a huge challenge for the banking system. In Chapter 7, Malcolm Harper estimates that, if such targets for the outreach of SHGs and of MFOs are met, by 2009 a quarter of all poor households will have access to micro-financial services through such intermediaries.

Finally, on micro-insurance, during the 1990s a large number of low-premium insurance schemes emerged, covering poor people against death, accidents, natural calamities, and loss of assets due to fire, theft, and so on. Livestock and asset insurance was extended along with the subsidised IRDP loans (now taken up in SJSY), and thus remained scheme-driven, with little awareness among clients. Livestock insurance, however, is quite expensive and its reach to poor people is negligible, except when linked to government schemes. Crop insurance, on the other hand, has been a great money-loser for the public sector provider, the General Insurance Corporation (GIC). There is therefore significant unmet demand for micro-insurance services also.

This brief overview of demand for micro-financial services suggests the huge challenges and opportunities the Indian market presents. While this book focuses largely on the role of SHGs, cooperatives and specialised MFOs in rising to these challenges and opportunities, it would be foolish to believe they could address all the demand. This can only be done if the mainstream financial sector also reaches out to millions of poor households to provide them with micro-financial services, both directly and through intermediaries. To conclude this chapter, we therefore summarise the organisational profile of the financial sector.

Summary of the organisational profile of the financial sector

Formal financial sector entities include:

- Branches of commercial banks and RRBs, which both take deposits and extend loans.
- Cooperative banks at the village, town and district levels, and urban cooperative banks, which both take deposits and extend loans, although a significant part of their lending funds come from NABARD.
- The Post Office, which provides savings as well as insurance services, and the National Small Savings Organisation, which sells deposit instruments.
- Non-banking finance companies (NBFCs), very few of which are allowed by the Reserve Bank of India (RBI), India's central bank, to take deposits. Within NBFCs, there is a special category called residuary non-banking companies, or RNBCs, which are allowed to raise an unlimited amount of deposits, as long as 80 per cent of it is put in government and bank deposits. Peerless, Sanchayani and Sahara are examples of such RNBCs.
- The Life and General Insurance Corporations.

The range of MFOs emerging comprise:

- Not-for-profit MFOs such as societies and trusts (legal forms of NGOs) that lend to borrowers, usually organised into SHGs or into Grameen Bank-style groups and centres.
- Mutual-benefit MFOs, especially cooperatives, some like the Self-employed Women's Association (SEWA) Bank registered as urban cooperative banks, while new ones, especially in Andhra Pradesh, are increasingly emerging as MACS under the new cooperative acts.
- For-profit MFOs incorporated as non-banking financial companies such as BASIX and SHARE Micro-finance Limited.

The overall financial system is summarised in Table 2.1.

Table 2.1: Present rural financial system in India

Traditional financial institutions		New financial institutions		
Formal sector	Informal sector	Formal sector		Informal sector
		Non-profit	For-profit	
1. Government departments and institutions (*Basic orientation: beneficiary identification and targeting of loans; Drawbacks: inappropriate choice of beneficiaries*) 2. Commercial banks & RRBs (*Basic orientation: obligation under priority-sector lending to achieve targeted numbers; Drawbacks: loans often doled out without proper appraisal*) 3. Cooperative banks (*Basic orientation: channels of government 'dole': neither internal financial nor internal governance strength; Drawbacks: can fold or stall once government funding stops*) 4. Registered non-banking finance companies that give loans but rarely deposits, except for residuary non-banking finance companies like Peerless, Sanchayani and Sahara (*Basic orientation: mobilisation of small savings, providing only a part of financial services needed; Drawback: unstable, might just disappear*)	1. Rural money-lenders, commission agents, traders (*Basic orientation: very short-term profit-maximising out-look; Drawbacks: may rip off poor borrowers*) 2. Unregistered local finance companies, if any (*Basic orientation: mobilisation of small savings, providing only a part of financial services needed; Drawbacks: unstable, might just disappear*)	1. SHGs promoted by NABARD, RMK and NGOs 2. Government-sponsored SHGs under DWCRA schemes 3. MFOs like *Sanghamitra* registered as a non-profit company under Section 25 of the Companies' Act	1. Rural non-banking finance companies like BASIX and SHARE 2. MACS, often called 'self-generating' or '*Swayam-bhoo*' co-operatives, including old ones that have converted to the new Acts 3. Commercial banks looking at microfinance as a profitable activity, such as ICICI Bank and Global Trust Bank	1. Un-registered self-managed financial organisations like local chit funds, *bishis*, etc.

Source: Datta and Sriram (2000).

Note: Formal sector institutions also include provident funds and insurance companies. Cooperative banks include both short-term structures (under State Cooperative Banks, District Central Cooperative Banks, and Primary Agricultural Credit Societies) and long-term structures (under State and Primary Land Development Banks). RMK and FWWB stand for Rashtriya Mahila Kosh and Friends of Women's World Banking. MACS stands for Mutually-aided Cooperative Societies registered under the new MACS Acts in Andhra Pradesh and other states.

Notes

1. The share of debt from informal sources stood at 58 per cent for the lowest asset group with less than Rs 5,000 in assets, compared to only 19 per cent for the highest asset group with assets of Rs 250,000 and above (Mahajan, 2000: 170).
2. The estimates in this section come from Mahajan (nd) and Mahajan and Nagasri (1999).
3. One survey showed that over 55 per cent of slum-dwellers surveyed in Delhi had lost money to one or other deposit-taker of this kind (Titus, 1995).

Notes

Part One

Micro-finance and development

Chapter 3

Micro-finance and social and economic security

Introduction

This book is titled 'Beyond micro-credit'. We are often blinded by the overwhelming policy support, in India and internationally, for 'directed credit' or micro-credit to poor people which simplistically assumes that, with an infusion of capital, poor households will be able to break out of the vicious cycle of poverty.

In reality, poor people need access to so many more financial services than just micro-credit, including a range of micro-savings and insurance products. Indeed, the first step for poor people on the path out of the poverty cycle is social and economic security. Appropriate savings and insurance, as well as loans for emergency expenditures or basic assets such as housing and education, can contribute significantly to such security, not least among poorer and more vulnerable households.

These services can *protect* poor people from the impact of unforeseen crises and emergencies in their households or micro-businesses, from falling yet further into debt, and enable poor households to plan and manage their limited resources more effectively to meet their basic needs (Johnson and Rogaly, 1997). Once poor households enjoy greater security, they may be able to access *promotional* micro-finance products that help them develop their livelihoods (see Chapter 4).

Rutherford (2000) has further demonstrated that, especially for the protective needs of poor households, there may be little difference between savings, loans and insurance:

... try to avoid sterile arguments about whether the poor need 'savings' or 'loans'.... It is much more helpful to think creatively about ways of collecting small sums (be they savings or repayments or insurance premiums) and then of ways of turning them into large sums (be they loans, or withdrawals from savings, or insurance pay-outs). The poor do not have a 'natural' preference for savings over loans, or vice versa—they have a need to turn small pay-ins into large take-outs. They will use the version of the three basic swaps [savings, loans or insurance] which happens to be on offer, and if all three are on offer they will take whichever is most convenient for them at that moment for that particular need (ibid.: 110).

Rutherford (2000: 4) rightly argues that poor households need relatively large sums of money for life-cycle needs (such as marriages, festivals and old age), emergencies (such as illness, the death of a bread-winner and floods) and investment opportunities (as much in assets and household goods, for example, as in investments in micro-businesses).

Poor households therefore need access to a basket of financial services. When looking at financial markets for poor people, we discover not only the lack of credit, but also that other financial services are unavailable.

This chapter focuses on the financial services offered by a range of micro-finance organisations (MFOs) to address the needs of poor households for social and economic security. A look at the basket of services offered by several MFOs featured in this chapter demonstrates that it is indeed desirable to offer a range of financial services that not only take care of the investment needs of poor households, but also address their needs for security.

We look in particular at savings, which are essentially a model of self-insurance, and explicit insurance products, as well as loans, and how these different products can be integrated into a comprehensive range of services to meet the needs of poor households. We feature most extensively the work of the Self-employed Women's Association (SEWA) Bank (see Box 3.1), the oldest MFO in India founded back in 1974, as well as look at emerging innovations in product design by more recent MFOs.

Box 3.1: SEWA Bank and the SEWA movement

SEWA Bank (Shri Mahila SEWA Sahakari Bank in full) was established in 1974 by 4,000 members of the Self-employed Women's Association (SEWA), a trade union that first started organising self-employed women in the slums of Ahmedabad in the state of Gujarat, but now has over 200,000 members in Ahmedabad, rural Gujarat and elsewhere in India. SEWA members are categorised into the following three groups:

(1) Hawkers and vendors, for example, vegetable and fruit vendors, small shopkeepers, vendors of flowers, fish, household goods and clothes;
(2) Home-based workers, like weavers, carpenters and other artisans, *bidi* rollers, garment workers and women who process agricultural produce;
(3) Manual labourers and service providers, like agricultural labourers, construction workers, head-loaders, paper-pickers and domestic workers.

Given that 93 per cent of the workforce in India is in the informal or unorganised sector, a union for such workers, especially women, was deemed essential to fight for their economic rights. However, economic rights are not sufficient in themselves. Women members also needed access to services, from health-care through financial services to business development. SEWA Bank is therefore part of a family of SEWA organisations: the union; the bank; a range of cooperatives (over 80) mostly organised around economic trades, but some providing health- and child-care; producer groups (some 200); rural savings and credit groups (1,600); federations of these cooperatives and groups; a housing trust and an academy for research and capacity-building.

The SEWA movement is committed to addressing a wide range of needs of its women members, known within SEWA as the '10 Points': enhancing their income, employment and their ownership of assets, improving housing, health-care and the intake of nutritious food, providing child-care, organising women and building leadership and greater self-reliance (both individual and collective).

The SEWA movement therefore undertakes a wide range of activities for its members, which can be classified broadly

(Contd)

(Box 3.1 Contd)

into organising (into the union, cooperatives and savings and credit groups), capacity-building (including leadership-building, training and skill-development), a range of economic activities (including not only financial services, but also business, housing, child- and health-care) and policy interventions (campaigning, communication, legal aid and research).

It is obvious that within such a context SEWA Bank is not just a provider of micro-credit. Its mission is to assist poor self-employed women in their overall struggle to live a life of dignity, while providing at least a minimum level of social and economic security. It was set up because commercial banks were not helpful in dealing with illiterate, poor women unfamiliar with banking procedures, while the women found those procedures complex and inflexible, with significant collateral requirements and inconvenient hours of business.

SEWA Bank is in fact a cooperative bank owned by 30,000 women holding over Rs 1.1 crore (11 million) in shares, who elect a board of 15 directors each representing members in a different trade. SEWA Bank has always focused more on savings products than micro-loans, and had close to 120,000 depositors at the end of 2001.

A recent survey (Chen and Snodgrass, 1999) suggested that SEWA Bank clients are likely to cluster around the poverty line, with most of them either just below or just above it.

Savings at SEWA Bank

Savings as an instrument of security

The SEWA movement believes that self-employed women in the informal sector are often trapped in a vicious cycle of poverty: their low incomes mean they have no capital to invest in assets that could enhance their incomes.

SEWA Bank was not set up to provide micro-loans to break this cycle, although such loans do play an important part of its strategy to address poverty (see further below). Within such a large movement, it would have in fact been easy for SEWA Bank to access deposits from other organisations within the movement and direct these as loans to its members.

Instead, the Bank assumed that poor women have a basic instinct for saving that needs to be cultivated and above all facilitated through good products. The Bank has therefore focused on building women's capital by providing convenient products for their savings to the extent that a recent study found that the 'bank puts more emphasis on savings accounts which involve 10 times as many members as the loan programme' (Chen and Snodgrass, 1999: 1).

SEWA Bank believes that savings can contribute in many ways to enhancing its members' security. Savings build members' capital for consumption, emergencies and investment and protect them against borrowing from moneylenders. They give access to loans (by providing collateral) as well as to insurance from the Bank. They also secure women's money, protecting it from their husbands when necessary, reducing wasteful consumption and instilling financial discipline. Through all these means savings not only give women a sense of security and hope, but can also provide them with greater self-esteem, giving them greater voice within their families and greater recognition and status both within and beyond their households.

The need to offer savings products also stems from the nature of income-flows in the areas where SEWA Bank first worked. It is in an urban setting, with members earning a regular daily or weekly flow of income through working as hawkers or labourers. These income-flows are small and not always regular, being dotted by days or weeks when women are unable to undertake or find work. The primary need of members is therefore to find mechanisms to smoothen their cash-flows by depositing part of their income in a safe place to be accessed in times of need.

However, such processes are not peculiar to urban areas alone. Women in rural areas also need access to such products because of the seasonality of their incomes. In partnership with other organisations within the SEWA movement, SEWA Bank supports 1,600 savings and credit groups (commonly known in India as self-help groups or SHGs) with 38,000 members in rural Gujarat. Each group deposits its members' savings in one common account at the Bank.

Ultimately, MFOs have to address the mismatch between income-flows and expenditure requirements, thereby providing a safety net at times of no or low income. Here are some comments from women involved in rural SHGs linked to SEWA Bank (Murthy, 1999: 44–45):

> I like to save with SEWA. I am a widow with responsibility for two children. I have to provide for their food and education, but when I think of their future, I save Rs 10 a month.
>
> Earlier we used to save Rs 10 a month, but now we save Rs 20 because it will be useful to us in our old age. Even if our sons don't keep us in the future, our own money will be useful to us. We keep aside Rs 2 when we go to buy vegetables; that is how we save.
>
> If we have savings of our own, then we do not have to beg before anybody in case we are in need.
>
> Now we feel there is money in our name and that brings self-respect.
>
> If we save Rs 10 a month, it can be useful to us some day. We get interest on the money and the savings are in our name. We don't have to ask for money from men.
>
> I like to save Rs 10 every month because by the end of the year it becomes Rs 120. We do not even realise it, but a small capital gets built in our name.
>
> If we save for two years and then withdraw it, we get interest. Otherwise at home we are likely to use it up.
>
> If we save, we can also get a loan.

Self-help groups in India and elsewhere are of course based on savings (see Chapters 5, 7 and 8). However, the difference between the SHG model and SEWA Bank's urban operations is in the attributes of the products offered. While self-help groups tend to have regimented and fixed savings on a weekly basis, thereby making savings very similar to regular repayment of loans, the SEWA model provides a range of flexible products for collecting voluntary savings to meet the needs of individual members. Accounts include daily deposits, savings accounts, recurring and fixed deposits.

SEWA Bank has sought to ensure that the range of these products provides sufficient flexibility, for both depositing and withdrawing savings, and adequate returns. Systems, such

as identification cards with photographs, have been introduced to suit the many illiterate clients. The formal regulated bank structure, as well as mutual ownership, provide
assurances to members on the security of their savings,
further enhanced by transparent systems such as regular
passbook entries.

To further encourage savings, SEWA Bank has long had
extension counters in Ahmedabad, including mobile ones
open on a regular day each week, for members to deposit their
savings (as well as repay any loans). Recently SEWA Bank
has gone a step further. It is now providing extension services
for those members who cannot make it to the Bank's extension
counters. It has set up teams of what it calls 'hand-holders'
who collect small amounts of savings and loan repayments
on a daily and voluntary basis but also counsel members on
how to deal with their finances. In this way the service for
small and regular savings has reached members' homes.

SEWA Bank is not the only MFO in India to provide savings products. Even MFOs like SHARE modelled on the
Grameen system (see Chapter 7) have not been satisfied with
the compulsory weekly savings collected in a group fund to
be lent out for smoothing consumption. SHARE also collects
voluntary deposits through a cooperative they have set up in
the state of Andhra Pradesh. These voluntary savings provide the flexibility of withdrawing cash, at weekly intervals in
the case of SHARE, at times of need, including for making
rather inflexible loan repayments.

However, evidence from a wide range of MFOs, including
SHG and Grameen-type programmes, suggests that SEWA's
approach encourages greater savings among poor women (see
Chapter 10). This is seen even when comparing SEWA Bank's
urban operations with its rural SHGs. Thus one survey
(Awano, 1996) found that urban members were saving 4.1 per
cent of their income, and rural members 1.9 per cent.

The advantages of savings to SEWA Bank

SEWA Bank not only addresses the needs of its members
through savings products. They also have significant advantages for the Bank itself. In the first place, they provide a

cheap and reliable source of funds that have meant that the Bank's financial operations have been sustainable since its inception. At the end of 2001, SEWA Bank had over Rs 30 crore (300 million) in 120,000 deposit accounts.

Indeed, along with other providers who focus on mobilising savings (like the savings and credit cooperatives promoted by the Cooperative Development Foundation as described in Chapter 5), SEWA Bank has discovered that deposits raise far more capital than it can easily lend back to members without significant complementary inputs to enhance their members' micro-businesses and hence their ability to absorb credit.

SEWA Bank's credit–deposit ratio currently stands at 31 per cent: in other words, of the Rs 30 crore it has available through deposits, only Rs 10 crore (100 million) are lent out to members. (Because of adequate investment opportunities, SEWA Bank still earns sufficient income on its loan and investment portfolio to cover its costs, generating a modest surplus.)

There may be organisational constraints here. For example, a loan applicant needs a recommendation from a SEWA leader or from one of the directors of the Bank. Those who borrow also tend to be less poor and thus able to utilise more credit, especially for investment.

Nevertheless, this experience seems to confirm Rutherford's argument cited above that for poor people savings and loans are essentially alternative mechanisms for of enabling them to make relatively large expenditures. When a financial-service provider gives its poor clients a choice of products, the clients are likely to choose those most suitable for their particular needs, which appear more often than not to be flexible savings rather than credit.

Savings products also bring SEWA Bank other advantages. They can reduce transaction costs on assessing potential borrowers, because savings provide a good indicator of members' ability to set aside part of their income for repayments. Each potential borrower has to save regularly for some time before they are eligible for loans. The savings then also reduce the risk on loans by acting as collateral.

In addition, savings in the form of shares underpin members' ownership of the bank. As 'hot money' from members and depositors, savings also provide the Bank strong incentives to ensure the security of those deposits. These incentives are reinforced by statutory regulation of deposit-takers.

To benefit from savings in these ways the Bank has of course to earn and maintain the trust of women and provide them a reliable service, although trust is helped by a structure of mutual ownership and being part of the wider SEWA movement. The Bank also has to manage a large number of accounts across a wide range of products, making demands on management, staff and information systems.

Insurance at SEWA Bank

Savings are one mode of self-insurance that members of SEWA Bank resort to. But savings may not be sufficient to address the complex needs of poor women to meet contingencies. Poor households are very vulnerable to events that are unplanned and beyond their control. A fire, theft, drought, cyclone or earthquake may destroy their home and other assets that are the means for their livelihoods. Poor households are also vulnerable to loss of earning power due to contingencies within the family—illness, death and, of course, pregnancy in the case of women.

These events bring very real and often high costs to poor households. Research on over 300 urban and rural members of the SEWA movement (Noponen and Kantor, 1996) looked at the incidence and cost of economic stress events, including positive ones such as the birth of a child, the marriage of a family member or a religious ceremony. It is important to recognise that for poor households each event, whether negative or positive, has economic consequences, and is not, for example, simply a social event with little consequence for the household's livelihood.

Table 3.1 sets out the results.[1] Illness was the event that most disrupted the household economy. Of the households surveyed, 87 per cent were affected by illnesses, with 1.2 incidents of illness in the household every month. The average monthly cost of such illness to a household was Rs 857, almost half of all costs caused by economic stress events.

Table 3.1: Incidence and cost of economic stress events

Stress event	Percentage of households affected at least once	Incidence rate per month per household	Total average Rs cost per month weighted by frequency of occurrence	Percentage of total costs weighted by frequency of occurrence
Illnesses	87	1.2	857	48
Rituals	75	0.6	301	17
Marriages	29	0.4	234	13
Other stresses	61	0.4	144	8
Repairs	49	0.2	87	5
Addictions	68	0.8	75	4
Deaths[1]	47	0.3	45	3
Births[2]	75	0.2	35	2
Calamities	9	0.04	4	0
Total				**100**

Source: Noponen and Kantor (1996).
Notes:
[1] The permanent loss of income from the death of a major bread-winner for the household is not included among the costs.
[2] The loss of female income because the woman giving birth cannot work, or the on-going expenses of an additional household member, are not included among the costs.

The research revealed that 20 per cent of the monthly costs imposed on households by such economic stress events were covered by savings, and that having a savings account with SEWA Bank in fact reduced the number of stress events a woman experienced. However, almost half the costs were covered by borrowing from a moneylender. This fact suggests that savings are unlikely to be sufficient to cover all the contingencies a poor household faces and that SEWA Bank needed to enhance its provision of emergency loans and insurance services.

At the time of this research, SEWA Bank's insurance services, started in 1992, were still in their early days, provided against premiums paid annually by members. Because of its orientation and focus on savings, and the outreach it has achieved through savings, SEWA Bank has increasingly linked its insurance services to savings. The Bank therefore provides insurance on an annual basis against a fixed deposit, as set out in Box 3.2.

Box 3.2: Insurance services provided by SEWA Bank in 2001

SEWA Bank currently has four schemes providing insurance services to over 25,000 women who have invested in fixed deposits that earn interest to cover the annual insurance premiums needed.

Scheme 1, which is currently being withdrawn, still has deposits of Rs 22,750 held by 91 women. The scheme provides cover for the woman's life (both accident and natural death). Each member deposited Rs 250 as a fixed deposit, which is withdrawable in any given year.

Scheme 2 has deposits of Rs 653,150, held by 200 men. The scheme is for husbands of members and covers death due to accidental and natural causes. The deposit required for this policy is Rs 200, shortly to be increased to Rs 650.

Scheme 3 has deposits totalling Rs 13,280,350, held by 21,319 women. This scheme provides comprehensive insurance coverage, including natural and accidental death (up to age 58); loss of property or equipment due to fire, theft, cyclone, earthquake and so on (up to age 70); health insurance and maternity benefits. The deposit required for this was initially Rs 500, and is being increased to Rs 1,000.

Scheme 4 has deposits of Rs 3,345,700, held by 3,639 women. This scheme is the same as the third, except that both the woman and her husband are covered for the same risks listed under Scheme 3. The deposit needed was initially Rs 700, but has been raised to Rs 1,150, and is to be increased further to Rs 1,650.

While SEWA Bank provides a single product to its members under each different scheme, some of the sub-components of the insurance coverage are provided by mainstream insurance companies (all within the public sector). Life insurance, for example, is provided through the Life Insurance Corporation of India. In these cases, SEWA Bank purchases coverage for its members in bulk, keeps records of policy-holders and helps them in settling claims.[2]

Other coverage, particularly for a broad range of diseases, including gynaecological disorders and occupational health, and maternity benefits, all of which are hardly covered by existing insurance companies, is provided by SEWA Bank out of its own funds. Maternity benefits are paid on receipt of a birth certificate, making the process very simple.

(Contd)

(Box 3.2 Contd)

> Thus SEWA Bank has been able to address specific needs of its women members, and has played a pioneering role in developing coverage for women-specific ailments and occupational health.

Box 3.2 shows that SEWA Bank provides insurance coverage for over 25,000 women, or about one in five of its depositors. In the survey conducted by Chen and Snodgrass (1999), only one respondent from the control group of those who were not SEWA Bank clients had a personal insurance policy.

According to an early survey (Srinivas, 1997), most of SEWA Bank's clients with insurance were urban rather than rural; the majority were also illiterate, which suggests that illiterate women are not deterred by procedural issues. Health cover was and continues to be limited to cases of hospitalisation only, which limits its effectiveness for self-employed women who can often not afford to be hospitalised. The health insurance covered about 40 per cent of costs incurred. Srinivas suggests,

'Yet without SEWA Bank's scheme, they would be approximately Rs 935 poorer *in addition* to the expenses they incur in their treatment. It is plausible, however, that increased small amounts are being spent on treatment (but less than the Rs 1,000 ceiling) precisely *because* of SEWA Bank's coverage. This indicates increased health-seeking behaviour and must only be encouraged.' The limit on health claims of Rs 1,000 a year represents something like 10 per cent of family income on the poverty line, therefore representing 'a significant saving' for the household.

In SEWA Bank's view, insurance services not only help women to sustain financial shocks and reduce their losses, they also enable them to continue the process of building their capital and assets, and inculcate habits of planning. They also help the Bank in providing some protection against defaults caused by accidents or emergencies, and insurance coverage is now compulsory for all the Bank's borrowers.

Insurance services have not come without their difficulties, with hassles in processing claims, mainstream companies providing coverage that is inappropriate or inadequate for poor self-employed women, claims being rejected by them, the need to back some insurance cover through SEWA Bank's own assets, the lack of understanding among women themselves and their high vulnerability to economic shocks.

Loans from SEWA Bank

At the end of 2001, SEWA Bank had Rs 10 crore (100 million) in outstanding loans to some 33,000 women. Of this, half was outstanding for working capital (33 per cent) and personal loans (17 per cent). This reflects the need for flexible credit by many women to sustain their micro-businesses and their household expenditure through periods of fluctuating incomes or lumpy expenditures.[3]

The other half of loans outstanding was not however for investment in equipment, which accounted for only 10 per cent of the loan amount outstanding. Even within the context of a large movement like SEWA, the challenge of using micro-credit effectively to promote livelihoods and micro-businesses, rather than just sustaining them at a minimal level of operations, remains (we address this challenge in Chapter 4).

So what of the remaining 40 per cent of outstandings? These were in fact for housing loans, used for such activities as repairing a wall or door, providing monsoon-proofing, adding a room, constructing or buying a new house. They also include loans for water or electricity connections, or building a toilet. As one example of an active borrower for housing, Dayavatiben has taken five loans from SEWA Bank, two (totalling Rs 9,000) for purchasing sheet metal and bricks to improve or expand her house, Rs 4,000 for fitting lights, and two larger loans totalling Rs 35,000 for renovation and repair.

Providing a roof over one's head is as much about security as insurance. For SEWA Bank, housing loans, like savings, also enable women to build their portfolio of assets which can provide both security and income.

Improving housing may provide better security and healthy living conditions for the household, potentially reducing the number of economic stress events, including illnesses that they face. In this sense housing loans seek to prevent some of the stress events which insurance seeks to cover.

At the same time, given that many self-employed women work from home, investment in housing is as much about investment in their businesses. For poor people to work from home, they need space to work. As SEWA says, 'their home is their workplace, their workshop, their storehouse'. In other words, seeing investment in housing as investment in business applies to many urban and rural workers, to vendors, cultivators, artisans or rag-pickers alike. In order for the economic activity to be successful, the work environment has to be conducive. For example, if a women makes pickles or *papads*, rolls *bidis*, or stores cloth, that obviously cannot be done effectively in a leaky hut! Thus, investment in housing safeguards their economic activities.

The Bank's housing portfolio is complemented by the activities of SEWA's Housing Trust and other organisations in supporting community-based partnerships to develop housing and other infrastructure in the urban slums of Ahmedabad. SEWA also has specialised lines of finance from KfW (Germany) and the Housing Development Finance Corporation (HDFC) and is working closely with organisations like the Housing and Urban Development Corporation (HUDCO) to address the shelter needs of poor women.

Integrating savings, loans and insurance

SEWA Bank provides savings, loans and insurance. These are not simply treated as different financial products, but linked in SEWA Bank's development paradigm.

Savings are the first step to break out of the vicious cycle of poverty enabling women to better manage their money and start investing in assets. Once poor women are able to accumulate savings they get used to financial assets and larger sums of money, but starting with their own money, they learn to use it responsibly. Savings can therefore be regarded as building assets and preparing the clients to take on loans as well. So as a strategy, savings can be seen as a first step in preparing poor women for greater credit absorption, which they can then deploy in activities that enhance their future assets and incomes. Insurance, as well as emergency loans, on the other hand, cover women against loss of assets and hence income, enabling them to continue to move upwards.

SEWA Bank has summarised its perspective schematically in Figure 3.1. Initially a poor woman has negative equity, in other words, debt (point 1). By accumulating savings she can move upwards out of negative equity (2). However, because of her vulnerability she is quite likely to fall back into debt (3), and needs insurance and emergency loans, as well as her accumulated savings, to guard against such a scenario. Further savings, and increasingly, loans for business investment, can then enable the woman to build positive equity as she moves from point 2 towards point 5. On the way, the woman continues to be vulnerable to shocks and emergencies, which could push her back to point 4, requiring an on-going need for her accumulated savings, insurance and emergency

Figure 3.1: Moving out of the vicious cycle of poverty

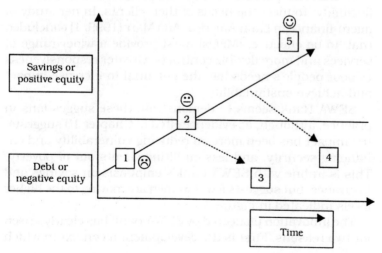

loans. In this way, poor women can gradually move out of the vicious cycle of poverty.

The whole paradigm is built around assets as much as income, as SEWA Bank believes it is assets that provide women not only a source of income but also security against economic shocks and dignity both inside and outside of the household. Throughout this process, financial advice and guidance are available to the Bank's clients, both in the Bank itself, as well as at women's doorsteps through the 'hand-holders', to show them ways of increasing their assets and incomes as well as enhancing their abilities to manage their limited resources effectively.

In the initial stages, savings are thus vital. Through savings women can reach point 2 where they have got rid of costly debt taken from informal sources. However, this may be a long process given their circumstances. A faster alternative is to start with cheaper loans that can replace existing costly debt, which enables indebted women to enhance their income by reducing the interest costs on their debt. SEWA Bank does indeed provide such loans, as do other MFOs in India, popularly called 'Mahajan Mukti' (salvation from the moneylender) loans. This model enables women to save more by providing them a lower-cost loan.

Few other MFOs anywhere in the world, however, provide such a diverse portfolio of financial products, and with such flexibility, to meet the needs of their clients. In her study of micro-finance in Latin America, Ana Marr (1999: 1) concluded that 'to be effective, [MFOs] must provide a wider range of services and more flexible contracts. Greater responsiveness to poor people's needs has the potential to increase impact and achieve sustainability'.

SEWA Bank seems to demonstrate these suggestions in practice, although, as evidence cited in Chapter 10 suggests, the impact has been more on reducing vulnerability and enhancing security, and less on lifting clients out of poverty. This is in line with SEWA Bank's emphasis on savings and insurance, but suggests fewer women are moving to the higher levels indicated in Figure 3.1.

The innovation pioneered by SEWA Bank has clearly arisen for two reasons. First is the developmental context in which

SEWA Bank operates. It is rooted in a democratic movement, and especially a trade union, which fights for the rights of poor self-employed women. Through this context it deeply understands its members' situation and hence needs. It has not emerged through the intervention of a professional MFO or non-governmental organisation (NGO). In 1974, two years before the Grameen Bank was first piloted, there were in any case few examples of MFOs to draw on.

Such a diverse range of flexible products has been made possible, second, because SEWA Bank is a full-fledged bank. If existing banks were not going to serve their needs effectively, then the founders of SEWA Bank were determined to set up their own bank. Only a proper bank could provide for most of their financial needs, and only a bank would give women as owners a real sense of dignity, a feature which lies at the heart of the SEWA movement.

Another interesting case of integrated services is *Safe*Save in Bangladesh, where financial products are built on Rutherford's analysis that savings, loans and insurance for poor households serve the same purpose of converting 'small pay-ins into large take-outs', and it is only the relationships between the pay-ins and the take-outs that are structured in different ways (Rutherford, 2000). The flexibility both SEWA Bank and *Safe*Save provide to their clients raises the challenge of discipline, which is reinforced in other systems through regular meetings and above all regular amounts of savings or loan repayments. In the case of *Safe*Save, collectors visit clients every day at their home or workplace to compensate, although savers can deposit any amount that day, including nothing. SEWA Bank has also recently introduced regular (weekly) collections at women's homes. However, SEWA Bank provides fewer such regular routines, and this is perhaps one reason that SEWA Bank may not have grown as much as other large or old MFOs.

Other insurance schemes

Insurance services can provide security to an MFO as much as to its clients. An MFO has to be sustainable and its sustainability depends largely on the sustainability of the client group it is catering to. This 'self-interested' strategy on the part of the MFO indirectly addresses the well-being of its clients also.

For instance, Grameen-style groups promoted by SHARE (see Chapter 7) and the savings and credit cooperatives promoted by the Cooperative Development Foundation (CDF; see Chapter 5) have funds set aside to meet contingencies. SHARE charges Re 1 from each member every week to maintain the contingency fund. In CDF cooperatives, members make 'interest-free' deposits under their Death Relief Assurance Scheme. These deposits are in turn invested in other securities, and the income earned on these is set aside for contingencies. Both funds are used to write-off outstanding loans if an existing member dies. This provides some immediate relief to the family of the deceased. In addition, both funds grant a certain amount towards funeral expenses. The CDF cooperatives also return the original deposit amount to the family of the deceased member.

In both cases, the primary motivation of having such a death-relief fund is to safeguard the loan portfolio from contingencies, while CDF has been able to extend this 'self-interested' policy to provide some additional benefits to the family of the deceased member. By safeguarding themselves, both organisations are also, to some extent, safeguarding the interests of their members.

What is important in this model is that there is no element of subsidy taken from any other source. Both the schemes are managed by the groups, and operate on the funds provided by poor members themselves. Both organisations have simply designed an effective framework for managing such contingencies.

Such an approach is different from that of SEWA Bank which, for developmental reasons, provides not only a much fuller range of insurance services but also covers some of the contingent liabilities through the Bank's assets which are not separated into a special fund. In this way, the more comprehensive insurance services come with greater risk to the MFO, which SEWA Bank is better able to bear than the SHARE groups or CDF cooperatives because it is an integrated bank with significant assets. However, it is not backed by the kind of assets most insurance companies seek.

Inspired by SEWA Bank, Friends of Women's World Banking (FWWB), India is spreading integrated social-security services among some of its partners. Four have already instituted life insurance and livestock insurance (provided at reduced rates by United India Insurance Company), covering 10,000 people. Two others are in the process of enrolling their members (FWWB, 2001).

BASIX, an MFO based in the city of Hyderabad, is also seeking to develop a more comprehensive range of insurance services. As an innovative organisation dealing with complex forms of financing for diverse rural needs, BASIX is exposed to greater risks than most other MFOs (see Chapter 4 for details).

BASIX has therefore identified three types of security needed by its client groups. The first is life insurance in the case of an unfortunate death. Second, the client has to be productive and able to work. This requires insurance in the case of accident to provide a lump sum to generate an alternative income-stream. So BASIX works in collaboration with insurance companies and encourages its clients to take life and accident cover. Since existing insurance companies provide appropriate products for these purposes, BASIX facilitates the process by acting as an agent or intermediary.

However, while there are scores of mainstream insurance products that cover various types of economic activities, there are few that efficiently provide security for the economic activities of poor rural producers. Conventional insurance products cover certain types of activities like livestock-rearing, but activities like farming do not have adequate risk cover.

BASIX has identified two types of risks (yield-risk and price-risk) that can both greatly affect the economic activities of its client groups. BASIX is therefore working to develop a product to cover yield-risks and is lobbying for micro-future markets that can cover price-risks. By experimenting or advocating these two products, BASIX is of course safeguarding its own interests as well as extending security cover to its clients.

A final example is the Mulkanoor cooperative in rural Andhra Pradesh, which is both an agricultural and a banking cooperative. Unlike most other cooperatives and indeed MFOs, this offers integrated banking services to its members. So it has traditionally laid equal emphasis on savings as well as credit. However, security cover was not available, except access to the voluntary and compulsory savings of members on termination of membership, either voluntarily or due to death. Recently, therefore, the cooperative started offering social-security cover to all its members and is bearing the cost of the premia on its own account. This is seen as a welfare measure by the cooperative after it had attained a certain financial strength and maturity. While safeguarding its own credit programme might have been one of the triggers, the product was introduced decades after the cooperative was set up. Here we see a mature organisation looking at ensuring its sustainability by enhancing its own salience in the lives of its members (Shah, 1995) through alternative routes, of which social security cover is just one.

In addition to SEWA Bank, these cases show that insurance services are an important part of micro-finance, at the very least to protect an MFO's loan portfolio against default on the death of a borrower. However, insurance services go well beyond this in terms of development impact. SEWA Bank provides an excellent case of fairly comprehensive coverage to meet the diverse needs of its clients, which is now being copied by others. BASIX and the Mulkanoor cooperative are two other MFOs that are going down the same route, in part to protect their loan portfolio (BASIX), in part to sustain themselves by enhancing member loyalty (Mulkanoor), in part to meet the needs of their clients or members (both).

Lending for housing

Housing finance is a popular product for mainstream financial intermediaries. The motivation for offering housing loans is, however, significantly different between mainstream banks and MFOs. In the former case, housing finance is seen as one of the safest and least risky products. A major part of the clientele comprises people who have a regular source of income and are able to pay monthly instalments without much difficulty. Housing finance can also enhance the income-stream of borrowers—either through increased rents if the new dwelling is let out, or through savings on rent, if the dwelling is self-occupied. The house also serves as loan collateral for the bank and gives the borrower several tax incentives.

None of the above attributes work for poor people, particularly not in rural areas. In most cases housing loans provided by MFOs are used to improve an existing dwelling and there is little enhanced income-stream from this activity. Poor people who do not pay tax cannot benefit from tax incentives either. Loan terms are usually shorter in the case of housing loans by MFOs, usually not exceeding three years, compared to a maximum of 20 years offered by mainstream banks. Why then do MFOs often encourage their clients to seek shelter-related loans?

The primary reason is what we discovered in the case of SEWA Bank. Housing loans enable clients to build their portfolio of assets that can provide both security as well as income if improvements to the house also improve a client's business premises. Another reason is that housing loans provide strong visual evidence of impact. Graduating a client from a thatched hut to a tiled-roof house to a concrete house provides a very powerful visual image of the impact created. This effect is not so visible in any other lending activity. Achieving such visual impact is important not only for the client's self-confidence and to attract further clients to the MFO, but also of course for funders of the MFO.

In most MFOs replicating the Grameen model, like SHARE, housing loans are possible only from the third or fourth cycle of lending. So if a client has been with the organisation for about three years, it is assumed that s/he has garnered enough financial power to invest in housing, which creates additional outflows without significantly enhancing cash-inflows.

However, while SEWA Bank and SHARE have large exposures to housing, many other Indian MFOs do not, suggesting that housing investment is being given far less emphasis than savings and insurance.

Other forms of security

Educating children can provide some of the greatest security for a family in the future. Many clients of SEWA Bank save to provide for their children's education. Likewise, FWWB (2001) is extending loans to its partners for on-lending for education through SHGs. Two partners, ASMITA, an urban NGO in Secunderabad in the state of Andhra Pradesh, and Development Organisation for Women (DOW), a rural NGO in the state of Tamil Nadu, have introduced such loans. So far, 1,375 children (of whom 1,158 were girls) have benefited from loans used primarily for paying term or tuition fees, and the purchase of books, uniforms, shoes and other related expenses. The programme is focused on educating girl children in particular in an attempt to shift attitudes on girls' education.

There are also other needs that can be addressed. An interesting example is that of Sanghamithra,[4] an MFO promoted by the NGO MYRADA in the state of Karnataka. While talking to members, Sanghamithra found that one of the important needs for which members wanted money was to carry out an annual pilgrimage to Tirupati in Andhra Pradesh. Sanghamithra was quick to respond positively to this need by developing a special loan product for it. Their argument was that since money is in any case fungible and members would in any case spend the money for an annual pilgrimage, what was the harm in designing a product for that? Another way of looking at this is that it is taking care of not only the physical but also mental well-being of members. Perhaps, a peaceful mind is happier working on an enterprise and repaying loans!

Conclusion

In this chapter we have taken the first step beyond micro-credit to explore a range of micro-financial services for poor people, including savings and insurance, with credit for emergencies and housing as much as for micro-enterprise. Such a range of services is important to meet the diverse financial needs of poor people and provide them greater social and economic security in the face of the many shocks that poor households face. Only once they enjoy such security will they be able to access micro-finance products that help them to develop rather than protect their livelihoods (as we explore in Chapter 4).

SEWA Bank, which has most successfully developed this range of micro-financial products, has integrated them into a coherent development framework to lift poor people out of poverty; first enabling them to get out of debt and build their savings until gradually they build their assets both at home and in their business, all the while protecting them from the loss of assets and from falling back into debt through insurance, savings and emergency loans. SEWA Bank has had greater impact on its members in the earlier rather than later stages of this framework, suggesting the need for more intensive work on supporting the development of micro-enterprise which would enable greater asset creation.

While other MFOs are also developing insurance products, insurance coverage for poor people in India is often unreliable (see Chapter 8) and still minuscule in scale, and is even more limited in terms of their long-term security in old age. The main lesson to draw from the review in this chapter is that the full range of micro-financial services needs to become much more widely available to the many poor households in India that need it. While MFOs are the pioneers here, such an agenda will clearly require the intensive engagement of the mainstream financial sector (see Chapter 11).

At the same time, MFOs are beginning to explore financial products for a range of other needs, including housing, education and even cultural needs. In the Indian context, where livelihood opportunities are significantly enhanced through educational achievements and skills, developing financial products to support education and vocational training may be particularly appropriate. While many MFOs and NGOs undertake capacity-building and technical assistance to support the purposes for which clients have borrowed, there are very few financial products we know of that enable clients themselves to acquire education and skills. Filling this gap could provide important additional security for poor households.

Notes

1. Chen and Snodgrass (1999: 29) found comparable results. 'Over the two years prior to the survey, nearly three-fourths of the total sample households (71%) experienced at least one economic shock and more than one-fifth (21%) suffered two or three shocks.... The most common type of shock experienced, reported by two-thirds of each sample group, was "serious illness". The next most common shock—reported by 15–20% of the respondents—was "marriage costs".' Sixty-three per cent of households experiencing shocks borrowed from non-SEWA sources to cover some of the costs; 23 per cent of households used personal savings. Households may of course have used more than one strategy to cope with the shock.

2. Chapter 8 reveals the extent of malpractice among insurance agents serving poor clients. The importance of SEWA Bank providing intermediation between some of the insurance companies and clients—making payments, keeping records, helping with claims—should not be underestimated.

3. Actual loan use (rather than the loan purpose) may be even more skewed towards such lending. For example, a survey of loans taken by members of rural SHGs supported by SEWA Bank (Murthy, 1999) revealed the following breakdown of the number of loans across the three different samples used in the survey: consumption (24–33 per cent); treatment for illness (20–26 per cent); marriage and rituals (15–18 per cent), trade (12–15 per cent); house repair (5–12 per cent); livestock (2–5 per cent); and other (1–3 per cent).

4. All the SHGs promoted by MYRADA are called *sanghas* (association in Kannada, the language in Karnataka). Sanghamithra ('friend of the associations') was formed as a company limited by guarantee engaging in financial services to support the SHGs promoted by MYRADA.

Chapter 4

Micro-finance and livelihoods: The challenge of BASIX[1]

Introduction

In the previous chapter we reviewed the role of micro-finance in providing a wide range of financial services, including savings and insurance, and not just credit, to meet the needs of poor people. Such services are particularly important for protecting poor households against the often severe consequences of fluctuating incomes, lumpy or emergency expenditures, ill-health, disability or death, and the costs of extortionate credit.

We provided examples, such as the Self-employed Women's Association (SEWA) Bank and the savings and credit cooperatives promoted by the Cooperative Development Foundation (CDF), that suggested poor people often value savings more than credit. Indeed, at the level of household consumption and enterprise, savings and credit both perform the same function, enabling smooth income-flows or lumpy expenditure, either by saving in advance or paying back in arrears (see the introduction to Chapter 3).

Like many micro-finance organisations (MFOs) providing appropriate savings products, SEWA Bank and the CDF cooperatives have found it much easier to accumulate deposits than give loans. At the core of this dilemma is the inability of MFOs to enhance the ability of borrowers to absorb credit beyond the needs of household consumption and minimal working capital for their micro-businesses.

Protective financial services may be critical for poverty alleviation, but do little for helping people out of poverty. For this, promotional financial services are required, primarily for enhancing livelihoods among poor people. As this chapter sets out, this is a far greater challenge than the delivery of micro-credit.

We explore this challenge primarily by reviewing the case of BASIX, India's second largest MFO in terms of outreach, which has been at the forefront of innovation and development in integrating micro-credit and livelihood promotion.

Livelihood promotion and the challenge for micro-finance

BASIX has defined a livelihood as ways of keeping oneself meaningfully occupied, by using one's endowments (human and material), to generate adequate resources to meet the requirements of the household in a sustainable manner.

In a manual on livelihood promotion, published in 2001 by BASIX and the New Economics Foundation (NEF) (Datta et al., 2001), the authors argue that livelihood promotion goes well beyond enhancing incomes. The goals of livelihood promotion may also incorporate creating assets or wealth, increasing food security, reducing risk, reducing variances in income, reducing rural to urban migration, organising producers to have greater control over their livelihoods, enhancing the money that circulates within the local economy. From this perspective, it becomes obvious that micro-finance can only be one input, however necessary, for promoting livelihoods.

Within the context of micro-finance, the resulting debate has usually been framed in terms of minimalist credit provision versus integrated services, the latter including both credit and business support services.

This debate is important, for both poorer and wealthier borrowers of MFOs. First, there is evidence that micro-credit can also harm poor people. Vijay Mahajan (1997: 9), the founder and Managing Director of the BASIX group, summarised the findings set out in Hulme and Mosley (1996) as follows:

> ... the increase in income of micro-credit borrowers is directly proportional to their starting level of income—

the poorer they were to start with, the less the impact of the loan. One could live with this finding in an imperfect world, but what is really troubling is that a vast majority of *those whose starting income was below the poverty-line actually end up with less income after getting a micro-loan, as compared to a control group which did not get the loan.* This should stop converts from offering micro-credit as the solution for poverty eradication, since it seems to do more harm than good to the poorest.

Can services in addition to credit prevent the poorest from being harmed by the provision of credit?

Second, poor borrowers from MFOs often do not graduate to higher and higher loans, and consequently to productive small enterprises. While credit may initially be the ruling constraint for micro-enterprises, for them to grow beyond a certain size, other constraints come into play, for example, of markets and managerial capacity. Micro-enterprises are therefore unlikely to grow significantly without inputs that can address these additional constraints. This is why MFOs using stepped lending methodologies (providing ever larger loans if earlier loans have been repaid on time) have often experienced that apparently good borrowers suddenly fail. The availability of credit has taken the entrepreneurs beyond their capacity to manage their businesses effectively.

However, even the debate on minimalist (credit) versus integrated services does not go far enough. Back in 1990, Tom Dichter and Vijay Mahajan argued that any approach to livelihood promotion should be contingent on the requirements of the situation, based on a systematic analysis. Micro-credit is necessary but not a sufficient condition for micro-enterprise promotion. The success of micro-enterprise depends on a whole range of resources (e.g., natural, human, social and financial) and opportunities (e.g., markets and the policy and institutional environment). Other inputs are therefore required, not just business support and training, but also the identification of livelihood opportunities, establishing market linkages for inputs and outputs, adapting technologies, organising producers, sub-sectoral analysis and policy reform.

The challenge for micro-finance practitioners is therefore that micro-credit must be coupled not only with business support to individual enterprises among their borrowers, but integrated within sectorally based technical support which can develop a large number of productive and sustainable livelihoods.

Similar insights emerged from the development of tools for sub-sectoral analysis (USAID, 1987) which clearly demonstrate that livelihood outcomes are often determined as part of larger systems (sub-sectors), and that a focus on the livelihoods of individual households may fall far short of having a significant and sustained impact on poor people.

In a recent review of BASIX, Dichter (2001: 5) writes:

> ... the desired outcome of development is aggregate and sustainable positive change in productivity and income that leads either directly or indirectly to economic possibility for growing numbers of poor and low-income people. This is where livelihood promotion should lead. Livelihood promotion is not ... just about generating income for the poor, but about generating additionality, long-term economic possibility and eventually mobility out of poverty. Lending Rs 1000 for consumption purposes does not fit this bill, even though it may be helpful to a poor woman and her household. Nor even does lending Rs 1000 so that a road-side seller can sell two dozen mangoes instead of one dozen, especially when he or she sits alongside 20 other mango-sellers in the same market. [There is no] convincing evidence [that] such loans ... are 'developmental'. Rather they suffice to alleviate poverty in the short run without necessarily reducing it. Thus I make a distinction between poverty alleviation and development. They are not the same.

The micro-finance industry has become fixated with micro-enterprise, as though it can shift many poor people out of poverty. The reality is that many micro-enterprises are not productive, but simply subsistence enterprises. Providing working capital may enable one micro-enterprise to expand, but often at the expense of another equally deserving enterprise.

Moreover, proponents of micro-credit often assume that poor people would all like to be self-employed. As Mahajan (1997: 8) argues, 'It is true that a certain proportion of poor people do like to take up micro-scale farming, processing, manufacturing or trading activities, but usually they do so to supplement their income from <u>wage-employment</u>. A majority of poor people, particularly the poorest (such as landless labourers in India) want steady wage-employment, on- or off-farm.'

Productive small enterprises, that can fill the missing middle between micro- and larger enterprises, that can provide wage-employment to poor people while often not being managed by them, need to come back into focus for livelihood development, as they were in the 1980s before the micro-finance industry emerged.

Such insights therefore provide a fundamental challenge to micro-credit practitioners. To be 'developmental', in the sense suggested by Dichter, they must not only go beyond the minimalist role of providing credit only, but also beyond the more integrated approach that provides business support services to their borrowers. Micro-credit must be used instrumentally as part of a strategy to effect a sustained change in the economic well-being of poor people.

Fortunately, the Indian economy provides many opportunities for this. Infrastructure development, whether revitalising old infrastructure that has fallen into disuse or was never properly used, or introducing new infrastructure like telephone booths (PCOs), provides significant opportunities for small and micro-enterprise, as does the improving climate for enterprise generally. The challenge is whether MFOs can harness such macro-changes to sub-sectors that have the potential to generate substantial livelihoods for poor people.

Developing livelihoods is thus far more challenging than providing financial services. As Dichter (2001: 8, 22–23) argues,

For the magic of micro-finance, with its promise to be self-financing while building economic capacity from the grassroots up, is far more seductive than the complex and more conceptually abstract realm of sub-sector analysis, rural infrastructure revitalisation, and technical support to enterprises.... As difficult as micro-finance is, it is not really rocket science and certainly not much an art. If the half dozen or so professional quality micro-finance manuals produced in the last 10 years were all to be followed carefully, many more good micro-finance organisations would now exist. The techniques of micro-finance can be learned, and imitated. In contrast the kind of work BASIX has pioneered in the enterprise development sphere and its continuing experimentation to find the best way of integrating financial services and sector-based enterprise development represents more of an art.

When BASIX was designed and set up in 1996, it called itself a 'new generation financial institution', largely to distinguish itself from the dominant practice within India of highly subsidised and directed credit (see Table 4.1).

Table 4.1: BASIX' seven I's of new generation development finance

Attribute	New generation behaviour
Image of rural small borrowers	Not see them as beneficiaries, but as entry-level customers.
Independence	No political interference, such as loan waivers, nor government ownership and bureaucratic control.
Interest rates	For deposits: high enough to attract savings; For loans: high enough to cover all costs.
Incentives	For staff: to ensure good customer service but prudent lending; For customers: to ensure deposits come in and loans are repaid on time.
Intermediation	Between local savers and borrowers; and Between local demand/surpluses and non-local financial markets.
Increased capacity	Larger scale of operations; Better systems for MIS and internal supervision; and greater ability to comply with regulation.
Integration	With social intermediation (e.g., by self-help groups) and technical assistance (e.g., by non-governmental organisations and government bodies in micro-enterprise promotion).

Within the current international context, the challenge of being a 'new generation financial institution' is to see whether a micro-finance organisation can go beyond the well analysed (if not practised) ground of minimalist versus integrated services, beyond seeking to combine outreach and sustainability, however necessary, to engage in genuine livelihood promotion.

By the mid-1990s many institutions in development came to believe that credit alone (aka 'minimalist credit') was a powerful mechanism of poverty alleviation and, it was assumed, of development. In many places and amongst many organisations lending money to the poor became a goal in itself. Urgency about outreach to the poor grew. At the same time sustainability of the lending operation became accepted as a necessary goal (though rigorous tests of sustainability were slow in being accepted).

By the late 1990s, especially within the micro-finance sector, we heard hardly any lively debate on large questions about development. Instead what debate there was in micro-finance focused almost exclusively on technique and scale, with purpose and impact having been taken largely for granted.

Inevitably a 'numbers game' began to be played. Who could reach more people, and more of the poorest people? Who could scale up fastest? Who could balance low transaction costs, high outreach, and high loan recovery the best? (Dichter, 2001: 10).

Can MFOs instead put livelihood development, not just poverty alleviation, at the heart of their mission? We now look at the experience of BASIX to see both what it has achieved and the many challenges it has faced in pioneering such objectives.

Introduction to BASIX: Mission and financials

BASIX was set up in 1996 as a group of companies which now comprises the holding company, a non-banking financial company, a not-for profit company and a Local Area Bank.[2] BASIX targets rural areas with the following mission:

> to promote a large number of sustainable livelihoods, including for the rural poor and women, through the provision of financial services and technical assistance in an integrated manner. BASIX will strive to yield a competitive rate of return to its investors so as to be able to access mainstream capital and human resources on a continuous basis.

BASIX has therefore made livelihood promotion its ultimate goal, not the delivery of credit. For this it needs to integrate financial and non-financial services to enterprises, and not just provide credit to the poorest of the poor. BASIX recognises that to generate large-scale rural employment, poor rural people will require wage-employment in small enterprises, in addition to self-employment through subsistence and micro-enterprises. To achieve such impact, the organisation must not only operate on sound business principles, and achieve financial viability, but must eventually become a mainstream player.

BASIX now has financial operations in 2,200 villages in 18 districts across four states in India, and works in a further five states,[3] with over 200 staff, including Field Executives and Customer Service Agents, based out of 11 units (branches). From June 1996 to September 2001, BASIX disbursed more than Rs 60 crore (600 million) in 58,000 loans. Loans outstanding on 30 September 2001 stood at Rs 20 crore among 21,000 active borrowers, with an on-time repayment rate of 91 per cent. BASIX' ratio of performing loan assets was 95 per cent of its outstanding, which is among the highest in the rural financial sector in India, and compares well with 60 to 80 per cent among cooperative and Regional Rural Banks (RRBs). This performance is in spite of the fact that the main region in which BASIX is working has faced severe drought conditions in two of BASIX' first five years of operations.

BASIX has been highly successful in attracting loans and equity from a wide range of development and banking sources, both national and international. As on 30 June 2001, BASIX had secured Rs 26.3 crore (263 million) of loans from international sources and Rs 12 crore (120 million) from national sources (including the first loan to an MFO in India from a private commercial bank). Interest rates on these loans range from 6 to 13.5 per cent. BASIX has also raised Rs 11.9 crore (119 million) in equity, including from the International Finance Corporation of the World Bank, as well as international and national financial institutions.[4] The equity deals in India were all firsts of their kind. Securing these loans and equity has been challenging, often involving new ways of doing things for donors and investors alike, and no other MFO in India has anything like this mix of investors.

BASIX seeks to achieve high financial performance, and therefore compares itself with averages of the fully sustainable micro-finance organisations across the world, as reported in the *Microbanking Bulletin* (see Table 4.2). These indicate that BASIX has maintained its operating costs at a much lower level than the average, while the return on its assets is 1.0 per cent compared to the average of 1.3 per cent. This has primarily happened as BASIX charges a much lower interest (21–24 per cent *per annum*, which along with loan processing fees and other income yields 26.4 per cent compared to 43.1 per cent for other fully sustainable MFOs).

Table 4.2: Comparing financial indicators for BASIX and fully sustainable micro-finance organisations reported in the Microbanking Bulletin (as on 31 March 2000)

	BASIX	Fully sustainable MFOs
Income to average loan outstanding	26.4%	43.1%
Operating cost to average loan outstanding	15.8%	21.9%
Interest cost of funds to average loan outstanding	7.7%	6.3%
Loan losses to average loan outstanding	1.5%	1.9%
Return on assets	1.0%	1.3%

To manage its financial performance, BASIX has developed a sophisticated Financial Accounting and Management Information System (FAMIS), enabling it to track its portfolio in detail: by borrower, by Customer Service Agent, by Field Executive, by unit (branch), and of course for the company.

BASIX has also developed sophisticated systems for human resource development, including elaborate selection processes, regular self-assessment and appraisals through line-managers, remuneration that rewards staff against performance targets, significant training both on-the-job and in special programmes, and involvement in developing the annual strategic plans which are made for each unit.

Within its first five years of operations, BASIX thus created and mastered a well-oiled financial machine, and, as described further below, pioneered a number of operational innovations that mark significant contributions to the field (Dichter, 2001: 8). This record is all the more remarkable in light of BASIX' ambitious objectives of livelihood promotion and its constant innovation in pursuit of these objectives. What then has BASIX achieved in terms of livelihoods?

Promoting livelihoods through BASIX

BASIX has ambitious objectives of both promoting livelihoods and becoming a sustainable and indeed mainstream organisation. To achieve these ambitions, the first five years of its operations focused on developing a sound and credible financial record, and innovating and developing a range of mechanisms for supporting livelihoods, in the spirit of seeing what worked in practice. While the first has been achieved and continues to improve, the innovation and development of livelihood support mechanisms continues with great experimentation and diversity, and cannot yet be judged to have achieved a steady state. So what is the record?

BASIX clientele

Let us first look at BASIX' clientele. In its focus on poor rural producers, BASIX has been careful to distinguish between survival activity and enterprise; between poverty-lending and enterprise-lending; between loans used for consumption and loans used for working capital; between micro-financial services and development (Dichter, 2001: 22). BASIX, therefore, addresses a wide range of rural clientele, distinguished both by the scale of their enterprises and by the sector in which these enterprises operate.

In terms of scale, BASIX reaches out to three categories, with different products designed for each group, as follows:

Figure 4.1: The pyramid of rural producers and BASIX clientele

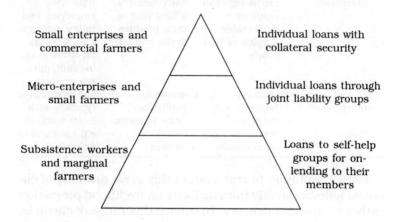

Small enterprises and commercial farmers — Individual loans with collateral security

Micro-enterprises and small farmers — Individual loans through joint liability groups

Subsistence workers and marginal farmers — Loans to self-help groups for on-lending to their members

Thus BASIX lends to a broad range of clientele, ranging from entrepreneurs (using direct loans with collateral) to landless poor women (via self-help groups [SHGs] and loans below Rs 50,000 with no collateral). Joint liability groups of five borrowers who mutually guarantee each other's loans are the mechanism to serve the group in the middle. The pyramid broadly reflects the numbers of rural producers in each of these categories, as well as in BASIX' loan portfolio.

Examples of each category of borrower, and the different sectors they operate in, are illustrated in Table 4.3. The table makes clear that while BASIX operates in rural areas, it by no means restricts itself to agricultural lending. Allied activities, such as livestock rearing, and non-farm activities, including services as well as manufacturing, are equally important for the development of a balanced rural economy which generates significant livelihoods for poor rural producers.

Table 4.3: BASIX clientele by type and sector

	Agriculture sector	Allied sectors	Non-farm sector
Subsistence workers	Marginal farmers and small farmers in semi-arid areas	Backyard poultry rearers; landless livestock rearers	Cottage units and artisan 'own account enterprises'; e.g., handloom weavers
Micro-enterprises	Small farmers producing cash crops or a marketable surplus of food crops	Small poultry/ dairy farmers, selling part of their produce to the market	Micro-enterprises typically employing two to five workers; e.g., wooden furniture making unit, auto-repair shop
Small and agro-enterprises	Plantation farmers; e.g., orchards, floriculture and aqua-culture	Commercial poultry and dairy farmers; fish-pond owners	Small enterprises, typically with 6–10 workers; e.g., stone-slab polishing unit

BASIX' ambition to reach out to this great diversity of clientele follows directly from its focus on livelihood promotion rather than credit delivery. To service this range of clientele, BASIX cannot rely on one or two products only. Instead, BASIX has developed a wide range of loan products, for farm and non-farm activities, as well as for general purposes (for example, in lending to SHGs) and housing. This product development continues. For example, BASIX is currently developing products for catering to the needs of large numbers of micro-entrepreneurs who sell in small rural towns or in weekly markets (*haat* or *shandy*) that operate in rural areas.

A key distinction among BASIX' loan products is between (i) direct loans and (ii) indirect loans. Direct loans are extended directly to rural producers by BASIX. Indirect loans are extended through intermediaries, who in turn on-lend to the ultimate users of the loan, often her/his customers. These intermediaries include not only the typical SHGs and other community-based financial organisations, but also market agents such as agricultural commission agents, input dealers, wholesale merchants, agro-processing firms, seed-production organisers, even in some cases moneylenders.

Using these agents helps BASIX to extend credit to a much larger number of rural producers, whom it would find difficult and far too costly to reach directly.

Almost all direct loans extended by BASIX are small loans below Rs 20,000, all without collateral. A small number, less than 5 per cent of the loans, are between Rs 20,000 to 50,000 and here BASIX does take some collateral. Eighty per cent of BASIX loans are originated and serviced by Customer Service Agents (CSAs), who receive incentive-based wages and follow a regular weekly route to service their customers. It is these CSAs that enable BASIX to reach out to borrowers dispersed over wide areas and in locations often not well connected.

Through these means BASIX has disbursed more than Rs 60 crore (600 million) in 58,000 loans since June 1996. Over half of BASIX' customers were below the official poverty line, which is austerely defined. In September 2001 the total loans outstanding stood at Rs 20 crore (200 million), of which 28 per cent were outstanding to women borrowers. In terms of purpose, about 40 per cent of the lending was to the non-farm sector, 20 per cent to dairy and other livestock and 30 per cent to agriculture. About 10 per cent of the lending was to women's SHGs and classified as 'general purpose' loans.

BASIX has developed estimates of employment generated by different types of loans, assuming 250 person-days of employment are equivalent to a full-time livelihood. According to these estimates, BASIX has supported over 40,000 livelihoods.

The latest Customer Satisfaction Audit revealed that:

- customers rate BASIX highest in terms of providing access to credit as BASIX lends for purposes not covered by others;
- customers cite BASIX' advantages as 'approachability, friendliness of procedures and timeliness of loans';
- two-thirds of customers reported the loan was adequate and cited flexibility in disbursement and recovery; and
- indirect loans reach poorer customers.

The areas of concern raised by the audit were:

- customers with access to formal sources find BASIX' interest rates high;

- transaction costs in certain categories are higher than alternate sources;
- the level of awareness of BASIX is low among indirect borrowers;
- some intermediaries are charging more than the rate of interest agreed with BASIX for on-lending.

Technical assistance and support services

The not-for-profit company within the BASIX group, which is called Indian Grameen Services (IGS), has been responsible for developing technical assistance and support services for BASIX' borrowers. BASIX has freely and widely interpreted technical assistance and support services. It has responded opportunistically during its first five years which has led to a broad range of activities.

BASIX estimates that about a third of its customers do not need technical assistance as they are quite adept at what they are doing. Indeed, some of them are used by BASIX as 'trainer borrowers' who provide practical advice to other borrowers engaged in a similar activity through BASIX' Inter-Borrower Expertise Exchange Programme.

About 50 per cent of BASIX borrowers who need assistance have received some form of technical assistance or support services, although such services are not a precondition nor even a supportive criterion for credit appraisal.

For BASIX to provide such services directly to each of its borrowers would have been hugely costly and made BASIX' operations unsustainable without huge grants. To avoid such costs BASIX initially made use of other market agents, including the trade intermediaries it used for on-lending.

Such intermediaries provide a range of other services to their customers, not least critical market linkages. For example, by extending loans through smaller commission agents who are constrained by their lack of working capital, small farmers are able to access more agricultural inputs. Likewise, seed-production organisers, who are also used as lending intermediaries, provide technical advice to their customers on improved cultivation practices.

BASIX has also linked up with other input-suppliers and purchasers of outputs who do not act as lending intermediaries. For example, BASIX has made agreements with seed, fertiliser and agro-chemical dealers to supply BASIX' clients as loans in kind. The economic interests of these parties are strong enough for them to provide specific inputs that can complement or replace the need for non-financial support from BASIX.

This method provides a cost-efficient way of delivering technical and market-linkage support to BASIX clients, including from entrepreneurs and companies specialising in specific activities where BASIX has no competitive advantage.

However, BASIX has also invested heavily in other technical assistance and support services, often delivered in partnership with relevant companies, research institutes and non-governmental organisations (NGOs). Such support includes building SHGs, introducing new agricultural practices, reviving defunct rural infrastructure, enabling borrowers to learn from each other, and reducing the risk they face through insurance and other measures. Box 4.1 provides a summary of these services.

Box 4.1: Summary of technical assistance and support services provided by BASIX from June 1996 to June 2001

Quality Improvement Programme for existing self-help groups (SHGs)

A significant proportion of BASIX credit extended to women is through SHGs and their federations. In collaboration with local NGOs, IGS has provided training to over 500 SHGs in accounting, loan appraisal, managing funds, setting interest rates and repayment schedules, and in linking up with livelihood opportunities.

Micro-finance Agents for forming new SHGs

This programme is innovative in using local individuals to form SHGs and paying them by results. Over 300 groups have been formed by this programme, of which 150 have graduated beyond the start-up phase and 110 have received loans from BASIX' non-banking financial company. Indian Grameen Services has also provided training to NGOs promoting SHGs.

(Contd)

(Box 4.1 Contd)

Dryland Agriculture Productivity Enhancement Programme

This has focused on *increasing yields through better seeds and practices* for various crops such as sunflower, cotton, chilli and groundnut (each in collaboration with specialised commercial companies, public universities and research institutes and NGOs). *Cost-saving pest control* measures have been diffused to farmers in collaboration with a range of NGOs, as have *lift, borewell and micro-drip irrigation* facilities, along with new practices for irrigated agriculture. *New crops* such as paprika, watermelon and tree crops have been introduced by commercial companies, and over 1,000 *improved variety buffaloes and cows* have been purchased by farmers, and *veterinary care* for these has been provided by cooperatives or NGOs.

Rural Infrastructure Revival Programme

Three *milk chilling plants* of the Andhra Pradesh Dairy Development Cooperative Federation (APDDCF) have been revived or made more viable by enhanced procurement of milk, itself made possible by intensive credit from BASIX in the villages along procurement routes. As a result, in the first case, daily procurement of milk, which had gone down to 270 litres a day in 1997, touched 10,000 litres a day in 2000. Bulk coolers have been installed in a number of locations.

A study of *defunct lift-irrigation schemes*, each with a command area of over 1,200 acres, has been undertaken for six schemes through a partner NGO. In the first case, an investment of Rs 100,000 enabled farmers to revitalise an irrigation system worth more than Rs 25 million. Other studies have looked at *rural electric-power distribution* and the *revival of traditional tanks*.

Inter-borrower Expertise Exchange Programme

Indian Grameen Services recognised that some of the successful local entrepreneurs could be the best counsellors for other entrepreneurs. Thus it initiated a programme to disseminate knowledge about efficient practices by arranging meetings for exchanging expertise among borrowers. It has identified over 90 expert borrowers in 23 activities, who provide training to others. Over 200 borrowers have been given such training in dairy, bakery, woodwork, repairs, better *kirana* (general and grocery) shop management, etc., as well as on SHGs and savings and credit cooperatives.

Market Linkage Programme

Under this programme, market studies are carried out for selected commodities produced by a large number of poor people—groundnut, pulses, vegetables and milk. Promising market segments are identified and pilot market-links established for these, for example, selling groundnut for confectionery rather than crushing into oil; vegetables to higher-income urban markets after sorting, grading and packing; and chilled liquid milk to local rural and small towns rather than pasteurised milk to distant markets already saturated with competition.

Risk Mitigation Programme

Crop insurance was facilitated by IGS based on mutual insurance and peer monitoring for two years in collaboration with an NGO working with dryland farmers. BASIX also offered *debt relief* upon the death of a borrower, and now *life cover* has been arranged through insurance companies. *Cattle insurance* has also been arranged through insurance companies. *Physical risk mitigation* has been achieved through improving irrigation systems, including the introduction of low-cost micro-drip irrigation systems in collaboration with a specialised NGO.

Institutional development for other MFOs

Indian Grameen Services has also been active in strategic planning, management support and capacity-building for other MFOs, including for an NGO promoting community-based MFOs, covering 10,100 borrowers with more than Rs 40 million of funds, as well as for other NGOs and 21 cooperatives. The total outreach of MFOs under this programme exceeds 100,000 borrowers.

The following two examples illustrate some of these support services which relate directly to livelihood promotion.

Indian Grameen Services (IGS) sought to demonstrate the usefulness of drip-irrigation technology in dryland agriculture. In Mahabubnagar district in the state of Andhra Pradesh it installed drip-irrigation systems for 35 farmers in the first year, in collaboration with an NGO called International Development Enterprises (which provided the low-cost drip-irrigation technology), UNDP's South Asia Poverty Alleviation Programme (which organised women from dryland farming households in the area) and Soubhagya Seeds Pvt Ltd (who took up distribution of the equipment on commercial terms). Farmers using drip-irrigation have reported a significant increase in production of chillies. Within a year of this demonstration, installation of drip-irrigation systems was taking place of its own accord, delivered by a range of commercial parties.

The collaboration of BASIX and the Andhra Pradesh Dairy Development Cooperative Federation (APDDCF) in Mahabubnagar district in Andhra Pradesh led to an increase of average milk collection by the cooperatives in the area. Daily procurement, which had gone down to 270 litres a day in 1997, touched 10,000 litres a day in 2000. Providing integrated extension services and credit through BASIX helped in this achievement. Following this experience, IGS helped to link dairy farmers with other APDDCF chilling plants in Kamareddy, Kurnool and Adilabad. Impressed with this turnaround, the top management of APDDCF has requested BASIX to extend similar services for their chilling plants at many other places.

In such cases, the innovation BASIX has undertaken to develop intermediaries, channels for on-lending and partners providing complementary services can have development multiplier effects in key sectors such as agriculture and dairy beyond the impact on individual clients of credit and complementary non-financial services. And some of these multiplier effects could be substantial, not only in terms of aggregate productivity, but in terms of creating new demand for financial services at a high enough volume to support BASIX' own financial development (Dichter, 2001: 15).

BASIX has also invested in medium-term consultancy on technology solutions. This work has led to developing and piloting several smart-card products. If the tests are successful, these technologies, especially the *Shabri* and *Sudama* cards, have enormous potential, not only to further reduce transaction costs, but to spread access to poor people hitherto unreached by micro-financial services (ibid.: 15).

Exploring new livelihood opportunities

Indian Grameen Services is also responsible for exploring new livelihood opportunities. Since the inception of BASIX, IGS has explored livelihood opportunities in new areas, designed and developed financial products for these areas, and created delivery channels for BASIX' services.

In most cases, BASIX used micro-credit as its entry point, supplemented with technical assistance and support services. However, in the states of Madhya Pradesh and Jharkhand, where economic development is very low, technical assistance and support services are preceding micro-credit in order to build capacity among rural producers.

In the states of Bihar, Maharashtra and Rajasthan, IGS initiated exploratory studies to understand the livelihood opportunities in these areas. This work included sub-sector studies of dairy, fishery, salt production and pulses.

In Dharwad district in the state of Karnataka, IGS has initiated a programme, Livelihood Initiatives in Northern Karnataka (LINK), as a part of its exploration of livelihood support opportunities. And in the state of Madhya Pradesh, it has been involved in the Madhya Pradesh Livelihood Enhancement Action Platform, with active participation of the government of Madhya Pradesh, which provides a platform for various stakeholders who can influence livelihoods in the state to come together and initiate joint action.

BASIX has also undertaken studies on a range of relevant topics, including defunct lift-irrigation schemes and traditional tanks, the distribution of rural electricity, financial products for servicing rural producers in watersheds that have been treated, estimating demand for credit for rural housing in Andhra Pradesh, and analysing livelihood opportunities for rehabilitating child labourers in parts of eastern Maharashtra.

Summary of the record

BASIX estimates that through its operations it has supported over 40,000 livelihoods in rural districts of India. BASIX has also been able to integrate a wide range of non-financial services within its lending operations, to the extent that one out of three borrowers have received some form of technical assistance or support services, which amounts to about half of the borrowers who need such services. The reason why BASIX has not yet reached the other half arises from the rapid expansion of its micro-credit operations, as it is only in the second or third year that borrowers develop enough confidence in BASIX to seek non-financial help as well.

By innovating significantly to develop cost-effective means of delivering such non-financial services, BASIX has also been able to deliver such support without an undue drain on its financial bottom-line. As on 30 June 2001 the main company within the BASIX group responsible for technical assistance and support services (IGS) had received grants that totalled about 12 to 13 per cent of the loans and equity BASIX had raised for its financial operations.

To what extent has BASIX been able to go beyond the integration of financial and non-financial services to its borrowers, to achieve the developmental impacts explored at the beginning of this chapter?

First, BASIX has been able to build on the extensive intellectual capital and experience of livelihood promotion which the promoters brought to the organisation, further deepening and enhancing these through numerous practical innovations in its operations and extensive research, from the functioning of cooperatives to detailed sub-sectoral analysis. As Dichter (2001: 11) comments, 'there are few if any major innovations or developments in micro-finance or enterprise development of which the founders are unaware'.

BASIX has also researched and engaged in its operations an extensive range of other market operators, so that its understanding of markets, and the impact of its operations, extends well beyond its own provision of financial services. Both these factors provide the necessary underpinning for significant livelihood interventions in the future.

This achievement should not be underestimated. It reflects the deep commitment of the promoters to engage in livelihood promotion in professional and systematic ways, and not just to operate financial services. Such commitment in practice (rather than just assuming financial services will have a developmental impact on poor people) is unusual among MFOs.

Second, BASIX has promoted specific activities whose impact on livelihoods goes well beyond its credit and non-financial support to individual borrowers. For example, micro-drip irrigation, now operating on a purely commercial basis in Mahabubnagar district in Andhra Pradesh, can reduce risk and enhance incomes to farmers, whether they are BASIX clients or not. Likewise, regular milk collections by chilling plants, and access to veterinary care, can enhance incomes to all poor producers supplying the plants. The latter case is particularly interesting as it is reviving existing but under-performing rural infrastructure or organisations, so that the costs for enhancing livelihoods are radically reduced in comparison to creating new facilities.

Such activities can have important multiplier effects, as Dichter (2001: 24) commented in his review of BASIX:

> To revive [moribund rural] infrastructure, bring it back to life, infuse it with workable business planning and good management can have powerful multiplier effects.... Using Rs 10,000 loans for cows and buffalos as the lever, linkages are strengthened with animal-husbandry extension, milk quality improves, the local milk-chilling plant adds value locally through job-creation, and other old plants in the region begin wanting the same thing. Moreover as the multiplier effects keep expanding, new demands for services and infrastructure may ensue, which could lead to new product development, new markets, and so on. And by breathing new viable economic life into an old moribund area of activity it also creates confidence, which in itself has real multiplier effects on individuals' lives.

At the same time, the proliferation of livelihood activities that BASIX has engaged in indicates that this part of its operations is still in an experimental and innovative phase. This is not surprising, granted that many years of livelihood promotion activities in India have still failed to produce clear guidelines on what works and what doesn't (see Datta et al., 2001).

It also raises the challenge for BASIX to become more strategic about its non-financial activities. It is not at all clear that its disparate support activities, however innovative each may be, make up a coherent livelihood promotion strategy. BASIX first needs to focus on those interventions that can produce significant livelihood gains and drop those that prove to be less effective. Second, it needs to ensure that different interventions can work together coherently for maximum impact.

For example, BASIX has not yet been able to fully use its deep understanding of sub-sectors which are significant for rural livelihoods to systematically intervene in these sub-sectors. Dichter (2001: 23) has recommended giving BASIX' sub-sector work more emphasis and rigour, providing 'innovative research and development on commodity sub-sectors that have potential to create new economies in rural areas.... The justification of such work is that it is one way to turn the threat of globalisation into opportunity. For over the long run, if India's farmers do not begin preparing for a larger market they will not be able to sustain themselves.'

The case of BASIX in fact demonstrates many challenges facing an MFO that focuses on livelihood promotion, challenges which should not be taken lightly. These challenges can be categorised into two key groups: (i) the complexity of livelihood promotion, and (ii) organisational challenges that the MFO will face.

First set of challenges: The complexity of livelihood promotion

As set out at the beginning of this chapter, livelihood promotion is complex, opening up multiple potential goals and interventions, and demanding an understanding of individual households and enterprises as well as the economic systems or sub-sectors in which they operate. Intervening in livelihood promotion is far more challenging than developing the efficient delivery of financial services.

The micro-finance industry has in fact moved away from livelihood promotion, even though the industry's roots go back to the enterprise development days of the 1980s. Instead, it has pursued financial sustainability through extending outreach and reducing costs, in particular shifting transaction costs to borrowers.

Using micro-credit to promote livelihoods may not be feasible with such a strategy. The necessary non-financial services that have to be added, and the investment in understanding the complexity of livelihood systems, incur significant costs.

Livelihood interventions may also require direct engagement with market actors, from households to exporters. They cannot therefore simply rely on loans and the financial record of borrowers as proxies of developmental impact as many MFOs have sought to do.

Nevertheless, BASIX has taken on the challenge, clearly stated in its mission, of both promoting livelihoods through the provision of integrated services and achieving financial sustainability to enable it to access mainstream capital and human resources. The record suggests that BASIX is some way down the road to achieving these ambitious goals.

BASIX is not alone in India in seeking to combine micro-credit and livelihood promotion. For example, SEWA Bank is part of the SEWA family of organisations, which has focused particularly on a rights-based approach to livelihood promotion.[5] The trade union of women slum dwellers working in the informal sector has organised over 200,000 of them and fought for their economic rights. These activities have been complemented by the provision of financial services, including savings, loans and insurance, provided through SEWA Bank.

The Cooperative Development Foundation has promoted savings and credit cooperatives, which have accumulated significant savings but have faced difficulty in lending these out (see further discussion in Chapter 5). The Foundation is now embarking on an ambitious programme of promoting dairy cooperatives, including a new processing plant in its area of operations, which will enable individuals to absorb credit for a tried and tested activity.

PRADAN, which has promoted SHGs in eastern India in particular (see further Chapters 5 and 9), has often linked these groups with water-user associations they have organised to manage lift-irrigation schemes to enhance agricultural development.

Nevertheless, BASIX has invested more than any other Indian MFO in systematically using micro-credit, integrated with technical assistance and support services, as an instrument for promoting livelihoods. BASIX has also sought to support some of the most challenging sectors, rural rather than urban, both agriculture and the non-farm sector, small as well as micro-enterprises. Each of these has presented particular challenges.

As Dichter (2001: 14–15) suggests,

It is worth noting that while there are others doing rural lending in India, on the worldwide scene, more micro-credit is aimed at urban or peri-urban populations than at rural ones. This is because rural lending is, again generally, inherently more costly, and agricultural lending more risky. But rural poverty is by far a greater problem for the developing world, and BASIX understands this. It takes on crop loans, agri-long term, and agri-allied loans, even though on-time repayment is bound to be lower in the first two categories. Likewise by tackling non-farm enterprise lending, some of which is aimed at genuine small enterprises rather than mere survival activities, it also incurs additional risk to its on time repayment. Still, it appears that BASIX methodology and careful monitoring have been generally successful in managing and balancing such risk.

Small enterprise lending has been particularly challenging, as other MFOs have also discovered. The on-time repayment rate of small-enterprise borrowers (both those who had taken on large loans to start with and those who had graduated to larger loans through stepped lending) fell sharply in 2000. For the present, BASIX has consequently stopped extending loans of over Rs 50,000 while it develops appropriate methodologies to lend to small enterprises without incurring such risk. This is a significant set-back for an organisation committed to lending to small enterprises to generate employment for poor people.

Lending to the non-farm sector has also proved challenging. BASIX emerged out of a long-term study led by Vijay Mahajan on the rural non-farm sector in India (see Fisher and Mahajan, 1997) which demonstrated that the real potential for rural livelihood promotion in India lay in the non-farm sector, not agriculture. BASIX was therefore set up in

1996 to lend to rural producers in all sectors, but in particular, to develop lending methodologies for the non-farm sector.

In the early years, BASIX' lending was, however, dominated by lending to agriculture, with a significant proportion going for crop loans. There was an immediate need for such loans at the time BASIX was set up, legally it was able to give only short-term loans because it initially developed its lending portfolio through its not-for-profit company IGS, and crop loans were well understood, if not practised, within the rural financial sector.

With continuous attention, given that market-demand for agricultural credit is effectively unlimited for a small financial organisation, BASIX has gradually been able to reduce the proportion of its portfolio allocated to crop loans and enhance its lending to long-term agricultural investment (e.g., irrigation), allied activities (e.g., dairying) and agro-processing, manufacturing (e.g., stone-polishing units) and services (e.g., repairs).

Lending for animal husbandry and other allied activities now accounts for around 20 per cent of BASIX' portfolio, and lending to the non-farm sector (processing, manufacturing and services), for around 40 per cent. However, at present, the latter is heavily concentrated on *kirana* shops (general and grocery stores), which represent as much as 9 per cent of all accounts. While lending to trading is so common among micro-credit portfolios around the world, BASIX has taken it one step further, focusing on proper shops, not just market stalls, which meet not only the basic needs of village populations but often operate as the main source of credit in villages. In this way, BASIX views *kirana* shops as a further channel for extending consumption credit to poorer rural households.

This record should be compared with other MFOs, for example, in South-East Asia. BAAC in Thailand lends largely for agriculture, while trading dominates the portfolio of rural lending by Bank Rakyat Indonesia (BRI). In the latter case, BRI achieved its impeccable rural micro-credit record in part by hiving off its poor performing agriculture and small enterprise loans from its micro-credit portfolio.

Second set of challenges: Organisational challenges

The first set of challenges focused on the external environment of rural livelihoods in India. The second set of challenges emerges from the first in terms of the challenges that face the organisation seeking to engage systematically in that environment.

At its simplest, BASIX has had to provide a wide range of both financial products and non-financial services and has developed a group structure to do this. Some of the inspiration for this came from the example of the group structure developed by Shorebank in the United States, again to address a wide range of products and services within a particular area (South Shore in Chicago).

Initially, the only financial vehicle open to BASIX was the non-banking finance company, and it set up two of these for micro-lending and small enterprise lending respectively. Over time, it became clear that this division of its financial services into two financial companies was not helpful, and BASIX conducted all its lending through one of the companies, while the ownership of the other company was transferred to a group of community SHG trusts in Tamil Nadu. In 2001, BASIX was finally, after years of negotiation with the regulators, able to set up a Local Area Bank (LAB) and has consolidated under the bank its financial operations in those three districts covered by the LAB.

The not-for-profit company, IGS, was established from the start to deliver on technical assistance, support services and research and development. At the very beginning, IGS even developed BASIX' lending portfolio before it was handed over to the main non-banking finance company which required a more secure portfolio than could have been achieved in the first years of experimental operations.

Behind this structure lay BASIX' unique vision of itself. As Dichter (2001: 11) comments, BASIX 'decidedly did not want to be an NGO, nor did it want to be a purely commercial bank. Yet it wanted aspects of both, because it felt that integrating livelihood promotion and financial services in a financially viable way required a more imaginative structure, one which could initially access both hot and cold monies, and then eventually use profits from the finance part to help support the non-finance part.'

Structure is in fact a reflection of identity, and it is at the level of identity that BASIX has faced more significant challenges as an organisation. By seeking to cut across the standard boundaries—between NGO and bank, development and commercial operations, micro-credit and livelihood promotion—BASIX has had to evolve an identity that is credible to a wide range of different constituencies, including the micro-finance industry, the anti-poverty community as well as the business and finance sector.

Dichter (2001), in his review of the first five years of BASIX, has set out clearly how BASIX had to proceed with a sense of sequence and priorities in its wide range of activities to achieve such credibility, concentrating first on lending, including developing new channels for reaching out to poor people, but all the while experimenting with its livelihood activities and wrestling with the ups and downs of regulatory constraints.

> The ultimate proof that BASIX has been able to keep its focus while juggling so many different activities at the same time is its financial performance. It has operated profitably. And this has meant a careful balancing of the parts in an unusually diverse portfolio.
>
> Financial services are the backbone of BASIX and should remain so. But there should be a shift in the way they are viewed. For they should become more pointedly instrumental. Lending has the huge value of being profit-making, adding clout and credibility, and eventually supporting part of the other work. That ... was part of the original vision of integration, and the rationale behind the holding company structure (ibid.: 14, 23).

In pursuit of its complex mission and of credibility among different constituencies, BASIX has had to be both strategic and opportunistic, to take risks, to experiment and innovate constantly, and to adapt flexibly to what worked and what did not, as well as to changes within its environment. For example, as BASIX has proved the viability of particular products and markets, or promoted effective SHGs, other providers have moved in, often offering cheaper but lower quality services. BASIX has made use of creative inspiration and opportunism, and has rarely fully standardised its products, instead allowing flexibility within a broad framework of uniform operations. For example, in an area with few SHGs, BASIX has started lending to traditional rotating savings and credit associations (ROSCAs).

While the outcomes have been broadly positive, we have already seen that BASIX has developed a range of disparate livelihood interventions that cannot yet be said to add up to a coherent strategy. Nor have the organisational processes that have arisen as a result been easy. For example, too much flexibility has sometimes led to significant innovation but widely differing standards of performance among different units, while shifts to more standardisation have upset those jealous of their freedom to innovate. BASIX has shifted back and forth on how much freedom and how much standardisation to give units.

Likewise, BASIX' operations have been through many changes, which have demanded a high degree of tolerance of change among both junior and senior staff. For example, the shift in the balance of BASIX' portfolio from agricultural to non-farm lending required a significant shift in mindset among staff in the field units. Such changes have not suited everyone within BASIX, leading to turnover and reorganisation of staff, not untypical for any innovative new organisation.

BASIX has also faced the constant challenge of translating its complex mission of livelihood promotion for the rural poor into something that can inform and motivate staff throughout the organisation, as well as the CSAs, who are not staff but paid on a commission basis. For them credit delivery has always been at the heart of their work, and BASIX' complex mission around supporting livelihoods has not always been fully understood. They are far more likely to judge a loan application on the basis of the ability and reliability of the borrower to repay than on the potential of the business to achieve livelihood outcomes. This can be serious, as it is precisely the Field Executives and CSAs who need, for example, to spot opportunities for micro-entrepreneurs to graduate to small enterprise and achieve the genuine developmental outcomes that BASIX seeks (see Chapter 12).

This is the challenge that lies at the heart of BASIX and indeed of this book, seeking to combine financial services with developmental outcomes. BASIX has discovered that it is all too easy for staff to become excited about financial parameters rather than the more complex issue of livelihoods, and for financial targets, for example of disbursements and repayments, to crowd out developmental tasks.

Financial targets are of course essential for the smooth running of its financial operations, and are reinforced by statutory requirements and auditors. However, developing incentives around developmental outcomes is far harder than using financial measures, and the same legal and even financial pressures do not exist for the non-financial part of BASIX' operations. Staff can thus become superb financial operators but lose sight of the wider purpose of the financial services. Within everyone's busy schedules, it has proved difficult to build regular time and incentives to reflect on BASIX' mission, not just its immediate operations.

Such tensions can never be resolved, but must be constantly managed as the organisation shifts back and forth between a focus on consolidating or expanding financial operations and pushing for real developmental outcomes.

Conclusion

BASIX has done more than most MFOs to integrate technical assistance and support services with its micro-credit operations. The challenge BASIX now faces is whether this is good enough. Does it need to go further, by building on its experimentation and innovation in livelihood promotion to go beyond the old debate of minimalist credit versus integrated services? Can it become a genuine developmental organisation promoting real livelihoods, by using micro-credit instrumentally as part of a wider strategy to effect a sustained change in the economic well-being of poor people? Only then can it really claim to be a 'new generation financial institution'.

The same challenge faces the micro-finance industry generally. Will it remain satisfied with merely providing credit, perhaps also financial intermediation for those who so desperately need it, perhaps adding some business-support services as well? Or will it rise to the challenge of using micro-credit instrumentally to develop livelihoods that can lift people out of poverty, not just alleviate it?

For this the industry will need to be informed by a strategy of getting the most long-term development bang for the buck and use not just the direct provision of financial services and technical assistance but also indirect interventions, artfully undertaken, that can have more powerful multiplier effects on the economic systems in which poor households and enterprises operate (Dichter, 2001). As BASIX is increasingly discovering, such a strategy cannot be achieved by one micro-finance or other organisation alone. It must involve extensive collaboration with a wide range of actors that influence those economic systems.

Clearly the micro-finance industry has much to learn from the pioneering work of BASIX, which shows both the potential and the challenges of such a strategy.

Notes

1. We have worked with BASIX for many years, but do not believe in reinventing the whole wheel when it comes to analysis and writing. In this chapter we have drawn heavily on Tom Dichter's organisational review of the first five years of BASIX' operations (Dichter, 2001), as well as on the case-study of BASIX' livelihood initiatives by the head of Indian Grameen Services (Datta and Thakur, 2001) and an article by the Managing Director of BASIX as a whole, Vijay Mahajan (1997). We are grateful to all these colleagues for their insights and inspiration over the years.

2. A non-banking financial company (NBFC) is initially not able to take deposits, until it has reached a certain scale and quality of operations. A Local Area Bank is a new type of bank in India, which can operate in three contiguous districts only. Formally, the BASIX group comprises: the holding company, Bhartiya Samruddhi Investments and Consulting Services Ltd (BASICS Ltd); the financial arm of the

group comprising the NBFC, Bhartiya Samruddhi Finance Ltd (Samruddhi) and the bank, Krishna Bhima Samruddhi Local Area Bank Ltd (LAB); and the not-for-profit company, Indian Grameen Services (IGS) which provides technical assistance and support services to BASIX' clients.

3. Financial operations are in the states of Andhra Pradesh, where BASIX is headquartered (in Hyderabad), Karnataka, Maharashtra and Orissa. BASIX also operates in Assam, Jharkhand, Madhya Pradesh, Rajasthan and Tamil Nadu in assisting other MFOs.

4. BASIX has secured Rs 26.3 crore (263 million) of loans from the Ford Foundation (USA), the Swiss Agency for Development and Cooperation (SDC), Shorebank Corporation (USA), Cordaid (The Netherlands) and DID (Canada), and Rs 12 crore (120 million) from Global Trust Bank Ltd, SIDBI, ICICI Bank and HDFC in India. BASIX has raised Rs 11.9 crore (119 million) in equity from IFC, the World Bank affiliate, Shorebank Corporation (USA), Hivos-Triodos Fund (The Netherlands), ICICI Bank and HDFC.

5. See further Chapters 3 and 6 of this book, the case study of SEWA Union in Datta et al. (2001) and Rose (1992).

Chapter 5

Micro-finance and people's organisations

Introduction

The need to promote groups and other social mechanisms for the effective delivery of micro-financial services has long been recognised. Whether Grameen-style groups, solidarity groups, self-help groups (SHGs), village banks or savings and credit cooperatives, all rely to a greater or lesser extent on trust or social capital that exist among members of the group. This social capital enables the micro-finance organisation (MFO) to reduce its transaction costs by giving the group the tasks of selecting and monitoring borrowers, exerting peer pressure when necessary, even guaranteeing each other's loans.

Such benefits to the micro-finance provider, which significantly reduce its costs, often do not come without some initial investment in promoting groups. This task is sometimes referred to as 'social intermediation':

> For individuals whose social and economic disadvantages place them 'beyond the frontier' of formal finance ..., successful financial intermediation is often accompanied by social intermediation. Social intermediation prepares marginalised groups or *individuals* to enter into solid business relationships with [MFOs].
>
> Evidence has shown that it is easier to establish sustainable financial intermediation systems with the poor in societies that encourage cooperative efforts through local clubs, temple associations, or work groups—in other words, societies with high levels of social capital.

Perhaps more than any other economic transaction, financial intermediation depends on social capital, because it depends on trust between the borrower and the lender. Where neither traditional systems nor modern institutions provide a basis for trust, financial intermediation systems are difficult to establish.

Social intermediation can thus be understood as the process of building the human and social capital required for sustainable financial intermediation with the poor (Ledgerwood, 1999: 76–77).

As this quotation makes clear, social intermediation is regarded as an instrument to enable effective delivery of micro-financial services. Micro-finance is the end, social intermediation the means.

Many practitioners in India might agree with this approach; many others would not. For the latter, enabling poor people to organise is the end, micro-financial services, the means. For example, both MYRADA and PRADAN, two major nongovernmental organisations (NGOs) in India, have long emphasised the need to promote organisations that poor people own, control and manage. Both discovered that to do this effectively, poor people need to organise around concrete activities in which they have a direct stake. For example, PRADAN has promoted many water-user associations of poor farmers to manage minor lift-irrigation schemes. Both discovered that micro-finance provides just such a concrete activity, and became engaged in the promotion of many small savings and credit groups, or self-help groups as they are known in India.

Is this reversal of ends and means, making micro-finance the instrument rather than the end, merely a game of semantics? Based on our assessment of practice, and the evidence cited in this chapter, the answer is no. While the process of organising on the one hand and the service delivered on the other are to some extent inseparable, the hierarchy of means and ends is important, and may lead to very different outcomes.

'Social intermediation', as commonly understood, is a means to enable the delivery of a technical solution. Organising poor people around concrete activities, micro-finance and others, has much wider goals in mind, of building assets and ownership, of developing opportunities, capacities and skills, of empowering marginalised people.

Al Fernandez, the Executive Director of MYRADA, is quite clear in the title of his book (2001) describing MYRADA's experience of promoting SHGs: *Putting institutions first—even in micro-finance.*

In this chapter we illustrate the practice of building organisations around micro-financial services. We look at SHGs promoted by leading NGOs such as MYRADA, PRADAN and the DHAN Foundation and the savings and credit cooperatives promoted by the Cooperative Development Foundation (CDF).

This does not mean that organising poor people comes without its own challenges, and it may not be an appropriate strategy in all contexts. In analysing the context in Bangladesh, Harry Blair (2000: 115) writes,

> ... rural credit programmes ... were long notorious for being subverted by the local rich, who had the collateral needed to secure loans and the political clout required to default successfully on their loans.... However, the micro-credit initiatives stemming most notably from the model pioneered by the Grameen Bank in Bangladesh have been eminently successful in steering resources to the poorest strata. The critical element in these programmes ... is that successful micro-credit programmes are invariably administered by outside agencies, not by local governments. Situating the loan-allocating process elsewhere precludes takeover by local elites.

In the strategies we review in this chapter, allocating loans is indeed done at the local level, although not by local governments. Promoting small organisations of poor people like SHGs may therefore make such groups vulnerable to political and bureaucratic capture, and we also look at strategies to protect such groups from such interference.

There has also been much debate within micro-finance around the implication that organising poor people into groups necessarily excludes non-members. Are these non-members the right ones to exclude, or are they the most vulnerable people who cannot take on the responsibilities and burdens that a group imposes? Are relatively poorer members in a group discriminated against in terms of access to loans, for example? The focus in this chapter on democratic organisations may present some alternative perspectives on this dilemma.

Given that the majority of micro-finance clients, in India and elsewhere, are often women, gender issues and impacts have also received significant attention. We review some of the evidence within the Indian context.

Self-help groups as people's organisations

The self-help group model

In Chapter 7, Malcolm Harper discusses the differences between two predominant group-based models used by MFOs in India. One is the model pioneered by the Grameen Bank of Bangladesh, in which implementation is largely driven from the top, with systems laid out well in advance and with little scope for variation. Likewise, most micro-finance models in India that target individual clients give little scope for these clients to participate in the overall design and management of the MFOs.

This contrasts with the second group-based model, of autonomous savings and credit groups, often known in India as SHGs, that have emerged in significant numbers. There are already hundreds of thousands of such groups across India. To what extent do such SHGs contribute not just to the delivery of micro-financial services, but also to wider goals of empowerment and organisation-building?

The SHG model, which was pioneered in the 1970s, has much more scope for members to participate in decision-making processes. Under the SHG model, the group of up to 20 members, usually women, is formed with the help of an external catalysing agent (typically an NGO) but the cycle of micro-finance starts with mutual savings and credit. It is only after a few cycles of mutual savings and credit have been successfully completed that an external financial agency may come into the picture by providing additional capital for on-lending to members of the group.

Although started by NGOs on an informal basis, indeed, partly learning from indigenous savings and credit systems, the SHG system is becoming increasingly mainstreamed, with organisations like the government and the National Bank for Agriculture and Rural Development (NABARD) developing specific programmes and targets for promoting SHGs and linking them to banks. Almost 300,000 SHGs have already taken loans from banks, and NABARD expects one million SHGs to be doing so by 2008.

Ownership and roles of self-help groups

It is important to recognise that SHGs are not merely efficient channels for delivering micro-financial services at lower transaction costs to an MFO, although many banks and MFOs may treat them in this way.

At best SHGs are autonomous organisations capitalised through members' savings, an innovation that was in strong contrast with earlier poverty-oriented credit-delivery systems offered by the state. As soon as groups are capitalised through members' own savings, it is essential that issues of ownership and governance be addressed.

Take, for example, the case of the 682 SHGs promoted by MYRADA in their Dharmapuri project in the state of Tamil Nadu (Fernandez, 2001: 10). Of their total funds, 53 per cent had come from members' savings, and 41 per cent from interest earned on loans. In the case of a bank or an MFO, this interest, amounting to almost Rs 2,000 a member, would have gone to the bank or MFO, not to capitalise a group owned by its members. As Malcolm Harper asks provocatively in Chapter 7, is this yet another way by which relatively elite bank employees sequester the hard-earned incomes of the poor?

As owners, members of SHGs also shoulder many more responsibilities. They are the decision-makers who collectively decide on savings, interest rates, the allocation of loans, distributing surpluses and other policies and systems. They are usually guided by the NGO promoter with wider experience of SHGs, but members are allowed to take their own decisions (although some banks and NGOs seek to impose their own policies on SHGs). In a sense, poor people are now taking the responsibility of managing their individual savings and borrowings through groups in which they are active participants and decision-makers.

This model has its roots in the strong democratic traditions within India. As Fernandez (2001: 7, 21) argues,

MYRADA believes that people's institutions, namely institutions whose functions and systems they have taken the lead in developing, and over which they have control in day-to-day operations, are the basis of a thriving democracy. Further such institutions have the potential to play a critical role in empowering the poor in a sustainable manner.

To achieve this broader objective, MYRADA assumed that it was necessary to invest in building institutions whose structure is appropriate to the functions and resource to be managed, and based on traditional and cultural norms and relationships [which MYRADA refers to as affinity[1]]. The structure of these appropriate institutions and their governance systems developed by the members would in turn foster the attitudes and skills required for sustained management, the ability to mobilise resources, to build linkages, and to become change agents—together these features form the basis of empowerment.

For PRADAN, SHGs are also far more than channels to deliver financial services. Narendranath (2001: 2, 4) of PRADAN describes their diverse potential roles as follows:

[SHGs help] women to gain increased access to and control over the economic resources of their families. As a group matures, it involves itself in wider social issues in the village. The social significance of SHG membership is no less than the financial benefits that flow from it.

The SHG has a bigger role besides financial intermediation. It is an institution based on the concept of 'peer

learning' as against learning that is externally controlled. This is a powerful process that enables growth
and progress in a community. Members learn from each
other in a group and SHGs learn from other SHGs, which
then leads to collective progress.
The cohesion that SHGs foster enables them to address issues such as health and education.... SHGs are
... an effective inter-face for the poor to deal constructively
with the external world, village society, the *panchayat*
[elected village council], the banks and the government.
The SHG is also a forum for solidarity and empowerment of women, providing them the space and voice to
negotiate and participate as equals both within the family and in society in general....
Therefore an SHG plays three roles simultaneously.
It provides mutual help and internal financial mediation.
It facilitates external financial mediation, and it empowers
women to make demands on the external world.

The DHAN Foundation in Tamil Nadu has similar broad
objectives (Narender, 1999). Its Kalanjiam Community Banking Programme promotes SHGs for women, which are
organised into cluster associations and federations.
Within the first 10 years of the programme's operations,
over 36,000 members of SHGs had saved over Rs 3.6 crore
(36 million), which contributed about a third of total funds
lent to members, particularly for consumption purposes.
Loans for income-generation, as well as for housing, are
often made from loans taken by the group from banks or from
the cluster associations and federations (see further).
The DHAN Foundation's philosophy is based on an exclusive focus on poor people, seeking to have a positive impact
on their poverty by (i) developing appropriate organisations
and services owned, controlled and managed by members,
and (ii) going beyond micro-finance to empower women and
develop their livelihoods.
As Narender (ibid.: 2, 11) argues, 'providing financial services should be seen as an instrument to address the overall
development of the poor. People need to be organised and
their internal capacity ... built to prepare them to address

the issues of their own development.... Providing financial services is a very effective and powerful entry programme to organise the community and bring out their inner potential. The ultimate focus is to make people set the agenda for their own development.'

Evidence of empowerment[2]

To what extent are these merely the lofty ideals of unrealistic NGOs? To what extent are these ideals used as an excuse for poor financial performance? There are clearly many cases of SHGs that function poorly or in a very limited way, and MFOs like BASIX (see Chapter 4) have had to provide significant capacity-building inputs to SHGs promoted by NGOs before they can lend the groups money.

In part, as Mathew Titus analyses in depth in Chapter 8, this arises from the enormous constraints imposed by the socio-economic environment, for example of illiteracy and low computational skills, and by significant imperfections in financial markets for poor people, including market distortions brought about by many corrupt or inefficient service-providers.

In part it may also already be the result of significant donor and policy interest. In pursuit of funding, NGOs without the necessary skills are taking up micro-financial services while banks, in pursuit of targets, are treating SHGs as delivery channels and even promoting some themselves.

However, there are also cases where autonomous SHGs have enabled poor people to take greater control of their own lives and of their groups to manage their own financial services, probably in a more effective manner than Grameen replicators. Within SHGs members control their own savings and funds, and this can have a larger pay-off when it comes to taking on other roles.

In Chapter 9, Ajit Kanitkar provides many illustrations of this, and analyses the empowerment reflected in the behaviour and performance of women leaders of SHGs promoted by PRADAN. Here we look at the results of studies of SHGs promoted by MYRADA (Fernandez, 2001: Chapter 12). The studies found evidence of empowerment along a range of indicators. Note that most of these indicators apply to women, as 85 per cent of SHGs promoted by MYRADA are women's groups, and a further 5 per cent are mixed groups of women and men.

- Dividing members among the upper, middle and lower poor, the studies found that members from each of these strata were as likely to take on the role of office-bearers (signatories) within their SHGs, suggesting that groups are providing opportunities for leadership even among their poorest members.
- Approximately 200 members of the SHGs had been elected to their village *panchayat* (council). These successful candidates indicated that they had developed the confidence to stand through managing their groups and having the support of their group members.
- In terms of impact on village life, half the SHGs in their third and fifth years of operations had been approached by other groups in the village to help solve social problems. Note that this is unusual for poor, marginalised and generally lower-caste women in a village, who are not usually accepted as agents of change.
- By the fifth year, 90 per cent of these groups were also in charge of maintaining at least two infrastructural assets in their village, and half the groups had members who had been elected to at least two public bodies.
- About 1,400 groups promoted by MYRADA have received a line of credit from a bank, which is more than two-thirds of groups that MYRADA considers eligible for such direct finance. Again, this indicator needs to be seen in a context where individual poor women would have at most received a government-mandated loan from a bank, and very rarely a commercial loan. Their ability to engage with banks comes from the confidence and skills (including basic skills like signing their name and use of the appropriate language) developed within the SHG, as well as from the support of the NGO.
- Individual members had sometimes left their SHG to borrow directly from the bank, or to engage in 'chit-funds', where interest rates are higher, but loan amounts larger than most SHGs are willing to extend.

• Many members, through frequent exposure to visitors, had gained the confidence to speak to such visitors, including government officials. They had acquired greater awareness of their rights in the welfare system, and of the procedures and requirements of negotiating the bureaucratic maze.

In these examples it is not the credit that is empowering, but the management of credit. Fernandez (2001: 16) argues:

> Models where credit provision is the fulcrum are not empowering. ... the **management of credit** does have the potential to be an empowering tool. This shifts the focus from credit provision to credit management and makes the model of credit management a critical factor.... for credit management to be an effective instrument of empowerment, it must first be a friendly instrument for institution building of the [SHGs]. It is only if it succeeds in fostering an institution which possesses all the features required for effective and sustained governance, that it will empower the members.

MYRADA has found that those groups that were promoted as autonomous groups, selecting their own membership and determining their own policies and procedures, have been better at sustaining their operations once MYRADA withdrew its support, in comparison to other groups that MYRADA had formed earlier, largely to implement activities determined by donors.

We should not, however, be blinded to the potential negative impacts of belonging to SHGs, even though there has been less research on this in India than in the case of Grameen Bank groups in Bangladesh. For example, there is evidence of such impacts on women members, such as the additional burdens (e.g., time commitments, managing finances and enhanced businesses, changes or conflicts within the household) that participation in SHGs may bring. Chapter 8 provides concrete examples of this, such as women who did not have the time or skills to adequately monitor the financial transactions of their SHGs and consequently put their savings at risk. The dividing line between micro-credit and micro-debt is also fine, and SHGs can push poor people into debts they cannot repay.

There has been no investigation we know of to see what the effect of specially formed groups on other community organising activities is. As Miller and Andrews (1998: 15) ask, 'to what extent do they displace traditional groupings which may have been more inclusive and also focused on a broader range of community issues?' To the extent that members of SHGs become more engaged in other traditional groupings, such as the *gram sabha* (the traditional meeting of all villagers), as we illustrate below, organising a range of groups can be mutually reinforcing, but this need not be the case, especially with the severe time constraints women in particular face.

Small autonomous organisations can also be highly vulnerable to capture, whether internal or external, or to gradual or sudden demise. Analysis of the performance of a wide range of MFOs, including SHG programmes, suggests that SHGs do not encourage members to save as much as they could (Chapter 10). Chapters 8 and 9 illustrate how the performance of SHGs can vary significantly, even when promoted by the same organisation. Members can become highly dependent on individual leaders and be largely unaware of their own responsibilities; leaders can capture a large share of the benefits; and SHGs can close down with the potential loss of savings and the severe disempowerment of their members.[3] Ownership brings freedom and benefits, but also greater responsibilities, and above all, risks.

MYRADA provides some of the most intensive capacity-building inputs of any promoter of SHGs within India, and while MYRADA's experience may point to the empowerment that can result, the quality of the promotional strategies and inputs is clearly critical.

Promotional strategies

To build effective people's organisations, therefore, requires effective strategies and high quality inputs on the part of the promotional agency. All three NGOs we focus on here (MYRADA, PRADAN and the DHAN Foundation) have developed a deep understanding of organisations and how to build them.

For example, based on its own experience, PRADAN has conceptualised the development of SHGs in five clearly defined stages (pre-formation, formation, stabilisation, growth and expansion), each with its own tasks, activities and milestones (see Table 9.1 in Chapter 9). PRADAN emphasises three key group values for SHGs to function effectively: equality (including democracy, participation, equal opportunities, sharing responsibilities, peer lending and influencing, confrontation), trust (norms, financial discipline, mutual help, risk-taking) and autonomy (independence, self-help and exercising choices) (Narendranath, 2001).

In promoting SHGs, MYRADA focuses on six features: vision or mission, organisational management systems, financial management systems, organisational accountability norms, linkages, and a culture of monitoring and learning. Capacity-building is a critical element of MYRADA's strategy, and involves a full range of inputs.[4]

Such inputs do not come cheaply, but are essential for building genuine people's organisations, with their additional benefits (rather than just creating delivery channels for micro-financial services), and for avoiding the potential failure of small and fragile local organisations.

Analysis of promoting SHGs, from urban slums in Delhi to tribal communities in some of the most resource-poor areas in eastern India (see Chapters 8 and 9), reveals the significant costs of promotion, which can, moreover, vary significantly according to the particular socio-economic conditions in which they operate. Chapter 8 analyses in detail some of the costs that may be involved. Likewise, the DHAN Foundation in south India argues that the costs of promoting SHGs and building their capacity need to be subsidised for at least one to two years before the SHGs become financially sustainable.

Most agencies promoting SHGs also seek to link them to banks or MFOs to access further capital, once the groups have stabilised their operations and their internal governance systems. It is important to note that the pioneers did not want to take on the role of providing credit themselves, i.e., becoming an MFO, a role unsuitable for an NGO, and for the development of the SHGs they were promoting. Fernandez (2001: 116) argues that it is the organisational demand to break even that forces MFOs to seek to limit their functions and those of SHGs to credit delivery and recovery. There is no time or resource for capacity-building that could empower women to play a wider role in society.

It is true that the roots of the SHG model stem from the growing frustration that mainstream financial intermediaries, including Regional Rural Banks (RRBs), deliberately set up to lend to the rural poor, were not delivering financial services effectively. However, NGOs have helped poor people manage their own groups and negotiate for lines of credit from mainstream financial intermediaries, which have a huge branch infrastructure and obligations to service poor people. Indeed, as MYRADA sees it, they were not seeking to mainstream the SHGs to suit the rules of banks, but persuade mainstream organisations to accept and engage with these alternative structures owned and managed by poor people.

Federating SHGs

Particularly if the promoting agency is to withdraw, the sustainability of SHGs, and their ability to avoid political or bureaucratic capture, can be enhanced by the support of federal structures formed by the primary groups. The three NGOs we feature here have different strategies towards such structures.[5]

In the case of PRADAN, different project locations may or may not promote secondary-level organisations of SHGs (see Chapter 9). If they do so, it is mainly to strengthen the process of peer-learning across groups, build solidarity and facilitate linkages. The secondary-level organisations do not play any financial role (Narendranath, 2001).

In the case of SHGs promoted by MYRADA, there are now over 100 federations enabling MYRADA in some cases to withdraw, leaving the primary groups to be guided by these federations while the primary groups themselves continue to access finance directly from the banks. The federations perform a wide range of functions, such as collecting information, providing training, helping to resolve conflicts and lobbying government. As with PRADAN, however, none of them have taken on managing finances or on-lending to groups (Fernandez, 2001: 46).

The DHAN Foundation, on the other hand, is building an elaborate structure of cluster associations and tertiary-level federations, each with distinct roles (see Table 5.1). Creating

Table 5.1: SHGs, their clusters & federations, promoted by the DHAN Foundation (adapted from Narender [1999])

Organisation	Membership	Function	Why
Savings and credit group	15–20 poor women	Managing savings and credit transactions; Meeting smaller credit needs through own savings; Leveraging money from other organisations.	To enable members to manage savings and credit independently at a hamlet level; Primary unit for handling transactions directly with members.
Cluster association (a) Promotional across 3–5 villages	10–15 primary groups from a homogenous socio-economic context	Promoting and strengthening groups in neighbouring villages within the vicinity of 5–10 km; Long-term sustainability for the primary groups through mutual support and cooperation.	To provide promotional support on a continuous basis at the local level for long-term continuity and growth of primary groups in a particular geographical area.
(b) Financial wing of cluster association		Creating greater access to credit for primary groups; Leveraging funds and on-lending them to primary groups; Strengthening the financial systems and managerial capability of primary groups.	To increase the ability of primary groups to meet higher-order credit needs and fill the gaps in credit demand at the local level [3–5 villages]; To channel funds to primary groups mobilised directly and through federation.
Federation (a) Promotional at block level	100–200 primary groups	Building solidarity for groups at block level (administrative division of districts); Relating with block-level development administration; Promotional activities for development of primary groups;	To provide block-level integration of community banking efforts; To promote continuity for the programme by women; To fill credit gaps not met by cluster associations;
(b) Financial at block level		Greater access to credit for primary groups; Leveraging loan funds from apex financial institutions.	To manage the collaboration with apex organisations focused on specific activities (housing, business).

people's organisations at different levels of a federated structure is seen as critical to address issues of powerlessness and isolation at the root of poverty. In addition to acting as local financial intermediaries for the primary groups, these organisations allow women to gain collective strength and power, and to influence both local banks and the government system (Narender, 1999).

While there may be different attitudes towards federal structures of SHGs, they often play a key role in building people's organisations, providing support services, sustaining their operations after the promoting agency has withdrawn (and in some cases accessing additional lines of credit), and protecting them from external interference while building collective visibility and influence as well.

Part Two of this book looks in greater detail at SHGs, comparing them with Grameen-type groups (Chapter 7), looking at a concrete case of the challenges of promoting effective SHGs in urban slums (Chapter 8), and at leadership and social entrepreneurship within SHGs (Chapter 9).

Micro-finance cooperatives: The CDF model

A huge number of SHGs, which are not formally registered, are emerging throughout India. However, the SHG model is not the only form of democratic local organisation available for micro-financial services. Formally registered cooperatives are an interesting alternative.

The history of cooperatives is also instructive for other people's organisations, not least SHGs. They were also promoted as democratic local organisations. However, once the government began treating them merely as efficient delivery channels for distributing government subsidies they became ineffectual and in most cases moribund (Shah, 1995). If SHGs are treated, by the government, banks or MFOs, merely as efficient channels for delivering micro-financial services, will their fate be any different?

For exploring the role of cooperatives in micro-finance, we take the example of the Cooperative Development Foundation in the state of Andhra Pradesh, that has worked with the mainstream cooperative structure throughout its existence (see Chapter 6). The Foundation's strategy has focused on empowering local organisations owned by members through strong democratic governance. It believes that only vibrant local economies can bring long-term sustainable development to local communities, and that local organisations, designed, managed and controlled by those expecting to benefit from them, are required for a sustainable impact on a local economy. Small groups are less likely to achieve this than cooperatives that capture a significant share of the local market in their line of business. Genuine cooperatives are also by definition managed and controlled by their members (CDF, 1999a).

The inspiration for CDF came from the farmers' cooperative in Mulkanoor in rural Andhra Pradesh that had thrived and grown to become a local organisation with real salience in the lives of its members and its local economy (Shah, 1995). The cooperative is a multi-purpose cooperative providing a range of services to its members, including input supplies, processing and marketing, as well as financial services and retailing. It has a membership of around 6,000 (with more than half being small and marginal farmers) and has a total turnover of Rs 32 crore (320 million) in trading and Rs 9 crore (90 million) outstanding in loans to members, a phenomenal average per member by Indian standards. Most of these loans are financed by member-savings accumulated over its 45-year history.

Initially, CDF sought to replicate the Mulkanoor example. The new cooperatives however performed poorly, primarily because of the hostile legal and policy environment (which we address in Chapter 6), but also because of the wide range of services they sought to offer. '... multi-purpose cooperatives ... were found to succeed only under extraordinary circumstances; cooperatives needed to work around single commodities' (CDF, 2000: 6).

Therefore, CDF focused on promoting cooperatives that focused on agricultural (paddy) processing and marketing only. These performed better, but faced the same legal obstacles. They also required significant promotional resources to get them up and running, not least in capital to invest in processing facilities.

The third activity around which CDF organised cooperatives was savings and credit. In fact, CDF calls them thrift cooperatives, distinguishing between thrift and savings (CDF, 1999b: 1):

> Thrift is a fixed amount, saved regularly throughout the working life of an individual and becomes available to support him/her financially to maintain the same standard of living in ... old age. The interest on thrift in a thrift cooperative gets compounded each year and the amount becomes substantial over a period of time. Savings [on the other hand] are those which are saved from the amount left over after expenditure or saved for a limited period with a specific purpose.

In other words, the cooperatives are seen more as an insurance mechanism than as a deposit-taking organisation, although they do take deposits and give loans (up to three times of a member's thrift *excluding* savings beyond their thrift). To emphasise the parallels as well as the differences across the different types of local organisations reviewed in this chapter, we will nevertheless call them savings and credit cooperatives.

The Foundation discovered that savings and credit cooperatives could emerge and grow much more quickly, in part because the capital needed came from savings. Within a decade these cooperatives in two backward districts of Andhra Pradesh had grown to 350 in number, with over 100,000 members and with Rs 12.5 crore (125 million) in savings. This figure is comparable to any large MFO with operations spread across a much larger area in India. What is more interesting is that not a single rupee of capital has come from external funding for these cooperatives.

The majority of these savings and credit cooperatives are for women only (although there are also ones for men), enabling CDF to promote cooperatives for rural women, not only men who dominate the farmers' cooperatives. CDF continues to promote savings and credit cooperatives vigorously.

The historical progression thus described is important because it demonstrates very clearly the instrumental use to which micro-finance can be put. The promoting agency was primarily interested in promoting effective democratic local organisations, in CDF's case, cooperatives.

CDF ... does not believe that it is in the business of providing credit or credit access to rural women. It thinks it is in the business of building rural women's financial institutions. Its energies have not gone into identifying women's credit needs—they have gone into, are going into, ensuring that women define their thrift coop, take responsibility for its operations and management, decide how they wish to interact with it and how they wish to control it (CDF, 1994: 3).

Organising cooperatives around micro-financial services was discovered to be particularly effective by CDF.

Because of their primary focus on effective local organisations, rather than just delivering micro-financial services, CDF places great emphasis on the effective running of the cooperatives. It has produced a long list of what characterises a good cooperative, which it has used to assess cooperatives for prizes for the best cooperative in an area. The list includes performance on legal registration; adherence to cooperative principles; growth and participation of membership; management; range of financial services; profitability; office infrastructure and environment; maintenance of accounts; internal controls and systems; education and training for members, staff and committee members; and relations with other cooperatives and associations.

Member control and service are at the heart of effective cooperatives (CDF, 1994). The activity around which a cooperative is organised is not the primary determinant of its performance. Democratic governance and control by members is more important.

The Foundation's argument has been that local organisations like cooperatives have so often failed because they have not been given a chance to govern themselves without external interference. Wherever government or other external

agencies have not interfered in the governance of cooperatives, they have almost always performed well. Mulkanoor was
the shining example, which had survived many a political on-
slaught by its sheer resilience and non-compromising attitude on democratic governance. The members had tremendous
financial stakes and a sense of ownership of their organisation which were the most important factors in its success.

Historically, however, while cooperatives in India had long
been a key vehicle available for organising rural producers,
they had largely been funded by the state, leading to frequent interference in their governance. The Foundation argued that there was no point in promoting cooperatives if
they did not honour the principles of cooperation that included democratic governance in keeping with their mutual
status. Unless poor rural people were given the opportunity
to manage themselves, they would be ever dependent on the
patronage of an external agency. The actions CDF has taken
to address these issues are described in Chapter 6.

This approach has also meant that CDF does not seek to
link the savings and credit cooperatives with banks or other
mainstream organisations (CDF, 1993; see also note 6). Because these cooperatives are much larger than SHGs, the
pooled savings of all members are usually sufficient to meet
their immediate credit needs, and most do not lend out all
the capital available to them from their savings. In CDF's
view, what is needed is effective management and control of
these resources. Of course, if the local organisation is strong,
it can always negotiate with mainstream organisations for
its residual capital needs. This strategy therefore reinforces
the autonomy of the cooperatives.

To ensure additional support and resources when necessary, CDF has also promoted associations of the primary cooperatives. These associations draw from the leaders of the
primary cooperatives for their own governance and manage
the function of balancing inter-group surpluses and deficits
of capital, as well as designing control systems, offering internal audit services, taking up welfare activities such
as life-insurance schemes, and enabling mutual learning.
They do not, however, attract external funding, as CDF had

discovered earlier that access to easy money tended to make associations irresponsible.[6]

Through the associations, governance, already built on the solid foundation of the primary cooperatives, is taken to greater heights to spread the benefits that can accrue from collaboration among several local-level organisations. Moreover, unlike a large micro-finance organisation, a failure of governance usually affects only the one organisation, thereby localising the problem rather than affecting the entire organisational system.

Some issues in people's organisations

Ownership and governance

Ownership and governance are often at the heart of such strategies to organise people, whether in SHGs or cooperatives. Micro-finance builds assets and may generate income-streams and profits, in addition to providing services. Who owns these assets, who gets these profits? These are critical questions in any development context where the unequal distribution of wealth, and hence of power that comes with wealth, often lies at the root of the need for development in the first place. We have already seen, in the case of SHGs promoted by MYRADA, that over time as much as 40 per cent of their capital can come from interest earned on loans.

It is striking, however, that many key texts on micro-financial services ignore some of the key aspects of ownership and governance. Let us take a typical example. In a World Bank handbook, the author (Ledgerwood, 1999) describes the many forms of cooperative financial organisations, explicitly referring to their key characteristic, that the members are the owners of the organisation (ibid.: 101–3). The section on governance and ownership, however (ibid.: 110–13), includes no reference to ownership by members of the organisation. Statements like 'it is important that members of the Board be independent from the [MFO]' are nonsense when referring to a democratically owned organisation where members elect their representatives on the board from amongst their membership.

Once again, commentators have turned any form of organisation into a mere efficient instrument to deliver financial services, disregarding issues of ownership and control, including who benefits from the assets and profits that such an organisation generates.

This does not mean that effective democratic ownership and governance come easily. As we have already suggested, ownership also brings greater responsibilities and risks. One comment on a democratically owned MFO was: 'While on the one hand, member control can be regarded as one of the factors behind [its] success, excessive emphasis on this aspect has had an adverse impact on its growth and expansion of operations.... As the directors have little exposure to strategic issues [related to financial services], less attention is paid to matters of governance of the [organisation] and other strategic concerns.'

However, ownership and governance cannot be ignored, and following the example of NGOs like CDF and MYRADA, the capacity of people to exercise effective governance of their own organisations has to be built over time.

Membership

There has been much debate internationally whether poorer people are excluded from self-managing groups. As Malcolm Harper argues in Chapter 7, they may be excluded by other members, or exclude themselves because they do not have the ability to take part in the financial operations of the group. Poorer members within a group may also be discriminated against in terms of access to services.

MYRADA provides evidence on the issue of discrimination among members within a group. MYRADA explicitly targets poor people for membership of SHGs. Nevertheless, they distinguish, through participatory exercises, among the lower, middle and upper poor members of SHGs. Studies found that the poorest members are not marginalised in terms of the number of loans they take. The record is mixed in terms of the total loan amount taken over three years; in some cases the poorest members took the same or even more than wealthier members, in others less. On the whole, however, the average size of individual loans was lower for the poorest members (Fernandez, 2001: Chapter 11).

The wide variations in these measures across different SHGs suggest that there is little discrimination against the poorest members in accessing loans. However, the poorest members do seem to have less ability to absorb credit, or less confidence in taking on the risks that come with it. The lack of discrimination is also confirmed by the evidence, cited above, that poorer members are equally likely to take on the role of office-bearers within the groups.

These results are encouraging. However, they may follow from the intensive capacity-building inputs that MYRADA provides, with their strong focus on autonomous democratic governance. Groups that do not receive such support may perform very differently in terms of access to services and leadership roles among members of a group.

In Chapter 9, Ajit Kanitkar observes that SHG leaders are likely to take a larger share than other members of the benefits from financial services, not least as an appropriate reward for the burdens and risks of leadership. However, if there is little discrimination by wealth on who becomes a leader, then this would not provide evidence of discrimination against the poorest members of the group. Kanitkar's evidence does not provide a firm conclusion either way, but does stress the need for effective leadership within SHGs.

Mathew Titus' analysis of SHGs in urban slums in Delhi, however (Chapter 8), provides concrete examples of deliberate exclusion of members, in this case on the legitimate grounds of their earlier repayment record, as well as a case of one family taking control of most SHGs in an area and using them to direct resources primarily to members of the family. In this case, discrimination is obvious, but happened without the promoting NGO at first noticing.

The Cooperative Development Foundation takes a very different line, which provides interesting insights into the inclusion or exclusion of potential members of a group. It has never subscribed to an exclusive focus on the poor or poorest.

It has focused on promoting democratic local organisations that are generally inclusive of members from different castes and classes. The Foundation further believes that, within such organisations, it is the democratic right of members to determine who is a member and who not. The promoting agency does not have the right to overrule this, a process that would only undermine local governance and enhance dependency.

The Cooperative Development Foundation is of course concerned about its impact on poor people, and has thus carefully studied whether its inclusive strategy discriminates against poorer members of the local community. The results are interesting (CDF, 1999a).

Over 75 per cent of members of the women's savings and credit cooperatives were from backward castes or Scheduled Castes or Scheduled Tribes, with the first being the dominant group (61 per cent), reflecting the overall caste profile of the villages. Upper caste women made up 13 per cent of members (with a further 12 per cent not classified).

The profile of leaders reflected a similar pattern, with Scheduled Castes and Tribes having a slightly higher proportion of leaders than of members. The proportion of borrowers was also closely aligned with membership, although those belonging to Scheduled Castes and Tribes took smaller loans than upper caste members. Moreover, eight out of 10 borrowers who missed one or other repayment were members from among the backward castes, Scheduled Castes and Tribes.

> It would appear, on the whole, ... that the practice of open and voluntary membership in [women's savings and credit coops] has resulted in women choosing to work together across castes, in a spirit of mutual trust and mutual give and take, possibly putting their common economic agenda above caste considerations (ibid.: 9).

To understand the class and wealth profile, CDF reviewed landholdings of the households from which women members came. Fifty-five per cent of members were from landless households, and a further 15 per cent from households with less than one acre of land. Thirteen per cent of members had more than three acres.

While the landless and those with less than one acre of land made up 70 per cent of the membership, they provided 67 per cent of the leadership, made up 67 per cent of borrowers and took 64 per cent of the total loan amount. There was even less variation when looking at all the poorer members of the cooperatives (from households with less than three acres of land).

This suggests that there is little discrimination within women cooperatives that have members from all caste and wealth backgrounds, and that all members are accessing their rights to opportunities from their cooperatives. The backward castes, in any case most numerous among the poor, make up 60 per cent of the membership, and 70 per cent of members are from landless or highly marginal farming households. Nevertheless, they have the same access to loans, although they tend to take smaller loans and miss repayments more often, while the landless are only slightly underrepresented in terms of leadership.

These results are likely to reflect the greater economic hardship that poorer households face. This applies first to their ability to absorb credit. As the cooperatives were not lending out all their capital, loan sizes were determined more by the level of individual savings (borrowers cannot borrow more than three times their thrift) and by their own assessment of their ability to absorb credit. The landless also have less time to spare for non-earning activities, which is essential for taking on leadership roles. The cooperatives are in fact thinking of compensating leaders for the loss of wages for days spent in committee meetings to enable more landless members to take part.

The profile of men's cooperatives was similar, although the upper castes were slightly more represented in the membership (18 per cent) and provided a significantly higher proportion of the leaders (33 per cent). The number of borrowers reflected the membership profile much more closely, although Scheduled Caste and Tribe members took smaller loans than members from upper castes.

In terms of land ownership, male cooperatives had fewer landless members (45 per cent) but more marginal farmers with up to three acres of land (41 per cent). Again, wealthier farmers with more than three acres provided a significantly higher proportion of leaders (44 per cent compared to 18 per cent of members). However, there seemed little distinction in terms of the number of loans, although again the landless took smaller loans than other members.

This suggests that in the men's cooperatives all members have access to the services of the cooperative, with poorer members being less able to absorb credit, while the leadership of the cooperatives is more dominated by wealthier members.

The case of CDF's cooperatives provides an interesting counterpoint to the more usual exclusive focus on poorer people, and suggests that there are opportunities for diverse groups to work together for their common and individual benefit. This may have a greater impact on the local economy as a whole, rather than just on members of individual groups, because the larger more inclusive groups are likely to capture a larger share of market demand and supply and hence have wider economic influence. For all of this to happen, however, effective democratic structures and governance are essential, and developing these is neither easy nor cheap.

Gender relations

As in Bangladesh, it is striking that micro-finance in India is growing most extensively and most rapidly among women members or clients. Even among those NGOs that are promoting both women's and men's groups, in each case the majority of groups are of women. The growth of micro-finance could have the potential therefore to create many opportunities for women's empowerment. To what extent is this actually the case in India?

Unfortunately, there has been less detailed research on the impact of micro-finance on gender relations in India than in Bangladesh, and much more analysis in the Indian context is required, especially as the provision of micro-financial services is growing rapidly to reach out to millions of women.

Some of the research in Bangladesh has focused on the impact on gender relations within the household, noting that women borrowers often do not retain control over the investment of the loan they have taken, but may use it to negotiate higher status within the household or less involvement in manual labour (Goetz and Sen Gupta, 1996). Rogaly et al. (1999: 82) summarise such evidence from Bangladesh by suggesting that 'micro-credit has not led to a transformation in gender relations, but has become an additional resource, around which negotiation occurs'.

A study of 64 women SHGs promoted by MYRADA showed that in three types of household decisions (on the purpose of loans taken by women members, on the adoption of household infrastructure, and on household purchases) the number of decisions made exclusively by the husband fell significantly over a five-year period. Indeed, more decisions were now taken exclusively by the wife, although many continued to be taken jointly (Fernandez, 2001: 97).

Another study found examples of women who had rarely been out alone going to banks, attending meetings and participating in the *gram sabha* (traditional meetings of all villagers). Some women members of SHGs were taking on activities new for women, such as driving auto-rickshaws and cars, becoming bus conductors or masons (most of these had also received training through MYRADA). Many husbands, although not all, had come to accept women going out of the home to attend meetings and other SHG-related work. On the other hand, some of the poorest members found the additional work required to participate in an SHG cumbersome (Fernandez, 2001: 98–100).

Chapter 9, which looks at leadership among SHGs promoted by PRADAN, provides concrete examples of women taking an active part in local governance bodies. It also illustrates the importance of having time to engage in SHG activities and provides cases of heightened tension between women and men caused by the SHG activities.

Such evidence falls within the first two of the three approaches to women's empowerment and micro-finance that Linda Mayoux (1998) sets out. Some initiatives adopt the first, the financial systems approach, that seeks to empower women through the expansion of their individual choice and capacities for self-reliance. They tend to focus on women rather than gender or class relations.

MYRADA falls more within the second community development approach, facilitating a wide range of other services within rural communities, in addition to savings and credit. In such cases, women are targeted because they are generally poorer than men and also more likely to spend income on the welfare of their families. The programmes seek to empower women in terms of community development and self-sufficiency, and tend to focus on households and communities rather than women alone or gender or class relations.

SEWA in Ahmedabad (see Box 3.1 in Chapter 3) and Working Women's Forum in Chennai (Madras) fall within the third approach, of feminist empowerment. As Mayoux argues, while both promoted micro-financial services early on, these are seen as only part of a strategy for wider social and political empowerment that is in turn seen as essential to sustained increases in incomes.

Both engage in unionising women working in the informal sector to fight for their rights, mobilising them for specific campaigns (see Chapter 6) and organising them into cooperatives. Advocacy focuses not only on the immediate rights of women, for example their economic rights to hawk wares or to access social benefits mandated by the state for *bidi* workers. It also incorporates a broader strategy to get wider recognition of the contribution that women in the informal sector make to the economy and, with that recognition, greater rights and benefits for all such women. In this sense, SEWA and Working Women's Forum are movements that are deliberately seeking to change gender relations within wider society.

Such categorisations are not clear cut, and probably a majority of MFOs working with women in South Asia see themselves operating to some degree within all three approaches (see, for example, Versluysen [1999: 225] on the Grameen Bank).[7]

Mayoux rightly cautions that all three approaches can support women's empowerment, but that they may not. As we have already suggested, there is evidence of potential negative impacts on women, for example the exclusion of the poorest or the additional burdens that participation in savings and credit groups may bring. Enhanced businesses and incomes may be marginal, especially when many women are competing with each other in the same line of business.

Even when women control the business and income-streams, this may lead to little change in gender relations, for example around girl children.

Thus we cannot determine *a priori* which approach is better. What is clear is that a narrow focus on the efficient delivery of micro-financial services only, focusing on their transaction costs, repayment rates and financial sustainability, is likely to leave less room for attention to women's empowerment and whether it is actually taking place. This is particularly the case if women's groups are seen merely as a vehicle to reduce costs for the MFO.

It is also apparent that programmes that give women greater ownership and decision-making powers may add to the responsibilities and potential burdens on members, but are also more likely to meet their needs, as perceived by women members themselves, than programmes delivered by a centralised MFO. This would suggest that the many anecdotes of individual and group empowerment seen around well-managed SHGs and savings and credit cooperatives point to changing realities on the ground.

The obvious response from those focusing more narrowly on the delivery of micro-financial services is that they introduced efficient systems in reaction to low performing microfinance programmes which reached few women and had little impact. However, efficient financial systems and organising women into democratic local organisations should not be seen as incompatible alternatives.

The Cooperative Development Foundation argues strongly that unless women (or male) members are enabled to manage efficient and effective cooperatives, little empowerment will take place. Most effective groups need to focus on pragmatic tools that bring immediate benefits to their members, and micro-financial services have proved to be a good tool for this. However, like MYRADA, CDF argues that it is not the financial services themselves, but the ownership and management of the savings and credit organisations, that are most empowering. To be so, ownership and management have to be effective, and CDF has introduced detailed systems, from governance structures to computer software, to enable women to manage their cooperatives well. Moreover, as the evidence from MYRADA suggests, the initial increased investment in capacity-building to ensure well-functioning local organisations may ensure longer-term organisational sustainability.

Most of the NGOs reviewed in this chapter are promoting federal structures to further strengthen the primary groups, both in terms of their efficiency and in terms of their collective visibility and power.

It is thus apparent that the primary focus on promoting people's organisations around micro-financial services, as well as other activities, is a key element of a strategy to empower poor people, especially women.

Within the Indian context, the development of microfinance moreover forms part of formal democratic processes. Even the mere visibility of groups representing and potentially mobilising large numbers of voters is important.

One of the areas most worthy of more detailed analysis is the opportunity for the leaders that are emerging from self-help and other groups to use their enhanced confidence, understanding and skills to enter mainstream democratic processes. In India, through constitutional mandate, a third of all seats on the tiered structure of *panchayats* (elected local councils) have been reserved for women. While there are plenty of examples of local elites manipulating these processes (the classic example is the village head getting his wife elected to the *gram panchayat* or village council), there are also a growing number of cases of women leaders from savings and credit groups being elected to the *gram panchayats*.

As Malcolm Harper calculates in Chapter 7, some 200 (about 2.5 per cent) of the total of 77,495 members of SHGs sponsored by MYRADA were elected to their *gram panchayats* in 2000. In 1999, 30 members, almost exactly the same percentage, of the 12,000 members of ASA's Grameen-type groups in the state of Tamil Nadu were similarly elected.

Likewise, in the last elections for the state assembly in Andhra Pradesh, the state that has by far the largest number of SHGs, it was not an uncommon sight to see political parties including the ruling Telugu Desam Party wooing SHG leaders with candidatures to fight the elections, a trend that is much more prevalent in the *panchayat* elections. This not only acknowledges the importance that the movement has had in day-to-day governance, but also in the popularity of SHGs, which have been seen to deliver effective services on the ground.

While the danger of political capture is obvious, as has happened so significantly to cooperatives in the past, the context of Indian democracy may also make the instrumental use of micro-finance to empower women easier, by providing formal and constitutional democratic channels through which women emerging from the thousands of savings and credit groups across the country can exercise greater influence and power.

Conclusion

Within the micro-finance industry 'social intermediation' is often seen as a necessary tool to ensure efficient delivery of micro-financial services. Indian practice featured within this chapter turns this argument on its head. Micro-financial services are an effective tool, among others, for organising and empowering poor people, especially women.

This is not surprising within the context of the very strong democratic traditions of India, which, moreover, provide formal democratic channels through which emerging women leaders can exercise greater influence and power. However, the lessons may apply equally to micro-finance practice elsewhere, whether in a democratic context or not.

It is often the unequal distribution of assets and wealth, and hence of power, that lies at the heart of the need for development interventions. For micro-financial services used in a developmental context, issues of ownership and control of resources cannot therefore be avoided. For example, who owns the financial assets, who receives the profits?

These questions are particularly important at a time when micro-financial services are becoming ever more mainstreamed and MFOs are taking on the characteristics of formal financial intermediaries. The mainstream financial sector is often a primary mechanism for maintaining the unequal distribution of wealth. For example, once most MFOs have learnt to provide effective savings products, will they do any better than the mainstream financial sector in collecting deposits that are then lent, usually elsewhere, to the already wealthy?

Local democratic management, control and governance are often the keys to empowerment at the local level, not least among women. It is not so much micro-financial services themselves that are empowering, but the effective management of them that enables poor women and men to learn skills and build capacities that they can use in other contexts beyond their savings and credit group, whether in the household, their community or in interacting with bankers and government officials.

The experience of the cooperative movement in India has shown that if local groups are treated merely as delivery channels controlled by a central organisation they do not build local capacity and often become moribund over time.

The experience of cooperatives also suggests that they need effective internal governance, which can only be achieved through appropriate investment in capacity building, to avoid being captured, whether internally by vested interests or externally by political and bureaucratic interests. Small SHGs are in many ways highly vulnerable, and cooperatives registered under the new 'mutually-aided' legal framework (see Chapter 6) may prove more resilient, as well as have access to larger resources accumulated through members' savings alone. Alternatively, SHGs are being federated into associations and federations, to provide support services, greater protection from external parties, and greater visibility and influence.

Building democratic people's organisations is not easy and requires significant resources, which are analysed in greater depth in Chapter 8. Achievements we have pointed to in this chapter have depended on intensive and high-quality promotional inputs by each of the NGOs involved. Organisations that have not been willing to invest these resources have not achieved the same results. Promoting democratic people's organisations is therefore not a quick fix. However, those that are well governed and managed are likely to be more empowering for their members, and more sustainable.

Notes

1. MYRADA has changed the way it refers to its groups, from 'self-help groups' to 'affinity groups', because of the wide use of the term 'self-help group' even by those who see them merely as delivery channels rather than as genuine people's organisations.
2. For a special bulletin of the NGO SEARCH on micro-credit and empowerment, see SEARCH (1999).
3. It is important to note that closing an SHG is not necessarily a bad outcome. As democratic organisations, they have the right to wind up their operations, if they feel that the SHG is no longer effective in meeting their needs as they change over time. This is an issue on which Rutherford (2000) encourages micro-finance practitioners to learn from informal financial-service groups that are often not designed to be permanent. Nevertheless, amongst almost all NGOs promoting SHGs, there is the presumption that organisational sustainability is an important goal.
4. Some 23 in fact! They are: structural analysis of society; analysis of local credit sources; the concept of SHGs; how to conduct a meeting; communication; affinity; vision-building; group goals; planning, resource mobilisation, implementation, monitoring and evaluation (PRIME); rules and regulations; members' responsibilities; book-keeping and auditing; leadership; conflict resolution; collective decision-making; common fund management; self-assessment; group graduation; linkages with other institutions; building credit linkages; federations; 'credit plus'; and analysing gender relations (Fernandez, 2001: Chapter 5; MYRADA, 2000).
5. The NGO Sharan has yet a different strategy for federating SHGs in the slums of Delhi (see Chapter 8).
6. '... CDF had learnt that for federations to be effective and member-sensitive, and to act from positions of responsibility and not power, they should not have access to easy money. Cooperatives, whether at primary or secondary levels, if dependent on high levels of member-participation, behaved responsibly, and elected persons of competence and integrity to their managements. Where, however, they were not dependent on member-participation for survival, and had access to soft funding of any form, they and their members tended to be irresponsible, and the need to be in control of the funds became of greater concern than the servicing of members' (CDF, 2000: 31).
7. 'When discussing credit as a tool for empowerment and social change, the first example that comes to mind is the Grameen Bank. It has taught landless unskilled women to fend for themselves, and is using its social constitution of Sixteen Decisions and group discipline to encourage its members to abandon the practice of dowry, control their fertility, and send their daughters to school. Grameen also

challenges the social and religious foundations of women's oppression and inferior status. But it has no monopoly on empowerment. BRAC, for one, has taken women's empowerment quite a bit further by helping village women defend their basic rights and offering legal advice' (Versluysen, 1999: 225).

Chapter 6

Micro-finance and system-wide change

Introduction

Eradicating poverty is surely a transcendent challenge for humanity,[1] on par with the challenges of achieving peace and sustainability. The micro-finance and other organisations we have featured in this book are clearly motivated at a deep personal and organisational level to play their part in addressing this transcendent challenge, and all recognise that the delivery of micro-financial services can only play a very small role.

To play even such a small role effectively, micro-finance organisations (MFOs) need to provide not only a range of financial services (savings, credit and insurance) to enhance social and economic security (Chapter 3), but also be linked to wider strategies to promote livelihoods (Chapter 4) or democratic people's organisations (Chapter 5). As a hard-headed review of poverty and micro-finance in Great Britain concluded, 'To maximise impact ... the cutting edge of micro-financial services ... must be integrated within wider strategies for social change and economic improvement' (Rogaly et al., 1999: 144).

It would be possible therefore to limit this review of micro-finance in India to only the most immediate developmental impacts. However, this would not do justice to the vision and motivation of many practitioners. Above all, it would not help us in understanding practical strategies and mechanisms that MFOs can adopt to make a difference well beyond the provision of financial services.

The reason that most micro-finance practitioners, and most development practitioners generally, shy away from such wider strategies is their 'awesome complexity and scale' (see

Lynton, 1998: Chapter 10). It is much easier to focus on the effective delivery of technical services (in this case, financial). However, while such a limited focus may help some poor people to cope better with their poverty (assuming any potential negative impacts are avoided), it will do little to contribute to development, let alone any transcendent challenge of eradicating poverty.

As we have already suggested, to achieve developmental impacts micro-finance practitioners must at the very least seek to integrate financial services with other measures to address the broader needs that poor people have, in terms of enhancing their security, their livelihoods or their power through individual empowerment and collective endeavour. To have any influence beyond this, MFOs must use micro-financial services, and themselves as organisations, as tools or instruments to effect wider system-level or institutional change.

We use the term 'institutions' here advisedly. '... the term "institution" has a much wider meaning than its common definition as a formal organisation of some significance. For example, Douglass North (1990: 3) describes institutions "as the rules of the game in a society or, more formally, ... the humanly devised constraints that shape human interaction". ... North (1981: 201–2) explains [that] "institutions are a set of rules, compliance procedures, and moral and ethical behavioural norms ..."' (Fisher and Mahajan, 1997: 86).

To achieve wider system-level or institutional change, MFOs do not have to become ever larger as though organisational scale alone could effect system-wide change. There is a

> strong possibility that work on a large scale will come with multiplying and interlinking well-functioning small (often local?) groupings, not by expanding into ever larger units. Masterful craftsmanship is involved in designing and managing the necessary connections. If this picture of going to large scale is even approximately correct, then quality work is not the alternative to quantity but its very means (Lynton, 1998: 286).[2]

We have looked at quality work in previous chapters, and will continue to do so in this one. To what extent can such work be multiplied and interlinked to have larger system-wide or institutional impacts?

First we look at BASIX, which has been a highly innovative organisation and a pioneer within the micro-finance sector in India (for more details, see Chapter 4). To push forward such innovation BASIX has had to establish a range of linkages, including with regulators, investors, promotional institutions, partners (who can act as intermediaries for or provide support to clients), small community-based organisations, such as self-help groups (SHGs), and so on.

Second, we look at the Self-employed Women's Association (SEWA) which has sought to use micro-financial services as well as other tools to empower women and change gender relations (for more details, see Chapters 3 and 5). SEWA has gone the route of organising poor women in the informal sector for collective action, and mobilised a range of campaigns, again with significant linkages to partner organisations as well as the organisations they seek to change.

Third, we feature the work of the Cooperative Development Foundation (CDF) in changing the legal environment for co-operatives, first in the state of Andhra Pradesh, and increasingly across the country (for more details of CDF's work with savings and credit cooperatives, see Chapter 5).

As we have seen in previous chapters, it is the instrumental use of micro-financial services, rather than treating them as an end in themselves, that leads to wider impacts, whether on livelihoods, empowerment, people's organisations or institutional change. In this chapter we analyse how wider impacts on institutions or large systems may be achieved in practice.

BASIX and the micro-finance sector

BASIX as an innovative pioneer

An organisation or enterprise has to engage with its environment, seeking to keep it at bay, or influencing and changing it in order that it can prosper. This challenge is growing as the environment most organisations face becomes more turbulent (Emery and Trist, 1965).

A *development* organisation also has to engage with its environment to prosper. In addition, it is often motivated by longing to create wider change beyond its own operations. In seeking to do so, it may become truly innovative: 'Innovative institutions aim to make a difference beyond themselves. *What* difference precisely and how, and how much it mattered in the light of history many forces will influence, as also the deliberate moves that took it there' (Lynton, 1998: 229).

BASIX has certainly been an innovative pioneer within the Indian micro-finance sector, and has deeply influenced that sector. Four areas stand out in particular.

First, as we saw in Chapter 4, BASIX has led innovation on leveraging micro-finance provision with a range of non-financial activities to promote rural livelihoods, including attempts to support small enterprises that can generate wage employment for poor people. BASIX has done this not just by attracting funding for business-support services, but also by working with existing market agents (e.g., input suppliers and dairy cooperatives), who respond to market incentives to support BASIX' borrowers, and whom BASIX can influence to provide higher-quality services. Through such mechanisms BASIX has, for example, helped in introducing new crops like paprika and technologies like micro-drip irrigation, revived existing under-performing infrastructure (e.g., lift-irrigation schemes) or organisations (e.g., dairy cooperatives), even created competition within moneylending markets.

Second, BASIX has been a pioneer in attracting mainstream finance to an MFO. This started with a soft loan from the Ford Foundation, a first for India, and led to the first loan to an Indian MFO from a private commercial bank, as well as debt and equity investments from around the world, including from the International Finance Corporation (IFC) of the World Bank (see Chapter 4, note 4).

Each step on what has been a long five-year journey has involved intensive negotiation, not only with Indian regulators to open up regulatory provisions to enable such investments, but also with the investors, for example to drop restrictions that would undermine BASIX' mission and to understand its unusual structure, not least as a development enterprise promoted with substantial sweat equity but less traditional financial capital.

In this area, as in its livelihood interventions, BASIX has been a pioneer not only in India but also internationally. As Dichter (2001: 12) comments: 'No other [MFO] on the scene has had anything like this mix of investors, this combination of loans and equity, nor has any such organisation made this kind of progress so early in its growth.'

Third, BASIX was the first MFO to set up a Local Area Bank, a new banking structure for banks seeking to operate in no more than three contiguous districts in India. Fourth, BASIX has developed highly sophisticated systems, including financial and management information systems, customer service agents, pay structures and staff development processes, and customer satisfaction audits, which are way ahead in the field of micro-finance in India and for the most part internationally also.

A pioneer opens up new terrain for others to follow. The first question to ask is how BASIX as one organisation could incorporate so much pioneering innovation.

An important factor here was the experience and intellectual capital that the promoters brought to BASIX (Dichter, 2001). This applies equally to the leaders of SEWA and CDF, who were deeply experienced and knowledgeable on union or cooperative activity respectively. However, to illustrate this feature, we elaborate on the promoters of BASIX. All had been through prestigious academic institutes. More important was the experience they brought.

The Managing Director had worked in the private sector; set up the non-governmental organisation (NGO) PRADAN committed to promoting rural livelihoods (see Chapters 5 and 9); was the national coordinator of a long-term and in-depth study on the rural non-farm sector in India (Fisher and Mahajan, 1997); and was a consultant and adviser on rural non-farm employment and rural finance to the Reserve Bank of India (RBI), the National Bank for Agriculture and Rural Development (NABARD), the World Bank, the Swiss Agency for Development and Cooperation and the Ford Foundation.

Another founder is a partner in corporate finance at PriceWaterhouseCoopers, with previous experience at the Industrial Credit and Investment Corporation of India (ICICI) and the Nehru Foundation for Development. The third founder had worked at the Ford Foundation for six years before becoming Programme Director and Executive Director (1987–92) at PRADAN.

Their depth of experience and understanding from the development and private sectors, across the disciplines of development, economics, finance, engineering and management, was complemented by a strong board and management team, again comprising members from the development and private sectors, as well as academic institutes. A deliberate policy to remunerate staff well, and the buzz of an innovative new organisation, were important factors in attracting high-quality staff.

More specifically, BASIX was designed after deliberate and intensive review of best practice in micro-finance in India and internationally. This involved, for example, an in-depth study of financial services for poor people provided through the banking system (Mahajan and Ramola, 1996); support, both technical and in strategic planning, for SEWA Bank; study visits to Bangladesh, Indonesia, Thailand and the United States; and review of practice elsewhere through research, international conferences and meetings with leading micro-finance practitioners. This work continued even after BASIX was established, for example in case-studies of MFOs in India produced for the International Fund for Agricultural Development (IFAD) (BASIX, 1999a). As Dichter (2001: 11) points out, 'There are few if any major innovations or developments in micro-finance or enterprise development of which the founders are unaware'.

However, in promoting a development enterprise, rather than a private business, even such experience and understanding is not sufficient. Equally important are the personal commitment and motivations of the social or development entrepreneurs involved. Alongside the ambition to take on the huge challenges of a pioneer, and to emerge from the development sector to become accepted as a legitimate and mainstream player in the Indian financial sector (Dichter, 2001), comes the deep commitment to the cause of development in India, shared by the founders, board members and many of the staff.

It is this ambition and commitment, combined with the deep understanding of the scale of the developmental challenges India faces, that continually drive BASIX never to rest, always to go one step further, to innovate and experiment, in pursuit of having a real development impact. This is not a fixed or static process. Each person interprets the mission in somewhat different ways, and the focus and emphasis of BASIX' work is constantly shifting as different energies and views are mediated through organisational processes.

A pioneer may open up new terrain for others to follow. However, that in itself does not ensure that others know about the innovation, can follow and learn from the pioneer and make their own contributions to developing the new terrain.

As inspiring as BASIX may be, inspiration alone is clearly not sufficient. It would of course be foolish to underestimate the power of such inspiration, as the case of the Grameen Bank shows. Like SEWA Bank, it demonstrated, against all conventional banking wisdom at the time it was established, that poor people are bankable (Rogaly et al., 1999: 126).

However, the huge number of pilot projects scattered all over India shows so clearly that innovation will not simply multiply or replicate of its own accord, even if successful. To ensure influence beyond the organisation itself requires deliberate strategies to exercise such influence.

For example, the Grameen Bank has been active in supporting the replication of its specific model of micro-finance through the Grameen Trust established for this purpose. As we have seen above, BASIX has adopted deliberate mechanisms to build its innovation, for example, the intensive review of best practice elsewhere, work with other Indian MFOs, remuneration policies to attract high-quality staff and so on.

What deliberate strategies has BASIX adopted to ensure that its innovations achieve wider influence beyond its own operations? A key factor of any such strategy must be to establish effective linkages that allow the organisation to exercise influence. It is also important to distinguish among different linkages for different purposes.

'Enabling' linkages provide the institution with legitimate authority to start and to operate, and to give it access to the funds and other support it needs. 'Functional' linkages provide for substantive exchanges with the environment. 'Normative' linkages deal with the establishment of standards in the institution and with its attempts to influence norms in the environment. 'Diffuse' linkages are for building widespread understanding and support for the institution. ... a fifth type of ('collegial') linkage provides at the institutional level what colleagueship does at the individual level, through exchanging experimental information and developing common strategies and common resources (Lynton and Pareek, 1992: 156; Lynton, 1998: 220).

In the case of BASIX, it has established strong enabling linkages, for example with a wide range of investors, as suggested above, and with the Reserve Bank of India, to enable BASIX to be the first MFO to establish a Local Area Bank. BASIX has established strong functional linkages as well, particularly with other market agents and other MFOs to support BASIX' borrowers and spread innovation in the field.

Normative linkages have been very prominent in the case of BASIX as it has sought to influence the regulatory and policy environment (see Box 6.1). Even before setting up BASIX, the promoters were seeking to use normative linkages to change the norms of rural banking practice, as captured in Table 6.1 (compare Table 4.1 in Chapter 4). A particularly important breakthrough that BASIX influenced came with the Task Force on a Supportive Policy and Regulatory Framework for Micro-finance (NABARD, 1999b), which created a much more positive policy environment for micro-financial services in India.

Of equal importance was probably the normative effect of one of BASIX' enabling linkages with Global Trust Bank (GTB), the first private commercial bank to make a loan to an MFO in India for on-lending to SHGs. Its significance lay in getting NABARD to refinance GTB's loan as priority-sector lending, setting an important precedent that lending to MFOs for on-lending to SHGs could be regarded by banks as meeting their priority-sector obligations.

Box 6.1: Policy work by BASIX

- The Managing Director (MD) had been a member of a working group on rural credit through non-governmental organisations (NGOs) and self-help groups (SHGs) in 1995 that boosted national efforts to link banks and SHGs.
- The idea of a Local Area Bank (LAB) was in part inspired by reports from study visits by BASIX' promoters, to Indonesia in particular, which were presented to the Deputy Governor of the Reserve Bank of India (RBI). This led to similar visits to South-East Asia by RBI staff, who developed the policy on LABs.
- BASIX' promoters had since 1995 been advocating important regulatory changes, in particular, the deregulation of interest rates, while working on the Indian Rural Finance Reform Project of the World Bank (which eventually did not materialise).
- BASIX assisted SIDBI in setting up the Foundation for Micro-credit through a study on the demand profile and cost-structure of well-established MFOs and reviewing the Foundation's business plan.
- BASIX was active in helping to establish Sa-Dhan, the Indian Association of Community Development Finance Institutions (see Box 6.2). Through Sa-Dhan, BASIX was also active in promoting the idea of the Task Force on a Supportive Policy and Regulatory Framework for Micro-finance, which was chaired by NABARD and reported to the Reserve Bank of India (NABARD, 1999b).
- BASIX carried out the feasibility study for the Andhra Pradesh Mahila Abhivruddhi Society or APMAS (BASIX, 1999c), which was established in 2001.
- The MD has worked on strategies to promote the rural micro-enterprise sector in the states of Andhra Pradesh, Rajasthan and Sikkim, and was a member of the Andhra Pradesh State-level Employment Generation Mission and the Rajiv Gandhi Mission on Livelihoods Security in the state of Madhya Pradesh (MP) which led to BASIX establishing an initiative called the MP Livelihoods Enhancement Action Platform. Most recently, the MD has become a member of the working group on poverty alleviation programmes for the Planning Commission and of the working group reviewing legislation and regulation of Regional Rural Banks.

**Table 6.1: BASIX' characterisation of existing and
new generation financial intermediaries**

Characteristic	Existing financial intermediaries	New generation MFOs
Self-concept	Credit delivery system, in which funds come from external sources.	Financial intermediary, linking micro-savers with borrowers.
Ownership and control	Mostly government owned. Even cooperatives, which are nominally member-owned, are often government controlled in practice.	Ownership will be with shareholders, largely micro-individuals and organisations.
Motivation	Saving the poor people from clutches of money-lenders using micro-savers as a source of funds; means of political patronage.	Making a reasonable profit, by providing competitive services to micro-customers.
Products and services	Few products that suit poor people's special needs: illiteracy, seasonality, mixed credit needs, livelihood diversity.	Savings and loan products will be designed to suit specific demand segments and customer attributes.
Main source of loanable funds	World Bank, RBI, NABARD, etc.; funds at low interest rates; also government funds, e.g., RMK.	Deposits, raised by giving real positive interest rates; also bulk borrowings.
Interest rate on loans	Lower than sustainable levels: cannot cover capital, operating and bad debt costs.	Interest rate must cover all three costs and also service the equity.
Repayment rates	On-time repayment rates are routinely 50 per cent or less.	On-time repayment rates of less than 95 per cent will lead to uneconomic operations.
Method of lending	Security-based lending; insistence on collateral; largely one-time basis.	Lending based on borrower's prior savings and credit history. Repeat loans are a key feature.
Attitude towards the poor	Seen as social obligation and intrinsically un-worthy of credit.	The poor seen as entry-level customers. If they prosper, the MFO prospers in leaps and bounds.
Operating methods	High cost, poor service, due to manual operations, over-staffing, bureaucratic functioning and poor industrial relations.	Lower level of cost, high level of service due to use of information technology, performance linked wages, and profes-sional orientation.

The promoters brought many diffuse linkages into BASIX, for example, within the wider development and academic sectors focusing on livelihood promotion. BASIX continues to build widespread understanding through these channels, for example, in collaborating on a resource book on livelihood promotion (in which BASIX also features as a case-study) (Datta et al., 2001).

Finally, BASIX has had strong collegiate linkages, both at an individual level (many colleagues are on the board or act as advisors and mentors to BASIX), and at an organisational level, where BASIX has worked with many other MFOs and played a leading role in establishing the Indian trade association for MFOs (see further).

Linkages need to be built and sustained (Lynton, 1998: 221). In the case of BASIX many of these linkages were brought into the organisation by the promoters. However, BASIX has also adopted deliberate strategies to develop such linkages. Here are some examples.

BASIX has formalised some of these linkages within the organisation, by inviting key individuals from both the development and private sectors to become members of the board, and using others as evaluators, advisers and mentors.

BASIX has allowed exposure to its work, to some extent through articles, studies and publications, but much more so through visits. BASIX brings together management staff from across the organisation to review its operations on a quarterly basis. This event is also used as the opportunity for visits by outsiders, who often go into the field prior to the event, and then attend some of the review sessions. This can of course also serve as a two-way process, enabling BASIX' managers to gain insights from external parties, some of whom bring significant experience and insight.

BASIX has given direct support to other MFOs in India. For example, BASIX has provided technical assistance and management support to a network of village banks set up by the NGO ASSEFA. It has provided strategic planning and training support to the NGO PRADAN, and advice to a range of development and financial entities. It has also developed strategies to promote and build capacity among the many grass-roots organisations like SHGs or mutually-aided cooperative societies (MACS). This work has led, for example, to further support for a capacity-building organisation for such groups in the state of Andhra Pradesh (called the Andhra Pradesh Mahila Abhivruddhi Society or APMAS).

Perhaps most important in the early years of its organisational life, BASIX has become deeply involved in policy processes around rural employment and finance. This has been in part around specific issues of policy that had a direct influence on BASIX' operations, such as foreign investment and the development of the Local Area Bank (LAB). As Box 6.1 shows, BASIX has also seized opportunities to influence policy more broadly. It has thereby contributed to the on-going development of a supportive policy-framework and environment for micro-finance in India well beyond itself, while also benefiting significantly from this improved environment.

The innovation of BASIX has therefore come from a range of factors such as the depth of experience and intellectual capital among BASIX' promoters and senior staff and their ambition and commitment to development, the entrepreneurship of the Managing Director and BASIX' ability to hire high-powered staff attracted to the buzz and the good remuneration. Influence has been achieved through the deliberate cultivation of a wide range of different linkages, and mechanisms to build and sustain these.

This has not come without its costs for the organisation. For example, constant innovation has led to constant change, and subjected the organisation to risk. It had to suspend lending over Rs 50,000 to small enterprises when that part of its portfolio performed badly. Some linkages have come with risks, for example, collaborating with commission agents, who have a very negative image within development circles in India.

The numerous innovations and linkages have also led to difficulties in maintaining focus, all of which have put pressure on the organisation and its staff. Some linkages, for example, some of the policy work, have at times distracted from business operations, not least for the Managing Director, and provided additional policy work when BASIX was already wrestling with policy and regulatory constraints that had a more direct impact on its operations.

Linkages, for example with other MFOs and development practitioners, have led to a range of engagements that may all have significant potential, but together may not necessarily reflect a strategic vision or the most effective portfolio of linkages for BASIX itself. Linkages therefore need to be built and used strategically, just as any other organisational mechanisms.

The review of BASIX' first five years (Dichter, 2001) suggested that BASIX had in fact, for strategic reasons, tried to be all things to all people, developing a huge set of linkages, but that it must now hone its identity (ibid.: 22):

> BASIX ... think[s] rigorously about important distinctions like that between survival activity and enterprise; between poverty-lending and enterprise lending; between loans used for consumption and loans used for working capital, and ... between micro-financial services and development.
>
> It is this understanding coupled with its integration of financial services and sectorally-based technical support which make it a new generation rural financial institution. And to the extent it can act on these aspects in more pointed ways and thus gain more experience, it will be far better positioned to influence not just regulatory policy for [MFOs], but development thinking.

The trade association Sa-Dhan

Many other individuals and organisations have been involved in influencing policy. Indeed, micro-finance practitioners have long been advocating relevant policy changes, at least since the 1980s. The openness to new measures that came about through the introduction of economic liberalisation in the early 1990s provided the environment for such advocacy to reach a critical mass and for the process of policy change around micro-finance to accelerate in the late 1990s.

For example, leading NGOs promoting SHGs (see Chapter 5) have been involved in influencing NABARD as it developed its 'linkage' programme through which banks lend to SHGs.

In particular, MYRADA, PRADAN, the DHAN Foundation and others have all been involved in training bankers about poor women clients and how to lend to their SHGs. For example, over nine years, MYRADA provided such training to over 4,000 bankers (Fernandez, 2001: 45).

However, such system-wide impacts are beyond the capacity of single organisations to meet. Moreover, each of the organisations seeking to bring about change may often be motivated to bring about change that benefits itself. It is hardly surprising that individual organisations see the sector as a whole through their own experience and often assume that the changes they seek for themselves must also benefit the sector as a whole. While this may sometimes be the case, it is unlikely to be the case all the time.[3]

> Complex societies in fast-changing environments give rise to sets or systems of problems (meta-problems) rather than discrete problems. These are beyond the capacity of single organisations to meet. Inter-organisational collaboration is required by groups of organisations at what is called the 'domain' level (Trist, 1983: 314–15).
>
> This means relationships that will maximise cooperation and which recognise that no one organisation can take over the role of 'the other' and become paramount (Emery and Trist, 1965: 153).

The broader vision and motivation of development organisations like MFOs to have an influence beyond their own operations may make such cooperation easier. At its simplest, such cooperation leads to the formation of an association, as has happened among MFOs in India that have promoted Sa-Dhan, the Association of Community Development Finance Institutions based in New Delhi (see Box 6.2).

An association is necessary to ensure that the interests of all are met, instead of the most powerful skewing the environment in their favour. Sa-Dhan has indeed been careful to build collegiate relationships amongst its members, setting up a range of working groups on policy, standards and capacity-building, and ensuring that it addresses the concerns of all its members, not just the larger MFOs that were initially involved in promoting the association.

Box 6.2: Sa-Dhan, the association of Indian MFOs

Sa-Dhan was established in 1998 by 10 leading micro-finance organisations (MFOs) in India, including SEWA Bank, BASIX, Friends of Women's World Banking (FWWB), Sanghamithra (set up by MYRADA), Rashtriya Gramin Vikas Nidhi (RGVN), Professional Assistance for Development Action (PRADAN), Society for Helping, Awakening Rural Pool through Education (SHARE) and the Development of Human Action (DHAN) Foundation.

Sa-Dhan is not model or ideologically specific in its approach. It is an apex membership body that brings together diverse views, models and concerns in the Indian micro-finance sector from a wide spectrum of stakeholders, including community-based development finance organisations. The association now has 49 members based in 15 states in India.

Sa-Dhan aims to establish an environment to accelerate the development of micro-finance in India. It seeks to encourage savings, credit and insurance services that are responsive to the needs of the lower and lowest income segments of society; to effect policy changes at the micro and macro-levels; to offer technical assistance and support to strengthen existing and promote new livelihoods; and finally to integrate micro-financial services with social development efforts to ensure that economic gains go hand in hand with improving the quality of life of poor households.

To take this agenda forward, the members have chosen to focus attention on three thematic areas: policy, standards and capacity-building. Sub-groups have formed on each of these thematic areas, and each sub-group meets formally three times a year, in addition to their participation at different programmes of the association. Following these meetings, the sub-group leaders, together with or through the Sa-Dhan secretariat, develop and implement programmes in collaboration with members.

To enhance participatory processes, Sa-Dhan enables policy-makers, academicians and field-level practitioners to brainstorm and work together on common platforms. The association works to create opportunities for policy-makers to observe and comprehend realities within the sector, and to enable greater accountability and transparency in the operations of the players in the sector. Towards this end, Sa-Dhan

(Contd)

(Box 6.2 Contd)

> develops operational standards and self-assessment, evaluates existing practices, and evolves consensus on minimum standards to ensure the sustainable growth of the sector.
>
> Sa-Dhan also organises events and programmes designed to bring people together to share their experience and adopt good practices from each other. It provides a common platform for leading practitioners to engage in dialogue and debate, developing learning materials containing insights from the field and supporting academics to transfer their knowledge and training skills to improve such materials available to practitioners.

Associations may seek to provide training and other inputs for their members. However, creating generally accepted standards, norms and values, in other words 'institutions' that influence a wide range of actors, in this case across the micro-finance sector, is key to their wider influence. As Emery and Trist (1965: 152–53) argue,

> [In turbulent environments,] individual organisations, however large, cannot expect to adapt successfully simply through their own direct actions.... Nevertheless, there are some indications of a solution.... This is the emergence of values that have overriding significance for all members of the field.

SEWA and self-employed women

The Self-employed Women's Association has also been trying to change social values, not just within the financial sector but primarily around women working in the unorganised or informal sector of the economy.

SEWA Bank is an important organisation within the broader SEWA family, which also includes the union; a range of cooperatives (over 80) mostly organised around economic trades, but some providing health- and child-care; producer groups (some 200); rural SHGs (1,600); federations of these cooperatives and groups; a housing trust and an academy for research and capacity-building (see Box 3.1 in Chapter 3).

It is important to note that SEWA Bank is therefore only part of a broader family of organisations. The union was established first, but soon discovered that to organise self-employed women effectively, members also needed access to practical services, among which financial services were particularly important. In essence, women members needed to take control of their lives, from their own finances to their collective endeavours.

As seen in Chapter 5, the micro-financial services provided by SEWA Bank therefore form part of a strategy for wider social and political empowerment of women that is in turn seen as essential to sustained increases in their incomes.

Like BASIX, SEWA has created a range of linkages to effect change beyond its own family of organisations. However, in an attempt to build a broader picture, we focus on other parts of its strategy here. Rolf Lynton (1998: 295) has argued that three components of a strategy to effect wider change are critical:

- the work is envisaged on a large enough scale to affect a transcendent challenge and commitments to action match it ...;
- the work is located where the challenge is actually encountered and the options are faced, and those situations will 'speak' as they develop. Fresh understandings will emerge; and
- connections have been built to the larger arenas of action so that local action will matter to the whole large system.

First, SEWA has focused on a large challenge: over 300 million people in India work in the unorganised sector of the economy, and more than nine out of 10 women workers. However, their contribution to the economy is often not recognised and their economic rights are largely non-existent. SEWA is therefore challenging both deep-seated gender relations and hard economic realities, a challenge indeed.

SEWA has also envisaged this challenge on a large enough scale right up to the international level, campaigning at the International Labour Organisation (ILO) for the rights of home-based workers across the world and collaborating with an international group, including economists, on how to recognise and measure the contribution of the unorganised sector to the economy.

Second, SEWA has located its work where the challenge is actually encountered, in the slums of Ahmedabad and surrounding rural areas. SEWA demonstrates more than any other organisation featured in this book a holistic view of its members' needs, rooted in a deep understanding of their lives that a membership organisation and constant work alongside members in their daily lives bring. SEWA's mission therefore incorporates a holistic view of its members' lives, from employment, income and assets, through food, nutrition and health, to leadership and self-reliance (see Box 3.1).

SEWA's approach will continue to challenge organisations promoted and controlled by professionals on how well they actually understand the needs of the people they seek to help. As we saw in the last chapter, power is critical here, and allowing women to own, control and manage their own democratic organisations is an obvious way to reverse power relations between poor people and development professionals.

It was this understanding that led the union to establish SEWA Bank within two years, to provide what had become clear were essential services without which women could not take control of their economic livelihoods, as well as to enable them to own and manage a formal organisation, no less than their own bank.

Third, SEWA has built connections to larger arenas of action. These involve not only collaborative relationships but also non-violent (and deeply Gandhian) confrontation in an activist mode. In a democratic context visible numbers often count, so mobilising women has been a key component of both collaboration and confrontation.

> While organising women and supporting them in building their own workers' organisations, the need for mass mobilisation through campaigns became evident. This mass mobilisation strengthens the SEWA movement and at the same time highlights their own pressing issues.
>
> All mobilisation is done as part of a campaign around a clearly identified issue. The issue is identified by the women and local leaders as one which affects large numbers of people, which [affects] them deeply or is felt as

unjust or intolerable, and is continually called to our attention. Mobilisation involves continuous meetings at the village or *mohalla* [neighbourhood] level.... It means follow-up of the strategy by local people supported by SEWA (SEWA, 1997: 9).

These quotations make clear how carefully SEWA seeks to build campaigns around local action where women encounter the challenges at the heart of these campaigns in their daily lives. Box 6.3 provides some examples of campaigns that SEWA has engaged in, in each case building linkages to enhance their impact.

Box 6.3: SEWA campaigns (SEWA, 1997)

The Home-based Workers Campaign, started by SEWA in the 1970s, reached its peak at the International Labour Organisation (ILO) in 1996, when the ILO voted for a convention to address the needs and priorities of home-based workers, according them full rights as workers. SEWA collaborated with unions in many countries and federations of unions like HOMENET. Extensive dialogue was also held with policymakers in the Indian Ministry of Labour and the equivalent department in the state of Gujarat.

The Water Campaign in northern Gujarat was launched after local women leaders organised *gram sabhas* (traditional meetings of all villagers) in 290 villages. The campaign involves not only mobilising women, but also engaging with the village *panchayats* (elected councils) and government schemes.

The Food Security Campaign was launched after the same *gram sabha* meetings, focusing on ration shops and alternatives to these, and has engaged significantly with the authorities for civil supplies.

The Vendors Campaign fights for the legal rights of vendors, ranging from work with municipal authorities in Ahmedabad through surveys in other Indian cities to an international declaration made by vendors from 11 mega-cities around the world.

The Clean Ahmedabad Campaign has involved organising women locally, working with residents' associations, corporate

(Contd)

(Box 6.3 Contd)

companies and municipal authorities, as well as organising paper-pickers who are members of SEWA and who depend for their livelihoods on recycling dry waste.

The Campaign for Recognition of Unorganised-Sector Workers led to the formation of the National Centre for Labour (NCL) in 1995, a labour federation of unorganised-sector workers, the first ever in the history of the labour movement. SEWA is the largest founder-member of the organisation, along with unions of construction workers, fisher-people, contract and domestic workers, forest and agricultural workers. The National Centre for Labour attended the Indian Labour Conference that brings together labour, employers and government to decide labour policies in the country.

Other campaigns include the Campaign for Minimum Wages pursued through NCL, the Campaign for Forest Workers, campaigning, in particular, for nursery-raising to be handed to local women, the Campaign for Land for Salt-workers, the Campaign for Recognition of *Dais* (traditional birth attendants) and the Campaign for Child-care as a Basic Service.

SEWA's advocacy has therefore focused not only on the immediate rights of women, for example their economic rights to hawk wares or to access social benefits mandated by the state for *bidi* workers. It also incorporates a broader strategy to get wider recognition of the contribution that women in the informal sector make to the economy and, with that recognition, greater rights and benefits for all such women, including SEWA's own members.

Where do micro-financial services come in all of this? Surely this is all about SEWA, not SEWA Bank? The achievement of SEWA has been to integrate the bank into the wider movement in a holistic way. It is not even so much that SEWA has used micro-financial services instrumentally in the way the Cooperative Development Foundation has done to change cooperative law (see the next section). Instead, SEWA started with a holistic perspective grounded in the overall needs of its members, and different organisations within the family were set upto meet particular needs.

Within this family SEWA Bank has of course had a very strong identity, accompanied by strong linkages of its own. SEWA Bank has played a leading role with other MFOs in promoting the association Sa-Dhan. More strikingly, SEWA Bank inspired the formation of Women's World Banking (WWB) located in New York to look at financial services affecting women worldwide (Rose, 1992). There is an affiliate of WWB in India, the Friends of Women's World Banking, which has been actively helping women to form and develop SHGs.

CDF and the cooperative sector

Wider economic impacts at the local level

The savings and credit cooperatives promoted by CDF were featured in Chapter 5. One way that CDF seeks to have an impact beyond individual cooperatives and its members is by saturating its area of operations in two districts with such cooperatives in order to have a sustained impact on the local economies as a whole.

> CDF feels that more work opportunities and choice of work will be available only if local purchasing power is increased, or if outside markets are explored.
>
> ... successful cooperatives share profit amongst members, and since members, by and large, tend to come from contiguous areas, such an action has, over a few years, significant economic impact on the area, increasing local wealth, increasing local demand for services since many families are benefited, increasing employment opportunities to meet the new demands, and improving quality of life.
>
> Significant profits in the hands of one or two individuals operating in rural areas as rice-millers, cotton-ginners, moneylenders, more often than not, result in their being unable, even if they so desired, to reinvest or utilise such amounts locally. On the other hand, profit in the hands of cooperatives engaged in any of these or other businesses results in that amount getting utilised locally and/or being reinvested in the business. Rural capitalisation and growth of rural employment opportunities are closely linked to processes by which large sections of people can increase their incomes....

The momentum generated by the activities of successful cooperatives [thus] leads to greater and more varied employment for men and women in the area. Income and employment opportunities come from the small service and trade enterprises which emerge in response to the growing needs of a rural community enjoying increased purchasing power. These economic opportunities are backed by secure access to both savings and credit facilities for rural entrepreneurs and others. Non-agricultural work opportunities leave their impact on agricultural wages (CDF, 1993: 6, 1996).

The DHAN Foundation, featured in Chapter 5, also seeks to saturate areas, such as administrative blocks, in this case with SHGs, to reduce the costs of operating the programme, to ensure a visible presence for the SHGs and their federations, to provide competition with both the formal and informal sector, and to prove that such operations can be a business proposition (Narender, 1999).

BASIX has discovered in practice that through its own operations it can influence the behaviour of other finance providers, including moneylenders who have sometimes lowered their interest rates and banks that have entered the micro-finance market once BASIX had demonstrated its viability (see Chapter 4).

All three illustrate strategies to have local impacts that go beyond the sum of their discrete interventions. More research on such strategies is urgently needed.

Reforming cooperative law

However, it is in reforming cooperative law in India that CDF has sought to bring about system-wide change. Initially, CDF used to work with cooperatives like the one in Mulkanoor (see Chapter 5), which had been established with state patronage. The Foundation tried very hard to free these cooperatives from state sponsorship and control, including engaging in activism and litigation. However, such strategies proved difficult since the state had significant financial stakes in many of the cooperatives (for a detailed description of the work done by CDF in this stage see Korten [1990]).

Therefore, CDF almost stopped its work with existing co-operatives and focused on a highly organised advocacy programme to get a new law for cooperatives enacted in the state of Andhra Pradesh (CDF, 2000). These efforts continued for more than 10 years, involving cooperatives, politicians, bureaucrats, bankers, lawyers, courts, academics, activists, the media, and even a model cooperative bill drafted for the national Planning Commission, all to little avail.

It was only around 1993 that CDF started turning its attention to a parallel law for cooperatives that did not seek or have government share capital. As a parallel law, rather than changing the existing law, it would not immediately challenge the vested interests of politicians and bureaucrats in existing cooperatives. This resulted at last in a historic change when, in May 1995, after intensive work by CDF with assembly members from the government and opposition, the state assembly in Andhra Pradesh unanimously adopted the Mutually-aided Cooperative Societies Act. The new act removed all state controls from cooperatives that did not seek state patronage and were registered under the new act.

The Foundation quickly followed up with the Chief Minister, using the most prestigious national figures in the cooperative movement, such as Shri L.C. Jain and Dr Kurien, to ensure that the law was notified and cooperatives, especially many savings and credit cooperatives, were registered under the new act. It also organised a series of workshops and press conferences across the state to educate officials from the department of cooperation, cooperators, NGOs, activists and potential cooperators on the new act, and worked with the department of cooperation to draft a range of publications on registration, by-laws, and so on. A new High Court judgement also confirmed the clear distinction between cooperatives under the old and new acts.

Ever since the new act was passed, there has been a large impetus for micro-finance as well as other cooperative activities in the state which have been enabled by a regulatory framework ideally suited to carry out activities for mutual benefit. Andhra Pradesh now has by far the largest number of mutually-aided savings and credit cooperatives, as well as almost 60 per cent of all SHGs in the country that are linked to commercial banks. The Cooperative Development Foundation is also helping other NGOs promoting micro-finance outside its own area of operations through exposure visits and training programmes, including sensitising them on the primacy of democratic governance in grassroots organisations. There are also other cooperatives emerging under the new act, or transferring from their old status to become mutually-aided cooperatives.

Building on its success in Andhra Pradesh, CDF has pursued its advocacy work to ensure that other states in India adopt similar liberal cooperative acts. For this it drafted a bill with commentary (the Self-reliant Cooperatives Bill) for states wanting to review their cooperative law (CDF, 2000). It also identified and built on the extensive cooperative networks throughout the country, providing expert information, conducting workshops, consulting with a wide range of stakeholders from cooperators to government officials, reviewing draft laws. The following report, on the state of Kerala, is not untypical:

> Senior cooperators, senior political leaders, academicians, professionals, trade union leaders and representatives of various voluntary organisations unanimously desired that a liberal parallel cooperative law should be enacted in the state. They participated in a series of workshops on the need for the enactment of a liberal parallel cooperative law in the state organised by Cooperative Initiative Panel, Anand, CDF and the South Indian Federation of Fishermen Societies ... (CDF, 2001).

Similar work, including in at least four cases the introduction of new liberal acts, has been taking place in numerous states across the country. In its newsletter for May 2000, CDF commented, 'during the month, CDF visited Himachal Pradesh, Punjab, Chandigarh (Union Territory), Haryana, Delhi (UT), Rajasthan, Gujarat, Madhya Pradesh, Bihar, West Bengal, Orissa, Tamil Nadu and Pondicherry (UT)'! Other states in which CDF has done similar work are Chhattisgarh, Goa, Jammu and Kashmir, Jharkhand, Karnataka, Maharashtra and Uttar Pradesh.

Change is now also occurring at the national level, with work on the legal framework for multi-state cooperatives, and a potential amendment to the Companies Act. The latter would enable cooperatives, whether registered under the multi-state act or any state act, to convert themselves into producer companies, which would retain the essential characteristics of a cooperative, but take them out of the purview of the Registrars of Cooperatives and enable them to tap capital markets for finance. The Prime Minister himself urged chief ministers and all political parties to help depoliticise, debureaucratise, democratise and professionalise cooperatives (CDF, 2001).

In all these activities, democratic governance has been at the heart of CDF's approach. It is effective cooperatives that are autonomous and make their own decisions that can lead to the democratic transformation of communities and, as suggested above, have an impact on the local economy as a whole, not just individual members of the cooperatives. The cooperatives to which CDF can point to demonstrate this in practice are mostly the savings and credit cooperatives in Andhra Pradesh.

The Cooperative Development Foundation also learnt from its many years of advocacy, concluding:

> It took CDF about two and a half years of concerted effort to get good court judgements, favouring cooperatives. It took it over a decade to get a good cooperative law in place. It will probably take it all of another decade to get enough states and the union to have good cooperative laws. CDF has learnt to work on several fronts at once to get the reforms that it seeks. It has also learnt that it is not important that it gets noticed, that its inputs get acknowledged.... What is important is to get the reform, and for that people formally responsible for the reform have to be convinced of what they are doing, and it is they who have to be in the forefront leading the cause. From fiery and self-righteous campaigns, CDF has moved to more strategic, and less visible planning and action. As CDF has refused to learn the skills of manipulation, where a government is not ready for change, [CDF] maintains a low level of pressure, waiting for better times, but moves on to another which wants change ... (CDF, 2000: 28).

The cooperative work done by CDF has also drawn it into other issues of governance. It campaigned against a union government proposal to introduce a statutory code of conduct for activists, and has engaged in work on legal aspects of societies, under which many NGOs, including CDF, are registered. The President of CDF is also actively involved in an organisation called the Foundation for Democratic Reforms that works in the arena of electoral politics and the overall democratic fabric of the country.

Learning from CDF

The Cooperative Development Foundation demonstrates the need to learn from experience, including failures, as it sought to replicate the superb example of the Mulkanoor cooperative. On realising, through its practical experience on the ground, that its endeavours could never work without a change in the legal environment, most of the organisation's attention was directed at bringing about just such a change, until finally the breakthrough came in 1995 with a new law in the state of Andhra Pradesh.

The Foundation did not, however, rest on its laurels at this point, but sought to deliver support to other states to adopt the same legal changes. Just as importantly, it returned with renewed vigour to its practical work on the ground, where many of the savings and credit cooperatives were registering under the new act. It has sought in particular to enhance the quality of these cooperatives, not just for the sake of their members but also to demonstrate in practice that cooperatives under the new law could perform better. The extensive linkages formed by CDF within the cooperative sector and its deliberate advocacy provide the channels through which such demonstration is communicated. In this way CDF is using the savings and credit cooperatives instrumentally to strengthen the case for system-wide change across the huge cooperative sector within India.

In these ways CDF, like SEWA, is following the strategy for system-wide change that Lynton (1998: 295) advocates. First, 'the work is envisaged on a large enough scale ... and commitments to action match it'. In CDF's case, it took up the challenge of transforming the huge cooperative sector in India, and developed a vision and strategies to match, working outwards by example from the one state in which it was based and therefore was most able to bring about positive change.

Second, 'the work is located where the challenge is actually encountered and the options are faced'. More by accident than design, CDF was based in a southern state of India where the political subversion of cooperatives into populist tools for political patronage was particularly rife (CDF, 2000: Chapter 2). At the same time it drew its inspiration from a highly successful cooperative in this environment, but it took actual practice on the ground to discover determinants of that success that could be replicated, and those which were simply unique. It was this experience that also led CDF to change its focus to the legal environment. More than most NGOs, CDF is above all reflective about its practice, learning from experience.

Third, 'connections have been built to the larger arenas of action so that local action will matter to the whole large system'. Here CDF has identified and established a wide range of relevant connections, including through membership of its board, with the grandees of the cooperative movement to whom politicians are more likely to listen, with sympathetic politicians and bureaucrats in the relevant state assemblies and government departments, with activists, lawyers and academics, and not least with a wide range of local cooperative leaders who were determined to ensure their cooperative worked and could provide evidence of 'the people's will'. It thus built systematically on the extensive cooperative networks throughout the country, providing vital, but often less visible, support to state-level campaigns for cooperative reform.

Above all, CDF established linkages between practice and policy, between sub-systems on the ground and the wider system. The understanding of what policy changes were needed was based on deep understanding of the realities on the ground. Likewise, when positive policy changes were introduced, CDF focused on the quality of cooperative practice on the ground to demonstrate that cooperatives under the new law could perform better. That is why micro-financial services, around which cooperatives could be organised effectively, became so important as an instrument to influence policy.

The costs and the time-scale of such strategies should not be underestimated. The Cooperative Development Foundation abandoned years of work on reforming existing cooperative law to focus on advocating parallel laws, years of work with existing cooperatives to focus primarily on promoting new cooperatives. It took CDF over 20 years to achieve its first-major breakthrough, which has opened up huge opportunities as well as demands to which the organisation is now responding, recognising that it will be many more years before it has achieved many of its goals. Persistence, in addition to learning and adapting, is clearly a necessary quality.

Conclusions

As development enterprises, MFOs face many challenges, including in engaging with their environment. First, an MFO must engage systematically with its environment through appropriate linkages in order to create an enabling environment for it to prosper. All the MFOs featured in this book do this to a lesser or greater extent, although few do so systematically.

Second, as a development enterprise an MFO must decide to what extent it reaches out beyond its own operations to effect change in its environment, not just from a 'self-centred' perspective of helping itself, but also from the perspective of contributing to a wider vision of social change of which its organisational goals are part.

This chapter has reviewed three cases of how MFOs, or organisations promoting micro-financial services, have systematically sought to effect change in their environment that has gone well beyond their own operations.

BASIX has been an innovative pioneer within the micro-finance sector in India, and built a wide range of linkages to enable it to introduce innovations that have pushed at the sector's boundaries, to open up and change the regulatory environment, and to play a major role in shaping the very identity of the sector, including through the new association, Sa-Dhan.

SEWA has integrated micro-finance within a holistic understanding of the needs of poor self-employed women. It has developed services, including micro-financial services, to meet their needs, and, building on these experiences on the ground, has mobilised and inspired a range of campaigns, from the local to the global, to fight for their economic and social rights. In SEWA's view, addressing all their needs is important, from access to savings and insurance to dignity, self-reliance and collective power.

The Cooperative Development Foundation has always had as its primary mission the promotion and support of cooperatives as democratic local organisations that can have a major impact on their local economies and thereby benefit almost everyone in the community. It has been influential in changing the legal environment for cooperatives in India, which had been highly restrictive and oppressive, enabling autonomous democratic cooperatives to emerge. As part of this strategy, CDF has used savings and credit cooperatives instrumentally to demonstrate in practice that mutually-aided cooperatives can perform better than the old cooperatives dependent on state patronage.

These cases demonstrate that MFOs and other organisations can use micro-financial services instrumentally as part of a strategy to bring about system-wide or institutional change that reaches well beyond their own operations. They also provide examples of how to do so, rooting their work where challenges are encountered in practice and systematically building linkages and connections to ensure that local action influences the whole system. Above all, they have not shied away from confronting the complexity and scale of system-wide or institutional change. Rather than falling into despair or cynicism, they have found practical ways in which they can play a constructive role in addressing transcendent challenges.

Such work does not come without cost. Their struggles have often been long, with many setbacks, and can easily become overwhelming. Seeking system-wide or institutional change can distract from the immediate needs of an organisation's operations. Indeed, achieving such change may undermine the organisation itself, for example, when mainstream financial intermediaries enter the market on the back of hard-won and costly innovations by MFOs, whom they then undercut.

Building cooperative relationships among such a diverse set of stakeholders, including those opposing the changes the organisation seeks, is also more challenging than building networks with like-minded organisations in an inward-looking sector. The wider the strategy, the more challenging it is to organise the stakeholders into cooperative relationships.

Yet it is in taking on such challenges that the innovative organisation—the development or social enterprise that most MFOs would like to be—marks itself out most clearly as different from ordinary organisations or enterprises. At the heart of a developmental organisation is the desire to bring about real and significant change, and the cases featured in this chapter demonstrate that, with careful and systematic practice and learning, this is indeed possible.

Notes

1. One 'that faces [humanity] within a thinkable timespan' (Robert Heilbronner, quoted in Lynton [1998: 284, 304]). Heilbronner was thinking in particular of 'making our economic peace with the demands of the environment'. The challenge of poverty has perhaps been with us much longer.

2. In this chapter we use the analytical framework of social change developed by Rolf Lynton, whose long and deep reflection and practice in organisational and institutional change (see Lynton, 1998), not least within the Indian context, has provided so much inspiration to so many of his colleagues.

3. One interesting example is the challenge that MFOs that are incorporated as non-banking financial companies (NBFCs) face. Many of them can no longer use this legal entity to take deposits, following scandals in which corrupt NBFCs swindled poor people of their savings. One of the policy changes that micro-finance practitioners are seeking is to be able to take deposits more easily again through their NBFCs. However, unless they can find a concrete mechanism to distinguish and isolate themselves from unethical providers, which is above all clearly identifiable by poor savers, such a change may not be for the good of poor savers as a whole.

Micro-finance: Organisations and institutions

Chapter 7

Self-help groups and Grameen Bank groups: What are the differences?

Malcolm Harper

Introduction

Most micro-finance organisations (MFOs) use a group system to distribute their services to their clients. There are
some exceptions, including the village unit system of Bank
Rakyat Indonesia (BRI), the world's biggest and most profitable provider of micro-financial services, but groups generally predominate.[1]

Many otherwise well-informed observers, and even some
senior bankers in India and elsewhere, appear to believe that
the group system pioneered in 1976 by the Grameen Bank in
Bangladesh is the predominant or even the only such system. One purpose of this chapter is to show that this is not
the case.

Group systems for micro-financial services evolved in particular in Bangladesh (the Grameen Bank method) and in
Latin America (solidarity groups and village banking), as well
as in India (self-help Groups or SHGs). While there are thus
many variants, there are broadly two very different ways of
using groups for financial intermediation. For convenience I
term these two systems the Grameen system and the SHG
system, using the terms that are familiar within the South
Asian context.

Both systems have their advantages and disadvantages,
and practitioners need to be aware of the options that are

available. In this chapter, I describe and explain each system, and compare their sustainability, their outreach and impact on the poor, including their empowerment impact, and their feasibility within their respective environments. My arguments are briefly summarised in Table 7.1 in the conclusion to this chapter.

Table 7.1: Summary of the pros and cons of the SHG and Grameen systems

	Self-help groups	Grameen groups
Plusses for clients	• Flexible • No need for bank at all • Highly empowering • Members can save and borrow as needed • Free to choose suppliers • No enforced loan ladder • Can evolve from existing groups, ROSCAs, chit-funds, etc. • Can access the full range of bank services • Can evolve into federations, and cooperatives	• No need for literacy • No need for members' initiative • Protected from internal and external exploiters • Poorer people are included • Belong to and are supported by the bank • Bank can offer a range of additional tailor-made services
Minuses for clients	• Need management skills and time • Depend on good accounts • Can be captured internally or externally • Cash may not be secure	• Must meet frequently • Little freedom or flexibility • Group composition not wholly under members' control • Pressure to borrow • Interest rates inflexible
Plusses for banks	• Lower transaction costs • Can fit into any branch • Graduation easier • Can build on existing groups • Savings mobilisation easier • Groups can absorb odium of expelling members	• Can resist subsidised 'schemes' • Tighter control • Standardised MIS • Standardised procedures • Easier to forecast need for funds • Can use lower-grade staff
Minuses for banks	• Hard to monitor • May be tempted by other banks or by politicians • Slow to develop	• Higher transaction costs • Need continuous guidance and presence • Need dedicated system

	• May form own federations • MIS more complex • Need NGOs or highly committed staff to develop groups	• Hard to evolve and change
Suitable conditions	• Existing bank network in rural and poor areas • Diffused communities, castes, wealth levels • Tradition of informal financial services • Wide variety of scale and nature of investment opportunities • Some local leadership • NGOs and/or committed bank staff	• Very poor, homogeneous communities • Highly marginalised people with little opportunity and/or initiative • Few traditional informal financial mechanisms • Lack of financial intermediaries • Resource poor, little hope of graduation • Large numbers of small business opportunities • Few NGOs

Both systems are dominated by female clients, but they differ in many other fundamental respects, which have important implications for their clients and for the organisations which use them. The systems are also implemented in many different ways, depending on local circumstances. The fundamental characteristics of each system, and the critical differences between them, are briefly described next. More detailed accounts of each system can be obtained from a number of sources, including Fugelsang and Chandler (1986), M. Harper (1998), Holcombe (1998) and Wahid (1995).

The Grameen system

Potential clients are asked by the MFO to organise themselves into 'groups' of five members which are in turn organised into 'centres' of around five to seven such groups. The members make regular savings with the MFO, according to a fixed compulsory schedule, and they also take regular loans. They each have individual savings and loan accounts with the MFO, and the main function of the groups and centres is to facilitate the financial intermediation process, through performing tasks such as:

- holding regular and usually weekly meetings which are supervised by an MFO worker, where savings and repayments are collected and handed over to the MFO worker who maintains the records;
- organising contributions to one or a number of group savings funds, which can be used by the group for a number of purposes, usually only with the agreement of the MFO which maintains the group fund accounts;
- guaranteeing loans to their individual members, by accepting joint and several liability, by raising group emergency funds and by accepting that no member of a group will be able to take a new loan if any members are in arrears; and
- arising from the above, appraising fellow members' loan applications, and ensuring their fellow members maintain their regular savings contributions and loan repayments.

The SHG system

The members form a group of up to 20 members. The group formation process may be facilitated by a non-governmental organisation (NGO) or by the MFO or bank itself, or it may evolve from a traditional rotating savings and credit group (ROSCA) or other locally initiated grouping. The process of formal 'linkage' to an MFO or bank usually goes through the following stages, which may be spread over many years or which may take place within a few months:

- The SHG members decide to make regular savings contributions. These may be kept by their elected head, in cash, or in kind, or they may be banked.
- The members start to borrow individually from the SHG, for purposes, on terms and at interest rates decided by the group itself.
- The SHG opens a savings account, in the group's name, with the MFO or bank, for funds that are not needed by members, or in order to qualify for a loan from the bank.
- The MFO or bank makes a loan to the SHG, in the name of the group, which is then used by the group to supplement its own funds for on-lending to its members.

The SHG need never go through all these stages; it may satisfy its members' needs quite effectively if it only goes to the second or even to the first stage, saving money and possibly not even withdrawing it (Harper, M., 2000: 39–42).

The SHG carries out all the same functions as those required by the Grameen system, but they do this on their own behalf, since the SHG is effectively a micro-bank, carrying out all the familiar intermediation tasks of savings mobilisation and lending.

The members have their accounts with the SHG, not with the MFO or bank, and the MFO or bank does not have any direct dealings with the members. The MFO or bank may assist the SHG in record-keeping; they may also demand to know who the members are and impose certain conditions on the uses of the loan which they make to the SHG. However, the SHG is an autonomous financial organisation in its own right (see Chapter 5).

Where, by whom and why are the two systems used?

The Grameen system

The Grameen system dominates the market in Bangladesh, where it has been widely imitated by a range of large and small MFOs. The system was pioneered by Professor Yunus in 1976, and has grown very rapidly since (Yunus, 1998).

° In addition to the originator, the Grameen Bank, with 3 million members, two other major users of the system, BRAC and Proshika, each have over a million clients. In 1998 there were some 30 other MFOs with over 10,000 members, and many hundreds of smaller organisations using the system (Credit and Development Forum, 1998). It has been estimated that some 10 million people in Bangladesh receive financial services through this system.

The system has also been widely replicated by MFOs elsewhere, including a small number in India and in more than 20 other countries in Asia, Africa and Latin America, as well as in disadvantaged rural and urban areas in North America and Europe. The Grameen Trust supports 'replicators' with funding and technical assistance; at the end of 1999, these replicators had 420,000 clients, including about 42,000 in India (Grameen Trust, 2000).

Low or no-cost foreign donations represent the largest source of on-lending funds for the large MFOs that use the Grameen system in Bangladesh, while members' savings and the accumulated surplus from operations each contribute some 20 per cent of the necessary funds. The interest rates vary, and it is difficult to estimate the actual rates because there are a number of fees, forced savings requirements and other charges. The methods of calculation also differ from one MFO to another. Broadly speaking, the cost to the final borrowers amounts to at least 2 per cent per month, and often substantially more.

The Grameen system requires a dedicated special pur-pose organisation. The success of the weekly or occasionally fortnightly or monthly meeting routine depends on tight dis-cipline and adherence to a regular schedule. It is difficult for a commercial bank which also has other financial products, to integrate such a Grameen system into its own operations.

One of the few banks which have done this is the Islami Bank of Bangladesh. By 1998, 45 of its more than 100 branches had financed over 12,000 people through groups and centres, more or less following the Grameen system (Alamgir, 1999: 72–75). One important difference, however, is that this is an Islamic Bank; most of its credit is disbursed in kind, and the Bank is far more intimately involved in its clients' use of their finance than Western-style banks. Al-though loans under the group system amounted to only about a quarter of 1 per cent of its total portfolio in 1998, the Islami Bank intended massively to expand this approach.

The SHG system

The SHG system is mainly found in India. There are also some important users in Indonesia, other parts of South-East Asia, Africa and elsewhere.

The SHG system in India was initiated by NGOs, and is used for financial intermediation by MFOs and by commercial banks. By April 2001 some 285,000 SHGs had taken loans from 41 Indian commercial banks, 166 regional rural banks and 111 cooperative banks. The average loan per group was about Rs 18,000, and the average loan per member was Rs 1,100, or just under US$25. During the year 2000–2001, 171,000 SHGs took loans, of which 149,000 were first time borrowers (National Bank for Agriculture and Rural Development or NABARD, personal communication).

The average membership is around 17 people per SHG, so these figures mean that at least 4.5 million people in India have access to formal savings facilities and loans through their SHG membership. While the vast majority of these members are saving regularly, not all of them will have taken a loan.

The formation of SHGs for savings and credit, and their linkage to commercial banks, was initiated in India by MYRADA in the mid-1980s (Fernandez, 1998). Around the same time the management of NABARD had had some exposure to similar experiences in Thailand and Indonesia, and they responded favourably to MYRADA's suggestion that this could be a useful way to bring formal financial services to the rural poor.

Since that time, the linkage of SHGs to banks has been vigorously promoted by NABARD and other organisations. Non-governmental organisations often play an important role in the linkage process, and have promoted some 80 per cent of SHGs linked to banks (Sa-Dhan, 2001: 15). However, NGOs usually do not play a financial role. They promote and train the groups, and assist them through the qualifying process of saving and internal lending. The groups are introduced to a bank to open a savings account, and later to take a loan. The NGO may remain heavily involved, assisting the members to manage their affairs, and possibly promoting higher-level clusters and federations of SHGs, or it may withdraw and work with other groups (see Chapters 5, 8 and 9 for detailed examples).

Other NGOs also act as financial intermediaries by borrowing from NABARD or elsewhere and on-lending to SHGs, either because they aim to become MFOs, or because this is the only way some groups can access finance, because many bankers still refuse to lend to SHGs directly, or even to open savings accounts for them. The financial margin on this business is, however, insufficient to cover more than a small part of the transaction costs incurred by these NGOs.

Over a third of the linked SHGs borrowed from MFOs rather than from banks in 1998, but this proportion dropped to a quarter in 1999 and is rapidly decreasing further as banks become more aware of the business opportunity represented by SHGs (NABARD, 1998 and 1999a).

In addition to paying the cost of training bankers as well as staff of NGOs, NABARD also encourages the banks to lend to SHGs by refinancing the loans they make to SHGs at a subsidised rate (currently 6.5 per cent). This subsidised finance was used to refinance 83 per cent of the loans made to SHGs in the year 2000–2001 (NABARD, personal communication).

Loans to SHGs are excluded from the maximum interest ceiling of 12 per cent that still applies to other loans under Rs 20,000 (Reserve Bank of India, 2000), but the banks have generally not taken advantage of this freedom, and most still lend to SHGs at about 12 per cent. They feel the resulting 5.5 per cent spread is enough to cover their transaction costs so long as the task of promoting, training and developing SHGs is carried out by an NGO, at no cost to the bank.

The on-time repayment rates on SHG loans are usually well over 95 per cent. This is so much higher than the normal performance of loans granted under government schemes to poorer people that the banks are generally satisfied with this form of intermediation, even if the spread is less than that which they usually obtain. The SHG members are free to charge themselves whatever rates of interest they choose; the annual rates can range from 12 to 60 per cent a year (Harper, M. et al., 1998: 76).

There is also a large and increasing number of MFOs in India, most of which use the SHG method. The portfolio of the approximately 35 larger MFOs which use the SHG system, and are doing business with the recently established SIDBI Foundation for Micro-credit (SFMC), amounts to almost Rs 850 million or US$13 million. These MFOs were said in early 2001 to be serving about 200,000 eventual clients, of whom 94 per cent were women (SFMC, personal communication). It is anticipated by SFMC that by 2009 their partner MFOs will be serving 1.3 million clients.

NABARD forecast in early 2001 that by 2008 about one million SHGs would be taking loans from banks, with a total membership of around 17 million people. This estimate was based on a forecast of 50,000 SHGs taking loans in 2001–2002, rising to a rate of 110,000 new groups a year taking loans from 2005 onwards.

In the event, 149,000 new SHGs took loans in the financial year ending in March 2001, so that these forecasts may be well below what is actually achieved. In terms of membership, using the same average of 17 members per group, this amounts to an addition in just one year of 2.5 million clients, almost equivalent to the total current membership of the Grameen Bank. This has been achieved by effective collaboration between the banks, NGOs, MFOs and NABARD, with the necessary recognition and authority from the Reserve Bank of India (RBI).

There are as yet no giant organisations comparable to the MFOs in Bangladesh, nor perhaps will there ever be; the SHG system reflects the scale, and the organisational diversity, of the Indian financial system.

A small number of Indian MFOs use the Grameen system. The total number of people in India served by the 18 MFOs using the Grameen system at the end of 1999 was approximately 50,000 (Grameen Trust, 2000: 72–78). SHARE in the state of Andhra Pradesh, the largest user of the Grameen system in India, projects that it will be reaching over 1.7 million women by early 2006.

If the figures for the growth of SHGs are even remotely realistic, and actual performance suggests that they may be under-estimated, micro-finance in India has finally reached take-off. Estimates of the numbers of people below the poverty line vary quite widely,[2] but the figure of 40 per cent of the population is quite commonly used. This amounts to 400 million people, or some 80 million households. It is unusual at the present time for more than one member of a household to be an SHG member. If the NABARD and SFMC forecasts are fulfilled, and if the present growth in the numbers of poor people does not accelerate, over a quarter of poorer Indian households will, by 2009, have access to formal financial services. The vast majority, even if SHARE's forecasts are achieved, will be using the SHG system.

Why Grameen in Bangladesh and SHGs in India?

The rural poor in India are not so different from their counterparts in Bangladesh. Indeed, the differences between northern and southern India are certainly more pronounced than those between poor rural communities in the Indian states of West Bengal, Uttar Pradesh, Bihar or Orissa and their neighbours in Bangladesh. It seems *prima facie* to be odd, therefore, that two such different systems have evolved, and that there are, as yet at any rate, so few examples of the SHG system in Bangladesh or of the Grameen system in India.

There are a number of possible explanations. None of them is probably sufficient on its own, but they may together account for the present situation. I start with political and social factors.

Bangladesh has less experience of democracy than India; its people are used to military governments, and may for that or other reasons be more disciplined and less individualist. The Grameen system is often criticised for being over-disciplined, or even militarist, with its tradition of saluting, of meetings with imposed seating systems and the necessity for strict adherence to pre-set schedules, by staff and members alike. It may, for that reason, be more acceptable in Bangladesh.

In India, on the other hand, many NGOs see credit as an entry point for wider goals, and there is strong emphasis on democratic organisation and decentralisation (see Chapter 5). Fernandez (2001: 6-7), for instance, mentions credit only as the third aspect of MYRADA's involvement in SHG promotion; the identification and strengthening of traditional social and institutional capital are given greater emphasis.

It is not surprising therefore that bank workers in the Grameen system visit every group, every week. Experiments with less frequent meetings have generally not been successful. In contrast, as illustrated in Chapter 9, the NGO field-worker or banker may visit an SHG even more frequently during the initial group promotion stage, but the aim is to help the group keep their own records and run their own meetings. Once this has been achieved, there is no further need for weekly or even monthly visits.

Clearly, the Grameen system is better suited for more densely populated areas. There are parts of India which are as densely populated as Bangladesh, while some parts of the Sundarbans in Bangladesh are fairly thinly populated. The population density in India is about 300 per square kilometre, whereas there are about 850 people per square kilometre in Bangladesh. It is unlikely that the Grameen system could have spread all over India as it has in Bangladesh.

Bangladeshi village communities are generally more socially and economically homogeneous, and less divided by caste, than their Hindu equivalents in India. It may therefore be easier in Bangladesh to persuade people to join together in groups and centres which follow a standardised system. The freer and more flexible SHG system may be more appropriate for the Indian situation.

However, neither of the two main exponents of the Grameen system in India, SHARE in Andhra Pradesh and neighbouring states, and the much newer Cashpor in eastern Uttar Pradesh, has reported any particular difficulty in introducing the Grameen system in India. Generalisations are therefore dangerous, since India is more diverse than some continents, and the differences between or within states in India are often greater than between other neighbouring countries.

Institutional factors are also likely to have strongly influenced differing practice in Bangladesh and India. For example, in Bangladesh the Grameen Bank itself is in part protected from undue regulatory interference by being formally constituted by an act of parliament whose influence extends to others using the same system. In India, self-help groups do not have more than 20 members to avoid the need to register themselves as legal bodies, which might bring with it a whole range of regulatory constraints.

In addition, the Indian banks have over 70,000 branches in rural areas, and there is a long if expensive and not particularly successful history of government-sponsored poverty alleviation programmes which have been delivered through the banking system (see Chapter 2). The Indian banks are also compelled to direct a substantial proportion of their credit to the so-called 'priority sectors' and 'weaker sections'. The SHG linkage system is ideal for banks; any branch can do business with one or a number of SHGs, without making significant changes to its operating procedures.

The SHG itself must of course be developed, but there is an increasing range of possible ways in which this can be done. If no NGO is active in the area of a given branch, the banks' staff themselves may perform this role. The Prathama Regional Rural Bank (RRB) in Moradabad in the state of Uttar Pradesh has mobilised local farmers' clubs to form over 1,100 SHGs (Prathama Bank, 2000). Government agencies are active in some states, and financial intermediaries such as BASIX (see Box 4.1 in Chapter 4) and the Jamuna Gramina Bank are experimenting with low-cost methods of promoting and training groups. As the scale of the SHG movement grows, groups, or their federations (as described in Chapter 5), are themselves spreading the message, and many people observe, learn from and copy their neighbours, without any external intervention.

It would have been difficult, if not impossible, to introduce the SHG system in Bangladesh, where bank-branch coverage is much less and banking management is in general less eager and under less compulsion to identify with new ways of reaching poor people. By the same token, it can be argued, it is unnecessary to introduce the Grameen system in India, since the banking network already exists. What is needed is a system for reaching poor people that demands the minimum of institutional change, and the SHG system is just that for India.

Funding sources have also played a key role. While early experiments with micro-finance in both countries began in the late 1970s without any donor assistance, micro-finance has been largely a donor-driven phenomenon, everywhere. The Grameen system was and indeed still is lavishly supported by donors in Bangladesh. It is an ideal channel for donor assistance, since it is relatively standardised and transferable, it is dominated by a few large MFOs, it depends mainly on subsidised funds and is more or less totally independent of existing local banks.

Development aid to India was US$1.90 per head of the population in 1985, and was at the same level in 1997. The equivalent figures for Bangladesh were US$11.40 and US$9.00 (World Bank, *World Development Reports*, 1987 and 1999). This difference may in itself account in part for the predominance of the Grameen system in Bangladesh.

Likewise, the two major apex financing bodies in each country have played an important part in determining which system predominates. NABARD in India is vigorously and successfully marketing the SHG-linkage system, through subsidised refinance, extensive training for bankers and for NGOs, and through exhortation. During the financial year 2000–2001, for example, NABARD organised 3,200 training courses on SHG linkage, with 166,000 participants (NABARD, personal communication). This single-product approach inevitably imposes some uniformity, and there has been some question whether MFOs which use the Grameen system are eligible for NABARD refinance at all.

In Bangladesh, the reverse may be true. The Palli Karma Sahayak Foundation (PKSF), the wholesale fund that provides almost 20 per cent of the on-lending finance to the country's MFOs (Credit and Development Forum, 1998: iv), has set criteria for its partner organisations that raise questions whether organisations that do not follow some variant of what I have called the Grameen system are eligible (Alamgir, 1999: 90). Institutional inflexibility may in both countries have played some part in determining which systems are used.

'Sustainability'

One of the main reasons for the popularity of micro-finance as a poverty alleviation tool is the belief that MFOs can eventually become 'sustainable'. This term has many meanings, ranging from the continuing ability to find and retain donors to the ability to cover all costs (including the cost of finance, the reduction in fund value caused by inflation and even a return on the investors' equity).

Donors appear willing to continue to extend large sums of money to cover the costs, and the funding needs, of micro-finance, even when this actually inhibits the development of unsubsidised MFOs serving poor people. Nevertheless, financial services for poor people must eventually cease to depend on subsidy. Only then will it be possible for all the people who need such services to receive them, and to continue to do so for as long as is required. It is therefore important to compare the sustainability of the two systems.

The recent M-CRIL Report (M-CRIL, 2001) contains information for 10 MFOs that use the Grameen system, three of which operate in India, and for 31 using the SHG system, all of which are Indian (for the detailed results, see Chapter 10). Much of the data is unfortunately not comparable, because the Grameen users are on average much older, and much larger. The differences in their scale and maturity conceal many of those that might arise from distinctions between the two systems.

The figures do show, however, the critical difference between the charges levied under each system. The average yield on the Grameen portfolio is 23.7 per cent, whereas the comparable figure for the MFO working through SHGs is only 8.9 per cent (M-CRIL, 2001: Annex Table 3).

Much of this difference arises because the younger MFOs promoting SHGs have large sums of un-lent funds on deposit, and because they are wholesaling funds to the SHGs that perform the retail function. Indeed, when SHG members use financial services for lumpy consumption, or even for micro-enterprise expenditure within a household budget, savings and loans may essentially perform the same role. Members may set aside either small amounts as savings to build up a lump sum or small repayments to repay a lump-sum loan they have taken (see the introduction to Chapter 3). A system that encourages savings first, as in the SHG system, is likely to accumulate far greater un-lent funds than a system that focuses on credit, accompanied by compulsory but inflexible savings products.

Nevertheless, the difference in yields shows that the Grameen system has to take a much larger proportion of the money out of the hands of its clients, to cover its higher staff costs.[3] As suggested in Chapter 5, the SHG system leaves more money with the communities, but, like any retailer, they have to perform many more of the transaction functions in return.

In the *Microbanking Bulletin's* issue on efficiency, Farrington (1999: 19) and Christen (1999: 41) concluded that efficiency does not depend on the methodology employed. Christen, however, suggests the 'efficiency drivers' are the average wage paid to staff, the average balance per loan and the number of clients per staff member. These variables are themselves to an extent dependent on the methodology.

The Grameen method tends to be able to use lower paid staff, since the system is rigidly structured and uniform within and even among MFOs. The SHG system is more flexible; the financial intermediary usually has less frequent contact with the groups, once they have reached the stage of taking loans, but assessing and guiding an autonomous micro-bank requires a higher level of skill than is needed in the Grameen system. It needs fewer, more highly paid staff.

The Grameen system requires more staff per client, because the MFO providing loans is acting as the retailer. In the SHG system, the SHG is the retailer, and thus loan balances from the bank or MFO to SHGs are much higher than those to Grameen group members. The amounts and balances of the loans an SHG makes to its individual members, and of any savings it mobilises from them, need not and usually cannot be recorded by the bank or MFO.

On the whole, therefore, the SHG system appears more likely to be associated with the two drivers of high average loan balances and high numbers of clients per staff member,[4] while the Grameen system requires less qualified and thus lower paid staff.

Ideally, we should compare the costs of two financial service providers serving the same numbers of clients, one of which works with SHGs and the other with the Grameen system. This is not easy. For example, under the system of linking SHGs to banks, loans are mainly extended by bankers for whom such loans are only one of a number of products, and it is difficult to separate out the costs of this product.

More importantly, the promotion of the groups themselves has, at least until recently, usually been undertaken by an NGO whose costs are not borne by the bank. Many of the bankers who have themselves developed SHGs have done this on their own initiative outside office hours, so that the costs are not recorded. In the Grameen system, however, the bank itself carries out the whole operation.

The financial performance of the MFOs that use the Grameen system is well documented. The Grameen Bank itself made a profit of just over 100 million taka in 1998, before taxes and after providing some 750 million taka against bad debts (Grameen Bank, 1999). This contrasted with a figure of only 14 million taka the previous year, and it represents a low return on the total capital employed of over 19,000 million taka. Over half this capital was provided from concessional sources, the majority at interest rates as low as 2 per cent.

SHARE in India is a much younger organisation, and it does not aim to reach 'financial self-sufficiency', which is micro-finance language for real profitability, until 2006, long after it has become a very substantial organisation. I can only conclude that the Grameen system has not, as yet, proved itself to be the basis of a genuinely profitable business, which can raise capital and loan funds on a commercial basis.

The Rudrapur branch of the Oriental Bank of Commerce (OBC), near Dehra Dun in India, is unusual if not unique in that its only customers are SHGs; it therefore makes it possible to assess the profitability of this type of customer. The SHGs have been promoted and developed by staff of the branch; no NGO has been involved so the branch's costs cover all aspects of the operation.

In March 2000, this branch had outstanding loans of about Rs 1 crore (10 million), over 80 per cent of which was funded by customers' deposits. The branch would have made a loss of just over Rs 5 lakh (500,000) without any subsidy, but the Bank was able to claim subsidised NABARD refinance against the loans. This subsidy meant that the branch approximately broke even. The members of the SHGs agreed that their groups would have been willing and able to pay well over the 12 per cent interest rate required by NABARD, had this been necessary. On this basis the branch would have broken even without subsidy.

It is more usual for SHGs to make up only a small proportion of a branch's business, and for the group promotion task to be undertaken by an NGO. The cost of initially developing and assessing an SHG has been variously estimated to range between about US$30 (Rs 1,350) and US$355 (Rs 16,000) (Harper, M. et al., 1998: 73; Fernandez, 2001: 35–36). Experiments with dedicated SHG development agents undertaken by BASIX (see Box 4.1) and others seem likely to significantly reduce the cost towards the lower end of the range. One Indian banker (Harper, M. et al., 1998: 64) stated that it was actually easier and thus less expensive to appraise an SHG loan application than an ordinary loan of a similar size.

It is also possible to compare the operation costs of the two systems, by reference to the Rudrapur branch of OBC and SHARE. The costs and overheads of the Rudrapur branch amounted to Rs 7 per Rs 100 lent, while the equivalent figure for SHARE in September 2000 was Rs 10. While this is obviously an over-simplified comparison, it seems to confirm the general impression that it costs less to do business through an SHG than through the Grameen system.

However, these cost calculations and comparisons take no account of the context in which micro-financial services are being developed, of the capacities of clients targeted or the level of development of the respective organisations, which can all contribute significantly to overall costs, as Mathew Titus analyses in depth in Chapter 8.

Likewise, the SHG system requires less long-term investment in organisations. Any existing bank branch can service an established SHG and its members. This in fact further complicates comparison as the full costs in the SHG system are likely to be higher upfront, during the promotion stage, but lower later on when SHGs have stabilised.

'Sustainability' is of course not only a matter of cost, but also of the price that is charged. SHARE and Cashpor, two of the main users of the Grameen system in India, charge their clients an effective annual rate of about 50 per cent a year, while most MFOs in Bangladesh charge well over 20 per cent. These figures are not directly comparable with the rate of 12 per cent that is charged to SHGs by most banks in India, since the SHG is a retailer.

The members of SHGs themselves pay their groups a wide range of different rates of interest. As Chapter 5 makes clear, although the individual member has to bear the cost, she is also a part owner of the SHG; she therefore benefits from the surplus it generates, whereas all the charges paid to MFOs using the Grameen system accrue to the MFO itself.

Self-help groups may be a less expensive distribution channel than Grameen groups, but they may also themselves be less durable. This has implications not only for their members, but also for the bank or MFO that must incur the investment of replacing them if they fail to survive. Like the ROSCAs from which many of them originate, SHGs will only last as long as the members continue to gain from them. As the cases in Chapters 8 and 9 clearly demonstrate, SHGs can be very fragile social entities; it is difficult for them to absorb the shocks of changes in membership, and they can easily be destroyed by minor disputes or disagreements.

Likewise, because SHGs are genuinely autonomous independent entities, they have little protection against hijacking or capture (either from within, or from outside) apart from their own internal solidarity or from whatever collective strength they can mobilise through coming together in clusters and federations (see Chapter 5).

The government, at the state and national level, has already identified the potential of SHGs as a channel for the delivery of subsidy. The new Swarna Jayanti Swarozgar Yojana (SJSY) initiative, which is designed to replace the massive but largely ineffective Integrated Rural Development Programme (IRDP) and other poverty alleviation programmes, is based on groups. Government development staff have already started to nominate existing SHGs for the receipt of support under this programme, and many bankers are alarmed at the possible effects this will have on their SHG clients who have thus far remained unpolluted by subsidy.

Indeed, well over half the SHGs that were financed in 2000–2001 were in the single state of Andhra Pradesh, where the state government has for some years been using SHGs for distributing subsidies. Some groups have turned down such offers, because their members are well aware of their destructive effects, and very strong groups can take advantage of subsidies without being damaged. Less mature groups can easily be destroyed by grants, however, and this has already happened in some cases (Harper, M., 1996: 88–89).

An SHG demands more management capabilities of its members, although probably less time, compared to those of a Grameen-type group. SHG members are running a bank, albeit on a very small scale. This demands significant additional responsibilities, not just of officers but also of members, who must at least understand issues such as interest rates and risk and be able to monitor the performance of their micro-bank. Such responsibilities can be significant for a poor, illiterate woman with limited time and computational skills (see Chapters 8 and 9 for many concrete examples).

A Grameen member, on the other hand, has to attend weekly meetings, and to maintain her regular saving and repayment schedule. The group and centre heads have only to ensure that the payments will be available on time; they are not bankers in any sense.

If the members of an SHG are lucky enough to identify and retain skilled officers, or if they can continue to enjoy the support of an NGO, the issue of management may not limit the life of their group; otherwise, it may collapse. Their bankers have many other customers, and cannot be expected to devote a great deal of time to sustaining their client SHGs. Grameen groups, on the other hand, are very much driven by the bank staff; they are the *raison d'être* of the bank, and staff are judged by their success in opening up new groups and preserving old ones.

SHGs may also switch to a different financial intermediary for their savings or loan requirements, and their new supplier may be able to offer a better deal partly because it has not had to incur the initial cost of customer development. Grameen groups, on the other hand, are tied to and kept alive by the MFO that created them. Members can and do switch to different suppliers, and groups do sometimes collapse, but they are on the whole more durable and longer-lasting than SHGs.

In summary, therefore, I tentatively conclude that at least in India the SHG system is more economical, and thus more financially sustainable, in the short to medium term at any rate, in spite of the fact that SHG members usually pay a lower price for their loans than members of Grameen groups. There is as yet, however, no proven method whereby new

SHGs can be developed at a cost that is low enough to make them into immediately profitable clients. As the analysis in Chapter 8 shows, the customer creation investment can be significant, and has to be undertaken by NGOs that benefit from external subsidy, or by the efforts of unusually committed bank staff. In addition, SHGs are more likely to deteriorate or collapse than Grameen groups which are an integral part of a larger and more rigorous system.

However, access is more important than price, and it is therefore necessary to enquire which system is most effective at reaching poorer people.

Outreach to and impact on the poorest

The primary aim of providing micro-financial services is not to maximise profits, nor even to cover all its costs. It is intended to alleviate poverty, and if some element of subsidy is needed to enable it to do this effectively, most would agree that such subsidy should be provided. Which of the two group systems reaches and benefits the poorest people most effectively?

There is little direct evidence as to whether the SHG or the Grameen system is more effective at reaching or benefiting the poorest people. It is now generally acknowledged that micro-finance in general does not reach the poorest of the poor, and that the poorer people whom it does reach benefit less from micro-finance than those who are better off. This applies to the SHG as well as to the Grameen system (Clar de Jesus, 1997: 21; Hulme and Mosley, 1996: 115; Wright, 2000: 56, 262).

Poorer people are excluded not only by better-off members, but they also exclude themselves. They are afraid that they will not be able to save regularly, their poverty means that they lack profitable investment opportunities, and they may also not be able to attend meetings regularly. Their exclusion may be in their own interest; poorer people benefit less than others from micro-finance, and many poorer micro-finance clients have suffered great hardship, and have even been driven to suicide, as a result of their micro-debt (Hulme, 2000: 26).

In comparing the Grameen and SHG systems, it is worth bearing in mind that the Grameen system is older and has been subjected to much more rigorous analysis and research. In contrast, there is little published material on the downside of the SHG system. Nevertheless, let us look, first, at the extent to which poorer people are included or excluded from the two different systems.

There is only one case known to me where both systems are operating in the same area. BASIX is working through SHGs in eastern Andhra Pradesh, and SHARE is working in the same part of the state through the Grameen system. Neither organisation can claim to have fully covered the market, and there have thus far been no instances where they have reached the same clients. No systematic attempt has been made to compare the wealth of their respective clients, but in brief meetings with both types of groups the SHG members appeared to be somewhat better off than the members of the Grameen-type groups.

The members of both types of groups are initially self-selected, as is necessary if they are to be willing to guarantee each others' loans. The staff of MFOs using the Grameen system, however, make a point of assessing the poverty level of the prospective members by visiting every member's home before their groups have been formally accepted (Fugelsang and Chandler, 1986: 110).

For example, Activists for Social Alternatives (ASA) in the state of Tamil Nadu, India serves 12,000 women using a modified Grameen system. It requires that potential members have less than 0.5 acres of irrigated land, or 1.5 acre of dry land, and household income of less than Rs 18,000 per annum. Their field-staff check poverty levels with a 16-point housing-quality index and a participatory wealth-ranking exercise (Hishigsuren, 2000: 29–30). ASA also ensure that the first groups formed in any village only include Dalits.

Grameen groups are therefore effectively formed or at least quite rigorously screened by bank or NGO staff before acceptance. There is, however, some evidence (Matin, 1997a: 50) that poorer people are gradually excluded from Grameen groups over time, as the staff have less influence over the recruitment of new members than they do when the groups are first formed.

In the SHG system, bankers and NGO staff who promote SHGs are more likely to accept their members without question. Many SHGs are formed from pre-existing groups (Harper, M. et al., 1998: 19), and neither NGO workers nor bankers are likely to demand that certain members leave because they are not poor enough, or that others are admitted on the basis of their poverty. Such issues are obviously of concern to many NGOs, but too much intervention here may undermine the democratic and autonomous functioning of groups that is so much part of the SHG system.

One study (Harper, M. et al., 1998: 27, 41) seems to confirm this. It found that the poorest people are excluded from SHGs, and indeed that many SHG members had suffered as a result of their membership.

There are, however, cases which suggest that the picture may not be as simple as this. Ashrai is one of the few MFOs in Bangladesh which effectively operates with the SHG system (Alamgir, 1999: 79–81). They work with over 1,000 groups of tribal people, who are from what are said to be the very poorest people in the country. Likewise, the NGO PRADAN (see Chapters 5 and 9) has promoted SHGs among some of the poorest tribal people in eastern India.

Part of the differences between the success of the two systems in including poorer people may arise from differing visions of how to tackle poverty. Unlike Grameen groups, which tend to focus more exclusively on poor people, Indian NGOs promoting SHGs may attempt to promote as many groups as possible in each village and to include every socio-economic level. This is part of their focus on building democratic people's organisations (explored in Chapter 5), not just delivering financial services.

Take the case of MYRADA. Fernandez (2001: Chapters 10 and 11) reports that in seeking to include different socio-economic groups from among poor people, MYRADA has found that over half of the poorest families are represented in SHGs after two or three years. Studies of these groups also suggest that there is little discrimination against the poorest members in terms of access to services and leadership (see Chapter 5). It may be significant that MYRADA is also one of the highest-cost promoters of SHGs (Fernandez, 2001: 35). Social inclusion has a high cost.

Finally, the basic unit of the Grameen system is in theory the five-member group, and it would appear *prima facie* to be easier for the MFO to influence who is or is not included in such a small group, as well as its operations, than it is to influence an SHG with 20 or 50 members.

In practice, however, it is suggested that the real unit of operations in the Grameen system is the centre, with 30 or more members (Matin, 1997b: 266). This is similar to an SHG, and suggests that the apparent benefits of the smaller group may be illusory. A larger group is more likely to be influenced by existing social and economic structures within a community, rather than by the poverty alleviation agenda of the financial intermediary. This influence can be benign, but is perhaps more likely to be oppressive (Harper, A., 1998 and 2000: 25).

In looking at the potential impact of the two different systems on poor people, the operations of Grameen groups beyond their formation remain very much under the control of the MFO. Grameen clients are in effect bound by a rigid and highly disciplined system. They have regular weekly contact with bank staff, and they have little discretion as to the amounts or terms of loans, or even as to who receives them. In effect, they have merely to do what they are told.

This regular supervision can serve to protect weaker members from exploitation by those who are stronger, and in particular to ensure that all members have equitable access to loans. It is also possible, as some experience in Bangladesh has shown, that pressure for high recoveries can lead the bank workers to act even more oppressively than fellow members. Regular supervision can be a two-edged sword.

In contrast, SHGs are much freer to manage their affairs as they wish. NGO or bank staff may attend their meetings, but as observers rather than managers, and the usual intention is to phase out regular attendance of this sort. The SHG system therefore requires its members to demonstrate a much higher level of management skill and initiative than the Grameen system. They have in effect to manage their own bank, financed by their own savings, by accumulated interest earnings and by institutional finance, and with a range of loans of different maturities and often at different interest rates. In Chapter 9, Ajit Kanitkar analyses the demands on local leadership that such a system makes, as well as its rewards.

It is possible that poorer people may be more likely to accept the rigid conditions of the Grameen system and to need the protection they imply, and be less able to cope with SHG membership, than those who are better off. This may indeed exclude the poorest from SHGs in the first place.

However, the impact of micro-finance depends in part on the differing needs of clients. As suggested in Chapter 3, poorer clients generally need greater protective services, such as savings, consumption loans and insurance, including loans to pay off higher-cost debt to moneylenders. The less poor, on the other hand, can benefit more from loans to build or expand their enterprise (see Chapter 4).

The SHG system is built on members' savings, and bank loans are taken only to increase the pool of capital available for lending to members, which can be for any purpose determined by individual groups themselves. In contrast, the Grameen system insists that loans be used for productive purposes (for investing in micro-enterprises) and demands compulsory savings as a condition of accessing loans.

The broader range of services which is provided by SHGs, and the greater flexibility of members in choosing which services to access, may thus be more appropriate to poorer people. MYRADA, for example (Fernandez, 2001), has found that while poorer members of SHGs enjoy as much access to loans as relatively better-off members, the poorer take smaller loans for consumption rather than investment.

In contrast, the insistence of Grameen-type organisations that loans be used for productive purposes risks forcing poorer members into taking loans for purposes they cannot manage effectively, and hence may push them into further debt.

However, these distinctions are becoming increasingly blurred. Recent experiments with voluntary savings by users of the Grameen system in Bangladesh (such as the Association for Social Advancement [ASA] and Buro Tangail) demonstrate that there is a substantial demand from members for such services, and that they can be integrated into the Grameen system without difficulty. The provision of voluntary savings is therefore expanding among Grameen-type organisations, including in India. For example, SHARE collects voluntary deposits through a cooperative they have set up in the state of Andhra Pradesh, and these voluntary savings can be withdrawn at weekly intervals.

As for loans, in practice, funds within a household are fungible, and, as Grameen-type organisations have discovered, it is often not possible (and usually not desirable) to prevent the 'diversion' of productive loans to other purposes. Moreover, Indian banks lending to SHGs insist that SHG members do not use these loans for consumption needs, making those SHGs that borrow from banks little different from Grameen groups in this regard. However, SHGs can often ignore this stipulation given that they have more flexibility because their initial loans are from their own group funds and their activities are less closely supervised by the banks.

In summary, the evidence seems on balance to suggest that SHGs are probably less likely to include poorer people than Grameen groups; neither system reaches the very poorest. The evidence on impact, however, is too unclear to make a conclusive judgement. Given the very rapid growth of the SHG system in India, more work is urgently needed to ascertain whether SHGs have the same damaging effects on their poorer members as some Grameen groups, and, if they do, how to minimise these effects.

'Empowerment'

Much is made of the way in which access to appropriate financial services has a non-economic empowering effect on poor and marginalised people, particularly women. 'Empowerment', like sustainability, can be variously defined, but there is little question that micro-financial services have enabled large numbers of poor people to improve their social and even their political status, as Chapters 5 and 9 illustrate.

This effect is closely related to the group-based methods of intermediation which are used. An individual woman may not be able to make much difference to her social position, even within her own family, if she improves her financial position, but if she has the support of her fellow group members she can do much more. Which of the two group-based systems under consideration is more likely to have this non-economic effect?

The members of an SHG are effectively the owners and managers of a small bank. This may place a heavy burden on their time and ability as Chapters 8 and 9 illustrate. However, if they are successful it seems obvious that this will enhance their status more than the fact of being a client of a bank or MFO, which is what the members of Grameen groups are. The bank of which they are clients has, at least until recently, often been far from customer-friendly. Although competition is forcing Grameen MFOs to be more flexible, they still have rigid loan rotas and repayment schedules. Although this is changing, freely withdrawable savings are still the exception rather than the rule. The analytical framework of sustainable livelihoods is increasing our understanding of the complexities of poor people's financial needs (see Chapters 3 and 4), and it is clear that the original rigid Grameen approach only satisfies a small part of those needs.

Members of SHGs can themselves decide who gets loans, when, and at what interest cost. They are indirectly remunerated for their management time and effort, in that the spread between their cost of funds and the interest they decide to charge themselves is retained by the micro-bank of which they are the owners. They build their own equity, whereas the high interest rates which Grameen clients must pay goes to pay the wages of the large numbers of staff that the system demands. It could indeed be claimed that the Grameen system is yet another way by which the relatively elite bank employees sequester the hard-earned incomes of poor people.

At the same time, as Chapters 8 and 9 clearly show, SHGs are more vulnerable to capture by vested interests, and to inequitable distribution of the benefits, because they are less closely supervised by the financial intermediary where they deposit their savings and from which they may take loans. While it may be possible to avoid such outcomes through effective promotion (see Chapter 5), this only adds to the overall promotional costs.

Moreover, as suggested earlier, there have been many cases in India where SHGs have been used as channels for government grants and other poverty alleviation programmes. These programmes can be very beneficial to members, and strong groups in particular can use such assistance to strengthen their own position. Assistance of this sort often comes at a price, however; political interests use them as a form of patronage to demand votes or other support; grants can also erode the sense of ownership and responsibility which are necessary for effective groups, and can even destroy the groups altogether.

Grameen groups are much better protected against internal or external threats; their members are less vulnerable, but also less empowered, since empowerment is freedom and this must also include freedom to face and, if possible, to overcome threats.

Both systems appear to empower their members in the literal sense of giving them the confidence to put themselves forward for membership of local government bodies, such as *panchayati raj* institutions. Fernandez (2001: 91) reports that some 200 (about 2.5 per cent) of the total of 77,495 members of SHGs sponsored by MYRADA were elected to their *gram panchayats* (elected village councils) in 2000. In 1999, 30 members, almost exactly the same percentage, of the 12,000 members of ASA's Grameen-type groups in Tamil Nadu were similarly elected (Hishigsuren, 2000: 71).

In addition, many Grameen-type groups in Bangladesh have switched their business from one bank to another, in search of better services; this is good evidence of their independence and empowerment.

Some Indian NGOs promoting SHGs, such as the DHAN Foundation and MYRADA, encourage and assist 'their' SHGs to come together in clusters and federations (see Chapters 5, 8 and 9). These bodies may or may not themselves be involved in financial intermediation, and some of them have become large and powerful democratic organisations in their own right, which may be able to empower members of their SHGs further.

Grameen groups have less need to come together in this way, since the members do not themselves perform the banking management tasks demanded of SHG members. Some Grameen replicators, however, such as ASA in Tamil Nadu (Hishigsuren, 2000: 27–28) also encourage their members to form similar apex groupings, for a variety of non-financial functions.

Membership of SHGs is thus more empowering, but at the same time more vulnerable. This serves to confirm our earlier tentative conclusion that Grameen groups are more suitable for poorer, more vulnerable groups. K-Rep in Kenya found that some Grameen or 'Juhudi' groups evolve into SHGs, and they also found that it was less expensive to service SHGs than to use the more labour-intensive Grameen method (Harper, M. et al., 1998: 107). Self-help groups are a more empowering instrument than Grameen groups, but they also demand more of their members, and expose them to greater risks. Freedom does not come without a cost.

Feasibility within a given environment

There is a great need and demand for micro-finance services throughout the world. Large sums of money are also available, whether from the savings of poor people themselves or from government and foreign sources.

The main constraint is the lack of organisational capacity to deliver the services to those who need them. Organisational capacity-building takes time and costs money. A system which requires less organisational development must therefore be attractive, even if it is not obviously less expensive to operate.

Self-help groups can evolve quite easily from existing ROSCAs or other traditional financial or non-financial groups, and any bank can do business with them, so long as its management are prepared to deal with this unfamiliar but potentially highly profitable market segment. If there are many pre-existing groups, and if there is a wide network of bank branches, which need new business opportunities, the environment would seem to be ideal for the SHG system.

It takes time to change management attitudes, and regulations may make it difficult to lend without collateral, or to do business with informal groups which have no legal status.

In the early years of the SHG movement in India many bankers showed that it is not impossible to overcome these constraints, and the regulatory environment has now changed so that there are no legal barriers to which a conservative banker can appeal as a reason for hesitation. It took some 7 years for Indian bankers to appreciate the potential of SHGs as customers, but the recent rapid expansion in the numbers of SHGs which have borrowed from banks shows that their not unreasonable scepticism is now being overcome.

Those few organisations which work with the Grameen method in India are also expanding very fast, and it is to be hoped that there will be many occasions in the future when people can make their own choice from two or more competing providers of micro-financial services. Then and only then will it be possible to determine which system is actually most suitable for which types of customer, so long of course as customer choice is not distorted by excessive or misplaced subsidy.

Until that time, my tentative conclusion is that the Grameen system is more expensive, but may nevertheless be more suitable for poorer communities, particularly in places where there are few NGOs to develop the groups, and few bank branches whose staff are willing to serve them. Elsewhere, the SHG system is probably better for Indian conditions, as the present and projected numbers seem to suggest.

Conclusions

I summarise the pros and cons of each system in Table 7.1. More broadly, Bangladesh is relatively homogeneous and very poor, and to the casual observer at least there seems to be little opportunity for progress. It may be an appropriate location for a rigid, autonomous, readily transferable and dependence-creating system that can alleviate poverty for large numbers.

India is fiercely diverse as a nation, and most communities are also diverse in caste, opinion and religion. Indians are also known for their sense of personal independence, which is often translated into indiscipline, whether on the roads, in political assemblies or elsewhere. The SHG system reflects this independence and diversity. It allows people to save and borrow according to their own timetable, not as the bank requires. Self-help groups can also play a part in a whole range of social, commercial or other activities. They can be vehicles for social and political action as well as for financial intermediation.

This flexibility and freedom also has its price. In making much greater demands on members of SHGs to manage themselves, such groups are more vulnerable to collapse. As small autonomous organisations they are also more exposed to capture, both from within and from without. In particular, politicians are driven by their need for popularity and power, and bureaucrats by their need to achieve numerical targets. Self-help groups can provide both with a ready-made vehicle.

If SHG members can identify and resist the disadvantages of being used by outsiders, and can exploit them rather than be exploited, the movement may in time play an important role in the reduction of poverty in India. If not, they will become no more than another milestone in the nation's long list of development failures.

Notes

1. Group systems are not only predominant within modern microfinance practice, but are also common in informal financial systems, especially the traditional rotating savings and credit associations (ROSCAs), chit-funds, etc., which are found throughout the world. As suggested later in this chapter, some self-help groups in India have emerged from ROSCAs and similar informal groups.
2. The Census of 2001 suggests that the proportion has fallen to 26 per cent, a significant reduction, although there is still much debate about this figure.
3. The analysis of operating performance in Chapter 10 seems to confirm that Grameen-type organisations have higher operating costs, largely because of staff costs.
4. The analysis provided in Chapter 10 suggests that this may not be the case, but that analysis looks only at the number of SHG borrowers that have borrowed as a result of SHGs taking loans from MFOs, and therefore does not include all the other financial transactions that take place in the SHGs, whether they borrow externally or not. Including these in the calculation would make the staff of SHG programmes more productive.

Chapter 8

Costs in micro-finance: What do urban Self-help Groups tell us?

Mathew Titus[1]

Introduction

As Malcolm Harper explained in Chapter 7, the most wide-spread model for micro-finance in India is that of self-help groups (SHGs). These groups of up to 20 members, usually women, are characterised by the mobilisation of savings and the subsequent disbursal of credit, either from their own savings or by accessing credit from the vast network of bank branches. The SHG movement has made dramatic progress: from 500 groups in 1992 there are now some 300,000 groups that have taken loans from banks under the 'linkage' programme of the National Bank for Agriculture and Rural Development (NABARD).

The programme rests on some strong assumptions that non-governmental organisations (NGOs) possess competencies to promote and provide support to SHGs, while banks are better able to manage finances. While these assumptions are in most cases right, there is little support to help NGOs meet the costs of promoting SHGs.

Unfortunately, discussion on costs has focused primarily on the costs of establishing the physical unit of the SHG, for example the costs of training programmes, while the expenditure on promoting groups has been attributed to the comparative advantage of the NGO (CGAP, 1998).

However, my decade-long experience in micro-finance suggests that the challenge is far more complex and difficult than such analysis would suggest. In this chapter I seek to unravel some of the complexity of costs in promoting and supporting SHGs.

I use insights from both economic and management theory to draw attention to three areas that contribute to these costs. The first set of costs arises from historical distortions as experienced by poor people using perverse or inefficient service-providers. The second set of costs arises from the need for efforts by poor, illiterate communities to establish effective financial contracts amongst themselves. Only the third set of costs relates to the ability of the promoting organisation to develop and manage a service and maintain its quality.

I illustrate each of these costs (Figure 8.1) from research on the performance of SHGs and their federations promoted by an NGO, Sharan, in the slums of Delhi. Identifying characteristics of the different federations and their SHGs enables taking a first step in managing financial services more effectively (Korten, 1980).

I therefore describe the experiences of members of these SHGs with other service-providers. I then focus on the growth and performance of the SHGs and their federations, drawing out factors that contribute to the other two sets of costs. First are the functional efforts of the community to overcome imperfections in credit markets and second are the efforts of the promoting NGO to manage effectiveness to produce a service of high and constant quality.

What emerges clearly is a web of elements that contribute to the costs of promoting SHGs among poor people. For example, research suggests that there is a strong rationale for high fixed costs in starting such initiatives. These arise from a variety of constraints, including distortions introduced by perverse and inefficient service-providers, and the efforts that members have to make to overcome imperfections in credit markets.

Costs of promoting SHGs will therefore vary from context to context. The SHGs promoted by Sharan are a case in point. They operate in urban slums of often new and transient migrants where traditional community and kinship ties, or even basic knowledge about other members of the community, may not exist. And yet it is precisely such ties and in-depth

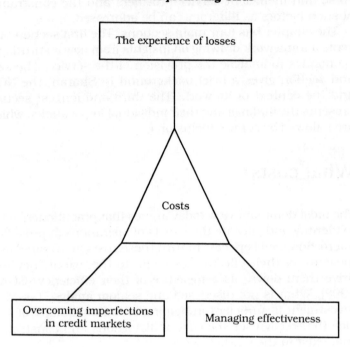

Figure 8.1: Three functions that contribute to the costs of promoting SHGs

knowledge to which the literature, primarily drawing on experience in rural areas, accords great significance in the functioning of any group mechanisms for savings and credit. This' will obviously have a major impact on the costs of promoting effective SHGs in urban areas.

Ignoring the need for investment to overcome such constraints will therefore lead both to members losing money and not receiving credit, and to the NGO losing the investments it made in promoting the SHGs. It will also contribute yet further to market imperfections and distortions that so undermine the provision of financial services among poor people.

It is important therefore that the micro-finance sector moves towards identifying and examining these costs and making the necessary investments. Progress with SHGs in the Indian context will depend not only on promoters driving down costs and maintaining services of high and constant quality, but also on the extent to which the problem of perverse and inefficient service-providers and the constraints of such factors as illiteracy can be addressed.

The chapter has four main sections. The first section presents a framework drawing on insights from new institutional economics to analyse the provision of the service. The second section gives a brief background to Sharan, the NGO and the context of its work. The third and longest section presents the findings and their individual implications, which are followed by some conclusions.

What costs?

The most dominant view today argues that practitioners need to identify and allocate their costs of operations in providing micro-financial services. In turn these costs are treated as a measure of their effectiveness and, to the extent they can drive them down, as a measure of their efficiency (CGAP, 1998). What is not discussed and seldom analysed is what investment is sufficient in helping to build a quality of service that recognises the cost of distortions and constraints that exist in the market.

The economic literature of costs has a well-developed and robust history. Its contribution to economics is borne out from the recent awards of Nobel prizes to some of its most vigorous proponents: Douglass North, George Akerlof and Joseph Stiglitz. By both working through historical changes and examining closely critical economic puzzles these theoreticians have systematically unravelled and identified functions that affect markets for services.

These economists have argued that constraints to participation in markets, especially for financial services, arise from three sets of conditions. The participation of agents in markets is contingent on (i) their historical experience of losses in their holdings, (ii) their ability to enter into contracts that are optimum in their functions, and (iii) the ability of service-providers to provide goods and services of constant quality (Akerlof, 1970; Hoff and Stiglitz, 1990; North, 1990).

These conditions generate transaction costs. Such costs arise from two sources: institutions and organisations. While institutions establish the context, organisations seek to overcome constraints that prevent the exchange of goods and services or addressing any other opportunity to meet the demand for a particular good or service.

Institutions, as defined by North, are the rules of the game that provide the structure to transactions and shape incentives. Institutions can be either formal or informal. A formal institution is one that is stated explicitly, such as, for purposes of this research, rules that define conditions under which credit may be extended. Informal constraints on the other hand are the conventions that determine the codes of behaviour—ideology, beliefs and social relationships—of agents. Both formal and informal institutions together form the basis on which people will participate in an exchange of goods or services.

What determines the character of the game in particular, including the level of compliance and the costs of enforcing contracts, is the ability of institutions to deal with intentional or unintentional violations. The ability of institutions to identify such violations and trigger remedial action to enforce contracts is an important contribution of their presence. The often discussed importance of 'reputation capital' in determining compliance and ultimately repayment, even in extreme cases at the cost of the death of small farmers in South India, is a classic example of the power of an informal institution. These institutions process information in a particular manner and partly contribute to the resulting action, in this case far from optimal.

In addition to the pressure of ensuring repayment to avoid damage to reputations, these institutions also provide the framework through which agents process information. These are the 'mental models' of participants. Understanding mental models makes it possible to understand decisions resulting from the processing of information. Institutions thus exist and contribute to actions in many ways.

Organisations too play a central role in determining costs. Their role has been more widely recognised in the literature. The critique of earlier directed credit-provision was forceful

in suggesting that organisational features (elaborate administrative procedures, different bodies for sanction and disbursement, and the absence of self-correcting mechanisms) partly
contributed to the failure of such initiatives (Adams and von
Pischke, 1992).

The allocation of costs arising from organisational functions, such as staff costs and administration, continue to
dominate the debate. Indeed, this is the only set of costs that
seems to get any recognition in discussion.

Given the difficulty that the dominant organisational form,
namely NGOs, faces in the provision of micro-financial services and given that very few have managed to truly cover
their costs, it is necessary to revisit the approach. The sector
needs to seriously examine what contributes to costs for
organisations providing micro-financial services to poor
people. Are there constraints that defeat all attempts at
lowering costs? Are there innovations that clients and
organisations need that contribute to efficiency? It is only
then that practice will move to a new level of performance.

Sharan: Structure and context of work

Rapid urbanisation in India in the late 1970s and early 1980s
caught most urban authorities unawares. Slums sprung up
in most open spaces, and became hazards, for example in
terms of health and crime. The main policy response in Delhi
was to raze slums to the ground and relocate squatters to
the outskirts of the city. It was in this environment that the
NGO Sharan registered in 1981.

Sharan's portfolio of activities initially focused on health
and education. Staff were directly involved in providing most
of these services, from being teachers in schools, to taking
patients to hospitals, to delivering medicines. Each of these
functions was intensive and relationship-based. As the
organisation learned from experience it shifted strategy and
started training community-workers who spearheaded interventions to introduce preventive and promotive measures in
health and education. A strategic evaluation that followed

recommended the need to change methodology and focus on increasing community participation with community resources. The assumption was that building community resources with community effort would result in the active management of the effort by the community.

By 1991 therefore, Sharan introduced the provision of financial services to its portfolio of projects, through the promotion of SHGs and their federations. The project staff for the area were responsible for mobilising and organising these groups, most of them of women, except in the Tamil community where mixed groups were promoted.

Following the completion of an orientation programme, new members fixed a meeting to launch a group. Each group had a maximum membership of 15 and a minimum of 5. At the first meeting each group fixed the interest rate on the savings and loans (1 and 3 per cent respectively) and chose a president and secretary. At each meeting each member had to save a minimum of Rs 10. The president and secretary of the group approved loan applications.

Geographical clusters of SHGs together established a federation. The federation board was made up of all the presidents and secretaries of the SHGs in an area. One among them would be the president and another the treasurer of the federation. A Sharan representative, usually the coordinator in the area, joined them on the board as the secretary and joint signatory to a bank account opened in the name of the federation (see Figure 8.2). All surplus savings and investments were placed in the bank account to provide larger returns on these funds. The bank account also provided legitimacy to the local organisation in attracting other resources if possible. Table 8.1 lists the areas and brief financial numbers.

This review draws on a survey of 80 respondents as well as focus groups to discuss their experiences of financial-service providers, both past and present. All this data is triangulated with the savings records of the groups over a five-year period. Savings are a much more sensitive barometer of the changes taking place within the service in a particular area. In particular, savings reflect much more accurately the level of confidence that clients have in the service.

Figure 8.2: Structure of SHGs and federations promoted by Sharan

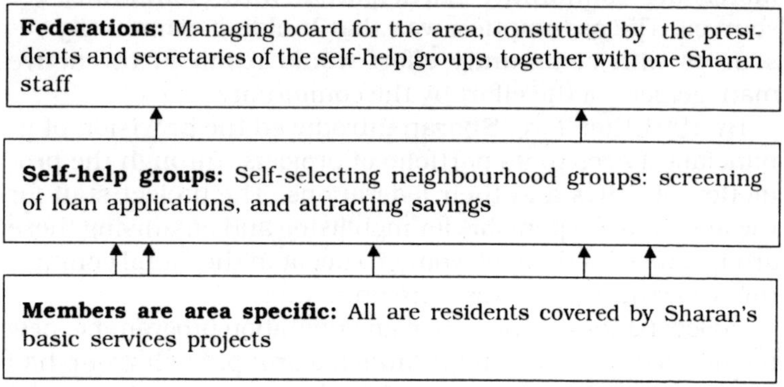

Federations: Managing board for the area, constituted by the presidents and secretaries of the self-help groups, together with one Sharan staff

Self-help groups: Self-selecting neighbourhood groups: screening of loan applications, and attracting savings

Members are area specific: All are residents covered by Sharan's basic services projects

Table 8.1: Areas and financials of Sharan's SHG programme (March 1996)

Federation	Location and ethnic mix	Date started	Total savings in Rs	Loans outstanding in Rs	Interest income for 1995–96 in Rs
Mongolpuri Y Block	Resettlement: mixed religious group	March 1992	157,914	112,900	18,528
Mongolpuri Q Block	Resettlement: Hindi-speaking migrants	December 1991	252,169	105,130	23,933
Sultanpuri federation	Temporary resettlement colony: Hindi-speaking migrants	January 1995	79,092	34,500	2,950
Tamil federation	Slum: Migrants from single district but with caste differences	December 1991	87,969	46,210	4,064
Gautam Nagar	Slum: Hindi-speaking migrants	December 1991	88,073	29,724	6,110

First cost set: The experience of losses

Poor people in urban contexts can suffer significant losses from engaging in the investment opportunities available to them. Respondents, recalling the previous two years, provided information on losses totalling Rs 75,000 (close to Rs 1,000 per person).

Of this total, 88 per cent was attributed to losses on investments, and 12 per cent to losses from extending personal credit. Two-thirds of the total amount lost was due to participation in rotating savings and credit associations (ROSCAs), which is not untypical (Rutherford and Arora, 1997: 366; Wright and Mutesasira, 2001). Most of these failures arose from the inability of managers of such investments to enforce contracts entered into by members. Formal-sector providers also generated losses for respondents: 11 per cent arose from investments in non-banking finance companies (NBFCs)[2] and 11 per cent from insurance or bank investments. Common to almost all losses seemed to be the inability to enforce contracts.

The analysis begins by examining cases drawn from a sample of SHG members that led to such losses. The cases reveal problems that confront residents of deprived urban areas as they enter into financial contracts. Understanding the reasons for such losses illustrates the institutional constraints.

ROSCAs and NBFCs

It was difficult for residents of the areas in which Sharan worked to differentiate among service-providers to see who might renege on a contract. These service-providers or agents invest time disseminating information about themselves and winning the confidence of the *basti* (slum) residents.

For example, members of the SHGs in Sultanpuri had saved with a ROSCA organised by a resident in the area whom they had known for well over a year. No one, however, was aware when he left the area or knew what happened to him. It was only when they did not find him for a few days that they realised that all their savings were lost.

The experience of SHG members with an NBFC in Mongolpuri Q was no different. Well-dressed agents of the NBFC regularly visited clients. They provided all account-holders with passbooks and made entries in registers described as 'important-looking'. Clients had access to their savings at the NBFC office. The close proximity of this office and the house-visits made the service extremely convenient for clients, and enhanced their confidence. However, finding the office shut continuously for a week, residents made investigations and found that none of the information given to them was true, nor did it enable them to trace the promoters.

Such experiences are not limited to poor slum-dwellers. Many middle-class residents in Delhi have experienced the same. Attempting to differentiate between service-providers with the information available is therefore a difficult task. It is made all the more difficult for residents of urban slums, where whatever information they have is largely restricted to the period of their residence in the settlement.

A second form of loss experienced by SHG members was due to the failure of ROSCAs to enforce contracts. In such cases, members of the ROSCAs borrowed large amounts and then did not repay the required monthly instalments. The organisers of the ROSCAs had no mechanism to ensure compliance. Efforts to exert pressure on the members' families, through local councils of elders in the area, failed. Unlike in rural areas, these local councils were not a regular body, but just brought together a few senior residents temporarily to resolve neighbourhood issues. From the survey there was little evidence of their success in ensuring repayment.

It is therefore not only the lack of information to differentiate among service-providers that characterises these markets, but also the weakness of existing mechanisms to ensure compliance to contracts entered into by different agents in urban areas.

Moneylenders and personal lending

Limitations in obtaining accurate information and the absence of enforcement mechanisms to ensure compliance in urban areas characterise the credit market also. This is very different from moneylending in rural areas. Those surveyed in the urban slums suggested that all moneylenders were resident outside their local blocks. Access to a loan was contingent on the person being introduced to the moneylenders and on the collateral offered. In the absence of either collateral or an acceptable guarantor, it was difficult to get access to such credit.

Time delays and demands for collateral diminish the competitive edge of the urban moneylender as an alternative service-provider. In one of the focus groups, members discussing the advantage of SHGs highlighted the difficulties of accessing credit from moneylenders:

> In the *basti* the moneylender charges Rs 10 as interest on every hundred rupees borrowed. Here [in the self-help groups] we can give only Rs 2 and get some money. We can get money in five minutes, and it can help in meeting our needs. It is like a bank of our own.
>
> When we go to the moneylender, we have to make 10 trips. Then we have to listen to different things, and there is still uncertainty whether we are going to receive the money.
>
> With the self-help groups we can return the money slowly, in smaller instalments. Even if we get the loan after one day, we at least get the loan after one day, we are almost sure of that.

This explanation highlights the constraints that moneylenders confront of verifying information and limiting default risk, resulting in delays and a large number of trips by clients before a final commitment to disburse funds can be made. The comments also illustrate the importance of low prices, smaller instalments and longer repayment periods that credit products of SHGs offer.

The survey suggested that repayment risks become even more acute in personal lending. In many cases of such lending mentioned by respondents, they had had personal information about the borrower, but once the money was given, the borrower reneged on the contract. There was little by way of remedial action any of the lenders could do.

Insurance

Residents experienced loss of investments with insurance as well. Though these losses are partially a result of the design and structure of the products, they also highlight important features of the market. Agents who are authorised to sell life-insurance receive as a commission approximately 20 per cent of the amounts deposited irrespective of providing any additional facilitation to the client, or not, beyond the first sale of the policy. Further, the client cannot transfer the commission to any other agent who provides better assistance in operating the account. The result is that while most of the agents are very active in opening accounts, there is little effort to provide any follow-up service or information to clients. The survey revealed that members who had made such investments were completely unaware of procedures in operating these insurance accounts.

In the absence of any monitoring by the insurance company of the agent–client relationship, further distortions become evident. For example, Nidhi, a resident of the area in which Sharan worked, invested in a policy from the Life Insurance Corporation (LIC). She made regular instalments to the agent in cash. However, the agent retained these cash payments, as there was no means of proving that Nidhi had made such cash deposits.

To Nidhi, an illiterate woman, the policy was operational as she made her deposits and received regular correspondence from LIC. When she showed the correspondence to a Sharan staff member, she was informed that her policy had lapsed due to non-payment of dues. Nidhi then made a trip to the LIC office to enquire about her policy and what remedial action she could take vis-à-vis the agent and LIC. The LIC officer suggested legal action after a lengthy procedure of filling in complaint forms. Recognising the futility and the high cost of initiating remedial action, Nidhi preferred to write off the investment as a loss.

There was mention too of losses of savings deposited in banks, although respondents provided little information to verify this.

These experiences with formal investments highlight investors' lack of ability to recognise the different attributes of the products on offer. When acquiring insurance products slum-dwellers are often not able to recognise the procedural requirements involved. Insurance policies assume that clients are literate and can understand the requirements of the policy.

Even in attempting recovery Nidhi faced similar difficulties. Having made the trip once to the local office of the insurance company, she recognised the need for assistance in filling the forms. The constant need for such assistance, together with the travel and time expended, would, according to Nidhi, outweigh the amount of money lost in the insurance policy.

In such cases, understanding the computational skills of agents becomes very vital. North (1990: 23) argues that it is possible to arrive at rational decisions by individuals provided we assume unlimited (perfect) computational skills. However, in instances such as these, where such skills are limited, it is difficult for investors to make correct decisions. Because she was illiterate, Nidhi was unable to recognise that her payments were not being deposited into her account, and unable to initiate any remedial action.

The failure to recognise the different attributes of the product being exchanged means that an informed decision in entering the contract is absent. Computational skills are thus a vital part in determining the success with which people enter contracts.

Conclusions

Two features stand out from this analysis. First, that losses extended over a range of service-providers and included public-sector providers. Second, that losses were not confined to savings markets, but were also found in credit markets. In urban areas NGOs like Sharan clearly confront some of the most acute deficiencies of markets for financial services.

Any initiative to provide financial services at low cost in these areas will therefore have to address specific constraints. Service-provision will have to address the asymmetries of information that exist between different agents in urban areas. In the case of Sharan, this is relevant to Sharan itself as the NGO-promoter, and to the members of the SHGs.

Within the micro-finance world there is increasing recognition of losses poor people in many parts of the world face in engaging in financial markets. What however is not discussed is 'not only the amount by which the purchaser is cheated; the cost must also include the loss incurred from driving legitimate business out of existence' (Akerlof, 1970: 495). The cases of losses cited above, and measures to overcome information asymmetries, have an impact on any new service-provider entering the market, not least in adding to the costs of launching their financial services. This insight was ratified during the field-work when one of the participants mentioned that it took a year before she could finally trust the federation and the NGO with her money.

The constraints therefore have an impact on both the financial intermediary and the potential members or clients. In the latter case, potential members or clients must first assess the risks to themselves. They need an adequate flow of information about the different attributes of the service. This flow of information, as well as the systems and procedures, has to match the computational skills of the clients. Not only does this requirement have cost implications for the financial intermediary, but any failure or variation in addressing information related to the attributes of the service can lead to an increase in uncertainty among members, potentially undermining the intermediary.

All the agents, whether promoters, members or clients, therefore need to enter such markets with great clarity. It is probable that similar behaviour as shown by members of ROSCAs will be present in the SHGs also. It is essential for members and the NGO supporting them not only to recognise that such behaviour is possible, but also to build in appropriate incentives into the lending mechanisms, and to ensure that these incentives are neither distorted nor diminished by the wealth-maximising behaviour of some members. The success of such an approach will depend on their ability to manage and recognise the flow of information that can alert them to possible violations.

Equally important to recognise is the weakness of most enforcement mechanisms in the Indian context, especially in urban contexts where reputations of members are not necessarily significant. This may require some form of collateral. Alternatively, it may require innovations in existing institutions that encourage people to honesty and repayment of credit (Akerlof, 1970).

Sharan and the SHGs clearly need to possess or invest in information about different members or clients. This information will enable them to evaluate accurately the potential risk of default. Failure to do so will lead to difficulties and delays in attracting investments or sanctioning loans. The success in gathering and managing such information could determine costs in moving quickly towards becoming a sustainable programme.

The following sections examine the performance of Sharan and the federations to determine the significance of these institutional constraints on the programme.

Second cost set: Overcoming imperfections in credit markets

The previous section drew attention to the experience of losses that poor people confront from different service-providers. I concluded that the experience of these losses was likely to drive up the costs of operations. In this section I identify specific costs that emerge around contracts within the SHGs, as poor members seek to meet the provision of financial services.

The theoretical literature suggests that limitations in the nature of the institutions that underpin credit markets can affect costs in the provision of financial services. The institutions perform multiple functions in contributing to the success of financial services. Most prominent among them are their roles in making information available about clients, establishing incentives and determining the quality of contract enforcement.

For example, information helps the lender in determining the likelihood with which the borrower will fulfil her/his part of the contract. Moreover, credit, especially small loans, is costly to monitor and enforce. Hence, incentives to repay and low-cost mechanisms to enforce contracts need to exist. Incentives can be of price, reputation or further access. Enforcement of contracts on the other hand can be done through traditional bodies of elders, kinship groups, or occupational groups that can ensure that people repay. The research on the SHGs promoted by Sharan provides real-life examples of such mechanisms, as analysed below.

Another important feature is the mental models of participants in markets. As suggested above, mental models are the frameworks that participants or agents in a market use to process information. These frameworks of course put in question the assumption that market participants possess perfect unlimited computational skills and that they will therefore arrive at rational decisions. Clearly, such assumptions about the levels of skills and abilities of participants are not always true.

It may therefore become necessary, for example, for regularised patterns of interactions to emerge, on the basis of which exchanges in complex situations can be built. Reliance on ideology or on the computational skills of others may be equally important. It is therefore necessary to recognise the elements of mental models that contribute to affecting the actions and the behaviour of participants in markets (North, 1990: 23). This applies as much to financial markets as any other markets, and I now look at the evidence provided by the SHGs promoted by Sharan.

The Sultanpuri federation: The absence of information

The Sultanpuri project was the first to be started and later shut down by Sharan. When the groups in the project were disbanded in 1993 they had total savings of Rs 40,573. The loans disbursed over the two-and-a-half years of their existence totalled Rs 61,511.

In 1995, after many petitions by some members of the community, a fresh initiative in savings and credit began. The second phase of the project performed much better. Within a year (by January 1996) the total savings of the groups had shot up to Rs 69,255 and loans disbursed in the same period to Rs 54,975. It is clear from these results that the experience of the first phase contributed to the performance in the second phase. What was going on?

The first savings and credit project was characterised by procedural and accounting discrepancies. Moreover, local Sharan staff were active with certain members of the groups in determining who would receive loans. Remedial action by the NGO resulted only in a few of the presidents, secretaries and even staff discrediting both the organisation and the savings and credit project.

The resulting confusion among members and the problems in managing the project led Sharan to close down the project and return all the money. Sharan, however, continued its welfare projects focusing on health and education.

The savings and credit project restarted in January of 1995. The most significant drivers were some of the old members. They felt there was a demand for such a service, but that it needed some changes. These old members determined the selection of new members of the groups. They actively used local information and the record of the older groups, particularly on default and delinquency in repayment, to determine membership.

So firm and rigorous was the screening process that those excluded petitioned staff members at Sharan to recommend their membership. Having learnt from the previous experience, the staff did not interfere with this selection process. Indeed, in circumstances when the local group leaders (SHG presidents and secretaries) found it difficult to refuse membership, staff members intervened to prevent membership.

Members consequently formed their SHGs around clearer evaluations of default. The experience of the first phase removed critical information asymmetries and provided members the confidence to make investment and credit decisions of much higher quality than that achieved in the first phase. In less than six months the federation had disbursed loans that totalled the same amount the federation had disbursed over a two-year period during the first phase, with groups in the second phase consequently earning much higher interest income on loans.

The Sultanpuri project illustrates one of the central problems confronting financial-service provision in urban areas, namely, the presence of uninformed members in SHGs. It points to the absence of relevant information in assessing risk, even though members had enjoyed proximity through long periods of residence in the community (in this case, over a decade on average).

By closing down the project and restarting it members could utilise information from the previous experience of members' performance within SHGs to achieve a better membership profile and performance. It led to members self-selecting their groups and excluding earlier defaulters. Members could also inform Sharan when default levels were questionable. Access to such information contributed to members investing and sanctioning finances at levels that would make a quick transition to sustainability more possible.

In drawing lessons for urban SHG initiatives it is therefore best to allow membership to move between groups to facilitate optimum group formation. Another solution could be to promote SHGs over two stages rather than one.

To conclude, it is important to recognise that the limited information available in transient communities or groups is not sufficient to provide the basis for effective performance within SHGs. In such communities, the necessary information can only come from building some critical experience within the community. All such measures give rise to additional costs for the promoting agency.

The Tamil federation: The absence of skills

After a consistent performance over four years the Tamil federation collapsed. An examination of the decline reveals important implications of building community-based organisations within illiterate communities with their limited monitoring skills.

The difficulties faced by the Tamil community reflected some basic urban characteristics. Being a small homogeneous community, migrants from the same district in Tamil Nadu, members possessed high levels of information about each other. However, as economic migrants with no language or social links beyond their immediate community, it was difficult for these Tamil residents to have access to any source of finance. Such limitations meant that their reliance on one another was extremely high.

When Angamuttu saw and understood the functioning of SHGs in other communities he quickly mobilised and established mixed SHGs of men and women within the Tamil community. Important to the acceptance of any alternative service by these residents was the need for trust. Trust would help them overcome the uncertainty faced in entering into a contract whose attributes they could not measure nor decipher. This was their condition to agreeing to join the SHGs. In doing so they trusted the person who was promoting the SHGs: Angamuttu.

From the perspective of the average resident of this Tamil *basti*, therefore, the main promoter was a local resident who was working with an organisation (Sharan) engaged in good works in the area. It was also agreed that members of the community would write the accounts for the groups. Sharan staff would work alongside these in maintaining a set of records. Assured by this process, and attracted to the low price of credit, members regularly put in their savings.

From their inception, the SHGs within the Tamil federation performed comparatively well. For the most part there was no problem with lending or borrowing, and most repayments came in on time. Attendance at meetings was good and members regularly updated their own bank records and those at the NGO office. The presidents typically signed all records that secretaries of the SHGs had verified.

Such a display of initiative marked out the Tamil community federation from the others and Sharan's focus now turned to strengthening what it saw as a people's movement. To reinforce and clarify group processes Sharan occasionally conducted training programmes, whenever Tamil-speaking staff were available. These training sessions addressed themselves to the formal rules that governed the SHGs. Distortions, if any, did not worry the organisation, as the results surpassed expectations.

However, after four years of such performance, monthly collections dropped drastically in most of the groups. The total annual collection of savings dropped from Rs 18,843 the previous year to Rs 8,754. For Sharan it was all too clear that something within this community-run operation had gone unnoticed.

All interviews and group discussions suggested the decline began around the departure of the main community-based promoter, Angamuttu. He was the pioneer who had convinced most of the members to participate in the SHGs.

Slowly, over time, Angamuttu had made loans to his coterie of associates. Although this could arguably have started the decline, it did not worry the other members as the repayments came in. When, however, it became widely known that the local accountant made wrong entries in the passbooks, the withdrawal from the groups began. Fear of further losses meant that savings dropped drastically.

For the NGO it seemed surprising that such events could have happened and that members who were so active could have condoned such action without so much as a discussion in the federation meetings. The findings challenged most of the assumptions made by the NGO in the build up of the project.

For most of the members, Angamuttu was the main promoter of the project. The role of the NGO seemed unclear to them and the training programmes did not help them recognise their ownership and consequent responsibilities and decision-making powers. While part of their dependence can be ascribed to the language barrier, the community regarded the SHGs as little different from ROSCAs, which were very common in this community, except for a different set of promoters.

In response to a more detailed exploration of ownership most of the women commented that their extensive household responsibilities and limited accounting skills ensured they did not pay attention. Rather than acquiring such skills or awareness, it was simpler (less costly) to hire somebody who could understand and be trusted to manage the group. In the absence of greater monitoring within the federation, presidents and secretaries of the SHGs were authenticating incorrect records that the community accountant entered. The inability of members to decipher and measure the attributes of the contracts was therefore at the root of the problem.

This case highlights again the high costs that confront any initiative to draw illiterate members into the provision of financial services. These costs can arise from the need to help them comprehend the important characteristics of the new organisation being built in the community and to develop their skill levels to comprehend and manage the different dimensions of accounting and monitoring within the groups.

The NGO can also attempt to identify and strengthen different modifications in procedures that members introduce. Many innovations, such as handing over money publicly, or the board of the federation processing loan applications from SHG presidents and secretaries, play a considerable role in determining the success of groups. In addition, by getting different local people to validate entries in books, it becomes possible to limit any distortions.

Such informal restraints introduced by community members themselves serve to overcome uncertainties among members arising from their lack of skills. Evidence of such behaviour even in ROSCAs, and the need to build such new mechanisms in community organisations, suggests that both the strengthening of new informal innovations and an improved understanding of SHGs by the community are central costs in the building of financial services among poor people (Bouman, 1995; Bennett et al., 1996).

The Mongolpuri Q Block federation: Building the repayment norm

By the end of March 1996 the Q Block federation was the largest of all those promoted by Sharan. Its cumulative savings had crossed two-and-a-half lakh (a quarter of a million) rupees and it had Rs 150,000 in different deposits. During the financial year ending March 1996 the federation had earned Rs 15,652 from these deposits and Rs 23,933 from its loan portfolio.

Every year in fact the Q Block federation disbursed and recovered large amounts of loan funds to and from its members. Starting from an annual disbursal of Rs 10,460 in 1991, it quickly passed one lakh (100,000) to peak in 1993–94 with disbursements of Rs 233,791. Over the five-year period reviewed under this research it had disbursed Rs 784,810 in loans and recovered Rs 697,672.

What operational strategies of the community contributed to such a robust loan portfolio? Successful loan portfolios crucially depend on the ability to enforce contracts. Such enforcement depends on having access to information that can recognise and alert members to any violations in a contract, in addition to having built-in incentives to repay. As the project structure in Q Block was the same as in other areas, I assume that such incentives were not the determinant of the comparative success in Q Block. Just as in other communities I have reviewed, systems and skills in accounting within both the NGO and the community were also weak. Alerting groups to possible defaults based on sophisticated management-information systems was not therefore possible.

In the absence of such internal information systems, the groups and the federation in particular had devised a proxy indicator that seemed to work well. Most of these SHGs were built and organised around the importance of cooperative values. Among others, these values included the need for consensus and participation of all individuals in decision-making processes. Such an approach was felt to strengthen the unity of the group and its ability to take action. The Q Block federation, more than any other, appropriated this idea and converted it into the basis for remedial action at the level of the federation itself. Such action contributed to strengthening the ability of groups to identify violations in contracts and impose a higher degree of enforcement.

Evidence of members reporting such violations to federation members and Sharan staff was available. Whenever individual members felt that the decision in a group was not acceptable to all members or that there was partiality in credit decisions, they reported this.

Based on one such complaint Sharan staff initiated an enquiry into a group's accounts. A scrutiny of the records led to the detection of a violation, a second loan to someone with a bad repayment record. Providing this data to the SHG made it possible for Sharan's coordinator to ask the office bearers in the group to desist from such decisions in future, as they violated the very effort of building shared visions.

In undertaking to relate to the groups through the prism of cooperative ideals, it became possible for the coordinator to recognise and respond quickly to infringements within groups, just as much as it contributed to members being able to recognise and inform staff about such violations.

In another instance, the president of an SHG had asked a member for a rent-charge for sanctioning the loan, over and above the existing interest-rate charges. When informed by the member of such a request, the federation called for a meeting and confronted the erring functionary. At the meeting, the president of the federation explained that such an action was against the rules of cooperation, which formed the very basis of the SHGs; the next time punitive action would follow. Besides this, group members also pointed out that such action decreased the price incentive for members to invest their savings and then seek loans from the SHGs.

Records of the federation demonstrate the close attention paid to reviewing infringements by members and remedial actions against them. The Q Block federation required its members (the SHG presidents and secretaries) to be active in screening applicants and in ensuring repayment. In case of default, SHG members who were guarantors lost their savings. According to the community worker, such appropriation of savings took place only twice. In both cases the member continued as a member of their SHG. The action, however, served to signal that enforcement was strict, after which there were no defaults.

This particular emphasis seems to have been the cumulative result of the inputs provided by the local Sharan team to the community leadership. These inputs stressed the norms that would contribute to the success of the SHGs (according to one community-worker, the most important was that rules must not be broken), and sought to build these values into the dynamic of the groups.[3] The effect of such clarity allowed the membership to recognise and reinforce features important to decision-making within the group. While the recognition of violations was important, equally critical were the discussions and the follow-up that resulted from such recognition. In most cases the coordinator and other staff talked about the need to discuss these issues in the federation meetings.

Consequently, the intolerance towards transgressors became clear and violations decreased.

The Q Block federation case reveals the dynamic relationship of institutional mechanisms to functional requirements of financial-service provision. In particular, it highlights the importance of ideology to the success of the service. Ideological infringements can serve as a simple mechanism for policing violations within SHGs.

The presence of ideology in NGOs has been recognised as contributing to their unique cultural characteristics. In microfinance its presence has been tolerated more as a carry-over of NGO values into the new area of micro-financial services. However, for the NGOs concerned it has been a very important tool in achieving successful performance among SHGs.

Two other studies point to similar insights. In the case of the Grameen Bank, Jain (1996: 83) recognised the importance of the 'enabling routine repetition of identical behaviour by all 30 members, week after week, 52 times a year'. In contrast, Hulme et al. (1994) concluded that the Buddhist context of open and participatory group processes and dynamic and voluntary leaders has contributed to the operations of SANASA in Sri Lanka.

While the importance of such ideological reinforcement on the performance of SHGs is widely accepted, its importance to transaction costs has not been widely recognised.

Formalising informal mechanisms and experiences

Clearly, efforts at overcoming imperfections in credit markets are not simple for members of SHGs. In that light there are many changes from the formal design of the service that micro-finance projects need to undergo. Typically, these changes begin as informal in nature. By opting to regroup, members in Sultanpuri made use of information to screen and include only 'good' members. In the Tamil group, by failing to adopt procedures that enabled members to recognise the true attributes of the service, the federation went into decline. In Q Block the emphasis of the community on building values of equity strengthened the enforcement of credit-contracts. These new structures and procedures relied on modifying institutions and mechanisms to make it possible for community members to measure attributes of clients or of the service. To capture these and formalise them into the provision of the service is important. The micro-finance sector therefore needs to reinforce its understanding of innovation as one that is designed to meet the needs of clients as they attempt to drive down the costs of their participation.

Third cost set: Managing effectiveness

So far I have analysed costs that arise from the losses poor people experience and from the efforts they make to overcome imperfections in credit markets. These two sets of costs fall outside the control of the promoting organisation. A third set of costs, reviewed in this section, arises from the effectiveness of organisations in providing a service. Only these costs are within the control of the organisations themselves.

This third set of costs arises from the challenge of entering particular markets. Institutional economics suggests that organisations must 'devise and discover markets, evaluate products and techniques, and manage actively the actions of employees; these are all tasks in which there is uncertainty and in which investment in information must be acquired' (North, 1990: 77).

These costs are threefold. The first is the ability of organisations to identify markets. For this they need to unravel (measure) local complexities and attributes, including their ability to gather information about their clients and what they require. This information then contributes to designing a product or service that results in meeting that demand.

The second arises from continuing or expanding provision for which the organisation must provide a service of standard quality. This relieves clients of the need to invest resources to assess service-provision of varying quality.

The third arises from the need to manage employees who are critical for building information and providing inputs of constant quality. In managing its employees, an organisation must focus on acquiring skills, knowledge and learning from doing. Skills relate to the particular requirements of the service; knowledge, both tacit and communicable, relates to the ability to understand and decipher local complexities of clients and inputs; and learning by doing relates to the organisation's ability to develop skills and routines that come from repeated interaction (North, 1990: 74).

As in the cases analysed above, I use evidence on the ground to demonstrate the importance of these tasks, identifying markets, providing a service of constant quality and managing staff, and how they can impact the performance of SHGs.

The Y Block federation: Building new kinship groups

The first case, of the federation in Y Block, illustrates the need to identify markets clearly to understand, and act upon, the complexities of local conditions and behaviour.

Though located in the proximity of Mongolpuri Q Block and Sultanpuri, the Y Block project got off to a slow start. By March 1993 the federation had savings of Rs 28,456. The groups, though few in number, seemed active and regular in their meetings.

Within a year, however, field-staff reported a declining trend in savings. In response, Sharan initiated an examination that revealed major deviations from the guidelines on member participation. Proxy membership was common and multiple membership from within the same family had led to loan decisions that favoured the few, often by ensuring they received the largest and greatest number of loans. One family had even managed to dominate the decision-making process of the federation.

While most members complained in private about this, the only evidence of the problems was the declining trend in cumulative savings and repayments during group meetings.

Following a new supportive intervention by Sharan staff, the project was back on track by early 1995. Savings at the federation had risen to Rs 84,273 by March 1995, and to Rs 157,914 by the end of the next financial year. This growth was the highest among all the federations for that year. The total loan amount outstanding at the end of the financial year was also the largest at Rs 112,900.

To understand potential costs better, it is important to identify the nature of the problem and recognise the corrective mechanisms adopted by the local Sharan team and by members of the SHGs.

While Sharan focused on promoting SHGs, few recognised the benefits of controlling the resources of the groups. One family (relatives of Bijli), however, played an active role in supporting the formation of SHGs by including their extended family across different groups. In two groups, this family included the name of a member who was not even residing in the area. Moreover, when Bijli and one of her relatives became the president and secretary of the federation, they were able to exercise even greater control of the funds. In the absence of information on relations among members, the NGO was unaware of this distortion. Consequently, the surplus funds at the federation were used to finance loans to groups where Bijli's family were members.

On recognising such behaviour, Sharan initiated remedial action. The first job of the staff was to change its interaction with the community. The project began a concerted thrust in investing time and resources to gather information about members. Proxy and double members, as well as those who did not qualify for membership, were removed, in part by ensuring that all members had to affix pictures of themselves to their cards.

Sharan also undertook steps to check the board of the federation. Most decisions were closely scrutinised until the end of the tenure of the existing board. The sanctioning of loan applications from SHG leaders was now done in meetings of all members of the federation rather than by the president of the federation. Such behaviour increased transparency and confidence in the transactions. In fostering such norms members also moved increasingly towards adopting honest behaviour. Sharan then actively promoted an alternative leadership from among the members.

The project staff also returned savings to whoever wanted them back, but followed this up with an intense period of personal home-visiting to explain the project and the current change process in detail. The new supervisor who joined the Sharan team actively explained to the SHGs how Sharan functioned as the promoting organisation, and why there was little opportunity for their savings to disappear. Specific attention was given to explaining the attributes of the service, including the responsibility of members and the process of sanctioning loans.

Given the schedules of poor working-class people, including many young mothers, it was not possible for all members to attend training programmes. Leaders of SHGs therefore undertook to educate and inform their members. This engagement increased the flow of information among households in a group.

Such information also made it easier for an SHG to offer flexible repayment contracts in response to delinquency without affecting the basic discipline of the group. As one leader put it: 'I explained, "what is your problem is our problem" and assured the member of a considerate response.' Such information therefore led to a better understanding of risk and improved the flexibility and hence lowered the price of the contract. Significantly, this behaviour contributed to a steady rise in, and repayment of, loans within the groups.

The training thus resulted in greater clarity among members about important attributes of the service. This increased flow of information and greater adherence to norms resulted in improving the operations of each of the groups and the federation, as seen in the increase in members of the groups and their savings.

The case of the Y Block federation demonstrates that organisations providing any service need to understand the complexities of local conditions and behaviour. The promoting organisation needs to acquire detailed information about the market and develop the necessary information to monitor any distortions that might emerge, all of which contribute to costs.

It is equally necessary for clients to understand the operating structure of the service. Particularly important when forming SHGs are high quality inputs from the promoting organisation that explain to members their rights and responsibilities, their functions and roles, and other information on the attributes of the service.

This information helps establish norms within SHGs. By recognising the importance of managing local information and enhancing the flow of information among members, Sharan helped the members of SHGs to establish new relationships amongst themselves. In practice, the new relationships mimicked kinship groups and thus established a new urban family and community. The approach therefore not only provided a clear understanding of the service, but also made available information that enhanced relationships among members.

The Gautam Nagar federation: Information and the maintenance of SHGs

The second case, of the federation in Gautam Nagar, illustrates the need to maintain information to provide constant service and the critical role staff play in terms of their skills, knowledge and learning.

From even a casual scrutiny of Sharan's intervention in Gautam Nagar, two points immediately attract attention. First, there was a large turnover of staff within the project, and, second, the fluctuation in savings of the federation was volatile.

On the first point, during the first four years of the savings and credit project in Gautam Nagar, there were four trainee-supervisors, none of whom stayed in the organisation for more than six months. It was these trainee-supervisors who supported groups in organising meetings and doing the accounts. The only two staff who had completed a year with the project were then sent for relief work following an earthquake in the state of Maharashtra. The greatest variation in staff occurred between 1993 and 1995.

On the second point, savings in Gautam Nagar witnessed the largest volatility among all of Sharan's projects. In the financial year 1991–92, there were barely three groups with savings of Rs 6,897. By the end of the next year, the number of groups and members had increased, with savings of Rs 52,018. In 1993–94 the federation reached its nadir with the membership of SHGs falling and savings dropping to Rs 13,089, with almost half of this amount coming from one group. Following the introduction of changes, the project turned around in 1995 and achieved total savings of Rs 52,323.

With a significant turnover of staff and large fluctuations in membership and savings, it becomes necessary to examine the relationship, if any, that existed between these two features of the project.

The success of Sharan's community development project in Gautam Nagar relied on close relationships of staff with the community. The isolation of new migrants and their inability to decipher urban systems often results in poor families relying intensely on NGO field-staff. In the case of Sharan, staff used the welfare activities (health and education) to build up close relationships with families. Such relationships form a contrast to what migrants generally face in their workplace, likely to be characterised by poor working conditions and exploitative contracts.

Critically, these close relationships helped establish the difference between Sharan and other service-providers, of great importance given the widespread experience of investment losses analysed above.

The relationships therefore enabled staff to attract participation in the SHGs, and to use their knowledge of families from the welfare activities to limit the possibility of inappropriate members joining groups and, in particular, of delinquency and defaults. This in turn gave members greater confidence in the groups.

All in all, as the local coordinator suggested, the SHGs were highly dependent on personal relationships, with 'an obvious premium on the [staff] person'. From the perspective of SHG members, individual staff members formed an important feature of the service. It was on this basis that the SHGs were able to mobilise some Rs 52,000 of savings by March 1993.

In 1993, Sharan undertook a general reorganisation of staff across the organisation. Given the limited resources the NGO possessed, it was difficult to ensure a clear overlap period when one team departed and another took over. The handover was therefore very cursory.

The new coordinator and team found that members of the SHGs in Gautam Nagar did not seem eager to participate.

The chorus was for old staff members to return and close the accounts. When visited, members would refuse to handover savings and more importantly their loan instalments. Unable to recognise the significance of what was happening, the team watched as members withdrew their savings and groups closed down. The team, charged with an agenda of growth, was confronting a decline.

Clearly, with the departure of the old staff, the close personal relationships that contributed to enforcement were lost. The decline in repayments only confirmed to group members some of their worst fears about the project.

The new team therefore had to restart the process of gathering information about members. In many instances the groups collapsed while the new staff groped for such information. While gathering information was time consuming, the more difficult task for the staff was to judge the likelihood of default among individual members, which was critical to maintain the confidence of members in their SHGs.

In an attempt to restrict the number of members leaving, the organisation deputed many new and inexperienced staff to attend meetings. In their enthusiasm, the new staff did not pay sufficient attention to what they said, or simply said the wrong things, introducing confusion in the minds of the members about the attributes of the service.

Poring over the financial records, holding training programmes for the community, and closely monitoring the SHGs did not seem to help either. On all counts (savings, repayments and interest earnings) the project experienced a rapid decline. Sound and active SHG members such as Menaka just seemed to want to withdraw their savings.

After much discussion, the team slowly defined a systematic response to the problems. In the first place, supervisors changed the way they functioned, informing members about the role of Sharan and the degree of its responsibility for the service. The project team moved towards standardising different processes, from the selection of group members to meeting procedures, and reviewed these regularly at project meetings. Arranging meetings within the community became compulsory to ensure the regular presence of members in all group meetings and that systems were in place within the groups. The team coordinator reinforced these changes by accompanying the team during field-visits and observing that procedures followed a fixed format.

This new structure contributed to diminishing the uncertainty and making good the loss of information the project had faced earlier. Within little more than a year of such efforts savings climbed back to their previous level of just over Rs 52,000.

Though perhaps an extreme case, the Gautam Nagar project and its difficulties direct attention to the relationship that exists between staff and the performance of an SHG project. While it is widely recognised in management theory that staff in organisations come to possess vital information, its importance among NGOs and more particularly in micro-finance has been less recognised.

There are three functional roles that field-staff provide in extending micro-financial services. First, they are crucial in helping clients overcome their diffidence to participate arising from their previous experience of losses. Second, in the absence of peer-information in urban settings, staff contribute to diminishing the probability of delinquency and default. Third, they can ensure a constant quality in the provision of the service. Together these functions form the basis on which the success of the service depends.

Any organisation promoting financial services must therefore be able to ensure that staff can deliver these functions. To achieve this will require greater attention to the resources and skills NGOs possess to recruit, instruct and equip staff to manage these functions. Only then will NGOs be effective in providing their service over the long term.

Some lessons

The cases of the federations in Y Block and Gautam Nagar illustrate well the third set of costs that arise from managing an organisation's effectiveness. The organisation must invest in gathering local information that provides the foundation on which it can devise, initiate and maintain services that are effective within local markets. In the case of financial services, such local information is particularly important in screening borrowers.

For investing in local information and maintaining service-quality, staff are of course critical. The case of Gautam Nagar makes it clear that it is not just the staff themselves who are important, but also the manner in which they are managed. Non-governmental organisations, like other development organisations, can focus excessively on understanding and servicing their clients to the detriment of building their staff and hence themselves as organisations.

Staff are therefore central in determining the effectiveness of an organisation in providing a service. Non-governmental organisations in particular need to develop systematic systems in managing their staff. This will require them to identify how they recruit, develop and replace their staff. It is only when such systems are in place that they will be able to offer a service of constant value to their clients over the long term. While it is evident that these requirements will drive up costs in the short term, they will contribute in the longer term to the ability of NGOs to capture the gains of their investments in the promotion of SHGs.

Conclusions

The provision of micro-financial services to poor people remains an abiding challenge for development in India. In recognition of the potential of SHGs to contribute to this objective, there is increasing support for their promotion. In tune with world-wide attempts at moving towards cost-recovery in micro-finance, there have also been efforts at identifying and recovering the expenditure incurred on the promotion of these groups.

Most service-providers working with poor people in remote or under-serviced areas are quickly discovering that the costs of service-provision are high, challenging their attempts at achieving sustainability. The sum of these costs unfortunately gets attributed to the comparative advantage of organisations in promoting SHGs. As this chapter demonstrates, such attribution of all the costs of building these community-based organisations is simplistic and the conclusions arising from it, therefore, potentially harmful.

I have argued that it is necessary to begin any exercise of cost-allocation by identifying what contributes to these costs.

This chapter is therefore a first attempt at outlining the factors that contribute to the costs of promoting SHGs. There are at least three sets of costs that need attention. First is the costs arising from historical losses; second, the costs of establishing a new set of organisations built by poor communities to overcome credit-market imperfections; and third, the ability of the promoting organisations to provide and maintain an effective service. Of these costs, only the last set can justifiably be included in the pricing strategy of the organisation.

Providing a reasonable service therefore requires service-providers to address market distortions and imperfections that drive up their overall costs of providing the service. The future of promoting community-based organisations for poor people will require further work in estimating the actual value of these costs, and in enhancing regulatory mechanisms and public investments to overcome these distortions and imperfections, as well as appropriate incentives that encourage service-providers to be effective and efficient within a given market context.

The regulatory challenge is difficult. While it is easier to restrict the entry of service-providers in these markets, the exercise might begin more appropriately by building an understanding of these markets. Such understanding must include sound knowledge on the demand for financial services by poor people, of issues that affect product design and monitoring, and of the role that different stakeholders can play in investing in service-providers. This will require systematic and close coordination among all the different stakeholders, as I outline in Chapter 11.

As important is the emergence of innovations to overcome distortions and imperfections. In most cases these are informal mechanisms that get introduced on the edges of the formal design of the service, often by field-staff and communities of poor, illiterate clients. The success of a promoting organisation in expanding and controlling its own costs will rest on its ability to recognise and formalise these innovations into its operating strategy.

Finally, supportive investments need to continue and expand. Public agencies and donors making such investments need to recognise that it is not only the provision of the service but its quality that is important. This is especially important to reduce the many uncertainties poor people face in imperfect markets.

Notes

1. This paper was written during a period of research generously supported by the India Education Foundation. I would like to thank Jean Schmid at the Foundation in particular for her support.
2. All NBFCs must register with the Reserve Bank of India (RBI). While a large number are registered, an equally large number claim to be registered. Since the time of the survey, and in response to a range of scandals, the RBI has restricted the ability of NBFCs to raise deposits (at least those that are registered!).
3. The key staff member explained the group values as follows: People understand each other's financial needs. Collective money needs to be handled in a fair manner, and those who are better off should not have undue influence. People have a tendency to change decisions and make decisions in favour of a few. They need to understand that the money belongs to 10 other people and the return of the money is very important because it will affect the other families.

Chapter 9

Exploring empowerment and leadership at the grassroots: Social entrepreneurship in the SHG movement in India

Ajit Kanitkar[1]

Introduction

The 1990s saw the emergence of a movement throughout India of thousands of poor women (and some men) organising themselves into self-help groups (SHGs) to access savings and loan products. As Malcolm Harper set out in Chapter 7, it is estimated that by 2008 at the latest there will be one million SHGs with a membership of some 17 million, mainly women.

This chapter focuses on a less researched aspect of this movement: the phenomenon of social entrepreneurship within the SHG movement. Based on a survey in the field, I explore what entrepreneurship means in the context of poor rural women setting up and leading SHGs. I set out what entrepreneurial traits are seen among women SHG leaders, and what challenges as well as rewards they receive for their leadership. Finally, I discuss the possibilities of developing and nurturing qualities of social entrepreneurship among women engaging in SHGs.

Given the lack of detailed research on these aspects of SHGs, the insights from this chapter can only be tentative. I hope nevertheless that they will stimulate further debate on this critical topic.

I also do not want to get bogged down in definitions about who is, or is not, a social entrepreneur. I have focused on those leading individuals, a few women always present in every group and community, who have taken the initiative of forming and sustaining an SHG in their village.

PRADAN and SHGs

The study draws on the rich experience of Professional Assistance for Development Action (PRADAN), a well reputed and professional non-governmental organisation (NGO) working in some of the most resource poor and difficult regions of India.

PRADAN began promoting SHGs (or savings and credit groups, as PRADAN usually calls them) in their Alwar project in the state of Rajasthan in 1987. What began as a way to revolve funds the project provided to buy cattle fodder evolved into a mechanism to provide savings and credit services to poor people, organising them into strong groups in the process. By mid-2001 PRADAN had promoted more than 3,000 SHGs with over 40,000 women members. Promoting SHGs has also become the launching pad for PRADAN's strategy to generate livelihoods (Narendranath, 2001).

As described in Chapter 5, PRADAN sees SHGs as far more than channels to deliver financial services:

The SHG has a bigger role besides financial intermediation. It is an institution based on the concept of 'peer learning' as against learning that is externally controlled. This is a powerful process that enables growth and progress in a community. Members learn from each other in a group and SHGs learn from other SHGs, which then leads to collective progress.

The cohesion that SHGs foster enables them to address issues such as health and education.... SHGs are ... an effective inter-face for the poor to deal constructively with the external world, village society, the *panchayat* [elected village council], the banks and the government.

The SHG is also a forum for solidarity and empowerment of women, providing them the space and voice to negotiate and participate as equals both within the family and in society in general.

Therefore an SHG plays three roles simultaneously. It provides mutual help and internal financial mediation. It facilitates external financial mediation, and it empowers women to make demands on the external world (Narendranath, 2001: 2,4).

The ability of SHGs to draw on external credit from banks, and the empowerment that this often entails, is a particularly important feature of PRADAN's strategy for building SHGs as self-sustaining and mature village organisations.

Leadership plays an important role in such groups. However, it is worth noting that PRADAN is not in the business of promoting social entrepreneurs, but democratically owned and managed groups, whether SHGs, water-user groups or groups with other functional roles. The insights reflected in this chapter arise from looking at the SHGs from a new angle, seeking out the role of *entrepreneurial* leadership within the groups. While this does not diminish from the role of the promoting agency, which remains critical to the emergence of SHGs, it does assume that leadership within the local community will be an important factor in the emergence and progress of healthy groups (see MYRADA, 2000: 121–28).

This issue is all the more important, first because the entrepreneurial traits of women SHG leaders have not been significantly explored, and are therefore not fully understood. Second, if the SHG movement is to grow as forecast to one million groups by 2008, it is likely to outstrip the promotional capacities of NGOs. Local leadership will be a critical factor in the quality of the SHGs that emerge, not least because SHGs are already spreading among women (and some men) without the intervention of external agencies.

The fieldwork

Fieldwork was undertaken with PRADAN professionals in May 2001 in two locations in the state of Jharkhand, first in Barhi block of Hazaribag district and second in Lohardaga district. PRADAN has been working in Jharkhand (formerly part of the state of Bihar) for some 14 years.

The population of villages in Barhi block consists primarily of members of Scheduled and Other Backward Castes. Complementing earlier and still on-going work on lift-irrigation schemes managed by groups or management committees of users, PRADAN began work on SHGs in this area in 1992. PRADAN has now promoted almost 500 SHGs for women in the area. It has also promoted clusters (currently 29) that cover the SHGs in about eight to 10 villages. A group of clusters then form a General Body or federation.

PRADAN took up SHG activities in the Lohardaga area a little later (in 1995), and has promoted about 270 SHGs for women there. The population in the area consists mostly of tribal people belonging to the Oraon and Munda communities. Here again PRADAN promoted lift-irrigation schemes. Unlike in Hazaribag, however, PRADAN did not actively promote a formal structure of clusters and a General Body for the SHGs in Lohardaga. Though cluster meetings were held at regular intervals, women took turns to attend these. This enabled more women to participate in the cluster meetings representing their own SHGs.

The rationale for choosing SHGs in the two areas was to compare the potentially different patterns of social entrepreneurship in Hazaribag, where a formal structure of clusters and a General Body was deliberately promoted and therefore leaders or social entrepreneurs consciously designated, and in Lohardaga where such structures were not institutionalised.

During the fieldwork we interacted with about 200 women in 17 groups and spoke to about 20 women social entrepreneurs who were taking an active lead in the running of the SHG in their respective villages. All these 20 had been to several cluster meetings, and in Hazaribag some of them were representatives of the General Body. I also held discussions with 10 PRADAN professionals involved in the promotion of SHGs and lift-irrigation in the area.

PRADAN selected the 17 villages and SHGs to include as much diversity as possible (by the age and performance of the SHGs, the communities represented in them, and in villages which also had lift-irrigation schemes and others which did not). In terms of age, groups varied from those promoted recently to at least three that PRADAN professionals had for some time stopped visiting and providing support to.

The analysis focused on three key aspects. The first relates to the evolution of the group and the role of the social entrepreneur or the lead person in steering the group to a desired objective. In setting out the results of this part I draw on concepts that have been widely discussed in the context of the performance of a team. The second part of the analysis looks at the social entrepreneur herself and the challenges and rewards that she experiences. The central question I explore is what makes this person tick in shouldering responsibility often accompanied by no apparent gains. The third analyses the qualities of the women social entrepreneurs, as perceived by SHG members and the social entrepreneurs themselves.

The evolution of an SHG and the role of the social entrepreneur

SHGs and the four-stage model of team dynamics

An SHG passes through a number of stages that might be called a life-cycle. The life-cycle of an SHG based on PRADAN's experience and analysis is presented in Table 9.1.

There is in fact a fifth stage of expansion (from 19 to 36 months and beyond) where the SHG lends more for income-generating programmes rather than just for consumption needs and PRADAN is able to withdraw its support.

Based on this framework, PRADAN has developed clear strategies to promote and support SHGs through their life-cycle until the final stage in which SHGs become mature village organisations, often engaging in more than financial intermediation, and PRADAN can withdraw. Here I focus on the role of the local leaders or social entrepreneurs within the SHGs.

The life-cycle of an SHG can be compared with the stages in the formation of a team, as developed in literature on organisation behaviour and development. An important

Table 9.1: The life-cycle of an SHG (as set out by PRADAN)

Stage	Time-frame	Tasks or activities		Major milestones
		PRADAN	SHG	
1.Pre-formation	0–1 month	• Identification of area to initiate project • Selection of village-hamlets	• No SHG. The potential members attend village meetings	• In-depth understanding of the socio-economic situation, markets, natural resources, occupations and skills • Decision whether to work in the area
2.Formation	2–4 months	• Rapport building • Participatory processes to identify group • Initiate weekly meetings • Start savings and credit • Introduce systems for meetings, transactions, etc. • To encourage autonomy and proaction by SHG, PRADAN provides or promises no subsidies	• Forms into an SHG of 10–20 members • Attend weekly meetings • Identify accountant • Formulate norms and rules	• Accountant identified • Systems in place
3.Stabilisation	5–8 months	• Staff attend alternate meetings to stabilise systems	• Attend regular meetings and conduct transactions as per norms and rules set	• Office bearers identified • Bank account opened • Meetings regularised

(Contd)

(Table 9.1 Contd)

Stage	Time-frame	Tasks or activities		Major milestones
		PRADAN	SHG	
4. Growth	9–18 months	• Train the accountant • Conduct exposure visits and training events for members • Initiate inter-group linkages like cluster meetings	• Inculcate values of strict financial discipline, participation, free exchange of views, etc. • Supervise accountant • Decide on roles and responsibilities of office bearers • Open bank account	• Systems streamlined
		• Assist a group in higher-level linkages like bank finance • Strengthen cluster level meetings of representatives	• Effective utilisation of internal credit and seek external finance for larger activities	• Transactions with external financial institutions start taking place • The SHG starts participating in larger social issues in the village

model suggests there are four dominant stages in building a high-performing team (Tuckman, 1965). These stages are: forming, storming, norming and performing.

- *Forming* is about providing orientation and generating commitment and acceptance through getting acquainted, setting goals, clarifying values and visioning.
- *Storming* is about overcoming resistance and conflict and generating clarification and belonging through active listening, conflict management, flexibility and creativity.
- *Norming* is about developing communication, cohesion and cooperation and generating involvement and support through communicating, feedback, affirmation and networking.

- *Performing* is about problem-solving and generating achievement and pride through decision-making, problem-solving and rewarding.

In addition to some promotional inputs from an NGO, a successful SHG needs quality inputs from its social entrepreneurs at each stage in its life-cycle. In the formation stage, a social entrepreneur needs in particular to demonstrate her skills in social mobilisation. This stage also demands initiative and risk-taking as the community is embarking upon a new venture. In many communities who have had bitter experiences of past failures and betrayals in financial ventures the task for a social entrepreneur is further complicated (see the case of Chamudevi later as well as Chapter 8).

Once the group is formed, many new dynamics emerge. On the one hand, social issues such as leadership, trust and participation need to be resolved. On the other, the SHG also starts undertaking business functions. The group needs to take a range of decisions on these business activities: how will they ensure the security of their savings, who will be given a loan and at what interest rate, and what actions need to be taken to ensure repayment? This stage of churning, also known as storming, presents significant challenges for the social entrepreneur who has to attend to not only social but also business dimensions.

After these two stages, the SHG may be more stable, but still needs to give on-going attention and reinforcement to norms of functioning both for group members and business activities. For example, when some members decide to pursue income-generating activities for which they need loans, the social entrepreneur in such a group is faced with critical choices. A good decision can lead to a positive precedence while a miscalculation could destroy the credibility and the reputation of the SHG.

What does the fourth stage of 'performing' involve? In the context of an SHG, this stage again brings uncertainties that require risk-taking and entrepreneurial behaviour on the part of the social entrepreneur. For example, when the SHG decides to link up and access loans from a bank or microfinance organisation (see Chapter 7), the SHG moves into a totally new and complex game plan. It is not only the volume of business and the associated risks that go up as a result of such linkages. It may also affect the inter-relationships and the cohesion among group members. The skill of a social entrepreneur is to take on these challenges.

Evidence from the field

Evidence from the field supports such analysis. For example, many SHGs had experienced churning in their membership as some dissatisfied members withdrew and others joined in their place. In particular, some SHGs had stabilised only after some of the initial members withdrew because the SHG had not fulfilled their expectations. In some villages, one big SHG had been replaced by two or three SHGs structured around geographical proximity or community membership (tribal, Scheduled Caste, etc.) or both. These examples of forming, storming and norming were critical in the stabilisation of the SHGs.

Some of the older SHGs, promoted by PRADAN more than five years ago, clearly demonstrated high performance. Some groups had successfully linked themselves with a bank. For example, two SHGs in Purhara village had each borrowed Rs 100,000 from the bank. In Urma Mor village, all the Muslim women of the seven-year old SHG actively participated in its lending operations, and had accumulated savings of Rs 20,000.

Other older SHGs were struggling because PRADAN had withdrawn almost all support such as visits, attending meetings and facilitation. For example, the first group promoted by PRADAN in Titirchanch village was functioning only haphazardly; many women did not remember the name of their SHG, some were unclear about their savings.

This difference was visible even in the same village. The SHG in one hamlet was struggling to function while another SHG in another hamlet of the same village was doing good business.

It became clear that SHGs need continuous re-engineering and that the responsibility for this often falls on the shoulders of the social entrepreneurs, especially when PRADAN professionals withdraw.

Task and maintenance functions

Another framework for team dynamics argues that in any team or group two processes simultaneously evolve as members come together to achieve common objectives (Pfieffer and Jones, 1976). The task processes (what it takes to do the job) involve behaviour and actions of members that contribute to the attainment of the group's objectives. Simultaneously, the maintenance processes (what it takes to strengthen and maintain the group) ensure the upkeep of the 'climate' and 'environment' that underpin a successful team. The framework argues that members need to be proficient in both the task and the maintenance processes. Imbalance in any one of these or over-emphasis on one at the cost of the other is likely to affect the well-being of the group in the long run.

Drawing upon this framework, SHGs clearly require a skilful balance of both the task (business) and maintenance (social) processes. The purpose of forming an SHG is to engage in the business of savings and credit. This necessarily involves financial transactions, record-keeping, setting interest rates, linking up with banks, diversifying into income-generating activities and so on.

Equally important as member involvement in these financial transactions are softer (and often invisible) issues such as group norms, discipline and climate. For an SHG the maintenance processes (the social dimension) are many, including, for instance, taking note of members who remain absent, members who deviate from norms of savings and/or repayment, members who attempt to hijack the benefits of the SHG for achieving their own personal ends and so on. The social dimension becomes more complex when factors such as gender, caste and community also influence the group's proceedings.

The task and maintenance processes may become more challenging if the SHG also takes on non-financial roles, engaging in other developmental issues in the village and acting as 'an effective inter-face for the poor to deal constructively with the external world', as Narendranath put it.

The role of a social entrepreneur in such a scenario becomes demanding as she has to skilfully balance both the business and social dimensions. The fieldwork suggested that this is not always easy.

For example, Draupadididi in Mahuva Tand village had played a leading role in her SHG for over seven years, and had been elected to the General Body in Barhi block. However, her group was finding it difficult to manage its business. There were at least three loans that had not yet been repaid since the SHG took a loan from the bank. Sakunadevi in the Harijan hamlet of Pandeywar village had been successful in mobilising all the members into the SHG. They were certainly aware of their rights and felt empowered. However, the SHG was not functioning as expected. All the women had found it difficult to repay the small loans they had taken from the group. Though the group was meeting regularly, the credit activity had almost stopped.

In some groups the SHGs had become dependent on external factors, such as an accountant who recorded the financial transactions of the SHG or a PRADAN professional whose on-going facilitation was expected.

However, wherever one or more social entrepreneurs were in command of both the social and the business dimensions, the SHG functioned smoothly, and was far less dependent on PRADAN's facilitation, the availability or otherwise of an accountant, and so on. The SHG in Jogidihi village led by Hemantididi and Manjudidi, the SHG in Purhara village led by Samrididi, the SHG and irrigation management committee in Gadbutoli village where Shivbidevi and Basantidevi were active, are some of the live illustrations that support this argument. The functioning of these groups makes clear that social entrepreneurs need to demonstrate capabilities in both business and social processes, and both those in abundance.

The social entrepreneur: Challenges and rewards

Management literature has devoted significant attention to understanding the psychological profile of entrepreneurial individuals. The need for achievement motivation has been seen as the driving force for an individual to take risks and venture into new business opportunities. The rewards for such entrepreneurial behaviour are indeed monetary, but researchers have put much more emphasis on the non-tangible rewards that an entrepreneur seeks.

How does this relate to the social entrepreneurs in action in the various groups we visited? The principle question we explored was what prompts these women to take an active part in the functioning of their SHG. What are the challenges and rewards these women associate with their active involvement in their SHG? Are these women motivated by achievement motivation, or by what some researchers on social entrepreneurs have described as extension motivation?

The case of Chamudevi of Kauvakhap village

The task of mobilising a community or group for savings and credit activities can be challenging, as the following example illustrates.

Kauvakhap is a small village in Kudu block of Lohardaga district. Most of the inhabitants are tribal people belonging to the Oraon community; there are also a few Muslim households in the village. Socio-economic conditions are typical of the region: rainfed agriculture, degraded land, lack of irrigation facilities, menfolk migrating to earn wages and so on.

Chamudevi, a resident of the village, approached PRADAN in January 2001. She had heard about the SHG movement spreading in neighbouring villages, and felt that such an activity could be useful for her village also. Samir, a PRADAN professional working in the area, made a couple of visits to the village. The response of the women in the community to the proposal of initiating an SHG was quite encouraging. Chamudevi, therefore, organised a series of weekly meetings with the prospective women members. Samir attended these initial meetings and facilitated whenever needed. After this initial preparation, the group was ready to form the SHG.

A few members were encouraged to attend a cluster meeting in the adjacent village. It was hoped that this exposure would boost the confidence and morale of the new group. In March, during *jatra*, an annual gathering or 'fair' in which women from all the SHGs in Lohardaga district participate, about 15 women from Kauvakhap were also invited. These women went to Lohardaga town about 15 km away in a jeep provided by PRADAN. A day-long training programme was organised at which Chamudevi and two of her colleagues from the village learnt basic concepts of accounting and record-keeping. Members also purchased a cashbook and individual passbooks.

Judging by the progress of the group, Samir thought that the group was now ready to take on further activities and that it no longer required regular visits and facilitation inputs from PRADAN.

We visited the group on Friday (18 May 2001) around two in the afternoon. This was the time scheduled for their weekly meeting. As expected, about 10 women had assembled under the tree near the village. After initial greetings and introductions, Samir asked how the group was doing, but there was complete silence. It was also clear that members did not have their passbooks with them. The register (cashbook) was not being used either. Instead, an old register was brought for the meeting.

Something was not working in the group and the women with whom Samir had established a good rapport were not forthcoming. With great persuasion, Samir requested the women to express what was on their minds. Slowly, one by one, women started sharing their concerns.

One member said that the group would decide later whether they wanted their group to go the 'PRADAN way' or the 'Aanganwadi' type. (Aanganwadi is a government-initiated scheme for supplementing the nutritional needs of children in the age-group from 2 to 6. The community organiser for Aanganwadi is also given responsibility for promoting new SHGs in the area.)

Some members shared their experience that after their visit to the *jatra*, a few men from the village abused them. The menfolk were agitated because apparently the women had not taken their 'permission' to visit the *jatra*. At this point, Samir pointed out that in fact a few women had boarded the jeep in front of their respective houses and, in some cases, their husbands had actually helped them to board.

Other women then said that some men were propagating rumours that outsiders would run away with their hard-earned money. Samir again patiently brought to their notice that the cash-box, the key to the cash-box and the pass-books and register were with them and nowhere else.

At this stage, another woman, Shantidevi, who was a little more articulate in her ideas, said that similar activities in the past had failed. She had taken responsibility for promoting and organising an SHG in the past. However, that attempt had failed and she had had to bear the brunt of public criticism. Villagers accused her of siphoning off money. So this time she would not take the lead and would go by the consensus of the group. It was becoming evident in the meeting that Shantidevi was affecting the group with her logic and subtle influence.

Samir then asked each and every woman to speak for herself whether she wanted to be in the group and whether she felt the need for continuing the SHG. Everyone except Shantidevi spoke in the affirmative. All of them wanted the SHG to continue and to develop further. Shantidevi was polite yet diplomatic. She said that she would follow whatever the group thought appropriate.

In further discussion it also became clear that lending had commenced in the group. The first loan of Rs 200 was taken by a woman whose husband needed it for medical treatment. The women also reviewed the two attempts to promote an SHG in the village in the past that had failed. The group resolved to be extra diligent about record-keeping and other functions.

In spite of all the preparations in the initial meetings and the subsequent inputs from PRADAN, it appeared that the group had come full-circle back to the beginning. Samir suggested to the group that they should not decide in haste to wind up the functioning of the group. If required, they should not hesitate to call him again for their next scheduled meeting on Friday next week. The women could also invite their menfolk to that meeting so that whatever apprehensions they had could be discussed in an open and transparent manner.

The meeting ended on this note and the women who had gathered continued for another hour depositing their savings of Rs 5 or 10. One member requested a loan of Rs 400 to purchase paddy, arguing that paddy prices go up by at least Rs 2 to 3 a kilo during the rainy season. And where was Chamudevi? We were told that she chose to remain absent from the meeting as she felt upset and hurt about these developments. Probably she also felt bad because it was at her initiative and request that PRADAN had facilitated the forming of the SHG. We left the village without meeting Chamudevi.

The challenges for a social entrepreneur

A detailed description of the events that took place in Kauvakhap suggests the manifold challenges that may confront a social entrepreneur forming an SHG. Building credibility for herself may itself be an important task, which may be helped by education, social standing or personal qualities such as honesty and integrity.

However, it is more daunting to build faith in the rationale and system of an SHG. The concept of SHGs is not new to village communities in India. It is the earlier failures and bad experiences of fraud, theft and malpractice in similar programmes that make the task of the social entrepreneur so difficult. How can the new system be fool-proof and tamper-free? Will it go the same way as earlier promises of other agencies and individuals had gone? The social entrepreneur needs to build the community's confidence in the face of such doubts lurking in everybody's minds. It may be relatively easy to be first in the field. It is more challenging to enter the field when other attempts have miserably failed. This is where the support of a trusted external agency already working in the area can prove so vital in inspiring confidence, as also seen in Chapter 8 on SHGs in urban slums.

Another dimension of the challenge is to manage processes both in and outside of the group. There are women and men in and outside the group that need to be convinced. Some of them may directly oppose the initiation of such a venture, others, like Shantidevi, through her lukewarm responses, can hamper the progress of the group.

As we were returning from Kauvakhap, a woman from the group joined us in the jeep for some distance. She alleged that Shantidevi had herself misutilised the money in one such earlier scheme and that her son was found stealing goods. If true, Shantidevi may have been concerned about a new group in the village that she could not control. If not true, it shows the depth of suspicion and lack of trust that can undermine a group.

For Chamudevi and other such social entrepreneurs, the battle is fought on both fronts: she has to influence and convince not only the women members of her group but also the larger community of men and women.

Another challenge is to promote a sound alternative in the midst of an environment that blatantly encourages populist and unsustainable operations. In Kauvakhap, the group probably thought of organising themselves through the government's Aanganwadi scheme (and not through PRADAN) because of expectations that the group would receive 'free gifts' of a *dholi* (a musical instrument), a *duri* (a carpet for meetings) and so on. Some women shared these thoughts in the meeting. It was also thought that the association with Aanganwadi would enable the village to get a *talab* (tank) from the government. Both the promotional agency and the local social entrepreneur who operate in such an environment have to convince group members on issues like sustainability, repayment, discipline, capacity-building, etc. This is swimming against the current!

Perhaps the biggest challenge in the work of a social entrepreneur is to keep going amidst adversity. This is easier said than done, especially in the context of a rural environment. Operationally, it means to sustain her own and the group's morale week after week after week when abuse and criticism, and lack of participation, cooperation and encouragement are amply present.

The challenge of continuity is indeed a tough one. On the way back from the village, we were discussing how many activities we as professionals have done voluntarily and continuously week after week in the last few years. We could not think of any! And yet this is what many of the social entrepreneurs mobilising SHGs keep doing.

The challenges faced by a social entrepreneur at the beginning of forming an SHG may be quite different from those at a later stage. For instance, in Kauvakhap the initial tasks for Chamudevi were to build credibility for the activity by convincing not only the women but also other stakeholders in the community. The challenges will change once the group matures, stabilises and gets into more advanced levels of financial transactions.

At such a stage, maybe two years after start-up, the social entrepreneur will encounter other challenges. For instance, if there is a possibility of a default or if a particular member who has taken a large loan is not following her repayment schedule and such behaviour starts affecting the performance of the group, the task for the social entrepreneur is to persuade and influence the behaviour of a recalcitrant member. The challenges will also be very different when the group decides to link itself to a bank.

What makes social entrepreneurs tick?
The social rewards

In all our meetings with SHGs in Hazaribag and Lohardaga, we deliberately provoked the key promoters and leaders of the SHGs by asking a standard question: 'In spite of being aware of the thankless job as a leader of the SHG, why do you continue to take up the responsibility of running and managing your group?' Based on the responses, I have drawn out certain conclusions. These are by no means the final words on the issue. However, it is important to debate them to achieve deeper insights into social entrepreneurs in general and the women leaders of SHGs in particular.

I begin with the social rewards. Invariably, all the women interviewed said they 'felt good' and 'happy' to take up the responsibilities of organising and managing their SHG. What specifically did they mean?

Initially, not all of the women had consciously thought about taking up these responsibilities. All of them were a little better off in terms of education compared to other women in the community. Some of them had greater exposure to the world outside the village, perhaps again through education.

For example, Kalavatidevi from Salagi village stayed in a hostel in Lohardaga town for her studies up to Class X (matriculation). Her father worked in a bauxite manufacturing company. Thedodidi from Saliya Kasitarn village went to school up to Class V. Both she and her sister Zibi are now leading SHGs in their respective villages. As a result of being educated, these women had been able to earn the respect and trust of the community, which made them 'feel good'. Through their role in the SHG, the community even looked to them as leaders and opinion-makers.

The women interviewed also mentioned that they were happy to take on the role of leading an SHG, though a difficult one, because they could use their expertise to improve their community. Jasvadevi from the Harijan hamlet in Jogidihi village was a member of the SHG led by Hemantididi and Manjudidi in the main village. Experiencing the functioning of this group and recognising the strength of such activities, she realised that such an intervention was required for her own people too. She said,

> Our people need SHGs the most. I saw our hamlet going deep into the red as a result of loans that were taken from the market. Menfolk were spending money on drinking and there were no savings. It is when seeing and realising this that I said I will promote a new SHG in my small hamlet.

Today she is happy and proud to say that her group has been functioning well. She continues to be a member of the SHG in the main village as well as leading the SHG in her own hamlet.

Thus both the recognition of their role by the larger village community and their involvement in developmental activities to improve their community were seen as a reward and a point of satisfaction.

This recognition and involvement can be seen in specific events. For example, Draupadidi of Mahuva Tand village recounted in great detail her participation in and contribution to the *gram sabha* (a meeting of all villagers). Earlier, no one bothered to consult the women. However, as a result of the strength their SHG has achieved, they are now consulted by the *gram sevak* (a government functionary in the village).

Draupadidi and three other women from the SHG in fact spoke in the *gram sabha*. They articulated their demands for ration cards for families below the poverty line, for pensions to widows and allowances for mothers who had one daughter. Draupadidi also enquired in the meeting about other developmental activities such as the construction of roads and the deepening of wells. As she narrated all these details, we could clearly see in her eyes a unique sense of satisfaction, confidence and self-expression, in other words, empowerment.

Another incident from Mayapur village is worth recounting. After our meeting with the women in the SHG, the two key leaders Satyadevi and Parvatidevi requested a lift in our vehicle to the main road, about 2 km from the village. We checked with them whether they had any specific work to do, and they said they wanted to visit some shops on the main road for buying food-grain. However, they also said that they wanted a ride in the jeep so that upper caste people of the village who had shops on the road could see them travelling in a vehicle with PRADAN professionals.

It was a simple five-minute ride. But on reflection, one can see what such a ride can mean to them. Later, the PRADAN professionals shared the struggles these two women had gone through, how the villagers had abused them in the past and how these women had gained confidence and self-assertion over a period of time. The jeep ride illustrates some of the 'social rewards' for poor and low-caste women of being a key member of an SHG in the village.

The financial rewards

While it was important to appreciate the social rewards such as satisfaction, recognition, self-esteem and confidence that a social entrepreneur receives from the community, we also explored any financial rewards they might receive.

In our meetings with SHGs, we asked the group to share information on the amount of loans taken by members, the frequency and size of loans, the on-lending of loans taken from a bank, and, in those villages with lift-irrigation schemes, the distribution of water (through the managed sale of coupons by the irrigation management committee). Here are four examples from among women social entrepreneurs leading the SHGs:

(1) I have already mentioned Draupadidi as a leader of the SHG in Mahuva Tand village. The SHG had linked up with the bank and taken a bank loan of Rs 20,000. Draupadidi took a loan of Rs 10,000 from the SHG after the linkage with the bank so that she could do business in selling fertilisers.

(2) Samrididi in Purhara village played a leading role in the SHGs in her village, as well as in the lift-irrigation management committee. There are three women SHGs in the village. Two of the groups had successful bank linkages. In both cases the first bank loans of Rs 25,000 each were repaid. Of the second repeat loans taken from the bank, Samrididi had taken a loan of Rs 50,000 to purchase a second-hand truck that her son drove. She also mentioned that she had purchased the largest number of coupons from the irrigation management committee.

(3) Bantididi had run the SHG in her village (Tiko Banda Toli) for the last three years. She took the first loan of Rs 200 from the SHG, and also had the largest outstanding loan of Rs 2,000 taken for medical treatment for members of her family.

(4) Kalavatidevi in Salagi village (who had been educated up to Class X in Lohardaga town) ran a group that was quite autonomous. The group had twice taken a loan from PRADAN's revolving fund for SHGs, and both loans were repaid. Kalavatidevi had taken a loan from the SHG for a marriage function in her family, and she hoped to repay it when she received money due to her from an insurance company.

It appeared to us that there were legitimate financial rewards associated with taking on the role of social entrepreneur in a women's SHG. We found that in most of the groups that we visited, the social entrepreneurs had been taking a large share of the associated benefits. Whenever an SHG had taken a loan from the bank, a significant proportion of the loan amount was on-lent to key social entrepreneurs and leaders in the group. They were also usually the largest buyers of coupons for water in those villages with lift-irrigation schemes.

I do not intend to pass any value judgement nor do I want to be critical and biased. While Mathew Titus in Chapter 8 cites examples where individuals had clearly captured most of the benefits from a cluster of SHGs for themselves or other family members, some financial rewards seem legitimate, especially when they do not undermine the functioning of the group.

One hypothesis that could be tested is that the distribution of the benefits reflects the risks taken by the social entrepreneurs in leading the SHG. I have already cited cases where the failure of an SHG brings reproach and rumours of misutilising funds. The responsibilities only increase when an SHG takes a bank loan, for example. The social entrepreneur may therefore derive legitimate benefits by accessing her claims on a priority basis in return for the additional responsibilities she takes on.

These are some of the financial rewards social entrepreneurs derive from tak]ing on a leadership role, and I hypothesise that a combination of the kind of social and financial rewards set out above continues to make them tick, year after year, in difficult situations.

Qualities of a social entrepreneur

During the fieldwork, we asked members of the SHGs a hypothetical question. If they were to select a woman among themselves to form new SHGs in neighbouring areas, who should be given that responsibility? We also asked them who was capable of shouldering the responsibility and what qualities made that person capable. In most of these meetings, the social entrepreneurs in that particular group were also present and contributed to the discussions.

Members attached a great deal of importance to a woman 'being educated'. For most members who are illiterate, a woman who had attended even some primary education classes made sense as a potential leader. In an environment where education seems to be a luxury for women, leadership roles therefore naturally come to a woman who is more qualified than others. Levels of education among SHG leaders we met ranged from Class III or IV to X (matriculation) and, in a rare case, graduation. The community looked upon them as a guide and friend in matters of money and business.

In addition to education, another basic criterion that was constantly referred to was the ability of a woman 'to talk' ('bolnewali chahiye'). We probed this aspect in greater detail and realised that it was not just about talking itself. The quality meant much more than this to women who had never interacted with an outsider. We heard stories in different villages about how they used to run away when any outsider came to their village. Many women also told us how difficult they found it to introduce themselves in a meeting. Some even now found it difficult to state their full name in front of everyone in a meeting. Thus this quality was not just about talking, but also captures a sense of confidence and belief that only a few women had. Those who had these qualities were encouraged by others to take a lead.

Managing consensus was seen as another important qualification for a social entrepreneur. Women described this characteristic in their own ways, for example, talking of a woman who led a joint family, one who had a sweet tongue, one who managed her household efficiently, one who had understanding and empathy for others. These qualities made her acceptable to the community at large. In other words, women expected the social entrepreneur to prove herself in her own family environment before stepping out to take on larger responsibility. A person who enjoyed the trust of everyone was seen as a natural choice to take up the responsibility of leading an SHG in the village.

Given household responsibilities, women were also quite practical about the ability of the social entrepreneur to take time out for the group. They were clear that not everyone could do this. A leading role within an SHG required a woman to have 'free' or 'extra' time away from their household chores. This is not easy in a rural environment. In one meeting, women narrated how they had to take turns to manage the household of Draupadidi, the SHG leader in Mahuva Tand village, when she had gone for three days of training and meetings organised by PRADAN. The time factor was thus a very important consideration for them.

Social entrepreneurs are the women who take a lead in community activities. Taking initiative and venturing into the unknown were thus important criteria that separated the leaders from other members of the SHGs. The women had their own ways of illustrating this. For example, Samrididi, the SHG leader from Purhara, explained, 'You are asking us who should qualify as a member of the General Body' (GB, the apex body or federation of SHGs in Barhi block in Hazaribag).

Do you plough a field with an old ox? This old ox will need to be whipped time and again; it will get bogged down in mud while ploughing. We don't need such an ox for the GB! If I go to the GB and sit quietly as if my tongue is locked, what is the use of attending the GB? I must talk, I must fight for my poor women members. If I sit in a meeting and people like you say one hundred and one new things, I must be capable of comprehending at least 10 such ideas. When we formed our group, we had to listen more than once to criticism and taunting from members of the upper-caste community. Male members used to say, don't behave like a bird that sleeps at night with its legs up thinking that it is holding the sky in its legs. We used to listen and ignore it. Now our SHG has become stronger, so the taunting has stopped.

Initiative and risk-taking may also be associated with empathy for the community and the need to exert oneself to do something for the community. Above I quoted Jasvadevi in Jogidihi village who saw a group functioning successfully in the main village and realised the need to initiate the same activity in her Harijan hamlet. She felt that her community badly needed such an intervention.

In general of course, leadership capabilities, trust and reliability were seen as the important characteristics of a social entrepreneur. What came out clearly through the stories women told was the challenge for the social entrepreneur to take everybody along with her. In Jogidihi, where the SHG in the main village had been functioning for over eight years and was running very well, the women members even went to the extent of saying that they had 'made' their leaders, Hemantididi and Manjudidi, and that the success of these two was the result of the collective support they derive from all members of the group.

The belief in the social entrepreneur's fair play and sense of justice was visible in a comment made by a group member in this village. 'Even if Hemantididi gives me a slap, I will take it sportingly because I know she wouldn't take such a drastic step unless I made some serious mistake.' Leaders and social entrepreneurs therefore command trust and respect.

Institutionalising social entrepreneurship: can it be done?

Is it possible to train individuals to take up the role of a social entrepreneur? PRADAN worked with two different approaches towards the SHG leaders in Jharkhand. In the first approach, in Lohardaga, PRADAN facilitators helped the groups designate leaders, who were then rotated consciously every year (for example, different members would attend cluster meetings, there would be a new secretary of the group each year). The rationale was that such rotation would provide enough space for new leadership to emerge. This was in a way an attempt to engineer social processes. In the second approach, in Hazaribag, PRADAN facilitated the emergence of leaders within a group and these leaders then took over responsibility for running the group.

On the basis of my observations, I believe that wherever the leadership of groups rotated by design, the groups in fact continued to be led by the main social entrepreneurs. In other words, only a few women took responsibility whether they were formally designated as leaders or not. Thus, while everyone may have abilities and competencies to take up leadership positions within the group, only a few may demonstrate these in large measure.

PRADAN's experience of Community-based Group Promoters

With its vast geographic spread and innumerable challenges India needs hundreds and thousands of social entrepreneurs at the grassroots. How can small and successful initiatives in one area be replicated for greater impact and reach? Any NGO that had successfully mobilised a few hundred SHGs in a particular block, would start thinking of scaling up its efforts.

The PRADAN team in Lohardaga experimented with one such initiative during 1999–2000. The initiative was called Community-based Group Promoters (CBGPs). This initiative was conceived and implemented as an alternative strategy for promoting more SHGs in a wider geographical area, in the hope that more SHGs could be formed in less time.

A group of five women and three men were informally selected. These Promoters were selected on the basis of their involvement, for at least one or two years, in a successful SHG. They were either directly associated with SHGs (women) or were supporting them in maintaining accounts (men). They were supposed to have both accounting and organising skills, and to be conversant with group dynamics. All of them were from the local community and had an educational background varying from Class VI to X. They were articulate and vocal, and had some capacity in convincing and communicating with others. They also had some free time that they could use for the formation of new SHGs.

To start the initiative, PRADAN conducted a one-day training event for these Promoters. In the meeting, through participative methodologies, potential areas (villages or hamlets) for forming new SHGs were identified, and geographical boundaries set. Generally, it was expected that a Promoter would work in villages or hamlets about 3 to 4 km from her/his place, a distance that could be covered on foot or bicycle. It was expected that each Promoter would be able to form and nurture about five to seven SHGs in a year.

At the meeting they also set indicators for measuring the performance of the Promoters, who were to be compensated with an honorarium that was linked to the performance indicators. The indicators were finalised for a year and performance assessed at the end of the third, sixth and twelfth months.

At the end of three months, for example, a group would have 10 to 20 members who had met 10 times sitting in a circle (to encourage equality) and could all say the name of their group. Member savings would be at least Rs 20 per member per month. Lending would have started, and interest payments on loans be regular. An accountant would have been selected and cash and passbook training would have started. For this, the Promoter would get Rs 200 a group.

The Promoter would get a further Rs 250 for each group that reached similar targets for the first six months, and another Rs 500 for each group that reached the targets for the first year. The latter included at least 45 meetings held, one round of dividends distributed, a bank account opened, the process for taking a bank loan at least initiated and a stable accountant writing perfect accounts, as well as meeting all the indicators for the first three and six month periods.

Initially, in the first six months, the performance of the Promoters was very positive. As they were from the same community, they were able to build a rapport almost immediately. Potential members of SHGs had more faith and trust in them as they shared their experiences of having been a member or supporter of a successful SHG in the neighbouring village or hamlet.

However, difficulties arose especially after the first six months. The Promoters did not have the necessary facilitation and capacity-building skills. For instance, the Promoters would correct an accounting mistake at a meeting themselves rather than explaining the mistake to the accountant who was writing the accounts and getting him to make the correction. The Promoters also found it difficult to handle the more complex tasks of higher-order transactions like the distribution of dividends. Thus PRADAN sometimes had to follow up later with the group when a Promoter did not have sufficient skills to deal with particular situations. Some of the Promoters also went about their work in a more restrictive manner, for example, focusing on collecting savings and lending, rather than being able to see the bigger picture of an SHG, its needs, its ability to empower and so on.

Some Promoters also could not understand the logic of honoraria being linked with the performance indicators. For instance, one of them thought that though the group was formed nine months ago, she was compensated for six month's work only.

As a result of these difficulties, PRADAN discontinued the scheme half way through. PRADAN feels that the CBGPs could have been more effective had they received further training and inputs beyond informal discussion and monitoring, and if PRADAN professionals had sometimes accompanied them to group meetings.

While this initiative was discontinued, the innovation involved is important. It attempted to build local capabilities that could spread the SHG movement in an area where the local capacities of tribal communities are emerging, but most development indicators, such as literacy, poverty and infrastructure, are very low.

The closure of the scheme also indicates limitations that would need to be addressed through additional training inputs. It may also have proved more effective to develop a cadre of professionals with higher educational backgrounds, say among any college graduates from the community.

BASIX has also sought to develop what they call microfinance agents (see Box 4.1 in Chapter 4). These are indeed often more educated than PRADAN's CBGPs, and over 300 groups have been formed under the programme, of which 150 have graduated beyond their start-up phase and 110 received loans from BASIX.

Conclusion

By 2008 at the latest India is expected to have 1 million SHGs with 17 million members, almost entirely women. All the three chapters on SHGs in this part of the book, as well as Chapter 5, suggest that SHGs are much more than just financial mechanisms for extending financial services to the poor. While they perform this function, SHGs are autonomous organisations that may have strong impacts on their members that go well beyond access to financial services.

As autonomous organisations they share the challenges and dynamics of other small organisations. For example, forming new groups requires significant energy, and the necessary group processes (in addition to financial tasks) cannot be bypassed. Likewise, if an SHG is not able to maintain itself as a well-functioning group, the financial intermediation it performs will collapse.

Governments, donors, policy-makers and resource-providers need to be aware of the dynamics involved in these small organisations. In their enthusiasm to promote and support a large number of SHGs and their anxiety to meet targets, they run the risk of turning these groups into 'state-helped groups', in the process destroying their very foundation of self-help and autonomy.

As more than financial organisations, SHGs can, at best, support better or new livelihoods for their members; empower them, including thousands and potentially millions of poor women; and form a major movement of grassroots democratic organisations.

This chapter has reviewed the role, qualities, challenges and rewards for the women leading SHGs in their respective villages. It is clear that their role is critical for SHGs to perform their task of delivering financial services to poor people, for maintaining and sustaining what are often fragile and vulnerable groups, and for ensuring they have wider impacts of economic development and democratic empowerment.

By approaching SHGs from a new angle, of social entrepreneurship, this chapter has taken a fresh look at what such leadership involves. It has revealed some of the challenges, in some cases perhaps realities, that underpin the leadership of SHGs that are emerging all over the country. For example, Draupadididi in Mahuva Tand village may be a very articulate and vocal leader, but her SHG was struggling, with three loans being behind in their repayments. A number of the groups had had long-standing leaders, even though many NGOs, including PRADAN and MYRADA, often encourage the rotation of leadership (MYRADA, 2000: 125–28) as an essential democratic feature of the group.

Likewise, the insights gained from the experience of the CBGPs suggest that local social entrepreneurs cannot easily take on the promotional role of an NGO which is so often essential for the emergence of well functioning groups. The promotional role requires more professional inputs, which are likely to demand higher educational and skill levels.

Nevertheless, already many women leaders are emerging from SHGs, fighting for their rights, promoting broader development in their villages or communities, and helping women to engage in democratic processes. A small number have already been elected to serve on their local *panchayati raj* institutions (local councils) (see the section on empowerment in Chapter 7).

Moreover, many of the organisations that promote SHGs in India are looking for more effective and cost-efficient ways to do so, and potential solutions are beginning to emerge from the experimentation by BASIX, PRADAN and others.

However, the main institutional challenges, which remain largely unanswered at present, are threefold:

1. How to support existing leaders and social entrepreneurs and nurture new ones; at least one million will be required!
2. How to ensure that SHGs remain autonomous and are not captured by political and bureaucratic interests pursuing votes or targets. Will the emerging movement of SHGs be any better at preventing this than previous movements, such as cooperatives?
3. How to support the SHG movement so that it can go beyond financial-service provision to support the development of a large number of livelihoods among SHG members. Some would argue this is inappropriate for such small organisations. Others, including PRADAN, would say it is essential given the livelihoods India needs to generate, not least for women.

Note

1. I am grateful to the professionals in the PRADAN offices in Ranchi, Barhi and Lohardaga in the state of Jharkhand, especially for the valuable interactions I had with Soumen, Sukanto, Ajay Kumar, Avijeet, Ramkishore, Dhiraj, Satish, Aparna, Meenakshi, Abdus, Samir, Vijay, Pavan and Rajnikant. I am thankful to all of them for managing the field-visits professionally and yet with modesty.

Chapter 10

Sustainability and development: Evaluating the performance of Indian micro-finance

Sanjay Sinha and Frances Sinha

The introduction to this book draws attention to the fact that most Indian practitioners of micro-finance have always worked from the assumption that developmental objectives need to be combined with financial sustainability. It also acknowledges that providing financial services to the millions of poor people in developing countries needs mass intermediation and that this can only be achieved through sustainability. Since all organisations must cope with changes in their operating conditions over time, organisational sustainability is not only important, but is an essential precondition for long-term financial sustainability.

At the same time, no account of micro-finance practice in India is complete without also considering the development agendas of the organisations providing or facilitating micro-financial services. These agendas include poverty alleviation at their core but also encompass livelihood promotion, empowerment (particularly of women), building people's organisations and changing the institutional environment.

This chapter seeks to address these different dimensions by bringing together analysis of the performance of the Indian micro-finance sector in terms of financial and organisational sustainability and of the available evidence on micro-finance organisations (MFOs) fulfilling their developmental agendas.

The first part of the chapter sets out the results on sustainability emerging from the rating of MFOs in India ('MFOs' in this context refers to organisations involved directly in the provision of financial services). As described in Box 10.1, the rating of MFOs is an innovative service introduced for the first time in late 1998 by Micro-Credit Ratings International Limited (M-CRIL), an organisation established by us for this purpose. It has, virtually for the first time in the world, enabled a systematic, detailed and standardised assessment of the performance of a large number of MFOs.

The latter part of the chapter examines the evidence available on the success of micro-finance in relation to wider developmental agendas. It discusses the challenges of assessment beyond the financial and organisational dimensions of providing micro-financial services, explores new trends in approaches to impact assessment and describes two current initiatives which build on these trends.

Box 10.1: Micro-Credit Ratings International Limited (M-CRIL)

An innovative organisational mechanism for Asian micro-finance

The issue of sustainability has become particularly important in micro-finance, not least in India, in recent years. This has happened as micro-finance portfolios have started to shift from being almost exclusively donor-funded to be significantly financed through debt. Loan funds are sourced increasingly from apex-level non-governmental organisations (NGOs), development banks and even, in a few cases, from commercial banks. Prominent amongst the organisations lending to micro-finance organisations (MFOs) in South Asia are the Palli Karma Sahayak Foundation (PKSF) and Sonali Bank in Bangladesh, the Pakistan Poverty Alleviation Fund, Friends of Women's World Banking-India (FWWB), and the Small Industries Development Bank of India (SIDBI). The encouraging experience of these organisations in revolving wholesale funds for micro-finance has led to growing interest in this activity, to more apex-level NGOs operating as wholesale lenders and to the involvement of banking organisations.

Since lending activity inevitably generates concerns about the borrower's cash-flows, viability and sustainability, the availability of skills for MFO appraisal and risk-analysis has, increasingly, become an issue. The response of the apex NGOs wholesaling development funds in micro-finance has been to attempt to develop the skills internally. Banks with large portfolios but relatively miniscule outstandings to the micro-finance sector have been more reluctant to undertake appraisals as purely internal exercises. There are two reasons for this. First, as custodians of commercial rather than development funds, they need a quality of risk-analysis that is more sophisticated than is customary in the development sector, at least in South Asia. Second, it is difficult for a bank with a loan-portfolio worth a billion dollars or more, invested in a diverse range of industrial and agricultural activities, to persuade many of its staff to specialise in MFO appraisals when the micro-finance portfolio is likely to be no larger than US$10–20 million in the immediate future. Yet, the potential for micro-finance lending in India alone is estimated to be in the range of US$6–8 billion if only the substantial (and liquid) resources of the banking system could be channelled in its direction.

Thus, the micro-finance funding situation in the region can be characterised as one of information asymmetry between banks that have funds but not the skills and experience to understand micro-finance operations, on the one hand, and MFOs that have a high demand for funds but many of which have doubtful records on issues like sustainability and viability. It is in this context that EDA Rural Systems Private Limited, an organisation with the reputation of a highly professional and competent provider of technical services to the development sector in South Asia, decided to develop a service for the credit rating of MFOs.

After around 18 months of research and field-testing, a credit-rating service for MFOs was introduced in South Asia, almost for the first time globally, by Micro-Credit Ratings International Limited (M-CRIL), a subsidiary company established by EDA Rural Systems specifically for this purpose.

In the three years since the launch of its credit-rating service in late 1998, M-CRIL has built up a specialised team for rating consisting of seven professionals. It has an active board of directors comprising professionals and academics with an intimate knowledge and experience of Asian micro-finance, and also uses the services of professionals as part of its Rating Committee to provide independent oversight of the ratings undertaken by the organisation. This vetting mechanism has served to ensure that no issues of prejudice, conflicts of interest or sins of omission arise to cloud the judgements made

(Contd)

(Box 10.1 Contd)

by M-CRIL's team. As a result, M-CRIL's MFO rating-service is increasingly accepted in the region as a highly reliable assessment of MFO credit-worthiness.

Until September 2001, M-CRIL had undertaken ratings of around 90 MFOs in South and South-East Asia. The ratings, based on intensive visits to MFO head-offices and clients in the field, have provided the detailed, independently verified information on MFO operations that financial investors need to make judgements on credit-worthiness. The opinions of M-CRIL as a professional organisation specialising in assessing the capacity of MFOs have served as a key factor in supplementing these judgements. In doing so, M-CRIL's innovative service has greatly accelerated the rate at which wholesale lending has emerged as a means of funding MFOs, particularly in India.

Lessons on sustainability from the rating experience

The M-CRIL database sample

Until the end of November 2000, some two years after its launch, M-CRIL had completed 53 rating assignments. Of these, one was a July 2000 update of a large Indian MFO first rated in March 1999 and another was the rating of an on-lender with many of its borrowers already included in the sample. At the end of November 2000, M-CRIL's database therefore contained information on 51 MFOs in the region. While the cross-sectional data for the 51 organisations covered by this analysis does not relate to a fixed point of time, it does serve the purpose of providing a broad picture of microfinance in the region as seen through M-CRIL's rating activity.

The 51 MFOs rated by M-CRIL included 44 MFOs in India, four in Nepal and three in Bangladesh. This discussion focuses on the information available for the Indian MFOs, although much of the data incorporates information from the entire database. These MFOs have an average age of just six years (although a few are over 20 years old) and follow different models of delivering micro-financial services. For the purpose of analysing the information in the database the following typology has been used for the sample MFOs.

(1) Pure Grameen-Bank type: Those following the model developed by the Grameen Bank of Bangladesh which essentially lends to individuals, but all borrowers are members of groups within which peer-pressure is a major factor in ensuring repayment. Collecting loans takes place at meetings of sets of seven to 10 groups, while disbursement is mostly from the branch-office and is made to clients as individuals (for more details, see Chapter 7).

(2) Individual-banking programmes (IBPs) where the relationship with clients is either fully individual or via joint-liability groups. The loan officer undertakes collection individually at the client's doorstep but disbursement is from the branch-office. These include cooperative societies and cooperative banks (such as the Self-employed Women's Association [SEWA] Bank described in Chapter 3) as MFOs as well as organisations that undertake predominantly individual lending through joint-liability groups (such as BASIX described in Chapter 4). It is a diverse category and performance issues here therefore need to be analysed carefully.

(3) Micro-finance organisations promoting and supporting self-help groups (SHGs, which function as informal village funds with support from the MFO). Here, SHGs borrow from the MFO and on-lend these external funds as well as revolve the savings of members amongst themselves. Whilst this is, in theory, the most economical of the micro-finance methodologies, in practice, the substantial capacity-building effort needed to ensure that SHGs function well (see Chapter 8) is very costly in the short to medium term. Further, the SHG methodology is predominantly used by MFOs with much wider development agendas, including both a strong focus on poverty alleviation and on building civil society, and this adds to the capacity-building effort required (see Chapter 5).

As described in Chapter 7, the major involvement by commercial banks in Indian micro-finance is through the SHG–bank linkage programme pioneered by the NGO MYRADA, and promoted by the National Bank for Agriculture and Rural Development (NABARD). This programme entails direct lending by banks to SHGs without financial intermediation by MFOs.

Some of the largest and best known NGOs in the country, such as MYRADA and PRADAN, have therefore focused on the promotion of SHGs as part of the linking programme but have specifically avoided becoming involved in financial intermediation. These NGOs have emphasised the civil society objective of ensuring that the banking system fulfils its social responsibility of providing financial services to poor people. Their strategy has, therefore, been to promote SHGs as autonomous local groups with self-governance capabilities that can act as local intermediaries for the financial services provided by the banking system.

Since the rating of thousands of SHGs by a single organisation is not possible at economically practical rates, M-CRIL's ratings have not covered them, and the SHG–bank linkage programme does not figure in this discussion. Even for MFOs working as financial intermediaries channelling funds to SHGs, M-CRIL's analysis covers the financial transactions conducted by the MFO as an intermediary rather than the sum of the financial transactions conducted by the members of the SHGs it serves. This is because most MFOs do not monitor SHG-level transactions that are not covered by funds intermediated by them. Any attempt by M-CRIL to include them in the analysis would, therefore, require an uneconomical, time-consuming effort with only a small bearing on the credit-worthiness of the MFO as an intermediary. To this extent, it is apparent that this analysis cannot fully reflect the financial services becoming available to members of SHGs as a result of the MFOs serving them.

Based on the above typology, Table 10.1 provides the coverage of MFOs in M-CRIL's database sample.

M-CRIL's rating incorporates a weighted scoring of key indicators on governance, management systems and financial aspects of an MFO's functioning. Based on this, at the time of assessment, only nine of the 51 sample organisations were able to reach the levels of performance (α or $\alpha+$ grades awarded by M-CRIL) to classify as highly credit-worthy, another

Table 10.1: MFOs rated by M-CRIL up to November 2000

Type of programme	Typology	No. of MFOs	Members	Active clients
Grameen Bank model	Grameen	10	212,000	150,000
Individual banking programmes	IBPs	10	139,000	67,000
Programmes working with self-help groups	SHG programmes	31	345,000	83,000
Total		**51**	**696,000**	**300,000**

22 were moderately credit-worthy (α – or β + grades), nine were marginal (β) and the remaining 11 were not credit-worthy.

Outreach: Grameen MFOs are dominant but total loans outstanding to clients are small

The outreach of the 51 sample MFOs is to some 700,000 people, although only 300,000 of these are borrowers from the MFOs. Others are all savers with MFOs, although some may also be borrowers from SHGs. The MFOs' total loans outstanding to client members amount to just US$23.7 million (see Table 10.2), a very small amount compared to the potential. Within the sample, the distribution is highly skewed; the best 10 MFOs of the sample in terms of performance (called Top 10 by M-CRIL)—also broadly but not invariably the largest—account for 64 per cent of this portfolio.

By model, the Grameen MFOs are dominant and account for nearly 50 per cent of the outstanding portfolio. Though this is partly on account of three relatively large Grameen programmes rated outside India, there are two or three fast growing Grameen programmes within India as well. Individual-banking programmes and mature SHG programmes (more than seven years old) in the sample each account for 22 per cent of the total portfolio.

Among MFOs in India, the number of new MFOs using the SHG model is quite substantial. This number should far exceed the 18 maturing organisations (three to seven years old) that make up a substantial part of the sample but, inevitably,

Table 10.2: M-CRIL sample totals

	M-CRIL		
	Full sample	India	Top 10
Sample size: number of MFOs	51	44	10
Membership: number of members	696,000	520,000	304,000
Loans outstanding: Rs crore	109.0	70.4	69.4
US$ million	23.7	15.3	15.1
Savings: Rs crore	56.7	46.0	35.8
US$ million	12.3	10.0	7.8
Staff: number	3,451	2,272	1,532
Cumulative disbursements:			
Rs crore	287.7	166.3	195.0
US$ million	62.5	36.2	42.4

most new organisations are not seen as mature enough to justify the cost of rating them. As a result, there are only five new MFOs in the sample and the remaining eight SHG programmes are mature organisations (with micro-finance operations that are more than seven years old). Maturing and new SHG programmes as well as newer IBPs are relatively small organisations with an average of around 5,000 members or clients each. The largest organisation in the sample has some 73,000 clients.

Savings mobilisation: There is potential to place greater emphasis on savings services

Not all MFOs in the sample are able to offer savings services, particularly the four organisations registered as 'for-profit' non-banking finance companies (NBFCs) and, therefore, regulated by the Reserve Bank of India (RBI), India's central bank. Further, the Grameen MFOs traditionally do not place much emphasis, beyond compulsory savings, on providing savings services to their members.

Nevertheless, deposits mobilised directly by the MFOs amount to US$8 million (or 34 per cent of the total amount lent to clients). Actual mobilisation—including amounts generated by SHGs for internal circulation but not deposited with the MFO—is nearly US$12.3 million (see Table 10.2) or more than 50 per cent of the amount outstanding.

This confirms the analysis in Chapter 3 by showing the value micro-finance clients place on savings services and demonstrating the potential for raising lending resources locally. As of now, the average savings of just US$18 per client are well below the US$26 average for the Top10 and US$52 for mature IBPs.

The average level of savings deposits with MFOs is mainly a function of three factors:

- implementation strategy
- age
- location

Thus the average savings deposits of Grameen programmes are just two-thirds of those of the IBPs and less than 40 per cent of the deposits of the older IBPs, despite having almost the same average memberships. While it is well known that Grameen programmes have traditionally not given much importance to savings as a source of funds, IBPs place considerable emphasis on this source.

The SHG programmes, by contrast, have compulsory deposit-schemes in which the members themselves determine the amount of the recurring savings deposit. This often results in minimalist norms and leads to deposits that are far lower than the members' savings potential. This is also reflected in the average figures that show that while individual banking clients have savings deposits of around US$38 each (over US$50 for mature IBPs), Grameen and SHG clients have saved only US$10 to 16 each. The Top10 average here of US$26 is driven almost entirely by the extraordinary performance of SEWA Bank on this indicator (see Chapter 3).

Staff productivity: SHG performance belies the expected efficiency of village banking

The 51 sample MFOs between them employ some 3,500 staff to provide micro-financial services. Staff productivity is highest amongst the mature IBPs, partly because the large ones are urban, slum-based programmes. However, even the newer

IBPs with 135 borrowers per member of staff fare better than the *Microbanking Bulletin* (*MBB*)[1] sample average of 111.

Grameen MFOs, with 94 borrowers per staff member, are well known to be relatively staff intensive, but it is the SHG programmes' 51 borrowers per staff member that really brings down the productivity profile of the sample. Even the mature SHG programmes are not able to achieve better than 66 borrowers per staff member and this seems to negate the expectation that village-banking programmes can be efficient in the long term as client representatives take over many staff functions.

However, such comparisons are difficult. Self-help groups may engage in many financial transactions that are not directly related to borrowing from MFOs, and may therefore not be captured by this analysis, making staff who promote SHGs appear less productive. Most of the SHGs in any case borrow from banks, not MFOs, which is not reflected in this analysis.

In Chapter 7, Malcolm Harper argues that, overall, SHG programmes are likely to be associated with higher numbers of clients, or at least of client transactions, per staff member. On the other hand, Chapters 8 and 9 make clear that promoting SHGs effectively presents many challenges, which are likely to lower the number of clients per staff member and drive up costs. This is all the more the case because, as described in Chapter 5, SHG programmes may aim to fulfil social objectives such as promoting the self-governance capabilities of members. They may, therefore, not be as strongly motivated to maximise productivity and limit operating costs, especially in the short term.

In terms of the number of loans serviced by MFOs within the M-CRIL sample, the 128 clients and US$9,900 per staff member of the Top 10 indicates the potential improvement that could be achieved by the others. Yet salary scales and other costs in the region are so low that the US$14 cost per borrower in the sample is less than one-tenth of the *MBB* sample's US$150 per borrower.

Portfolio quality: Grameen-type MFOs are the best performers

M-CRIL measures portfolio at risk (PAR) at the 60-day level (loans with overdues more than 60 days beyond the designated date of payment are regarded as being at risk of default). Grameen MFOs are the best performers in the sample with an average PAR of 3.9 per cent. The poor performers in this case, as in the case of cost coverage, are the mature programmes. This is largely on account of the stronger welfare (rather than commercial) orientation of the early entrants into micro-finance. Many of the older MFOs in the sample place less emphasis on credit-discipline within their financial-service activities.

Some of the newer IBPs have suffered not so much from methodological or ideological constraints as from lack of experience in the management of risk associated with different types of loan products, particularly crop loans. The sample average of 15 per cent and the India average of over 20 per cent are far higher than the *MBB* sample PAR (>90 days) of 2 per cent and emphasise the impression that MFOs in the region do not pay enough attention to portfolio quality. Further, they are reluctant to write off unrecoverable loans for fear of giving clients the impression that loans remaining unpaid for extended periods of time will not be recovered by the organisation. However, this gives the MFO management an unrealistic picture of its asset quality and tends to confuse decision-making.

Financing: Donor funds are pre-eminent; efficiency in the deployment of funds needs improvement

Micro-finance organisations in the region have historically been heavily dependent on donor funding for financing both their portfolios and their operations. As much as 47 per cent of the total of US$38.1 million currently deployed in the sample MFOs consists of the organisations' net worth, made up primarily of donated equity (see Figure 10.1). Accumulated losses amounting to US$3.2 million in 42 of the 51 organisations have contributed to erosion of the equity.

Some 21 per cent of the funds deployed in micro-finance by sample MFOs could be described as member-funds consisting of both withdrawable and non-withdrawable savings and emergency funds accumulated to cover loan losses due

Figure 10.1: MFOs' sources of funds

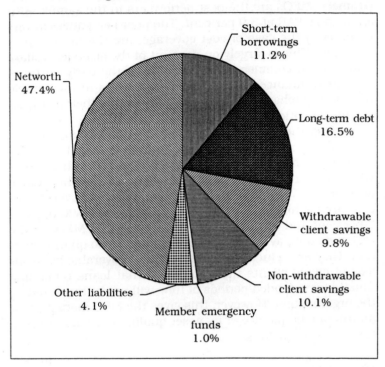

to disasters affecting MFO clients.[2] While a large proportion of these savings is generated by cooperative organisations with a legal mandate to generate these funds for lending to members (for examples see Chapters 3 and 5), in South Asia even MFOs with charitable status are able to generate savings for on-lending purposes. There are three reasons for this. First, the regulatory authorities accept that there is a dearth of financial services for poor people. Second, they recognise their own inability to regulate hundreds of MFOs in any effective manner, and third, there has not so far been any significant case of default or misappropriation by any MFO in the region.

Given that a large proportion of the best MFOs have been rated so far, our analysis shows that micro-finance in the region has a long way to go before it can achieve any form of commercial viability. However, M-CRIL's experience also shows that the importance of donor funds is declining and that MFO managers are increasingly aware of the need to obtain more resources both from members and from various types of institutional lenders.

Since MFOs in the region generally do not see themselves as commercially viable entities, their preference is to obtain resources from development loan funds on 'soft' terms. Therefore, it is not surprising that 28 per cent of the funds raised by MFOs for their activities are accounted for by soft loans from development banks and dedicated micro-finance wholesalers. The share of commercial banks in this total is negligible.

As mentioned earlier, the commercial banks' involvement in micro-finance is currently mainly under the NABARD promoted SHG-bank linkage programme. According to information published by NABARD, the banks had provided Rs 1.93 billion (US$42 million) as loans to 82,000 SHGs and 1.9 million families under this programme until March 2000 (NABARD, 2000). Unfortunately, these figures are cumulative and the numbers for outstanding loans are not available, so they cannot be compared directly to the M-CRIL sample. Since 2000 the cumulative figures have also increased sharply. As Chapter 7 makes clear, some 300,000 SHGs have borrowed from banks.

It is striking that only 57 per cent of the total resources of US$38 million available have been deployed by sample MFOs in loans to clients, while as much as 23 per cent has been placed in short- and long-term investments, mainly with banks (see Figure 10.2). These investments, even in long-term bank deposits, earn no more than 8 to 11 per cent. Yet the conditions on MFO loans to clients amount to annual effective interest rates of 18 to 45 per cent and could potentially yield them very high returns. It is apparent that MFOs are being inefficient in sourcing debt finance and then failing to apply it to the intended purpose of lending to clients.

Many MFOs have discovered that it is difficult to lend to clients beyond animal husbandry and consumption loans. Typical micro-finance clients find it difficult to enhance or launch business activities and often require technical support services that MFOs are generally not able to provide (for an exception, see Chapter 4). In addition, savings products tend to reduce the demand for consumption and emergency

Figure 10.2: Utilisation of funds by MFOs

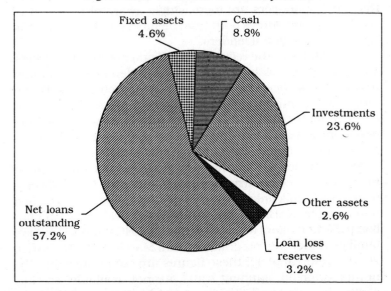

Fixed assets
4.6%

Cash
8.8%

Investments
23.6%

Net loans
outstanding
57.2%

Other assets
2.6%

Loan loss
reserves
3.2%

loans since both perform the same role. In the case of savings, clients set aside small amounts in advance; in the case of loans they pay small amounts in arrears (see the introduction to Chapter 3).

Portfolio management: IBPs manage funds well

The efficient, effective and prudential management of an MFO's assets is also important for achieving financial sustainability. Such management depends on a number of factors:

• the use of member deposits as a (relatively cheap) source of funds;
• the minimisation of the need for fixed assets relative to total assets;
• the maximum investment of financial resources either in the loan portfolio or in high return, long-term investments; and

- limiting the risk associated with the MFO's financial assets to levels consistent with the organisation's own funds or net worth.

M-CRIL's analysis of the management of the sample MFOs' assets shows that IBPs are amongst the most efficiently managed, the mature ones particularly so. The mature IBPs are savings-based organisations with high deposit–credit ratios (200 per cent), reasonable fixed to total assets ratios (4 per cent) and low ratios of liquid to total assets (3 per cent).

While the average for the total sample of 5 per cent fixed assets is reasonable, 9 per cent liquid assets is relatively high and, as the earlier discussion showed, the deposit–credit ratio of 34 per cent could certainly be improved. Another important concern here is that at least four, not very small MFOs, have actually eroded their equity to the extent that they have negative net worth.

Operating performance: Operating costs are low but portfolio yields are even lower

Surprisingly, in the context of many management deficiencies within MFOs in the region, the database shows that operating efficiency compares well with international best-practice norms. Operating-cost[3] ratios of many of the rated MFOs are less than 30 per cent. Though Grameen-type MFOs record a slightly higher average operating-cost ratio of 27 per cent, the sample average is just 23 per cent and the average for Indian MFOs less than 20 per cent. This compares with the equivalent average of 31 per cent for the *Microbanking Bulletin* (*MBB*) sample of 90 MFOs.

On the other hand, the average portfolio yield (the actual revenues generated from lending to clients as a proportion of the average portfolio) for the M-CRIL sample is just 17 per cent (India only 14 per cent) compared to the *MBB's* 40 per cent. So low is the portfolio yield, indeed, that the financial spread[4] being earned by MFOs in the region is less than 8 per cent, leaving a 15 per cent gap between it and the operating cost level of 23 per cent of average portfolio.

Figure 10.3: Relationship between portfolio size and efficiency

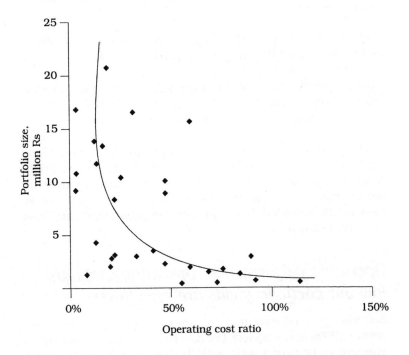

Since economies of scale are generally expected in any economic activity, the relationship between the operating-cost ratio and portfolio size of individual MFOs is outlined in Figure 10.3. Though the correlation is not perfect, a clear inverse relationship between portfolio size and operating-cost ratio emerges from the sample information.

It is also interesting to note here that there is apparently a minimum operating-cost ratio (around 10 per cent) below which it is all but impossible for MFOs to function. Further, even MFOs with relatively small portfolios of Rs 46 lakhs (US$100,000) or less are able to achieve low operating-cost ratios of 10 to 15 per cent if they make an effort. This finding is methodology-neutral.

At the same time, it is important to remember, as Mathew Titus analyses in Chapter 8, that operating costs are not only determined by factors within the control of the service-provider, but in part depend on the socio-economic context and the extent of market distortions and imperfections.

Return on assets: In a bleak scenario, the newer IBPs perform better

The lack of commercial viability of MFOs in the region becomes clear in considering the return on their assets. The sample average loss of 4.8 per cent on total assets is much worse than the *MBB* sample profit of 1.5 per cent. The M-CRIL Top 10 average of –1.3 per cent indicates the ground that MFOs in the region still have to cover in comparison with the *MBB* sample's 6.2 per cent profit for fully sustainable organisations.

The situation is not uniformly bleak, however. The disaggregated information from the database shows that four MFOs in the M-CRIL sample earn more than 3 per cent returns on loanable funds and as many as 13 MFOs earn positive returns. On account of their relatively good fund management, the IBPs perform better than other types of MFOs and have average losses of just 0.6 per cent of total assets.

Dependence on subsidies is high

Operational self-sufficiency (OSS) measures the ability of an MFO to meet all its operational and financial costs out of its income from operations. As expected from the above discussion, IBPs as a group are fairly close to full OSS (96 per cent), although the distribution of 10 such MFOs indicates that three of them are still quite far from that target. Of the Grameen programmes, four are still quite far from self-sufficiency but two of the 10 are able to cover all their costs. Out of the 31 SHG programmes, only seven are approaching self-sufficiency while just one is able to cover all its costs.

A calculation of the Subsidy Dependence Index (SDI) shows that the average subsidy dependence of newer IBPs is the best at 37 per cent. Unlike the case of OSS, however, the SDI of Grameen programmes (58 per cent) is better than that of mature IBPs (91 per cent).

The average of 72.7 per cent for OSS and 83.4 per cent for SDI for sample MFOs in the region compares poorly with the *MBB* average of 129.7 per cent OSS for 63 fully sustainable MFOs and 106.6 per cent for the full sample of 92 MFOs. The Top 10 MFOs in the region have an average OSS of 91.4 per cent and SDI of 48.9 per cent. However, with relatively low operating cost ratios, there are still enough MFOs in the M-CRIL sample with positive returns to provide grounds to hope for better overall performance in the future.

Organisational issues: The sustainability of MFOs is critically affected by the self-perception of the promoting NGOs

It is apparent from the discussion in this chapter that the performance of the rated MFOs in India in terms of financial sustainability has been relatively weak. Though systematic information on sectoral trends is not presently available, the experience of M-CRIL's team with the performance of MFOs in the region over the past few years indicates that the message of sustainability is starting to permeate through the micro-finance sector. Consequently, there is a positive trend in overall performance both in terms of sustainability and in terms of growth.

There are, however, a number of organisational and systemic issues that affect the sustainability of MFOs in the region. These issues include staff quality, scale of operations and geographical focus, the quality of information systems, financial control systems and, above all, the orientation of most CEOs of MFOs within a development perspective.

Staff quality. Many of the staff of MFOs do not have the skills and incentives necessary to work in a more productive and cost-effective manner. By and large, remuneration in the sector is uncompetitive with the public sector and significantly lower than much of the private commercial sector. This results in a high turnover of competent junior staff and a capacity mismatch at supervisory levels. The few organisations that have introduced appropriate remuneration and incentive systems are also the best functioning MFOs in the region.

Scale of operations and geographical spread. The typical number of borrowers of sample MFOs in India is no more than 3,000 to 4,000 with average loan sizes of just US$100 to 125. While M-CRIL is convinced that their scale is not the only cause of low financial sustainability of MFOs in the region, it is certainly a factor. For this reason, 27 (53 per cent) of the 51 MFOs in the sample were urged by M-CRIL to expand their lending activities.

At the same time, in many cases, there is a concern that the geographical spread of programmes affects their operational efficiency. Many MFO leaders, in their concern to work with particular communities or reach especially poor regions, spread their programmes over distances—often in excess of a 100 km radius—which, for small organisations, substantially adds to the cost of operations and hampers managerial supervision.[5] M-CRIL has recommended consolidation of operations in 19 (37 per cent) cases within the sample. Five of the sample MFOs were found to be both small and spread thinly over a wide area.

MIS and portfolio quality. Amongst the least satisfactory aspects of MFO operations in the region is the quality of management information systems (MIS). A number of organisations do not have adequate systems even to track basic member and borrower information in a manner that will enable an accurate enumeration of clients served. Others suffer from inconsistencies at various levels of operation so that appropriate information is either not available at head-office level or at branch level. Many do not even collate information on the quality of their portfolio.

Only eight of the sample MFOs were found by M-CRIL to have a fully effective MIS, while 18 (35 per cent of the total) have adequate systems for tracking portfolio quality. In the latter case, this is related to the predominant (and inappropriate) use of the cumulative repayment rate as an indicator of the quality of the portfolio. In this scenario, greater than 90 per cent repayment rates are regarded as satisfactory on the part of MFO managers and breed complacency despite being (often) associated with a 15 to 20 per cent portfolio-at-risk ratio.

Financial control systems. Overall accounting systems in sample MFOs are reasonably satisfactory. However, only 39 per cent have internal audit mechanisms in place, a risky situation in the context of the failure of most (62 per cent) even to undertake any formal budgeting or cash-planning. As discussed earlier, liquidity management is also an area of concern in the operations of many MFOs with inefficiencies in the sourcing of funds from lenders or donors, in the transfer of cash between branches and head-office, and in placing idle funds in short-term investments.

Development orientation of CEOs. This approach to micro-finance management is largely a reflection of the social-development oriented background of most MFO CEOs who may not have recognised the full potential of micro-financial services as a business, albeit with a social purpose.

Most MFOs in India have either evolved from NGOs undertaking a wide range of development activities or continue to be divisions of such organisations. In this situation, discussion with CEOs during assessment visits revealed that the development orientation of such leaders tends to be strong and, though there is an increasing recognition of the need for sustainability as well, this is yet to become a priority in the practice of micro-finance in the region. The potential to achieve sustainability and thereby reach larger numbers of people is therefore considerable, but such a goal may conflict with other developmental agendas of the promoters.

The analysis of developmental objectives set out in this book brings this issue to the fore. Some promoters may not pursue a limited focus of delivering micro-financial services to the largest number of people as their primary goal (although all would probably subscribe to the need in the Indian context to reach out to a large number of poor people, and therefore increasingly understand the need for greater sustainability). They may well add other inputs, for example, around the quality of self-governance, that may inevitably drive up costs and slow down expansion, at least in the short term. This brings us critically to the issue of a more refined understanding of the purpose of micro-financial services and their impact.

The difficult task of assessing impact

Why impact assessment?

Complementary to financial and organisational performance are questions relating to development impact. As this book demonstrates so clearly, for most if not all actors in India—NGOs, MFOs, donors, even bankers—micro-finance is not only about the efficient and sustainable delivery of micro-financial services. Micro-finance is a means, not an end. The ultimate goal is to reduce poverty. And, in India, the development strategy includes (for many NGOs) savings and credit management by SHGs not as a system for delivering micro-financial services *per se* but as a tool for building people's organisations and empowering women (Chapter 5).

Impact assessment in this context implies questions about outreach and effectiveness in meeting development objectives. What changes does micro-finance lead to? Are providers of micro-financial services reaching poor people? If so, do they serve to move poor people out of poverty? What is the role of women in micro-finance—is it empowering and how is that defined? How strong are the groups as social organisations?

Micro-finance is often defined in terms of the local provision of financial services in small amounts that meet the needs of the poor with a special focus on women. In the early days, it was sometimes assumed, given the nature of the service, that data on client outreach, the involvement of women and timely repayments were adequate indicators of impact. The argument for this assumption went something like this: only poor people are interested in small ('micro') amounts, therefore they must be the clients; clients exercise market choice and therefore an increase in clients means that the service is meeting their needs on acceptable terms, whilst the ability to repay on time and take repeat loans must mean that the loan was being used productively and profitably, enabling an increase in income. Moreover, the involvement of women as clients with direct access to financial services implied a significant contribution to gender equity and women's empowerment.

Such assumptions have been explored and questioned as researchers and practitioners have looked more closely at these issues. Evaluations and case-studies in different parts of the world have highlighted some important issues:

- the fungibility of finance at the household level in the context of varying financial needs and strategies which are not only enterprise related; what then is the role of micro-finance in relation to these needs?
- gender issues: does the role of women as clients for micro-financial services translate into empowerment for them or is this merely a pragmatic means of ensuring repayments and group discipline (see further the analysis in Chapter 5)?
- different levels of poverty: is micro-finance reaching mainly the moderately poor, and not the more vulnerable?

The issue of impact assessment has therefore assumed significance, and has been expanded to address questions not only of what is being achieved by micro-financial services, but also, as in this book, how micro-finance can be more effective in achieving development objectives. In other words not only (or even!) *proving* impact but also *improving* practice for better impact (Hulme, 1999).

Proving or improving

Seeking to prove the impact of an intervention involves distinguishing cause and effect and this is conventionally done through large-scale sample surveys (of clients and a 'control group' of non-clients, before and after an intervention) and statistical analysis of the different data sets. This kind of assessment is data intensive, it takes time for the results to emerge and, even then, it is not clear how to interpret the results: what do the numbers really mean? who understands them?

Increasingly, therefore, there has been a shift to adapting and down-scaling survey techniques and using different (more qualitative and participatory) tools. The aim here is to arrive at results more quickly and to explore (assess rather than measure) dimensions of change that are relevant to local stakeholders (practitioners and the community).

In terms of the extremes, different approaches to impact assessment can be categorised as in Table 10.3 (compare Simanowitz, 2001 and Noponen, 2001).

Table 10.3: Different approaches to impact assessment

	The 'old' way	New trend
Why?	Proving: establish change due to the programme, to know what is happening and to justify funding	Improving: information relevant and useful for improving programme practice; strengthening organisations through a process of self-evaluation
What?	Structured survey: results quantified (numbers, averages, frequencies)	Participatory process: qualitative understanding (patterns, differences, perceptions)
When?	One-off cross-sectional study	Long-term process: on-going monitoring as well as longitudinal studies
Who?	External consultants	Clients, staff, all stakeholders
How much?	Main focus on programme activity only, i.e., micro-enterprise	Wider set of impact indicators on individuals, households, communities

The practice of impact assessment must lie in-between these extremes, with a pragmatic mix of both approaches, as donors (to some extent) and researchers become more interested in the alternatives, whilst practitioners (NGOs, MFOs) look for information about their programmes for their own use and to serve their development objectives.

So what is the impact?

Reports of impact assessment available from India are relatively few. Table 10.4 summarises eight available studies. They relate to some of the most reputed organisations engaged in micro-financial services in the country, and reflect different micro-finance models and contexts.

These are very different studies in terms of scope and approach, depending partly on the type of organisation, the impact questions they seek to answer and the amount of time and money spent on the studies. They usually include one or more of the following impacts: effects on the poverty of

Table 10.4: Summary of impact assessment studies of micro-finance in India

Context	SEWA	FWWB	NABARD	MYRADA	BASIX	SHARE	ASA	CDF
Registered status	Cooperative bank	Apex MFO-society	Apex bank	Society	NBFC	NBFC	MFO-society	Trust
Type of client	Individual savers and borrowers	MFO partners (study is of four MFOs)	Banks who lend to SHGs	SHGs linked to banks	Mainly individual borrowers; also lending through intermediaries and SHGs	Grameen model groups of borrowers	Grameen model groups of borrowers	Thrift and credit cooperatives
Approach	Banking services plus gender empowerment	Loans and capacity-building of MFOs	Refinancing	SHG capacity-building, empowerment of poor people	Micro- and other finance, with technical assistance and support services	Micro-finance	Micro-finance plus community empowerment	Enhancing women's skills for cooperative management
Date started micro-finance	1974	1991	1992	1984	1996	1993	1993	1990
Date of study	1998–99 & 2000–2001	2001	1999–2000	2001	1999	2000–2001	2000	1995–96
Outreach: members at time of study	120.000		1.9 million	77.500	10.200	84.000	12.000	12.500

Context	SEWA	FWWB	NABARD	MYRADA	BASIX	SHARE	ASA	CDF
Study method	Question-naire; Case-studies; panel data	Case-studies; focus groups; question-naire	Recall: Question-naire	Recall: (i) participa-tory assess-ment; (ii) question-naire	Recall: Question-naire and focus groups	Question-naire	Practitioner-led AIMS tools: Case-studies (recall)	Case-studies (recall)
Sample	Clients: 600 Control: 300 Panel: 800 Case-studies: 12	Case-studies: 20 Survey: 125 clients	560 members of more than 220 SHGs in 11 states	(i) 6 groups (ii) 64 groups	187 clients	125 mature clients; 104 new clients	40 clients	2 primary coops
Basis for poverty assess-ment	(i) 'Local' poverty line (ii) 'US$1'/ day	Income—but poverty level not specified	'Official' poverty line	(i) Participa-tory wealth ranking (ii) 'Official' poverty line	Poverty line index (survey based)	Poverty index and relative ranking (survey based)		Not applica-ble—open membership

(Contd)

(Table 10.4 Contd)

Findings	SEWA	FWWB	NABARD	MYRADA	BASIX	SHARE	ASA	CDF
Poverty outreach (% sample)	By (i) ~10% By (ii) 45%*	~46%	42%*	100%	52%	100%*	–	–
Poverty reduction	Between rounds 1 and 2: change of less than 1%. Increase in average household income by 14% (mainly attributed to male salaries)	Graduation to a sustainable or increased level of income less likely than providing a 'safety net' and reducing vulnerability	22% moved above poverty line. Increase in assets (59%), savings (×3), annual income (from Rs 20,000 to 26,800)	(i) 75% have improved status to middle or upper poor after three years (least change for the poorest) (ii) 86% cross poverty line after five years	Inconclusive: 61% report some increase in incomes at household level and 29% report some increase in employment, but magnitudes not estimated	38% no longer poor; 38% shifted from very poor to moderately poor; high correlation with number of household earners and sources of income	Increased income through new/expanded income generating activities; increase in food intake; improved housing condition; purchase of household assets	–
Financial services	Clients' informal debt continues at similar levels; overall debt increases by borrowing from SEWA	More than half of MFO clients continue to borrow from moneylenders	Decline in average interest rate of borrowings; improvement in repayment of bank loans	Groups increasingly linked to banks, or ready to be linked	Additionality: increased volumes of credit (by ~24%) to client households, with 4% reduction in overall cost of credit; 20% now access formal credit		Client suggestions for MFO services from separate 'client satisfaction' focus group discussions	Women appreciate easy access to money at reasonable rates; helps to reduce interest rates of informal credit

Findings	SEWA	FWWB	NABARD	MYRADA	BASIX	SHARE	ASA	CDF
Empower-ment	Women have personal savings accounts and plans for the future Overall self-image same for clients as for control group		Attitude changes (self-worth; ability to communicate) Object to, e.g., alcohol and wife-beating Decline in domestic violence (37%)	Groups increasingly involved in social problem solving and maintaining village infrastructure; members elected to local *panchayats* Increase in self-confidence among members; learn to sign, approach bank, speak to visitors Increased predominance of wives in household decisions regarding purpose of loans, purchase of assets			Improved self-confidence (mobility, dress, jewellery, ability to plan, decisions for self and family) Access to medical facilities Take action on social issues Increase in inter-caste interaction	Women can spend on own needs Able to manage personal finances better Self-confidence and respect Awareness of community issues

* 'before' participation in MFO or group, or at time of baseline. Other figures relate to study results.

client households, on financial services (in terms of access and terms), and on empowerment for women clients.

The study approaches include questionnaire-based surveys only, or a mix of survey questionnaires, focus group discussions and case-studies, or only the last (to capture empowerment issues). All base their assessment of change on recall of 'before' and 'after' joining a programme, except for the SEWA Bank study which has used panel data at two different points in time.

These studies indicate that outreach to the poor among most of the MFOs studied is about 42 to 52 per cent, that is, around half of the sample are categorised as poor when they joined the programme; in two cases 100 per cent are assumed to be poor.

Evidence for reductions in poverty is mixed. Three studies quantify significant shifts from 'poor' to 'non-poor', of 22 per cent in the case of the NABARD study after three years and 38 per cent in the case of SHARE. The SHARE study also differentiates between different categories of the poor, and shows a similar 38 per cent shift from being 'very poor' to 'moderately poor'.

In the case of MYRADA, two studies are available. The survey-based study of 64 groups shows 70 per cent of the sample crossing the poverty line after three years, and 86 per cent crossing in five years. The participatory wealth-ranking of six groups, on the other hand, suggests somewhat differently that 75 per cent of members have improved their status over five years, but have not moved out of poverty.

In the case of BASIX (see Chapter 4), a high proportion of the sample (61 per cent) report an increase in household incomes, and 29 per cent report some increase in employment. However, the magnitude of the increases is not estimated and the study is not conclusive in relation to effects on levels of poverty.

The study of SEWA Bank (see Chapter 3), using panel data over a period of two years (a baseline carried out in 1998 and a follow-up survey in 2000) reports marginal changes in poverty status (of less than 1 per cent). There has been an increase in average real household income of 14 per cent, but this increase is attributed largely to the increase in salaries of male members of the clients' household rather than to participation in SEWA Bank.

Overall, across all the studies, a significant proportion of clients remain poor, however poverty is defined. This lends credence to the observation of the FWWB study (of four of its partner MFOs) that graduation to an increased and sustainable level of income (poverty reduction) is less likely than micro-finance providing a safety net and thereby helping clients to reduce vulnerability (see Box 10.2 and Chapter 3).

Box 10.2: Clients have diverse credit needs (FWWB, 2001)

Credit needs for activities not related to income-generation are as important as ones with potential for bringing in higher economic returns. Therefore, clients are likely to continue to access loans from multiple sources, through different modes for a wide range of consumption needs. As one elderly respondent put it (ibid.: 75):

> When the river is dry one fetches water from several sources and collects in larger containers to use for different purposes. What matters is its judicious use at home for so many tasks, and not who carries it home and from where. Money raised through loans from moneylenders, pawn-brokers, relatives, friends, neighbours, employers or whoever, is like this pooled water which gets used as the needs arise.... correctly used, it quenches your thirst and wrongly used, it spills away.

Enterprise effects are not specifically covered in these studies, but tend to be subsumed within an assessment of changes in household income. However, the SHARE study links evidence for shifts out of poverty to a reduced dependency burden and an increase in productive assets, and these are assumed to result from the micro-finance activities.

The SEWA Bank study, on the other hand, tested hypotheses on increased revenues, fixed assets and employment at the enterprise level, but did not find the links significant: micro-enterprises operated by women generally raised their revenues between rounds of the survey, but the increase was smaller than the rise in household income and was not clearly linked to participation in financial services.

The impact on financial services for the client is seen partly in terms of additionality. Thus the BASIX study reports increased volumes of credit (by up to 24 per cent) to client households with a 4 per cent reduction in the overall cost of credit (based on interest rates), and an increase (20 per cent) in clients accessing formal bank credit.

Other studies found similar results with the NABARD study reporting a 29 per cent increase in bank repayments, and MYRADA having 1,400 groups already linked to banks, and another 2,000 ready to be linked. Two studies (FWWB and SEWA Bank) comment on the continuing indebtedness of MFO clients to informal providers of finance, due to diverse credit needs related not only to productive activity but to a wide range of consumption needs.

Evidence of impact in terms of empowerment indicators comes from four of the studies (for the case of MYRADA see Chapter 5). Changes for clients as individuals are reported in all four in terms of improved self-confidence and mobility contrasting with rural traditions. For example, women say they are now able to sign their names, go to a bank, speak to visitors and government officials, talk in meetings; they can spend on their own needs (health-care, clothing, jewellery) and play an enhanced role in household decision-making. In the case of MYRADA and Activists for Social Alternatives (ASA), there is also evidence of empowerment at the community-level in terms of inter-caste interaction, women taking action on social issues and members being elected to local *panchayats* (village councils).

The SEWA Bank study (which covers urban working women) found little difference between clients and the control group in the survey, but found significant evidence of impact in the detailed case-studies. These tend to reflect the supporting activities of the SEWA union (collective bargaining for increased piece-rates, a scholarship for a daughter, subsidised housing) and also mention appreciation of a secure place to save money ('out of the reach of a gambler husband'). This strongly confirms the integrated strategy that SEWA pursues, as described in Chapters 3 and 6.

Emerging issues

The variations between these studies suggest we need to look more closely at certain issues in order to understand the impact of micro-finance in practice.

A central issue is the question of poverty, in impact assessment no less than in development strategy, which is also reflected in national-level debate in India. How can we understand and measure poverty and poverty reduction? Who are the poor? When does a poor person become non-poor? What about vulnerability? Is the non-poor status sustainable?

The standard methods (income or expenditure measurements) pose a number of methodological problems. Even when incomes are measured, who are the poor? The SEWA study rejected the local poverty line in favour of the World Bank's US$1 a day as being more 'plausible'.

Participatory wealth-ranking is more interesting, as it reflects local realities, indicators and perceptions, and captures significant aspects of the quality of life apart from income and expenditure. However, whilst capturing relative poverty, it does not necessarily reflect absolute poverty, as in the MYRADA example where all categories are poor.

The SHARE study uses a four-indicator index (sources of income, household-dependency burden, productive assets, and housing quality—all easier and quicker to measure than income or expenditure) with three categories: non-poor, moderately poor and very poor. The category cut-offs are calculated based on a broad relative profiling of a control population, divided into equal thirds as follows: top 33 per cent = 'non-poor', bottom 33 per cent = 'very poor', middle 33 per cent = 'moderately poor' (as in the Consultative Group to Assist the Poorest [CGAP] poverty-assessment tool). This proxy index is a handy tool, but the categories remain relative ones, and the impact may be over-reflected when some of the indicators are effectively direct inputs of the MFO.

A related question is what time-scale is appropriate: how long does it take for change to take place; change that is sustainable? Is the two-year time frame of the SEWA Bank study sufficient to assess impact? Or are even three years not sufficient to assess sustainable change, as noted in the MYRADA study? At the very least, the impact assessment must include the period clients have been involved with the programme as part of its analysis.

Impact is also linked to organisational performance: how does programme design or micro-finance methodology affect impact? Does a focus on the financial sustainability of an organisation reduce its outreach to poor people and other development impacts? In Chapter 8, Mathew Titus analyses convincingly that the socio-economic context and organisational design and performance have a strong impact on the costs of operations. It is thus highly likely that they will also affect the overall impact of any programme.

Other issues relate to the selection of tools for impact assessment. There is a tendency to assume that quantitative surveys using standardised sampling and statistical techniques are more reliable and rigorous (accurate) but are high-cost and time-consuming, in comparison with qualitative methods that provide more in-depth information more quickly. The challenge is to have a judicious mix of both. Quantitative techniques can provide a useful assessment of scale and patterns. Qualitative techniques are necessary for a deeper understanding of context, processes and issues such as perceptions of poverty, empowerment and client priorities.

Whatever the approach, rigour is important. The reliability and utility of surveys depends on representative sampling with careful analysis and use of data. The same goes for qualitative techniques (focus group discussions and case-studies) which need to be rigorous in terms of selecting participants (i.e., sampling), exploring issues, triangulation, documenting what people say, recording differences and analysing patterns. Similarly, truly participatory processes that involve clients in analysing their own situation and defining their own needs require balance and facilitation.

None of the studies we feature here covered dropouts. There are usually some people who drop out of the programme because it is not useful for them, or because they cannot cope with the demands of the programme. There are also people who graduate, who use micro-financial services and then move on. All are relevant to an assessment of outreach (is it the poorest who drop out and why have they dropped out?) and impact. Similarly, it would be useful to include case-studies of less successful clients alongside the success stories.

New initiatives

Market research is increasingly seen as a significant aspect of impact assessment. BASIX commissions periodic 'Customer Satisfaction Audits' carried out as a market survey by external consultants. An alternative approach is for staff themselves to explore customer satisfaction through focus group discussions. For example, ASA has used the customer satisfaction tool (one of the Assessing the Impact of Microenterprise Services [AIMS] [2000] tools intended for use by micro-finance practitioners) to obtain detailed feedback on its products (Hishigsuren, 2000). This is an approach that has now been developed in more detail and is being promoted as participatory market-research by Microsave Africa through its training programmes.

The new trend in impact assessment includes an interest in impact monitoring by the practitioner as part of an internal system, implemented by existing staff, that tracks trends over time and is part of the regular information system of the organisation. Examples of such systems come from outside India: the client monitoring system (Jamaica) uses an access database that provides baseline data on health, education and financial status of individual clients at the time of the first loan and at subsequent points thereafter; the monitoring and evaluation system developed by the Small Enterprise Foundation in South Africa is based on regular questions to borrowers by loan officers, complemented by more detailed case-studies and surveys. There are no examples yet of such systems in India, although a few NGOs are experimenting with pictorial diaries used by group members (Chaitanya) and as part of an integrated learning system which is aggregated upwards (ASA again) (Noponen, 2001).

Alongside many interesting on-going initiatives by individual organisations, two wider initiatives have been recently launched in India.

One is Improving Impact of Micro-finance on Poverty (ImpAct), an action research programme funded by the Ford Foundation. Part of an international three-year project and steered for India by the Institute of Development Studies (IDS) at the University of Sussex in the UK, the aim of this research programme is to improve and develop impact assessment systems, building on the priorities and agendas of microfinance organisations, and empowering these organisations to be more pro-active in developing their own learning systems, both to inform internal decision-making and to satisfy the requirements of external stakeholders. Three Indian organisations (of about 20 globally), including PRADAN and SHARE are participating in the programme and are being facilitated by resource persons from IDS to think through their objectives in undertaking impact assessment, reviewing alternative tools and methodologies, and applying these effectively within their own management systems. This represents a significant attempt to strengthen practitioner systems for impact assessment in order to improve their impact.

The second initiative is a national impact assessment of the micro-finance support programme of SIDBI's Foundation for Micro-Credit, supported by the Department for International Development (DfID) (UK). This is being carried out by EDA Rural Systems in association with the Institute for Development Policy and Management at Manchester University in the UK. This exercise is a longitudinal study, incorporating a number of features:

- consultations with different levels of stakeholders (practitioners, clients as well as funders) on their objectives and priorities, the impact hypotheses to be explored, and the indicators that are relevant to them (similar to a social or development audit approach);[6]
- a sample drawn from different regions of the country, reflecting different micro-finance models and approaches, levels of organisational sustainability as well as variations in socio-economic context;
- equity analysis drawing on participatory wealth-ranking in all sample areas and comparing local indicators across areas to arrive at a comparable assessment of poverty levels;

- tracking panel data over a seven-year period, with a base-line in the first two years, followed by revisits to the same areas and samples in subsequent years;
- extensive use of focus group discussions with qualitative and participatory methods, carefully documented, to in-form and provide depth to a full-scale sample survey;
- involving local staff of MFOs in field-level research, to the extent that MFO resources permit;
- reporting back to all stakeholder levels.

Both these initiatives are in an early 'pre-test' phase. They hold considerable potential for increasing our understanding of the outreach and impact of micro-finance in India, and developing capacity to assess this.

Conclusions

This chapter presents a number of challenges to micro-finance practice in India. While the book has primarily focused on the developmental purposes for which micro-financial services can be used, issues of sustainability and measuring impact cannot be avoided.

The performance in terms of financial sustainability of the rated MFOs in India, likely to be among the better performers, has been relatively weak. Likewise, little systematic analysis of impact, whether on incomes, vulnerability, empowerment, people's organisations, institutional change or any other variables, is available. The limited evidence of impact is also quite mixed, from significantly positive outcomes to almost no change at all.

This does not mean that wider developmental purposes and impacts are not important. It would be foolhardy to suggest that because they cannot be measured easily they should not be a focus of on-going attention. Previous chapters have illustrated many cases of good practice and also positive im-pacts. In this chapter we have made clear that the earlier reliance on proxy indicators (like outreach and repayment rates) is not sufficient to support good micro-finance prac-tice, with all its potential for such varied impacts. Even straightforward costs may vary dramatically according to different market contexts (see Chapter 8).

Part of the apparent divergence between the analysis in this chapter and the case-studies in previous chapters is that many of the latter have deliberately been selected to illustrate some of the best practice within India. It is these that can lead the way, that can open up space and possibilities for others to follow, especially when the best-practice organisations have been able to dissolve some of the tensions between developmental purpose and organisational efficiency, for example. As suggested in Chapter 5, for instance, people's organisations cannot be empowering unless they are well managed.

At the same time, this chapter makes very clear that all practitioners, including from among the best-practice organisations, need to enhance their standards of financial and organisational sustainability, and of assessing impact to improve their practice to achieve greater and better impact.

Fortunately, as the micro-finance sector grows in India, so do systems that can help organisations and practitioners in these endeavours. The emergence of a rigorous rating agency, and the launch of two major initiatives, one to strengthen organisational systems for impact, the other a long-term study widely defined to include a range of assessment tools and potential impacts, will significantly enhance understanding and hopefully practice. Results from all these studies over the next few years will provide a wealth of information that will help to deepen the understanding of the reality of micro-finance as a tool for poverty reduction.

Notes

1. The *Microbanking Bulletin* is a CGAP-sponsored six-monthly publication that *inter alia* collates data from MFOs around the world. The *MBB's* sample of more than 100 MFOs contains information that is mostly self-reported by (usually) the better known and more successful MFOs. M-CRIL's information, on the other hand, is obtained from MFOs that have applied for loans, are not necessarily the best ones and, most importantly, have had their data subjected to the close scrutiny and verification that is typical of a rating exercise. The comparisons made between the two sets of averages, therefore, need to

be viewed with caution. The M-CRIL averages may appear significantly worse than the status of MFOs in the South Asian region relative to global micro-finance.

2. This refers specifically to funds deployed by MFOs (and taken on their balance sheets) rather than those managed and rotated internally amongst members of SHGs.

3. Staff, travel and other expenses incurred in MFO operations (excluding financial costs) as a proportion of the average loan portfolio.

4. Portfolio yield minus financial costs (the total cost of funds for the period plus loan-loss provision expenses divided by the average portfolio).

5. Some programmes, however, deliberately concentrate their operations within a confined geographic area. See Chapter 6 for the examples of the Cooperative Development Foundation and the DHAN Foundation, which seek to saturate their areas of operations to enhance the overall impact on the local economy.

6. See www.edarural.com (DA resources).

Chapter 11

Rising to the challenge of scale in India: Growing the micro-finance sector

Mathew Titus

The focus of the book so far has primarily been on micro-finance organisations (MFOs) and various community-based savings and credit groups, which the Indian association Sa-Dhan calls 'community development finance institutions'. It would be extremely optimistic to expect such specialised and community-based intermediaries alone to meet all the demand for micro-savings, credit and insurance.

This draws attention to the particular challenges for increasing outreach in a systematic manner in India. To begin with, it is important to recognise, as the literature on enterprise promotion also suggests, that promoting individual organisations is often not sufficient or effective. Promoting the micro-finance sector, within which a large number and diversity of providers of micro-financial services can flourish, therefore requires a different approach.

The approach requires the active participation of a range of different stakeholders, including regulators, policy-makers, investors, retailers, MFOs, community-based service-providers and their support organisations. Only when all these stakeholders are working effectively for the growth of micro-finance will there be any hope of meeting the pressing need for financial services among the large number of poor people in India.

The contribution of different stakeholders in affecting the success and potential expansion of micro-financial services across different market segments is therefore critical if progress is to be systematic and sustained. This demands debate on key factors affecting growth, and recognition and encouragement of the roles of different stakeholders.

The demand for micro-financial services

The first step in any mapping of roles is to understand the demand for micro-financial services. The potential demand in India is huge (see Chapter 2 for more details and Mahajan and Nagasri [1999] for the figures quoted here). While banks have provided access to deposit facilities for large numbers of small depositors, total demand is far from being met, especially for more flexible micro-savings. This is clear from the fact that many poor people continue to turn to informal service-providers or financial companies, many of which are unreliable (as illustrated in Chapter 8).

As for credit, credit *usage* among poor households in 1998 was estimated to be almost Rs 50,000 crore (500,000 million) or US$11 billion. It is clear from the rapid growth of self-help groups (SHGs) and other community-based intermediaries that if credit were more readily available, credit usage would only go up, suggesting that much demand for credit among poor households is also not being met.

The supply of insurance services to poor people is increasing, including low-premium schemes covering death, accidents, natural calamities, loss of assets, etc. However, attributes of these products are often not appropriate (for example, for illiterate clients) and poor people therefore face significant risks in purchasing insurance (see Chapter 8 for illustrations). Moreover, much of the expansion has been driven by government schemes, such as the Integrated Rural Development Programme (IRDP), while crop and livestock insurance are largely unavailable to poor households.

Not only is the total current demand for micro-financial services not being met, but there is likely to be significant additional latent demand. Market imperfections, such as the inability of poor people to assess the reliability and quality of deposit or insurance providers (see Chapter 8 again), and market distortions such as subsidised credit which has negatively influenced both lender and borrower behaviour, mean that many poor households will not express their demand for micro-financial services until such market imperfections and distortions are overcome or removed.

In addition, demand needs to be enhanced by supporting the growth of micro-producers and community-based organisations that will enhance their need and capacity for absorbing credit, as well as other financial services. While systematic livelihood interventions are still not well understood (Datta et al., 2001), interventions like those of the National Dairy Development Board that has influenced the lives of nine million dairy farmers and of the Bharatiya Agro-Industries Foundation's cattle cross-breeding programme supporting one million livelihoods, can have a significant impact on demand for financial services, whether for credit, (livestock) insurance, or enhanced savings. Likewise, reviving the cooperative infrastructure throughout India, as CDF and BASIX have started (see Chapters 4 and 6), could also have a huge impact on demand.

It is clear, therefore, that there is no lack of demand for micro-financial services. However, in addition to strategies to meet that demand, market imperfections and distortions need to be overcome and further demand built through systematic livelihood interventions.

The supply of micro-financial services

The total outreach of specialised providers of micro-financial services is estimated to fall well below 1 per cent of credit usage by poor households (Mahajan and Nagasri, 1999). While banks have given a very large number of small loans, the proportion of rural credit usage supplied by the formal sector stood at 56.6 per cent in 1991, and much lower for the poorest households. The latter accessed 58 per cent of their debt from informal sources (see Chapter 2, note 1). Moreover, banks have not delivered effective micro-financial services, but been driven by mandatory targets and subsidies resulting 'in low repayment rates, leading to a vicious cycle of non-availability and non-repayment' (Mahajan and Nagasri, 1999: 4). The number of small loans they are extending is also falling.

As described in Chapter 7, bank lending to SHGs is increasing, and some 300,000 groups have now taken a bank loan. Mahajan and Nagasri estimate that if the National Bank for Agriculture and Rural Development (NABARD) meets its target of one million SHGs borrowing from banks by 2008, that will absorb at least Rs 5,000 crore (50,000 million) worth of funds, or about 10 per cent of current credit usage. As suggested above, this can only act as a conservative estimate of demand for micro-financial services. Whether even this target is achieved will depend on the cooperation of the increasingly independent and profit-oriented banks in NABARD's 'linkage' programme.

In terms of refinance or other capital available to banks, MFOs and non-governmental organisations (NGOs) for micro-financial services, current outstandings are around Rs 320 crore (3,200 million), of which Rs 250 crore (2,500 million) from NABARD's linkage programme are with banks, and the balance with MFOs and NGOs. Both could expand significantly, with NABARD's programme expanding and SIDBI investing more of its new corpus fund of Rs 200 crore (2,000 million). However, even with such expansion, refinance capital would cover only well under 2 per cent of total current credit usage! Moving outstandings close to meeting even 10 or 20 per cent of the needs of poor households will require something more than just letting operations drift along as they currently exist.

Developing the supply of micro-financial services

Specialised MFOs alone cannot meet the total demand for micro-financial services in India. Instead, a three-track approach is required (Mahajan and Nagasri, 1999) to:

- incentivise existing mainstream financial-service providers;
- encourage new MFOs with a supportive policy and regulatory framework and financial resources to enlarge and expand their services; and

- to build, from the grassroots up, a network of community-based financial intermediaries.

All of these will clearly require better regulation and policy to create the appropriate enabling environment.

Policy

Perhaps the most immediate policy initiative that is required is the transformation of the repayment culture. Any expansion of micro-financial services will need not only appropriate and efficient micro-products on a very large scale, but also customers who are willing to pay the full costs of those services. This will not be easy for politicians and bureaucrats, and the many vested interests, who are addicted to subsidies and targets, rather than developing a genuine market. Moreover, as a result, many bankers have become cynical about lending to poor people because of the low repayments of government-subsidised loans, attitudes that are only just beginning to change with experiences of lending to SHGs. Bankers must therefore also change their attitude towards small loans to poor people, including poor women, from seeing them as a social obligation to treating them as potential business opportunities.

Equally important, policy-makers need to recognise the potential of micro-financial services to support investment and growth in key economic sectors and hence to contribute significantly to national economic growth. It is only such a recognition that will draw the necessary attention, skills and resources to understand, disseminate information and invest in these markets. The rural non-farm sector has the most potential to grow (see Fisher and Mahajan, 1997), especially services which now contribute close to half of India's gross domestic product.[1] However, the non-farm sector cannot thrive if the agricultural sector and rural demand generally, especially among poor people, stagnate.

Policy, however, needs to go much further than just recognising lending for micro-finance as priority-sector lending, to address the ultimate engine driving demand for micro-credit, which are micro-enterprises themselves. This will require identifying and understanding growth and emergent sub-sectors within the economy, from the national to the local level, and enabling and supporting the entry and growth of micro- and small-entrepreneurs, including those who employ poor people. Finance itself will not provide adequate support for this. For example, beyond a particular scale of operations a micro-business may be more constrained by entrepreneurial ability or the lack of access to non-local markets, which restricts the ability of many borrowers to move to larger loans. Micro-enterprises also face a wide range of policy and economic risks.

Such a strategy will further strengthen the micro-finance sector by generating wider knowledge about the linkages that exist in particular sub-sectors and about critical points at which effective interventions can be made. Such information can then enable a more informed engagement by mainstream financial intermediaries and MFOs.

Regulation

Regulation of micro-financial services is often necessary (Fisher et al., 2001). As Mahajan and Nagasri (1999: 7) argue, regulation

> helps in long-term sustainability, even though MFOs may chafe under it in the initial years. The need for regulation and supervision of MFOs arises from several considerations like protecting the interests of small savers, ensuring proper terms of credit, instilling financial discipline and having a proper reporting and supervision system. Regulation and supervision ensure that MFOs are run prudently and cases of poor people losing their money due to fraud or incompetence are minimised.

Significant progress in the regulatory environment for micro-financial services has already been achieved. For example, micro-credit was recognised as a specific strategy in the credit policy announced in 1999, and new organisational forms, like the Local Area Bank (LAB), have been created. Most interest rate ceilings have also been removed.

However, there is still a long way to go. For example, interest-rate ceilings still apply to the smallest loans below Rs 200,000, even though, because of cost structures, interest rates on micro-loans are going to be higher than on larger loans.

All the different micro-finance providers therefore face significant obstacles to developing their services. In terms of banks, in addition to the restrictions on interest rates on small loans, the Regional Rural Banks (RRBs) cannot take any private equity, and the cooperative acts of all states only allow the state government to set up district-level cooperative banks. The result of these laws is that rural credit has been a monopoly of state-owned intermediaries. Private finance 'companies' are not allowed to take deposits, and due to their unincorporated status, they cannot borrow from banks to grow their operations (Mahajan and Nagasri, 1999).

Non-profit MFOs face the following constraints:

- In most states the Registrar of Societies has not recognised micro-finance as a permitted activity for societies.
- The Income Tax Act (Section 2[15]) does not define micro-finance as a charitable activity, so that NGOs engaging in micro-finance risk losing their charitable status.
- The Income Tax Act (Section 11[5]) does not allow NGOs to promote mutual-benefit or commercial MFOs as they are not allowed to invest in equity.
- The Foreign Contribution Regulation Act is ambiguous about receiving funds for micro-finance, whether the foreign funds are used as grants or loans.
- Non-profit MFOs have difficulty in raising deposits without contravening the Reserve Bank of India (RBI) Act.

Moreover, both societies and not-for-profit companies (Section 25 companies) do not recognise their capital. Subsequently, lenders have difficulty assessing the levels to which they should take an exposure to them, the kind of collateral that they must ask for and most importantly, how to assess the soundness of the operations for which the organisations are borrowing funds.

Mutual-benefit MFOs also face significant constraints. To begin with, since 1995 only five states have enacted liberal acts for mutually-aided cooperatives free of government control (Andhra Pradesh, Bihar, Madhya Pradesh, Jammu and Kashmir and Punjab; see Chapter 6). Even though there are now many savings and credit cooperatives registered under these acts, NABARD does not extend refinance to them, nor has the RBI amended its rules to support such progressive cooperatives. Other mutual benefit structures (such as *nidhis*)[2] also need to be encouraged.

Commercial MFOs that seek to attract loan and equity funds operate in an uncertain environment, and the RBI needs to create a policy for such commercial entities. Currently they have to register as non-banking finance companies (NBFCs), requiring minimum start-up equity of Rs 2 crore (20 million). The RBI prohibits deposit-taking by NBFCs that do not have ratings by two different rating agencies, both of which must be above investment grade, which obviously takes a significant time to achieve. This makes the NBFC route very difficult for MFOs, unless they can attract foreign equity.

However, not only are there few Indian sources of equity (for example, NABARD is not allowed to make equity investments), taking foreign equity has been fraught with legal and bureaucratic obstacles. Likewise, tax benefits available to housing and infrastructure finance companies, and some to banks (under Sections 10 and 36 of the Income Tax Act), are not available to commercial MFOs.

Even the apex finance institutions are constrained. For example, NABARD cannot refinance any private-sector financial intermediary or any bank lending to SHGs in urban areas, while SIDBI cannot extend loans to the agricultural and allied sectors, even though many members of SHGs are engaged in such activities. And HUDCO is restricted to lending for housing only.

There has been some progress in these areas. For example, non-profit (Section 25) companies were exempted from regulations for NBFCs in January 2000, which was taken further in February 2000 to allow any organisations, of whatever legal form, working with poor people and providing them financial services to access loans, refinance and other capital to on-lend to their clients in whatever way they choose (legal form neutrality, product diversity). Lending for micro-finance was classified as priority-sector lending at the same time, and foreign equity allowed in August 2000.

Further progress needs to be made, for example, in lifting interest-rate ceilings on all loans, and above all in developing a more enabling environment for savings. Effective micro-savings products are urgently needed to meet the security needs of poor people and to raise adequate capital to lend to them. Most MFOs that offer flexible savings products, as well as banks, have discovered that the pool of savings that can be accumulated from poor micro-savers often exceeds their capacity to absorb credit (see Chapter 3).

However, because of restrictions introduced to curb corrupt finance companies, most MFOs, including those registered as NBFCs, are unable to raise deposits. A regulatory structure allowing degrees of regulation as the number and amounts of deposits grow would be a more appropriate response. A new form of micro-finance company requiring less start-up capital would also help. In either case, MFOs would have to be able to distinguish themselves clearly, not least to their poor clients, from corrupt or inefficient service-providers.

All of these issues relate to the regulation of micro-finance as a whole, which has not yet been resolved in the Indian context (Sa-Dhan, 2001). Should MFOs fall under mainstream regulation, enjoy special regulation under a new chapter in the RBI Act of 1934 (as proposed by the micro-finance task force, NABARD [1999b]) or a new act altogether, regulate themselves, or come under a graduated regulatory framework depending on the scale of their operations? Should MFOs which provide only credit be regulated at all?

A graduated framework might be appropriate to ensure only light regulation on the smallest micro-finance providers, including NGOs, with regulation intensifying as operations expand, requiring conversion to a more appropriate status like a cooperative or company.

The emergence of a large number of SHGs (as described in Chapters 5 and 7 to 9) will also need attention. Many of the SHGs that started 5 to 10 years ago have moved on to enlarge their operations. They are borrowing much more and collecting higher levels of deposits from their members. What are the financial and operational risks emerging within these groups? And who is responsible for some form of supervision, the promoting NGO, the bank lending to the SHG, any federations of SHGs, or some other body?

As democratic local organisations, members are of course primarily responsible, and the fate of cooperatives should warn officials off seeking to interfere, which will lead to the inevitable stagnation of the movement. However, attention to the performance of SHGs, and on how to protect micro-savers from corrupt promoters, will become an ever more important issue.

Resources

Equally important as the overall policy and regulatory environment are the availability of promotional resources and how the delivery of these is organised. Most of the promotional resources for developing micro-financial services still come from donors, often based abroad. Many domestic sources are restricted to funding state-promoted organisations.

As suggested above, there are also severe restrictions on accessing equity (whether domestic or foreign), key apex financial intermediaries are restricted in what they can refinance, and, because of the overall reputation of NBFCs, micro-finance providers incorporated as NBFCs have significant difficulties in accessing debt finance from banks and other financial intermediaries. Micro-finance, in contrast to other financial services, is also not eligible for tax incentives. Unblocking these many restrictions could significantly enhance the resources available to the sector.

In terms of resources for promotion, NGOs and other agencies promoting SHGs have at best received Rs 25 crore (Rs 250 million or US$5 million) from domestic resources over the past decade. Compare this to the over US$150 million of grants and soft loans that the Grameen Bank alone has received, and to the Rs 250 crore (2,500 million) of outstanding loans from banks to SHGs.[3]

The growth of bank loans to SHGs suggests that, in addition to members' savings, the capital needed for growth of micro-finance in India will be resourced from within the formal financial sector. However, where will the resources for promoting SHGs and other community-based providers come from? With massive expansion, NGOs and other promoting agencies will also face the challenge of whether to rely entirely on donor grants, or progressively to move towards first identifying (see Chapter 8) and later attempting to cover their own costs.

With massive expansion, the performance of SHGs also becomes ever more critical, especially as many SHGs are being promoted by governments and banks. Ensuring good performance and sustainability across such a vast number of small local organisations is a real challenge, and will require significant resources for support and development.

Likewise, as specialised MFOs grow, whether NGOs, cooperatives or companies, they will require increasing resources not just for capital, but also for organisational and human resource development to ensure they become effective financial and developmental organisations. Such resources will have to come from a range of organisations, including donors, the mainstream financial sector, NGOs and training institutes. The emergence of support organisations like the Andhra Pradesh Mahila Abhivruddhi Society (APMAS) for capacity-building for savings and credit groups is a promising sign of developments here. As the sector grows, the effectiveness of such resources will also have to be assessed.

Even within the formal sector, RRBs have been going through significant change, but investment in organisational development will need to continue if they are to become effective providers of micro-financial services.

A further challenge is that the vast majority of resources are channelled through public agencies, which can be slow, rule-bound and risk-averse. Almost no attempt has been made to build more independent organisations for resourcing and supporting providers of micro-financial services that must emerge if the sector is going to massively expand and develop.

It is even more unfortunate that the provision of these funds has been made to organisations that are ostensibly credit-disbursing organisations. This often dilutes the intensity of the credit contract the lending organisation has with the borrowing organisation and leads to potential conflicts of interest between the management of loan funds on the one hand and capacity-building funds on the other. Indeed, the patient and slower investments and risks required for developing a wide range of MFOs do not come easily to lenders. Ironically, this strategy among public support agencies mixes credit with other development activities, even though the very same donors and promotional agencies generally encourage MFOs at the retail level to focus more clearly on one or the other.

Capacity and performance of MFOs and community-based intermediaries

Critical to the expansion of micro-financial services is the ability of retail organisations to grow. This however is easier said than done. As this book demonstrates, most agencies are pursuing distinct strategies in developing financial services for poor people. Reinforcing effectiveness and improving efficiencies will therefore require skill in weaving appropriate measures into the diverse fabric of existing operations and innovation.

Developing any new and innovative instruments of support must therefore be based on a systematic understanding of the requirements of the service-providers which incorporates their socio-economic context, their developmental objectives, governance structures, management quality and functional competencies. Such understanding will enable a set of good practices, appropriate to different providers, to emerge. These good practices and their constant improvement can perform a critical function in enhancing effectiveness and efficiency, and provide the basis for instruments and support that can strengthen retail organisations, in terms of both the scale and quality of their services.

Within this broad approach there are areas that require specific attention. Prominent among these is the development of products and services. Evidence emerging from the different interventions presented in this book suggests that overcoming market imperfections and distortions is a difficult and challenging task, as is the appropriate use of resources, both subsidised and commercial. In many cases this has been achieved through the development of robust methodologies within existing programme designs. Such innovations, with their resulting modifications in product design and pricing, need to be adopted more widely.

This applies equally to the growing understanding of the financial needs of poor people and not least the development impacts of micro-finance on them, an important focus of this book. As Rutherford points out (in Oberdorf, 1999: 88–89), such understanding has rarely led to better product design to enhance the performance and impact of MFOs. It is urgent that this gap between research on needs and impact on the one hand and the technical design of products on the other is closed.

Another critical area is upgrading the skill levels of staff. For example, Chapters 5, 8 and 9 have demonstrated the importance of high-quality staff to promote effective SHGs, and illustrated the wide variations that can exist not just between different NGOs but even within the same NGO.

Any strategy to upgrade skills needs to begin by seeking to understand the quality of human resources the MFOs are currently recruiting, and the quality available to them in the long term. On the basis of such understanding, it is possible to design programmes to upgrade skills that equip staff first with the necessary minimum level of understanding, and thereafter enable them to constantly improve their skills and the effectiveness of the services they provide. Some of the specific skills that require enhancement are the ability to integrate financial-service provision and developmental objectives, to mobilise resources, to identify and manage elements of costs, and to maintain financial discipline.

The challenge here is that, while many micro-finance initiatives have emerged, there are as yet few agreed standards. Some issues are achieving greater clarity. Few practitioners would argue anymore in favour of subsidised credit if it undermines lending and means, for example, that savings and credit groups or cooperatives managed by members themselves cannot achieve sustainability and hence independence from external support. However, the challenge of standards and measurement that adequately address the great diversity of micro-finance practice in India, as we illustrate in this book, remains. Financial performance can be measured using a range of ratios. However, their meaning can remain contested and means of assessing development impact illusive.

Overcoming these obstacles is important not only for individual retailers, but also for the development of micro-finance markets generally. First, it will enable retailers to adopt good practices from each other. In particular, methodological innovations that reduce costs will enable many more service-providers to enter the market, from mainstream banks to NGOs.

Second, the understanding achieved through these means will also enhance the ability of promotional agencies, of third parties such as auditors, rating agencies and others and not least of regulators to better support and enable the sector through appropriate and effective measures. This is critical to support good practice more widely and enable the expansion of micro-finance markets that is essential if a larger proportion of the many poor people that need them in India is to benefit.

The role of different stakeholders

Table 11.1 summarises and develops this analysis by providing an assessment of the different stakeholders involved in the micro-finance sector in India, their respective actions, and how these help or restrain the healthy growth of the sector. Building on the table I briefly outline the key roles of each stakeholder.

Government

The government is one of the most powerful stakeholders, with overall responsibility for policy and policy instruments. It is clear from the analysis above that there are specific measures that the government needs to introduce.

In broad terms, the government has to withdraw from credit disbursal, whether directly or through the banking system, which has caused severe market distortions. Product design has been wrong, costs have gone up, rent-seeking and

Table 11.1: The role of stakeholders in developing the micro-finance sector

Stakeholder	Action	Constructive	Distortive
Government	(1) Policy priorities: (a) Identifying areas in line with political preferences (b) Monitoring efficiencies (2) Policy instruments (a) Policy measures (b) Resource allocation (c) Incentives such as tax-breaks	• Allocating appropriate resources • Defining priorities and increasing allocations • Sharing knowledge and information with other stakeholders	• Only working with government-owned agencies • Expecting diverse competencies from single agencies rather than seeing the need for a wider range of diverse organisations within the sector • Concentrating resources • Piece-meal and reactive policy-making structures • Not focused on markets and demands of poor clients
Regulators	Regulation and supervision, including defining financial and legal forms	• Removing distortions (interest rates, etc.) in markets • Increasing acceptance of the diversity of financial intermediaries that is neutral to the model adopted and also allows product diversity • Investments in understanding entities and their assets and liabilities	• Primary reliance on mainstream ideas and primary attention to formal mainstream intermediaries, both of which may not be appropriate to micro-finance organisations • Lack of investment in internal capacity among regulators and supervisors
Apex bodies	Resource flows for • public goods • debt • equity	• Sharpening organisational competencies. Develop skill-sets to match objective of instruments and resources (e.g., through bank linkage programme)	• Conflict of interest between different resource functions, such as lending, capacity-building and supervisory functions

Actor	Function	Strengths	Weaknesses
		• Monitoring and improving asset quality	• Many of the same distortive characteristics that apply to government also apply to the publicly owned apex bodies
Banks	Providing debt and equity	• Improving service quality and costs • Potentially taking up equity positions	• Only understand collateral-based debt appraisal • May view lending to micro-enterprises as an obligation rather than business opportunity
Donors	Resource flows for • public goods • debt • equity	• Increasing flows to appropriate bodies and intermediaries • Resources for specialisation	• Limited instruments for interventions • Concentrating both loan and development funding in the same organisations • Limited allocation of resources for learning-by-doing
MFOs, community-based service-providers	Service provision	• Innovative and risk-taking • Focus on expansion, targeting, experimentation, etc., with client-group • Building of skills and products to suit client-group	• Weak MIS and monitoring • Limited learning from operations and peers • Inadequate attention to micro-enterprise demand and to demand constraints
Support (third party) organisations	Bridging different experiences; Audit and data verification, rating; Organisation and human resource development; Evaluation, impact assessment; etc.	• Verifying information and data • Establishing quality benchmarks • Investing in research and refinement	• Limited specialisation • Inappropriate application of tools and methods

corruption have become widespread, and bankers have become cynical about lending to poor people. The government needs to establish an enabling environment for a diverse range of providers, not deliver credit itself.

Second, the government needs to give the micro-finance sector greater attention, in particular seeing its potential to support poverty alleviation, economic development and even local democracy, but not in the traditional interventionist and controlling way. It needs to free up the regulatory environment, for example ensuring many more states adopt liberal cooperative laws. It also needs to understand the diversity of service-providers, and hence avoid simplistic and standardised solutions.

Attention to micro-financial services must be part of a wider policy engagement with poverty alleviation and, as I suggested above, with micro-enterprise, including a deep understanding of their role in providing livelihoods and contributing to national economic development.

In terms of resources targeted at the micro-finance sector, these are required not only for strengthening existing providers, whether MFOs or their support organisations, but also, if massive expansion is to be achievable, for promoting many new ones.

Critical for such an endeavour is the better allocation of resources, in particular moving significant resources from public sector entities, that are sitting on huge resources for capacity-building, to effective service-deliverers and their promoters in the private, non-profit or community sectors, whether banks, specialised MFOs, cooperatives, NGOs or SHGs. Developing a strong tier of support organisations will be critical. Allocation of resources can be done through budgetary allocations as well as incentives, for example through the tax system.

Changing or clarifying tax laws is in fact critical. For example, NGOs must have the confidence that micro-financial services are regarded as charitable if they are going to expand their operations beyond being mere financial service boutiques. The tax laws must not undermine the building of reserves and other provisions to contribute to financial strength.

Regulators

The Reserve Bank of India and NABARD have both worked on developing a more favourable regulatory environment for micro-finance (NABARD, 1999b). However, much change is still needed. Choices on how best to regulate providers of micro-financial services need to be taken, which do not hamper the development of existing providers or the entry of new ones, but do protect poor savers in particular. Such regulation must recognise the need for a great diversity of service-providers if the sector is to have any chance of meeting the huge demand for micro-financial services among poor people.

Equally important, the micro-finance sector continues to be buffeted by regulatory changes introduced to address the needs of the mainstream financial sector, but that do not take their impact on MFOs into consideration. This needs to change. Regulation must be developed based on a clear understanding of micro-finance providers, their diverse developmental goals, legal and governance structures, management capacities, clients, activities and future growth plans. Only then will regulation not only provide the necessary protection for clients but also actively contribute to the development of the sector that provides an essential service to them.

The focus of regulation must therefore be on the soundness of the diverse range of MFOs, rather than trying to accommodate them into existing regulatory provisions that may not be appropriate. The key principles underlying such regulation must be:

- maintaining the interests of clients;
- making a range of services available;
- creating a stable image for the sector that can provide confidence to clients;
- providing access to investment funds and refinance;
- increasing the capacity and performance of service-providers;
- supporting their sustainability in the broadest sense set out above;
- pre-empting any repressive action by politicians, bureaucrats or regulators.

One further essential regulatory change, controlled by the government rather than the Reserve Bank, is to facilitate the flow of investments in micro-finance from abroad, which are more readily available and at cheaper cost. A new scheme, possibly called 'External Developmental Borrowings (EDB)', could be established on the lines of the External Commercial Borrowings (ECB) scheme.

Apex financial institutions

Apex financial bodies need to perform a range of specialised functions, including lending (debt), providing technical services, providing capacity-building inputs as well as playing supervisory roles. The key point to emphasise is that these are all specialised functions in their own right, often requiring highly specialised skills. It is inappropriate to mix them within one agency, which tends to create tensions and conflicts. Sound lending requires a very different approach from effective capacity-building, for example.

Unfortunately, policy-makers and donors have tended to prefer a small number of apex bodies to interact with and support, saddling them with a wide range of objectives and functions, which makes it challenging for them to deliver these objectives and functions effectively, however laudable they may be.

Apex bodies also have an important role in building up relevant knowledge. Analysis of their portfolios, for example, would yield very useful information and insights into performance among MFOs, which, if shared, could assist in building the sector as a whole.

Banks and other mainstream intermediaries

The banking sector to date has done a commendable job in the bank–SHG linkage programme. The total number of SHGs that have received loans from banks exceeds 300,000. The programme involves over 300 banks and 1,000 NGOs, and cumulative loans from the banking system exceed Rs 500 crore (Rs 5,000 million or some US$95 million) (see Chapter 7).

It is important therefore that, as this programme expands rapidly, the linkage mechanism improves. Some new efforts are emerging, such as internal appraisal tools that can help bankers differentiate the good from the bad. New and innovative instruments for lending and support are also emerging, for example, bulk lending through federations and marketing support. What is still lacking is the emergence of more equity-based products. In addition, the challenge of expanding such activities to a very different scale of operations remains, as does the need to understand the enterprises poor people invest in and that ultimately determine the soundness of the emerging portfolio. Such information and learning-by-doing can contribute dramatically to enhancing the quality and the scale of the overall linkage programme.

It would be wrong, however, to suggest that the role of banks is limited to loans to SHGs. Self-help groups can only address a distinct segment of the market, and are not appropriate, for example, to larger micro- and small-enterprise lending. Likewise, the analysis in Chapter 10 suggested that SHGs encourage only limited savings, well below the savings capacity of many poor people. Ultimately, if the demand for micro-financial services—savings, credit and insurance—is to be met more than marginally, the mainstream financial sector will have to engage much more extensively in providing such services.

It is therefore essential that banks develop more appropriate and flexible savings products and a far greater range of loan products that can meet the diverse needs of poor people. These could be delivered directly or in collaboration with specialised MFOs. Likewise, insurance companies need to develop services that not only incorporate appropriate products but also ensure their delivery is intelligible and secure for poor people, even those who are illiterate, for example.

The case of Bank Rakyat Indonesia (BRI) suggests that it is possible for mainstream financial intermediaries to develop such services as part of their commercial operations. It is critical therefore that the mainstream financial sector understands the business opportunities in micro-financial services.

Donors

Donors play a critical role in providing resources, and are in some cases better able to take on the risks of supporting innovation in pursuit of their developmental objectives. Most donors also recognise the diversity of stakeholders (regulators, policy-makers, bankers, NGOs, etc.) and their needs that require attention if markets for micro-finance are to develop. Their contribution in calling attention to the need for developing the competencies of different stakeholders is therefore significant.

However, translating this understanding into a viable strategy for their own interventions has proved more challenging. Any large funds are usually placed with public-sector organisations, and often require such organisations to take on multiple roles that may conflict with each other. For example, enabling the same agency to both lend and provide capacity-building inputs to MFOs can lead to serious conflicts in their strategies and operations. Donors need to develop a greater diversity of investment channels for their funds, as well as a range of non-financial interventions, that are in tune with their understanding of the organisational diversity and complexity among the sector's many different stakeholders.

Donors, who are accustomed to give grants, also urgently need to develop more alternative mechanisms to provide debt and equity support, like the programme-related investments of the Ford Foundation. The Government of India should encourage such alternative mechanisms as a valuable source of capital.

Retail providers of micro-financial services

As outlined in Chapter 2, there are three different types of specialised retailers outside of the mainstream financial sector:

- Not-for-profit MFOs such as societies and trusts (legal forms of NGOs) that lend to borrowers, usually organised into groups (SHGs or Grameen-style).
- Mutual-benefit MFOs, especially cooperatives; a few urban cooperative banks like SEWA Bank and a growing number

of mutually-aided cooperative societies (MACS) under the new cooperative acts.

- For-profit MFOs incorporated as non-banking financial companies such as BASIX and SHARE Micro-finance Limited.

In each of these categories MFOs need to grow and enhance the quality of their services. The data on the bank–SHG linkage programme suggests that there are at least a thousand small and large NGOs involved in the promotion of SHGs. The quality of their work varies significantly, as evidence from this book shows. The need to enhance the promotional capacities of these NGOs is therefore urgent if the SHG movement is to grow, and above all if SHGs are to provide high-quality services and sustain them effectively into the future.

In addition, some of the NGOs are not just linking SHGs to banks but also providing them credit directly. Such credit is drawn from a variety of sources, mostly government bodies and banks. This requires a very different range of skills, not least for managing their own financial-service operations, which many of these NGOs do not currently have, as the evidence from Chapter 10 makes very clear.

It is important that the emphasis on meeting the demands of poor clients does not cloud understanding of the need to build not just SHGs but also the NGOs that promote and support them.

Mutual-benefit MFOs are expanding rapidly, especially under the new mutually-aided cooperative acts. However, there is a long history of cooperatives being undermined by external entities. These MFOs will therefore have to build their internal capacities to withstand such interference and take on the full responsibilities that come with owning and managing one's own organisation. At the time of writing, urban cooperative banks were facing major challenges, so for the time-being they are unlikely to serve as an effective avenue for the expansion of micro-financial services.

Finally, there are still very few for-profit MFOs registered as NBFCs and only one LAB committed to micro-finance. Finding effective ways of expanding this segment is therefore a priority.

For all categories, the need to develop standards is essential, as has begun to happen through the association of MFOs, Sa-Dhan.

Support organisations

Support organisations are central to the performance of the sector. There are a range of them, such as auditors, consultancies, rating agencies, providers of technical services, organisation development experts, etc. One of their key contributions is to intermediate in the demand for information and skills.

For retail agencies, they provide a road map, set standards, draw attention to difficulties, highlight opportunities and contribute to enhancing their operational abilities. For investors, they demystify operations, translate them into categories that make sense, thereby enabling investments. For regulators, they provide essential market information, not least on financial performance, and signal dangers. In performing these tasks, they can provide independent assessments that provide the crucial affirmation to information supplied by the retail providers themselves.

The main challenge is their limited numbers. As in the case of apex bodies, such a shortage can give rise to the concentration of too many resources and too many different functions in a few organisations, and some functions can conflict with each other. Far too little attention has been paid to such organisations and to initiatives to help them improve and expand their skills and services. Most of these organisations will also be in the private sector, not the public sector, making it more difficult for them to attract development resources while the sector is still emerging.

For all the stakeholders set out above, gathering and sharing market information is critical. This responsibility falls to the government, the mainstream financial intermediaries, including at the apex level, the MFOs (especially through their association) and the support organisations that are often well placed to process the information (see, for example, the analysis provided in Chapter 10). Without sound market information, the sector will not be able to grow effectively.

Conclusion

This chapter argues that the optimum expansion of the market for micro-financial services can only come about as a result of active participation by all the relevant stakeholders. It suggests that there are roles different agencies must play, for example, in overcoming information asymmetries, strengthening organisations at the retail level, and increasing the flow of resources, both for capital and organisation development.

Much progress has already been made. As the sector has shifted from its nascent to its growing phase, mainstream financial intermediaries have become more engaged, an association has emerged, supporting organisations are coming up for training, capacity-building and rating, for example, and discussions on performance standards are under way.

While there is increasing support for developing the micro-finance sector in this way, there is also a dangerous trend of concentrating or appropriating too many roles around a few lead agencies. Building or improving the institutional efficiency of all stakeholders, including regulators, policy-makers and retailers as well as support agencies in the private sector, is a necessary and concomitant task that is not attracting sufficient attention and resources.

The opportunity provided by such an approach is of course that the impact can extend across all providers of micro-financial services, whether banks and other mainstream financial intermediaries, specialised MFOs or community-based financial intermediaries. Only such a three-pronged strategy has any chance of making progress in meeting the vast need for micro-financial services among poor people in India.

Such a sectoral strategy needs to balance the need for greater standardisation to ensure significant impact, replication and projection with the need to ensure diversity to meet a wide range of needs and engage a wide range of creative energies of social entrepreneurs.

As this book demonstrates very clearly, the need for diversity extends well beyond the diversity of particular models, systems and technologies. Perhaps two factors stand out in particular: the diversity in socio-economic environments and the diversity of developmental missions espoused by different MFOs. For example, it makes little sense to assess the performance of MFOs according to the ratio of their staff to clients, if the number of staff needed varies significantly according to literacy levels among clients.

This also suggests that the overall design of a sectoral strategy must be informed by the development of an effective market, for which interventions on the demand side are as important as supply-side measures. Appropriate policy and support for livelihoods, micro-enterprises and community-based organisations are therefore as important as resourcing the suppliers of financial services.

Notes

1. As reported in *The Economic Times*, Hyderabad, 27 November 2001.
2. *Nidhis* are mutual-benefit societies, incorporated under an act of 1913 that allowed neighbours to save money and secure loans at favourable rates of interest, made up of poor and middle-class people. They are now incorporated under Section 620a of the new Companies Act.
3. These comparisons are instructive. In spite of receiving far fewer resources, the membership of SHGs is expanding very rapidly. In Chapter 7, Malcolm Harper estimates that, in one year alone (2000–2001), the SHGs that took their first loan from a bank had almost as many members (2.5 million) as the Grameen Bank (3 million +).

Chapter 12

Emerging lessons and challenges

Thomas Fisher

In this concluding chapter, I look at 10 lessons and challenges that emerge from our analysis. I begin with the following five: micro-financial services must be used as an instrument of development; those services must be adapted to their context; non-governmental organisations (NGOs) have a distinct role to play; practitioners and supporting agencies must learn to deal with wider systems; and, building on the last point, the fast emerging savings and credit groups in India make up a system that urgently requires system-wide attention. I deal with each of these in turn in the first half of this chapter. In the second half, I take up five additional challenges of capacity-building, a topic that has often failed to attract sufficient reflective analysis.

Five lessons

At the broadest level, this book suggests that micro-financial services must be integrated into wider strategies and systems. It shows that this can be done effectively in practice to meet the diverse needs of poor people, integrating micro-financial services into broader strategies to achieve developmental outcomes, into existing local markets, into the existing institutional and infrastructural context. Integration is a key concept that underlies many of the specific points I take up below.

It is not a coincidence that the provision of micro-financial services raises such issues. On the one hand, micro-financial services are a 'hard' technical and economic instrument, which brings to the fore tensions with 'softer' developmental goals. On the other hand, underlying the provision of all financial services, more than any other economic activity, is the need for trust or social capital. 'Credit' after all means 'trust'. Without trust, no financial intermediation would take place. This recognition has been built into the extensive use of groups in micro-financial services, and in the concept of social intermediation explored in Chapter 5.

This book pushes the door opened by the need for trust much further to incorporate a broader range and depth of 'softer' developmental goals. For example, trust or social capital is as important for democratic organisation as for the delivery of financial services. By combining the two, trust developed through the former can help support the latter, and *vice versa*. The analysis in Chapter 5 in fact may reverse the logic of social intermediation. Rather than using social intermediation to prepare for the delivery of financial services, organising poor people around a concrete activity like financial intermediation enables them to build social capital. This leads into my first and most important lesson.

1. Micro-financial services are a means or instrument of development, not an end in themselves

With the growth of an international micro-finance industry with access to significant resources, and with the attraction of a technical 'solution' or 'fix', micro-finance can all too easily become an end in itself. However, micro-finance by itself is only developmental inasmuch as many poor people clearly need access to financial services through effective financial intermediation. If realistic within a given context, an effective banking system is by far the best way of achieving this developmental end, as has happened to a large extent in Indonesia, for example.

To achieve any other developmental goals through micro-finance, whether enhancing social and economic security, promoting livelihoods, reviving local economies, empowering women and poor people, building democratic organisations or bringing about wider institutional change, micro-finance has to be seen as an instrument within wider strategies. For example, as both the Cooperative Development Foundation and MYRADA argue, it is the management of financial services, not the financial services themselves, that is empowering. To be empowering in this way, any promotional strategy must incorporate capacity-building inputs to ensure effective ownership, governance and management by poor people of democratic organisations that provide micro-financial services (Chapter 5).

Likewise, Chapters 3 and 4 have shown that micro-financial services can do little in themselves to promote poor people's livelihoods. For this they must be integrated as instruments within wider livelihood strategies. Ironically, the micro-finance industry grew out of wider development efforts to promote enterprises in particular, but the seduction of an easy technical fix that micro-finance provides has meant that practitioners have often lost sight of those wider strategies. As Dichter (2001: 8, 22–23) comments:

> For the magic of micro-finance, with its promise to be self-financing while building economic capacity from the grassroots up, is far more seductive than the complex and more conceptually abstract realm of sub-sector analysis, rural infrastructure revitalisation, and technical support to enterprises.... As difficult as micro-finance is, it is not really rocket science and certainly not much an art. If the half dozen or so professional quality micro-finance manuals produced in the last 10 years were all to be followed carefully, many more good micro-finance organisations would now exist. The techniques of micro-finance can be learned, and imitated. In contrast the kind of work BASIX has pioneered in the enterprise development sphere and its continuing experimentation to find the best way of integrating financial services and sector-based enterprise development represents more of an art.

As soon as we entertain the potential instrumentality of micro-finance to meet a wide range of developmental goals, the situation becomes complex. Development after all is complex. It is perhaps not surprising that the leading Indian economist,

Amartya Sen, has deeply challenged existing economic frameworks with their emphasis on income, growth, utility and efficiency (ODI, 2001). How easily the micro-finance industry often slips into such a narrow paradigm. However, Sen draws attention to individual entitlements, capabilities, freedoms and rights as key to economic development.

For example, given income disparities within India, it is unlikely that the economic growth that India is experiencing will by itself enhance the economic security of many of the 400 million poor people in India, unless they can gain entitlements to share in the benefits of such growth. Sen argues that civil and political rights can reduce the risk of major social and economic disasters and thereby significantly enhance poor people's security. Even the World Bank's *World Development Report* for 2000–01 acknowledges 'that poverty is more than inadequate income and human development—it is also vulnerability and lack of voice, power and representation' (ODI, 2001: 2).

To what extent does micro-finance contribute to these wider issues of entitlements, rights, voice, representation, power? An initial response might be to suggest not loading micro-finance with developmental goals that it cannot hope to address. This is perhaps the greatest danger of the approach taken in this book, that MFOs seek to take on a range of different developmental goals, achieving none of them well, rather than focusing strategically on one or two.

However, evidence suggests that, used strategically and in a focused manner, micro-finance can contribute to these wider goals. We have seen in Chapters 5 and 9 how the provision of micro-financial services can be designed in practice to build democratic people's organisations that give women, in particular, greater voice and representation, and in Chapter 6 how micro-financial services can be integrated into coherent strategies to enhance the entitlements and rights of poor producers.

Design inputs required for such interventions, however, go well beyond the efficient delivery of financial services. The key design challenge is integrating financial services within those broader strategies. Again, practice reviewed in this book suggests that this need not be a matter of coupling together disparate objectives and techniques. It is possible to integrate them into a coherent whole. For example, as suggested above, it is managing financial services well that is empowering. Designing the efficient delivery of micro-financial services can therefore contribute as much to empowerment agendas as to service-provision itself.

2. Adapt the provision of micro-finance to its context

Designing developmental micro-financial services cannot be done without proper attention and adaptation to the environment in which those services will operate; there cannot be a design blueprint to suit every condition. The analysis in this book has made this abundantly clear by reviewing a wide range of different methods for providing micro-financial services already in practice in India, from informal local groups to banks. Here I draw attention to five specific points.

First, any micro-finance interventions need to fit the overall institutional context (Chapter 7). This can apply to cultural and political factors, such as the strong commitment in India to democratic organisation and decentralisation, to diversity and personal independence, which may make the self-help group (SHG) design, rather than Grameen Bank-style groups, particularly appropriate in the Indian context. It also applies to the existence of formal infrastructure that can be tapped, in particular the huge network of bank branches (see further below).

Second, potential micro-finance clients already have access to a range of financial services, both formal and informal. It is not just that any new micro-financial services need to take account of existing provision, and the impact the new services are likely to have on the existing market. The experience of those markets will also deeply influence the willingness of potential clients to engage in any new services, and the way in which they participate. The design of any new services therefore has to take the previous experience of potential clients, and the behavioural patterns that are likely to arise from such experience, into account.[1] These factors may also have a significant impact on the cost of developing micro-financial services (Chapter 8).

Third, it is important to understand the local community. Indian communities are often deeply divided into groups by caste, religion and opinion, and economic power rests with the most powerful groups. Targeting the provision of micro-financial services at the poorer and more disadvantaged groups, as many NGOs in particular do, may therefore be appropriate in many contexts.

However, it should not be assumed that this is always the best strategy. Evidence in this book has shown that SHGs can bring together different groups among the poor and benefit all of them, and that some savings and credit cooperatives have brought together members from across the whole community, from poor to rich, for mutual benefit (Chapter 5). Within a political context that is ever ready to divide one group from another, such interventions may be particularly appropriate in building local democracy.

Fourth, it is equally important to understand the local economy. This goes beyond a deep understanding of local financial markets to embrace other features of the local economy. For example, given the choice, most poor people prefer wage-employment to the risks of self-employment. Supporting small enterprises that can provide wage-employment, even though most will not be managed by poor people, may therefore be an important strategy (Chapter 4).

Likewise, if designed correctly, micro-financial services can have a wider impact on the local economy that benefits almost all economic actors. The Mulkanoor cooperative, providing both agricultural and financial services from which all farmers in the village benefit, has been able to raise purchasing power across the community, which has led to demand for other goods and services provided locally. Strategies that seek to saturate a local economy with micro-financial services are more likely to have these second-order effects (Chapter 6).

Greater understanding of how micro-financial services can impact money-flows and economic activities within the local economy as a whole is thus urgently required.

Finally, mapping the existing community and economy, the provision of financial services and the institutional environment, also provides the baseline information needed to assess impacts on development processes, which I address further below.

3. NGOs have a distinct role to play

Much micro-finance practice was developed by NGOs. However, with the increasing critiques of NGOs in development, not least of their effectiveness, management and efficiency, they have often come to be more tolerated than admired. This is particularly the case within the micro-finance sector, where many doubt the ability of NGOs to manage the provision of micro-financial services, and alternative organisational structures like financial companies and banks are regarded as preferable.

> [NGOs] themselves are losing their sense of self and are beginning to see themselves through the criteria of other sectors and organisational forms. The exhortations to 'go to scale', to deliver according to the needs of government, to become profitable—or at least financially self-sustaining—all take their toll. And judged according to these criteria, [NGOs] are found wanting, relegated to the status of bit-players, cast in the mould of naïve and irrelevant youth disturbing the serious and 'real-world' concerns of adults (CDRA, 1996: 9).

It is time to recognise the distinct role of NGOs in micro-finance, rather than forcing them to become what they are not, to emulate the practices of other organisational forms that they will never be able to match. As the Community Development Resource Association (CDRA, 1996: 9) in South Africa puts it, NGOs 'are something more than merely inadequate enterprises or small-scale delivery-vehicles'.

First, in line with the dominant perspective on NGOs, they can provide a useful transitional organisational form that is more flexible than companies or banks. Even BASIX, with its strong commitment to becoming commercially viable and attracting mainstream resources, first developed its portfolio through the non-profit company within the group. The innovation required, the potential losses that might be incurred, and the ability to attract grant and low-cost capital would have been constrained by the legal form of a for-profit company.

Second, in strategies which focus on maintaining the delivery of high-quality micro-financial services in a local area (rather than going to scale through geographic expansion), some legal form of NGO may be more appropriate, especially if the governance of the NGO can be rooted in the local context. The governance issue may be more appropriately addressed through mutual ownership at the local level, although it is precisely here that the role of the NGO often becomes so important. The third area where NGOs often enjoy a comparative advantage is therefore in facilitating the emergence and performance of community-based financial organisations such as SHGs and savings and credit cooperatives, the fastest growing part of the micro-finance sector in India. Banks are much more likely to treat SHGs as efficient delivery channels for their loans, a strategy that often fails to deliver many of the potential empowerment impacts that such groups can bring (see Chapter 5). Non-governmental organisations still need to enhance their understanding and skills in finance for playing this role within the micro-finance sector, but the centrality of their value-base, for example of democracy, inclusivity, empowerment, equity and justice, is often conducive to facilitating developmental groups at the community level.

Fourth, the values that NGOs bring to the table should be used as a resource, rather than seeing them only as a hindrance to hard-nosed financial-service delivery. As Mathew Titus illustrates in Chapter 8, a cooperative group ideology facilitated by NGO promoters may prove a highly effective and efficient mechanism to spot violations in financial contracts which could not be detected through other mechanisms given the low computational skills of members. Indeed, financial markets can be severely constrained by inadequate computational skills, and developing literacy and education may therefore be as important to the widespread development of financial services for poor people as to addressing other human needs of theirs. Here again, NGOs are likely to play an important role.

Finally, as analysis in Chapter 6 revealed, NGOs like the Cooperative Development Foundation (CDF) and other non-commercial legal forms like the Self-employed Women's Association (SEWA) union can prove highly effective in creating a more conducive environment for micro-financial services and their developmental impacts through effective advocacy and other interventions in wider systems and institutions that influence the micro-finance sector.

4. Deal with systems

The need to go beyond individual organisations to systems has in fact become apparent over and over again in this book. For the foreseeable future most MFOs are going to remain very small relative to the wider systems in which they operate. To achieve greater developmental impacts therefore they will have to work out how to influence those wider systems.

In Chapter 6, we explored the strategy of three MFOs to do just this, and noted their ability to conceive of the challenges on a large enough scale, but to locate their work on the ground where the challenges are actually faced, and then to connect their work to wider systems through the strategic use of linkages. In Chapter 11, we also explored the micro-finance sector as a wider system and how each stakeholder group has a distinct and vital role to play if the sector as a whole is to grow.

However, there are many other examples of systems in which MFOs need to intervene.

Micro-finance organisations can influence local markets. For example, if they can capture enough of the local market for credit they may be able to influence the interest rates and policies of other financial-service providers, including moneylenders. Likewise, as I have already mentioned, if they saturate a local economy with micro-financial services, they may be able to enhance purchasing power generally within the local economy.

Micro-finance organisations can also seek to influence economic sub-sectors in order to have a far greater impact on livelihoods than would be possible through the support of individual micro-enterprises alone. Intervening strategically at points of leverage in sub-sectors is a well developed analytical framework (see Datta et al., 2001; USAID, 1987). Chapter 4 also points to the potential to revive rural infrastructure and organisations that can have a dramatic impact on livelihoods, in part because the costs of creating such infrastructure have already been sunk.

Within the Indian context, the banking infrastructure, including the extensive network of rural branches, is also a large system which has huge resources that could be put to good use in micro-finance. The rapidly expanding 'linkage' programme to get banks to lend to SHGs is particularly exciting (Chapter 7). It not only provides a mechanism for bankers to engage with micro-finance that suits their capacities and incentives, but it is also transforming the way bankers see poor and women borrowers, undoing the damage done by past use of the banking system as a channel for directed and highly subsidised lending. Building systematically on these linkages, and on the new understanding gained by bankers, could lead to huge additional opportunities in the future for the banking system to better serve the needs of poor clients.

In Chapter 5, we also saw that the systems of local democratic governance within India may provide opportunities for achieving developmental goals through micro-finance, by providing a channel for women who have become more empowered through participating in savings and credit groups to achieve greater voice and representation.

All of these examples, therefore, provide cases of wider systems in which micro-financial services can operate, and have wider impacts, if micro-finance practitioners and organisations can find effective ways of connecting their micro-finance operations to influence those systems.

5. Deal with savings and credit groups as a system

The rapid expansion of the SHG movement, as well as of savings and credit cooperatives, is itself becoming a system that urgently needs attention at the system-level, not just at the level of individual groups and loans from their local bank branch. Otherwise they are likely to go the way of credit unions in Latin America (if not necessarily elsewhere):

> The original idea behind credit unions was that each one would be a little, self-contained financial [organisation],

and there'd be hundreds of them across a country. But what they found was that the skill development required to do that was so great that they're now promoting the idea of having a few large, strong credit unions that can afford professional management. The lesson is that it's not efficient to have a lot of little, tiny micro-finance [organisations] (Elizabeth Rhyne in Oberdorf, 1999: 32–33).

In India there are already far more than hundreds of tiny savings and credit groups. Self-help groups are of course somewhat different from credit unions, smaller, less structured and more adaptable according to their members' wishes. The savings and credit cooperatives, however, are basically credit unions and have, at least in the case of CDF, performed well. Nevertheless the challenge that Rhyne throws out is still valid to the Indian context of savings and credit groups.

A broad and enabling regulatory and policy framework is already in place, not least through NABARD's linkage programme for SHGs. At least five states have adopted acts for mutually-aided cooperatives free from government interference. Many NGOs are also engaged in the promotion of SHGs and, to some extent, savings and credit cooperatives. Unfortunately, however, this is far from sufficient for the healthy growth of such groups as a system.

As we have seen in Chapters 7 to 9, SHGs in particular can be very fragile organisations, and can easily be captured, both internally by powerful members, and externally by politicians and bureaucrats. The latter is already a clear threat in the state of Andhra Pradesh, where political and government involvement with SHGs is extensive.

The primary strategy to address this threat is perhaps the creation of associations or federations of SHGs, although there is no consensus among NGOs on what mix of roles such higher-tier organisations should play. Indeed, while they provide strength in numbers to individual SHGs, they also make capture of the whole tiered structure all the more attractive to external parties. Bankers must also be mobilised. They have an incentive to protect their loan portfolio and know all too well from long experience how damaging political interference can be on their clients' repayment performance.

Finding effective ways to ensure the performance and quality of the savings and credit groups is an urgent need. Issues extend well beyond the financial performance of such groups to developing effective ownership and management and ensuring that inputs provided by external parties do not jeopardise the autonomy of the groups by making them dependent on external support. Building the groups' capacities both to perform their tasks (financial services, interactions with external bodies such as banks, etc.) and to maintain effective group processes and dynamics are equally important if the groups are to grow and to empower their members (see Chapter 9).

The emergence of a dedicated non-profit capacity-building organisation in Andhra Pradesh (Chapter 6) is a step in the right direction, as are the associations and federations that can also play a significant role in capacity-building and providing supportive services, such as internal auditing. However, the number of SHGs in particular has already grown well beyond the capacity of such organisations and NGOs to support, and strategies to address this gap are urgently needed. The development of organisations that can support the primary groups is therefore as important at this stage as the promotion of the primary groups themselves.

A key part of this challenge is how to spread innovation and good practice within the system. As we saw in Chapter 8, much innovation is happening on the ground within individual SHGs, but there are few mechanisms in place to spread such innovation even within the operations of a single promoting organisation! Likewise, NGOs are experimenting with effective promotional strategies, pursuing both intensive strategies to ensure the highest quality (see Chapter 5) as well as the most cost-effective strategies (see Box 4.1 and Chapter 9). However, there are few mechanisms for other organisations to learn from such experiments that are adequate to the scale of the challenge that one million potential groups present.

The same applies also to the role of the banks, where apex bodies are not particularly effective at sharing best practice emerging within the banking sector, although it is clearly their role to do this. At least the linkage programme is also providing opportunities for the most experienced promoters from NGOs to deliver training to a large number of bankers.

If the movement of SHGs and cooperatives is to achieve its true potential for delivering micro-financial services to a large number of poor women (at least 17 million is the current target), and for empowering them in the process, then system-wide mechanisms, whether for sharing innovation and good practice, for providing support services, for protecting SHGs from external interference, or any other function, will need to be addressed. In building on a fast and in some cases self-expanding movement, in other words on existing and growing organisational infrastructure, such inputs are likely to be a good investment, even though it is challenging to reach so many small groups.

Five challenges of organisation and capacity-building

A review for the Ford Foundation on the scale, scope and impact of community development finance in the United States and micro-finance in developing countries concluded (Miller and Andrews, 1998: 19):

> The authors do not believe a shortage of capital is the biggest constraint facing the [community development finance] field. We suggest that while the growth of [community development finance organisations] has been solid, especially in developing countries, the field is not seeing the formation and maturation of as many [organisations] as are warranted by what has been achieved. This is a very big question to which we do not yet have good answers.

This rings true, both in India and internationally. The lack of professionalism and technical expertise among many organisations providing micro-financial services, which we identified most clearly in Chapter 10, has prevented them from achieving scale, impact or sustainability. It is striking that among the thousands of MFOs operating across the world, only a small proportion are pursuing best practice in the technical aspects of micro-finance provision.

However, the challenges of the organisation of micro-finance provision, and of capacity-building for it, become all the more acute when we incorporate the range of developmental goals for micro-finance that we have covered in this book. At the same time, these challenges open up space for fresh insight and approaches that could resolve some of the tensions and controversies that seem constantly to surround micro-finance, not least on whether it is achieving any developmental impact.

Capacity and organisation building for micro-finance provision is often conceived in terms of staff, the role of the Managing Director, product design, cost control, systems, incentives and bonuses, access to capital, and governance through an effective board. A publication on micro-finance called 'conversations with the experts' from around the world (Oberdorf, 1999) provides some of the most reflective insights on this range of issues, suggesting that on many there is no consensus or clear solution, but nevertheless there is much to learn from these practitioners to aid one's own reflection and practice.

Approaching the challenges of capacity and organisation-building through a list of items helps only to a limited extent to address the developmental purposes of micro-finance. Here broader, less technical approaches are required, and in the rest of this chapter I summarise five of these challenges, based on my own experience of micro-finance in India. These are in addition to some of the approaches I have already set out, like designing micro-financial services that are appropriate to their context, and also working on wider systems that influence the delivery of those services. (See also Sinha [1999] for a good practical overview of the challenges and frustrations of capacity-building for micro-finance in India.)

6. Embrace both financial-service provision and developmental purpose

As suggested above, it is all too easy to see the provision of micro-financial services as an end in itself rather than as an instrument for achieving developmental goals. An exclusively technical approach to micro-finance provision seeks to reduce development to the delivery of resources, which it is not, and to mask the political economy of development, where resources are contested.

The first step to enable the match of micro-finance provision with developmental purpose is to consciously acknowledge and communicate that this is what is being sought. Micro-finance organisations are development enterprises (or social enterprises as they are increasingly called in northern countries). Such enterprises combine developmental aims, and often a strong focus on ethical values, with an enterprise orientation (Social Enterprise London, 2001).[2]

As development enterprises, MFOs must also recognise and embrace the likely organisational tensions, even contradictions, that their structure will entail, demanding choices or innovative reconciliation. For example, there is often tension between the standardisation that efficiency demands and the diversity and innovation that complex development issues seem to require. Financial parameters and targets can all too easily dominate, not least because they are also reinforced through statutory accounting and auditing requirements, leaving tracking developmental outcomes on the margins of the organisation.

Likewise, operating within a technical financial framework, it may make a lot of sense to access cheaper external capital and then lend this on to clients. On the other hand, if a micro-finance cooperative has been promoted to empower village women to pool and manage their financial resources, then external resources may well undermine this purpose by reducing their stake in the organisation.

Ignoring the potential contradictions between the overall developmental mission of an MFO and the technical demands of delivering financial services efficiently will lead to unresolved tensions. As CDRA puts it, 'when organisational contradictions are dismissed or ignored they sap our energy in spite of ourselves; when they are taken on as a challenge they become a creative force' (CDRA, 1996: 5).

In a series of workshops to help an NGO with its strategy to promote SHGs, the unresolved tension between a vision that saw autonomous SHGs performing a range of different roles for their members within the community, going well beyond micro-finance and enterprise, and the demands for standardising financial-service provision across the NGO's programme to improve the financial performance and efficiency of the SHGs, kept interfering with and undermining other strategic decisions. Only when the participants had gone through a difficult internal debate, without facilitators, to resolve this issue, could the strategy evolve further.

Sustaining the development mission of the organisation is perhaps one of the greatest challenges. In the micro-finance industry this tension has usually been illustrated by the drift towards larger loans that are likely to make the MFO more sustainable but exclude its poorest clients (see the analysis of this in CGAP [1997a]). This is a genuine dilemma as an MFO struggles to adapt to the growth and changes within its clientele group, for example seeking to maintain its good borrowers. With the more sophisticated understanding of potential developmental purposes this book has encouraged, the challenge for MFOs to maintain their mission and focus becomes all the more complex.

Given that development is as much a process as an outcome, maintaining developmental values is also demanding. As Cheney (1999) suggested of the Mondragon cooperatives, of what value are the characteristics of a development enterprise, if they become indistinguishable from those of mainstream organisations? Where are the additional benefits that justify the efforts to create a different type of organisation?

To take a concrete example from India, Al Fernandez (2001: 6–7) reports on the pressures the NGO MYRADA was placed under to promote Grameen Bank-style groups, rather than autonomous SHGs which require much longer to grow, but, he argues, can deliver better on MYRADA's goals of empowering poor rural people (see Chapter 5).

There are strong historical precedents to demonstrate the validity of such concerns within micro-finance. The history of mutual 'building societies' in Britain goes back to the end of the 18th century when they were set up by poor people pooling their micro-savings to enable them to take loans to build houses. Over time these building societies became very large, any genuine sense of membership was lost and, following regulatory changes introduced in the 1980s, they became indistinguishable from commercial banks, and many have indeed converted themselves into banks. They have long failed to serve any developmental purpose, even though financial exclusion again became an important public issue in Britain in the 1990s.

This example is instructive in other ways. It is often assumed that MFOs are developing markets that mainstream providers can eventually serve. Community development finance organisations in the United States and Britain, for example, have often focused on near-bankable clients, seeking to demonstrate that they can be viable bank customers.

However, as mainstream providers begin to serve such customers, the community development finance organisations are likely to shift the focus of their operations to the next group of clients who are excluded from access to mainstream financial services, rather than competing with the banks. Such shifts may not appear to make the best sense for the sustainability and growth of the organisations concerned, but are in tune with their developmental missions. From this perspective, MFOs should not be seen just as steps on the road to full commercial and mainstream operations,[3] but as organisations constantly seeking to bring those on the margins of the economy to access mainstream markets.

Micro-finance practitioners should not imagine that such challenges are not familiar to other organisations. Organisations can be seen as pyramids, as in Figure 12.1, in which

Figure 12.1: The organisational pyramid

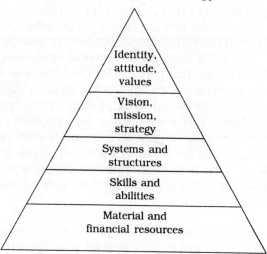

each level needs to fit with the other for the whole to be fully functional (adapted from Fowler et al. [1995] as quoted in Eade [1997]). It is simply that the 'hard-nosed' attitudes needed for the delivery of micro-financial services bring the tensions to the fore more explicitly.

How can these tensions be addressed in practice? One of the leading Indian practitioners puts it as follows (Oberdorf, 1999: 21, 70):

... while micro-finance [organisations] need to live up to financial standards, it's not good enough to measure them only by those. You have to have a combination of financial and developmental standards, and you have to fulfil both. That's the challenge.

Leadership is key, and I don't mean just the CEO. The promoters and directors and key investors have to steer that difficult course between, you know, 'Hey, we got 98-percent repayment and an 18-percent return on investment' and those who say, 'Hey, we've reached the poorest of the poor and it doesn't matter whether we're haemorrhaging money'. It's in between these two that you've got to steer the course. And that then gets built into the organisation design. I mean, you need it in your [management information system], you need to monitor both financial and developmental performance. You need to build it into your training and your recruitment. You've got to ensure that you are taking people who are hard-nosed but at the same time empathetic to your plans. It has to run right through the vertical cross-section of the organisation, this concern for dual objectives.

About governance, I'd say the key issue is managing that tension between development and financial sustainability. Investors need to just get that right. I mean, occasionally you can get someone like Shore Bank [in Chicago] who knows both sides, but ideally it's best to balance your board with different people who represent different interests and then be very transparent about the trade-offs.

In embracing financial-service provision and development purpose, we also need to recognise creative opportunities for integration, where successful development outcomes are essential for financial performance, for example by ensuring the ability of clients to repay, and where, as suggested above, the effective management of financial services leads to positive development outcomes.

We also need to recognise the advantages that MFOs as development enterprises may have, not just the challenges they face. They may be particularly effective at identifying new opportunities to serve those at the margins of the economy, and at diversifying their products to meet the needs of different clients in different local contexts, rather than delivering standardised products regardless of the local context. Indeed, in the midst of complex and dynamic challenges, the strong values and purpose that development enterprises may have can serve as a constant centre of gravity and a clear framework for action (Harding, 1997).

As the analysis in Chapter 8 showed, they may also be good at fostering financial discipline in contexts characterised by information asymmetries, severe market distortions and the lack of a repayment culture. Given the often on-going need for subsidies to genuinely reach and impact poor clients (Miller and Andrews, 1998: 14–15), MFOs as development enterprises may also be better able to attract goodwill and hence the low-cost capital and subsidies required.

7. Put practice at the heart of the organisation

The practice of an organisation 'concerns the particular discipline it offers, its methodology, the way in which it pursues its work in the world' (CDRA, 2000: 8). In the micro-finance sector it is all too easy to slip into regarding the delivery of micro-financial services as the organisation's practice, as though even on a technical level such provision is easy to define. However, in this book we have seen that micro-finance provision is highly diverse, using a range of different organisational structures from informal groups to mainstream banks, being delivered for a wide range of different purposes, from security through livelihoods and developing the local economy to democratic empowerment.

It is here that we find one of the deepest challenges confronting the micro-finance sector if it wants to achieve developmental impact. The technology of delivering financial services resides only in the three lower rungs of the organisational pyramid set out in Figure 12.1. This cannot be seen as the organisation's core purpose or practice, because these have also to be rooted in the organisation's identity, values, vision and mission which define its developmental purpose in particular.

An organisation's practice will differ according to what its core purpose is (CDRA, 2000: 6). The practice of an MFO seeking to provide its members with social and economic security through a full range of financial services will differ significantly from the practice of the MFO promoting livelihoods and not least from the NGO that does not engage in financial service provision at all, but promotes democratic community-based organisations to undertake financial intermediation.

Because such practice is developmental, it is far less precise and more complex than the technology of delivering financial services. There are few manuals, little insightful analysis, that are readily available to practitioners to help in building their developmental practice. Indeed, some practitioners may be scared of such a focus. The delivery of financial services remains in the control of those delivering them; interventions in complex development processes do not.

So what does all of this talk about organisational practice mean in practice for an MFO? As CDRA (2000: 8) says, 'The essence of developmental practice lies at the interface between practitioner and client'. It is at the interface between the MFO's staff, particularly field-staff, and the client or member, whether she is saving, borrowing, purchasing insurance or managing her own group, that the developmental processes an MFO seeks are likely to take place.

In a workshop for an Indian MFO, a role-play on the interaction between field-staff and client revealed the rather domineering, almost patronising, attitude of one field-staff towards the borrower. This may, to a small extent, have been important to signal that this MFO was different from public banks or NGOs which were soft in their lending, to make clear that this MFO would demand repayment. However, it is difficult to see how such an interaction could be developmental for the client.

In all the cases analysed in this book it is the field-staff who interact directly with clients or members who are the key to MFOs achieving their developmental mission. It is the 'hand-holders' at SEWA Bank who go out regularly to visit members in their homes who have the best opportunities to help the self-employed women to enhance their financial security (Chapter 3). It is the Customer Service Agents (CSAs) and Field Executives at BASIX who are most likely to spot the micro-enterprise that can grow to generate employment or provide an essential service in the local economy. It is the Unit Manager who is most likely to identify rural infrastructure or organisations in the area that could be revived through the judicious use of financial services (Chapter 4).

And, as we have seen in Chapters 5, 8 and 9, it is the quality of the field-staff that plays a major role, although by no means the only role, in determining the performance of savings and credit groups. In a workshop for CDF, field-staff spent much of the workshop exploring their relationship with the cooperatives they were promoting. Were they behaving as experts, 'doctors' or facilitators (see Chapter 1 in Schein [1999]), or even activists, in their interactions with the cooperatives? Which role was most helpful, and when, in achieving their developmental mission of high-performing democratic and autonomous people's organisations?

If financial intermediation is the only developmental purpose sought, then it may be possible to do without greater attention to the quality of field-staff. As Stuart Rutherford (Oberdorf, 1999: 28–29) reports on the Association for Social Advancement (ASA) in Bangladesh, '... all its procedures are extremely simple and well documented. ASA has a wonderful combination of maximum delegation with minimum responsibility.... everything's so automatic, it's quite clear whether or not this client is eligible for this loan or not, and of what size.... It's so standardised that it can be delegated to the lowest level.'

However, for most MFOs, because they achieve their developmental purposes at the interface between staff and clients or members, it is here that their organisational practice needs to be built most. In Chapter 4, we provided the following analysis of BASIX:

BASIX has ... faced the constant challenge of translating its complex mission of livelihood promotion for the rural poor into something that can inform and motivate staff throughout the organisation, as well as the Customer Service Agents (CSAs), who are not staff but paid on a commission basis. For them credit delivery has always been at the heart of their work, and BASIX' complex mission around supporting livelihoods has not always been fully understood. They are far more likely to judge a loan application on the basis of the ability and reliability of the borrower to repay than on the potential of the business to achieve livelihood outcomes. This can be serious, as it is precisely the Field Executives and CSAs who need, for example, to spot opportunities for micro-entrepreneurs to graduate to small enterprise and achieve the genuine developmental outcomes that BASIX seeks.

The analysis in this chapter might suggest that the approach needs to be turned on its head. If field-staff are the most likely to facilitate developmental processes on the ground, then they of course need to have their perspectives and insights on development enhanced to do their job more effectively. I have not conducted a workshop for any MFO in India where field-staff were not enthusiastic about enhancing their understanding of developmental processes.

However, the challenge is likely to lie not just with the lack of developmental perspectives among field-staff, assuming they have been well selected, but as much with the lack of organisational mechanisms to acknowledge and value the centrality of development practice, and to help those who need to deliver it on the ground to build that practice.

It is also the organisation's development practice that will provide the necessary learning for the organisation to enhance its developmental impact, and reviewing and learning from that practice must therefore play a key role in designing, reviewing and refining the organisation's strategy (rather than the other way round).[4]

But what space does the organisation provide for field-staff to review, reflect on and learn from their practice on a regular basis, amidst the huge pressures of delivery that most of them are placed under? Do they have opportunities for reflecting for themselves, with peers or a mentor? How safe is such space for staff? Once you have acknowledged to your peers how you practice, you cannot take that knowledge back, unlike a position in a debate from which you can always re-treat (CDRA, 2000: 9). But without such safety and above all trust, reflection and learning cannot take place.

I remember sitting in on a loan committee meeting of an MFO where field-staff presented their loan applications to the committee for review and, they hoped, approval. In the absence of many other organisational mechanisms for this purpose, this committee had become a major vehicle for learning what was going on in the field. However, it was not a safe space for field-staff to be open about their practice. Instead they spent most of their time ensuring that they looked good, and attempting to get as many loans approved as possible, which would reflect well on them. They even calculated the most effective order to present the applications to the committee to ensure that the majority, or at least the really important loans to them, were approved.

In the micro-finance industry, which is often fond of incentives and bonuses, how can these be structured in such a way that they encourage reflection on developmental outcomes, not just on the outputs of financial services? If an MFO is serious about its developmental purpose, it will not hide behind the easy position that developmental outcomes are so much harder to measure than financial parameters.

In Chapter 10, Frances Sinha outlines some emerging methodologies and processes to enable MFOs to better measure their developmental impact. Some of these developments are being supported by funding from the Ford Foundation, in part guided by a paper (Miller and Andrews, 1998: 14) that concluded:

> After more than a quarter of a century of [community development finance] we don't yet have enough objective information on impacts.... If we do not assess impact we run the danger of accepting positive output measures as indicators of success, when there is a far more important story to be told. Further, a focus on outputs

risks skewing the field away from its fundamental mission. You get what you measure, and so far we have not been measuring the most important part of our work.

Appropriate methodologies and processes must clearly involve much more than the standard case studies to which so many micro-finance practitioners turn, often it would seem in desperation, to demonstrate their impact (with the often instinctive response from listeners: 'we don't believe you; why do you never show us any case studies of failures?').

The industry needs to move beyond such limited assessment of developmental impact. However, case studies do emphasise that developmental impact must happen among people, whether on their security, livelihoods, empowerment, democratic representation or any other area of their lives. This is about relationships and power. As Muhammad Yunus (1998: 234) puts it, 'credit creates an entitlement to resources.... Since credit creates economic power, and hence social power, the institution which is responsible for deciding who should and should not get credit ... can really make or break an individual, a group of individuals, or even a whole segment of society by favouring them or by rejecting them.'

So how do we move on? This is CDRA's perspective (2000: 11–13) on developmental organisations generally, of which MFOs are part:

> It is often said that development—human development—is difficult, even impossible, to measure and for that reason other, related, indicators of success are sought. This is simply not true. In a developmental approach, practitioners intervene into complex development processes; they do not bring them into being. Through whatever resources, projects, or services they bring, they aim to effect change in the power relations of their beneficiaries. These shifts do not come about as a result of the efficient delivery of the resource or service, but through the developmental process employed.
>
> Where a shift in relationship becomes the aim of practice, and its measure, neat deliverables and packages cease to occupy centre stage. Instead, measurement

comes to be seen as beginning with the ability to make developmental assessments. This involves analysing and understanding each situation being intervened into as a living, dynamic, changing process with a rich history, a present reality and a future potential. A central component of this assessment includes qualitative and descriptive pictures of the formative relationships surrounding the subject of intervention.... As development practitioners develop the art of describing relationships before and after their intervention, as they learn to tell the stories of change, so their ability to do so with greater precision grows.

The organisation that best supports developmental practice is receptive to these measures and descriptions and makes central use of them in the course of strategising.... Out of various accounts, a picture emerges that isolates the central themes—both in practice and in impact in the field. It is these pictures of the essence of developmental practice that inform further work on practice as well as the next steps in organisational strategy.

Such reflective measuring processes are also likely to motivate and support staff, especially field-staff, rather than proving an additional task or burden for them to deliver.

Key to any such learning are feedback mechanisms and information systems. For example, what mechanisms does the organisation put in place for managers and head-office staff to learn from review and reflection on development practice in the field? When SEWA Bank introduced the system of 'hand-holders' whereby staff visited members regularly at their home to review their finances and their livelihoods (Chapter 3), the staff involved met regularly to exchange their experiences. This was a useful mechanism for peer-learning among colleagues. However, fewer systems were developed for the organisation as a whole to learn and change its operations in the light of insights on developmental processes that emerged from the 'hand-holding' system.

All organisational systems in fact need to be geared towards supporting practice and learning. The check always is on whether organisational systems and procedures support or hinder the two primary processes: direct contact in the field and learning towards improved practice and strategy' (CDRA, 2000: 16).

8. Learn by doing

The environment in which most providers of micro-financial services operate is often messy, with much uncertainty and change, and a complex range of developmental needs, only a few of which can be addressed directly through micro-financial services. The best illustration of this comes from Chapter 8, where the transient nature of temporary slum communities brings the uncertainties and complexities into sharp focus. However, the development context in a village is likely to be equally complex.

In such environments a technical solution by itself is unlikely to deliver the goods. Members or clients may not join, groups may collapse, unforeseen competitors may enter the market, micro-financial services may have unforeseen consequences, within households or within local enterprise markets, the regulatory and policy environment may change, and so on. The more exclusive the pursuit of technical excellence, the less relevant the services provided may become from a developmental perspective.

What is needed is reflective practice. In his book, *The reflective practitioner*, Donald Schon (1983) shows how, across many disciplines, apparent experts muddle through, forever reflecting on their experience, on what they are doing and on what the outcomes turn out to be. In this process of learning by doing, of trial and error, they use much intuition and tacit knowledge, as well as their formal knowledge, and welcome the surprises and puzzlement of unforeseen dynamics or outcomes.

Such a process is much closer to my experience of microfinance practitioners, and is well illustrated in the development of the Grameen Bank, as described by Muhammad Yunus in Part II of his autobiography (1998).

Two features stand out clearly in this framework. First, the problems need to be set and the ends agreed. With the great diversity of contexts and practice illustrated in this book, it is clear that there will not necessarily be a consensus on the problem that needs solving and the end that needs to be achieved. The way that this book is structured suggests that the simplistic assumption that the lack of credit is the problem that needs solving requires scrutiny. What other financial services are needed, how will micro-credit benefit livelihoods, how can micro-financial services be empowering, and so on? Going even deeper, why do poor people not have access to financial services? Does this relate to information asymmetries, lack of entitlements or the perspectives of elites managing financial intermediaries? In each case the problem and the end may turn out to be different.

Second is the need for innovation, for learning by doing, for trial and error. Chapter 6 analysed the innovation undertaken by BASIX to promote livelihoods, Chapter 8 revealed cases where learning by doing was an essential prerequisite for high-performing SHGs. Only by finding out who were good borrowers in practice could members recreate groups with good repayment rates.

It is the need to learn from doing that has informed the strategy of a range of different MFOs to hire fresh graduates rather than already experienced recruits, to provide them with only short introductory courses before making them shadow existing workers, and let the good ones rise through the ranks so they know exactly what is involved at the 'coalface' (Oberdorf, 1999: 9, 27–38). At later stages of their organisational development, MFOs may need to recruit existing professionals from outside the organisation, with all the potential cultural conflicts this can give rise to.

It is only through learning by doing that most organisations will be able to weld together their delivery of micro-financial services and their developmental missions. This should not be seen as an abstract process, or one where research and development is separated out from operations. As Stuart Rutherford rightly laments (Oberdorf, 1999: 88–89),

One of the things that I find curious ... is that if I look at the considerable amount of research that's been done in Bangladesh by academics, very, very little of it is about the product itself. I can read endless reports about where the Grameen Bank members send their children to school, whether they use contraceptives, whether the women are empowered, whether they have a bigger voice in their households or their communities, et cetera, et cetera. But I don't find much telling me about the product, how people really use it, what is it used for, what if we changed the product?

Learning by doing, in contrast, is based on reflection in action, testing what works and what doesn't, and learning from that to improve operations, systems and products or to refine, even change, developmental objectives in view of experience on the ground. Indeed, nothing of what I outline here should be taken as an excuse for fuzzy development interventions, for woolly thinking or navel-gazing (see Sinha, 1999), attending workshops to bear all about one's practice, and then returning, with a weight off one's mind, to the same old practice! Reflective practice is very different and far more demanding: the quality of reflection can be judged from whether it leads to learning, and learning to changes in practice.

Continuous innovation, adapting to lessons learnt in practice, is challenging for organisations (see Chapter 6). As Schon (1983: 328) writes: 'Significant organisational learning—learning which involves significant change in underlying values and knowledge structure—is always the subject of an *organisational predicament*. It is necessary to effective organisational adaptation, but it disrupts the constancies on which manageable organisational life depends.'

Learning by doing also presents challenges at the system level, as we suggested above. How can learning and innovation be transmitted to other parts of the system? The growing SHG movement, for example, could be seen as a huge research and development programme, but how will lessons learnt spread across small, highly dispersed and autonomous organisations?

This is all the more important as the micro-finance sector matures. While all MFOs must remain reflective and adapt to changing realities, this applies in particular to the innovative pioneers. However, there is little point reinventing the wheel each time. SEWA Bank and the Grameen Bank in many ways muddled along because there was little good practice for them to draw on. A key feature of the development of the Grameen

Bank, as Muhammad Yunus points out (1998: 142), was going slowly. 'A guiding principle of our work is to start low-key and in a small way.' This enables greater learning by doing.

On the other hand, BASIX, coming much later, was able to systematically assess good practice within India and internationally, and build in lessons from such analysis into its organisational design. The Association for Social Advancement (ASA) in Bangladesh in many ways did the same. Given the scale of the challenge of meeting the demand for micro-financial services among poor people in India, such learning processes are essential, and need to be encouraged and facilitated.

9. Move towards resolving the issue of ownership and control

The discussions of the expert practitioners on ownership and governance of MFOs (Oberdorf, 1999) are interesting. Perhaps the best summary is that 'in this sector there are no true investors so far and there are no true owners so far' (ibid.: 86). The practitioners list a range of potential board members for an MFO, from development visionaries to bankers, and including experts, business-people and small investors, and speak of the need to have a board that balances hard-nosed and softer approaches (compare CGAP [1997b], which provides a good overview of some of the challenges of governance).

What is striking is the lack of any consensus, or even detailed attention, to issues of ownership and control. SafeSave in Bangladesh is registered as a cooperative, but its promoter does not elaborate at all on any sense of ownership that such a structure might provide, pointing instead to the need for regulators to control financial-service provision on behalf of depositors; 'this is really no different from formal banks, is it?' (ibid.: 71).

Only one practitioner (ibid.: 65) suggests, 'I would like to think that they should be the ones to own it. I mean, the clients', although another warns (ibid.: 70) that

> I think it is a pretence to imagine that micro-finance [organisations] such as the Grameen Bank are really

owned and managed by, you know, poor women. I mean, they are basically professional oligarchies ... and we are very lucky that there are people like Professor Yunus running them. But we should be prepared for a situation where, in future if not already, people use the fig leaf of member control to run professional oligarchies. And the best way to control this is not through the pretence of member control but through a governance structure where other stakeholders keep the organisation on the straight and narrow. In that sense, it's not very different from large corporations.

At the time of writing, when the huge corporation Enron had just collapsed, such an analogy is perhaps less appropriate. However, this extensive muddling among leading practitioners suggests that ownership and control is very much an unresolved issue in micro-finance.

This is unfortunate, for two reasons as we saw in Chapter 5. First, ownership gives entitlements to benefits, including the profits of micro-finance provision, which can be significant. Second, ownership and control is at the heart of most of the empowerment strategies through micro-finance that are used in India, especially the SHGs and the savings and credit cooperatives.

Above, I argued that the developmental impact of MFOs will be determined largely at the interface between the organisation and its clients or members. The structure of ownership and control is in fact a key parameter in determining different forms of organisation, and therefore the relationship between the organisation and its customers, clients, members or citizens (Mintzberg, 1996). Ownership will therefore also be a key determinant of the development impact of MFOs. At its simplest, the control over resources and the power that this brings are critical in almost any development context. Can micro-finance really afford to ignore it? I suggest three steps that can be taken to explore in practice, to learn from doing, to move towards resolving this issue.

The first step is to acknowledge and support the role and potential benefits of mutual ownership structures within micro-finance, both informal (SHGs) and formal (cooperatives and credit unions). As we illustrated in Chapter 5, all too often, issues arising from mutual ownership are simply ignored in much of the literature on micro-finance. However, mutual ownership not only brings members potential benefits, but may also overcome information asymmetries and reinforce financial discipline, not least because members are dealing with their own 'hot' money.

Moreover, given that micro-finance is ultimately about development, and that must mean of people, structures that give additional control and empowerment to people deserve attention. 'Development as an outcome is inextricably linked to the processes used in its delivery. This indivisibility of process and product, of cause and effect, [means that] to "get" development, we have to work in a particular way, that is, developmentally' (CDRA, 2000: 1). Mutual ownership structures may serve well as a development process to deliver micro-financial products.

This is not a call for all MFOs to become mutual entities. However, if the industry is going to learn from practice, from doing, then its portfolio of practice must include mutual ownership, and serious investigation and support for such ownership, to draw out lessons, and to see to what extent such structures meet the developmental needs of members. Chapters 5 and 6 provided examples of what such support might mean in practice, including strategies to promote effective ownership within savings and credit groups and the work of CDF in creating an enabling regulatory framework for cooperatives.

There is also much analysis to draw on. The Cooperative Development Foundation has built an effective cooperative micro-finance practice on the basis of its deep understanding of cooperatives developed over many years. Credit unions of course have a long and chequered history internationally, and have been much studied. In India there has also been in-depth analysis of the functioning of cooperatives, for example, in Shah (1995) and Fisher and Mahajan (1997: Chapter 7), which have also had a chequered history, allowing analysis of both successes and failures. And, as suggested above, the SHG movement can provide a huge scope for exploring issues of ownership and leadership within democratic financial organisations (see Chapters 5 and 9). The industry can no longer hide behind simplistic generalisations, neither that cooperatives are the only solution to ownership, nor that mutual ownership never works.

A second step is to build more experience on managing equity and other investments, and particularly differentiated rights of control that may come with different forms of investments. Many MFOs are set up by entrepreneurs who have great developmental vision but little financial capital. In traditional equity structures, the sweat equity of the promoters is not recognised, and large investors can all too easily push out others. As one practitioner warns, 'if you've got one very large shareholder with a representative on the board of the [MFO], especially if that [MFO] is majority-owned by that one shareholder, it is very difficult for the other board members to have any significant role. If the one shareholder doesn't like something and would withdraw his funds if the [MFO] goes ahead with it ...' (Oberdorf, 1999: 70–71).

This is particularly unfortunate if it is the developmental promoters who have the greatest commitment to the developmental mission of the organisation, but no capital to allow them to exercise control over the MFO. Equity mechanisms that come with differentiated rights, even recognition of sweat equity, clearly need greater exploration. So do holding company structures, like the equity of Triodos Bank in Europe, for example, that is held by a trust to protect the social and environmental aims of the bank, while the bank itself is regulated like any other bank to ensure sound financial management. This example provides a positive case, as opposed to the crisis that befell Corposal and Finansol so often cited in the micro-finance literature (CGAP, 1997b).

The challenge here is not so much legal (almost any structure of investments and the rights that come with them is already available), but of building experience through individual negotiations between MFOs and their investors, and, through example, expanding the range of rights that investors are willing to accept.[5] Donors also have a particular role to play here. It is not appropriate to invest in and endow organisations that have no proper investors or owners in the hope that the chickens will not come home to roost too soon. Nor is it appropriate to rely on institutional investors, by directing grants and investments through apex public bodies, who often tend to be conservative and bureaucratic.

A third avenue of practice is to explore what happens when MFOs float their equity on open markets. Some NGOs providing micro-financial services have already converted to banks, some financial companies like BASIX are looking to float on stock-markets in the future. If lessons are to be learnt in practice on how effective the resulting traditional company or banking structures are in maintaining the developmental focus of the MFO, then careful attention and reflection will need to be given to such cases (see CGAP [1997a], for example).

Such suggestions do not provide solutions, but in the spirit of learning from practice, learning from doing, they would enable the industry to move forward constructively on this vital issue.

10. Develop the art of capacity-building

Micro-finance organisations obviously need a range of technical inputs from experts, on systems, accounts, financial management, cost control, and so on. However, a focus on the developmental goals of micro-finance introduces more complex and messier issues for MFOs to deal with, of framing appropriate goals within a given context and strategies to meet them, of tracking progress towards them, of adapting and innovating as the organisation learns from doing and meets with unforeseen consequences of its actions, and all the time maintaining a developmental vision among often rapid changes in the environment, of managing the organisational tensions that arise from change and innovation as well as diversity among staff motivations and skills, and so on.

Here a strongly rational, analytical and technical approach of management may not be adequate. Indeed it may divert attention from the dynamic and unstable challenges of development (and the strong identity and purpose required to address these) by focusing on the security and control that technical models of financial-service delivery appear to provide. Instead, as Schon (1983) argues, professionals must develop an artistry or craftsmanship in their practice which allows them to work constructively and reflectively with the uncertainty, conflicts and unique situations they often face (Harding and Chapman, 2000). As Harding (1997: 4–5) suggests, such an approach is an art not a science. It requires years of patient practice and experience; the ability to reflect critically on that experience; creativity in response to difficult issues; the ability to bring good intuition and judgement in alongside rational thought; and the qualities and strengths to work well with people, to stay open to learning, and be confident about meeting the unknown.... It is more like white-water rafting (the course is very unpredictable, the ride is rough, change is all around you, you need to adapt constantly and fast, and you need a skilled crew who can think for themselves). Whitewater rafting is scary—but it can also be exhilarating [!].

This also changes the role of the external consultant, where uncertainty limits the scope of technical expertise. Schein (1999) describes the need for process consultation, the helping relationship, that passes on the skills of how to diagnose and constructively intervene so that organisations become better able to respond on their own to new development challenges. It generates space and opportunities for learning and reflection, so often pushed out by the frenzy of action, for reflection on insights and lessons emerging from practice on the ground where development processes are encountered. It creates a climate where difficulties and mistakes can be surfaced and discussed without fear, as otherwise learning by doing, which necessarily involves mistakes as well as breakthroughs, cannot take place. It facilitates learning, rethinking and adaptation. It builds on the work and experiences of the organisation, rather than imposing external frameworks and solutions that often demotivate or are simply ignored (Harding and Chapman, 2000).

It draws attention to values, identity and purpose, which are at the heart of any development practice, as well as to the whole picture, and helps organisations explore tensions at this level, for example when they overburden themselves with too many developmental objectives. It may encourage new ways of looking at things. As just one small but pertinent example, one MFO wanted to develop new indicators and generate more information to better assess its performance and impact. Process consultation enabled it to see that it was not the lack of information that was the problem, but its inability to use the substantial information the organisation's rapidly improving accounting and management information systems were already generating. Technical systems that generate information the organisation cannot process are not an effective strategy for organisational performance or impact.

Process consultation is not an alternative to technical expertise. All the MFOs I know need to upgrade their technical competencies and systems to deliver financial services effectively. However, MFOs also require additional and different skills and inputs if they are to develop their capacity to deliver not only efficient financial services but also development outcomes. BASIX has been able to access and put to good use a wide range of help from technical experts, challenging advisors, experienced board members, process consultants and reflective mentors, as well as formal organisational processes such as an innovative 'organisational learning and evolution process' after the first five years of its operations. It is recognising the help it can derive from all of these in steering a difficult course through complex development situations that has helped BASIX to progress so rapidly.

For some it will come as a surprise to conclude a book about micro-finance with a focus on practice at the interface between staff and clients, on embracing organisational contradictions, on learning by doing, on exploring ownership, on reflective practice and process consultation. However, all of these are critical for building the necessary insight, creativity, capacity and, above all, impact to enable MFOs to move beyond financial-service delivery to achieve genuine developmental outcomes.

Notes

1. This should not imply that in every context new provision is required. Where feasible, building on existing provision is likely to be more efficient than seeking to set up new organisations.
2. It is important to distinguish development or social enterprises from socially responsible business, which is a growing and welcome trend internationally among businesses. India, of course, has a long tradition of such responsible business, with the Tata group of companies perhaps the most celebrated example. The Indian tradition, like elsewhere

in the world, has often been dominated by philanthropic and paternalistic motivations, but there is a gradual trend internationally to placing such responsibilities at the core of the business activity, which is described in a recent publication from the New Economics Foundation called 'The civil corporation' (Zadek, 2001). Development enterprises are different from socially responsible businesses because their primary purpose is defined by their developmental aims, which they have decided to pursue through enterprise (and often profitable) activity, while socially responsible businesses continue to pursue profits as their primary goal but in an increasingly responsible or ethical way.

3. Indeed, the need to raise commercial capital may divert from their developmental purpose, as even the very earliest Rochdale cooperatives discovered (see Cheney, 1999: 39).

4. All too often, strategy is divorced from such review and learning processes, determined centrally for field-staff to deliver, and when the inevitable gaps open up between strategy and implementation, it is the field-staff that are hounded for their underperformance (CDRA, 2000).

5. I am grateful to Bharti Ramola for this insight.

Appendix: Capacity-building and organisational learning project for development finance in India

This project, funded by the Ford Foundation with close to $400,000 over more than five years (end of 1996 to early 2002), involved collaboration between the New Economics Foundation in London (NEF) and four Indian micro-finance organisations: BASIX, Cooperative Development Foundation (CDF), PRADAN and SEWA Bank. The final output of the project is this book reflecting on development and organisational challenges in micro-finance. This appendix brings together some of the reflections by Thomas Fisher, the Project Director, drawing on internal reports.

Project inputs

The project provided a wide range of inputs to different organisations:

- Training workshops on impact and financial indicators; subsectoral and cluster analysis for enterprise promotion; the local economy and money-flows; basic economics; and social auditing.
- Organisational workshops to develop visions and future scenarios; strategic plans; strategies for implementing a capacity-building programme; organisational assessment and development for co-operatives; financial statements; understanding of information and research results; presentation materials.
- The training and organisational workshops were geared to enhance the training, facilitation and process skills of staff who in most cases co-designed and co-facilitated the workshops concerned.
- Review, observation and feedback on documentation and organisational processes, including on: field visits; review and loan committee meetings; financial systems; internal documentation; and assessment, evaluation and research material.

- Other process and capacity-building inputs including mentoring and co-mentoring sessions (for senior staff); team-building sessions (both among senior and junior staff); long-term assistance in building the role, research skills and other capacities of the Research Department at SEWA Bank; and formal and informal sessions and inputs for individual staff.
- Other inputs, including learning visits and presentations by Indian organisations in the UK; participation in relevant organisational development events; and regular mentoring sessions for the Project Director.
- Workshops to draw together leading experts, case-studies and other materials from across India on livelihood promotion; for the first time drawing together lessons and practices from over a decade of experience in India into a resource book for livelihood promotion; and trialling and revising this resource book at a training workshop (see Datta et al., 2001). This work also involved a capacity-building process, enabling both the senior and junior staff involved to significantly enhance their understanding of livelihood promotion.

These inputs were provided by a range of staff from NEF, although increasingly over the course of the project, also from relevant Indian consultants, including among the project partners. BASIX staff in particular worked with NEF on inputs for PRADAN, SEWA Bank and the resource book for livelihood promotion.

Key characteristics of the project

Flexibility

A key feature of the project was its flexibility in responding to the needs and wishes of the Indian organisations involved. This began with two initial visits by NEF to India (under an exploratory grant from the Ford Foundation) to explore what working together might involve. It continued throughout the course of the project, giving rise to diverse and changing activities, many of which did not feature in the original proposal. That this was likely to happen was in fact acknowledged in the original proposal itself.

Such flexibility was a critical feature for enabling effective organisational and capacity-building inputs, allowing the project to shift responsively to the greater understanding of needs developed during the project and to the organisational dynamics of the partners at any particular time. It also allowed adequate trust to develop. For example, initially, work between CDF and NEF, who knew each other least at the beginning of the project, began on the basis of 'let's see how things go, how useful we find it; we can always decide to part ways'.

Such flexibility is not only essential for effective organisational collaboration, but also unusual for a development project (hence the difficulties many capacity-building projects have run into). The Ford Foundation made a very significant contribution in allowing such flexibility.

The drawback of such flexibility, involving work with four different Indian organisations, was that the diverse and changing activities did not always make up a coherent project as a whole. This was particularly the case given that the project, at the suggestion of the Indian organisations involved, deliberately excluded networking among them, in which NEF as a foreign organisation had less of a role to play. Even with work with individual organisations, the changes meant that the collaboration sometimes lacked continuity. This occasional lack of coherence and continuity also caused some dissonance for the staff of NEF involved in the project; who had to be very flexible and open to change.

Learning as you go along—responding to organisational dynamics

Flexibility allowed the project to respond to the greater understanding of needs that arose during the project. For example, in working with SEWA Bank on new indicators, including of impact, it became clear that it would be more appropriate to first develop effective use of financial indicators that could be drawn from the existing computerised accounts rather than develop new ones. Likewise, at the beginning of the project, NEF conducted a workshop on social auditing for PRADAN. In the light of what the PRADAN participants had learnt about social auditing, they decided that it was not a priority for their organisation.

Equally important, the project was able to respond to the organisational dynamics and changes of the partners involved. In the case of BASIX, working together generally involved work with the senior management team, and the particular content and method of such work was determined by the immediate needs and opportunities of the organisation and the senior managers at the time. In the case of SEWA Bank, the 25th anniversary provided a suitable opportunity to launch a strategic planning process rather than returning at that stage to new indicators, as originally envisaged.

Responding to organisational dynamics also led to times when work together was put on hold, and some expected outcomes were not achieved. For example, it took a while for active work with PRADAN to resume after the social auditing workshop, as both sides explored the best options for collaboration and PRADAN focused on its own internal changes and developments. Likewise, resumption of work on indicators with CDF was planned for their review process to draw up their next five-year strategic plan, which was then postponed as a result of internal changes within the organisation. With collaboration among dynamic organisations, such ebbing and flowing was inevitable, and it would have been foolish to expect otherwise.

Long-term commitments

Including the early work under the exploratory grant, the project was planned to run for at least three and a half years (and was then extended to allow completion of capacity-building inputs for some organisations and development of important publications arising out of the project). Even as first planned, this involved a significant span of time, allowing the kind of flexibility, enhanced understanding and responsiveness already described, without endangering the organisational relationships. For example, it enabled NEF and individual Indian organisations to work through tensions that arose, knowing that such a process was worthwhile. Indeed, without the long-term commitment, some of the organisations may not have been willing to engage in the project in the first place.

Such a long-term commitment also allowed activities and inputs to be adjusted to the organisational rhythms and changes of the partners. For example, some activities took longer than expected due to enhanced understanding of the processes involved or unforeseen complexities or bottlenecks. The long-term commitment enabled the project to respond to such dynamics, allowing pauses in the process and time extensions (although without any additional financial resources from the donor). It is almost certain that without such a long time-frame, the project would have failed to achieve some of its outcomes. For example, some of the workshops that led to organisational changes would have remained just workshops which everyone enjoyed but ultimately led to few changes. Long-term commitments also allowed understanding and trust to develop, which proved critical to the development of the project.

Regularity

The regularity of three-monthly visits from NEF proved useful in allowing work to progress effectively without overburdening the time commitments of the staff of the organisations involved. At least two of the Indian organisations involved explicitly stated that more frequent visits would have proved impossible.

However, it is questionable whether all the types of organisational inputs provided under this project could have the fullest impact when their timing was confined to one visit every three months, especially by staff of a foreign organisation. The ideal kind of flexibility would have allowed additional visits, responding to particular needs and opportunities as they arose. This does not apply to all the inputs provided, and to some extent the long timeframe of the project compensated for this. For example, changes in organisational practices at SEWA Bank, as for most organisations, arose as a result of the cumulative impact of the regular visits over time, so that some new practices became more instinctive.

Trust

The long-term commitment and regularity allowed significant trust to develop between NEF and each of the Indian organisations. Such trust was critical to the project, especially for the more sensitive organisational inputs, and was developed on the basis of the Project Director's extensive prior work with at least two of the Indian partners. It is such trust, as well as the diverse range of expertise that NEF brought to the project, that were the main justification for NEF, rather than an Indian organisation (which would have been the ideal) playing a role in the project.

For trust in organisational collaboration to develop, it was also crucial that the project was divorced from monitoring and evaluation, particularly in relation to the programme related investments and grants that the Ford Foundation was considering at the time the project was designed. To uphold this principle, some of the more confidential reports to the individual organisations were not shared with the Foundation.

Reflections on impact

The project generated a range of outputs, some concrete, others harder to specify, in part because they were based on process inputs. Concrete outputs included:

- a strategic plan for PRADAN's savings and credit programme, which was then adapted to develop its strategy for capacity-building, funded again by the Ford Foundation, to enable PRADAN to significantly expand this programme;
- various documentation, processes and presentation materials, a monthly financial statement, and a participatory strategic plan for SEWA Bank;
- a resource book on livelihood promotion, drawing together relevant experience for the first time; and
- this book.

The project also contributed to a range of organisational processes, for example:

- building the capacity and understanding of the Research Department and staff across SEWA Bank (although two key members of the staff from the Research Department later left for personal reasons—husband transferred and marriage);
- the extensive use of cross-departmental teams by SEWA Bank;
- for a period, a fortnightly management meeting at BASIX;
- enhanced training, facilitation and process skills among some staff;
- greater professionalism (e.g., in financial and strategic analysis; recording and report writing; presentations, etc.) among some staff, both management and field-staff;
- enhanced ambitions among some staff for their organisation; and
- significant support to key individuals.

The project also provided

- opportunities and space for significant reflection, discussion and processing of organisational processes, issues and dilemmas, not least around growth and strategic processes, personal issues and team interactions; and
- enhanced understanding and technical skills in a range of areas, for example, livelihood promotion, strategic planning, processes to promote people's organisations, research, and economics.

It is difficult to measure to what extent new organisational processes, support to individuals, significant reflection and processing, and enhanced understanding contributed to the effectiveness of the organisations concerned and to their impact on those they seek to serve. While organisations reviewed and fed back regularly on project inputs and processes in order to adapt the project as it progressed, including at one mid-term review with all the partners and the donor, there was no formal or external evaluation at the end of the project.

All the formal feedback from the numerous workshops touched on gaining important insights and learning as well as including more critical feedback. Some workshops had an impact on the participants' organisations, others turned out with hindsight to be workshops that enhanced understanding but clearly had little sustained organisational impact.

There is also much anecdotal evidence on the collaboration contributing to changes in organisational culture and skills, for example, staff at SEWA Bank having a greater understanding of financial and other issues beyond their own department. The same staff now use participatory teams for many tasks, and are able to design and facilitate workshops for such teams independently of NEF.

Likewise, CDF used frameworks developed in the project to reflect deeply on its interaction with the cooperatives it promotes, interaction which is at the very core of its practice. The project, alongside inputs from many others, allowed significant processing of organisational and management issues and dilemmas within BASIX, ranging, for example, from insights on staff processes to co-mentoring within the management team. PRADAN received funding to implement part of its strategic plan developed under the project, and the project assisted PRADAN in launching this process, which has contributed to greater systematisation as well as growth in the outreach of PRADAN's programme.

The manual on livelihood promotion, in particular, which has already been taken up by NGOs, donors, support organisations and management institutes in India, including translation into at least two local languages, all without any marketing by the project, is also contributing to enhanced understanding, skills and, hopefully, practice in livelihood promotion. It marks a concrete step towards the idea of a school for livelihoods in India, an idea that predates the project, and was discussed as one of the potential processes that the project could facilitate. The resource book is now being used concretely by BASIX as part of the exploration for turning this idea into reality.

To some extent, the value to the micro-finance sector of the understanding that emerged through the project must be judged by the quality of this book, and its contribution to learning from Indian micro-finance practice, both inside and outside of India.

It is also important to put the project in the right context. In its flexibility and responsiveness, it sought to meet the organisations involved where they were at the time. Some of the organisations involved had extensive and sophisticated research and evaluations done of their effectiveness and impact, but these had little influence on them. This was in part because the organisations did not respond positively to the results of those assessments, and in part because they were not able to absorb the results. In other words, the interventions were not geared towards the conditions of those organisations, and some such work was thus wasted.

This was by and large not the case with the project under review, which sought throughout to respond to the needs and opportunities of the organisations involved, adapting the inputs as understanding and trust developed. At times this meant that progress appeared slow, although the pace of intervention must itself be adapted to the condition of the organisation concerned.

On the downside, as suggested above, it also meant that some activities initiated were not completed. For example, one organisation came close to developing a simple index for assessing development in a village, but this was not adopted because of changes within the organisation's strategy. Likewise, work between NEF and two of the Indian organisations was put on hold for a while as the organisations concerned focused on other organisational challenges in which they did not want involvement from NEF.

Some of the following might best have been done differently:

- Managing collaboration between NEF and four individual organisations was difficult. It might have been easier to reduce the number of partners, or to work with several of the organisations together, for example, through their association, although this only emerged during the course of the project. On the other hand, ideas from one organisation often contributed to inputs provided to another, and the ebbs and flows in the collaboration with individual organisations always meant there was plenty to do, even when some work was on hold.
- Longer and more substantive activities could sometimes have been planned further in advance to ensure greater continuity. The downside of responding to immediate needs and opportunities was that the project sometimes lost coherence.
- It would have been much easier if NEF had been based in India, rather than in the UK. This would have allowed more continuous and frequent inputs, with their timing and length adapted to the requirements at the time.
- While the start of collaboration with each partner was carefully negotiated, there was less attention to closure. Work with some

of the organisations was formally closed, with others it was less well planned.

- Formal monitoring and evaluation processes, aside from the mid-term review, could have been built into the project. On the other hand, the partners did not want to involve the donor in this, as the Ford Foundation was supporting the same organisations through other projects and investments.

Glossary

Aanganwadi	a government-initiated scheme for supplementing the nutritional needs of children
basti	slum
bidi	an indigenous Indian cigarette
bishi	kitty run by informal group
block	administrative areas into which districts are divided
crore	10 million
Dalit	disadvantaged groups (castes and tribes)
dholi	musical instrument
duri	carpet for meetings
gram panchayat	elected village council
gram sabha	traditional meeting of all villagers
gram sevak	government functionary in a village
grameen	(of the) village
haat	weekly market
Harijan	Gandhi's term for untouchables (Scheduled Castes)
jatra	village fair
kirana shop	general and grocery store
lakh	100,000
mahajan mukti	'salvation from the moneylender', a loan to enable an MFO client or member to pay off her/his debt to moneylenders
mohalla	neighbourhood
nidhi	mutual-benefit society, incorporated under an act of 1913, that allowed neighbours to save money and secure loans at favourable rates of interest; now incorporated under the new Companies Act
Other Backward Castes	formal classification of disadvantaged castes other than Scheduled Castes
Panchayat	local council
Panchayati raj institutions	three-tier system of panchayats from village to district level

papad	popadum
Scheduled Castes	castes which are officially recognised as backward
shandy	weekly market
talab	tank

Bibliography

Adams, D.W. and **J.D. von Pischke** (1992), 'Micro-enterprise credit programs: Déjà vu', *World Development* 20(10): 1463–70.

AIMS (Assessing the Impact of Microenterprise Services) (2000), *Learning from clients: Assessment tools for micro-finance practitioners*, Management Systems International, Washington, D.C.

_____ (2001), *Managing resources, activities and risk in urban India (Executive summary)* (report on SEWA Bank), Management Systems International, Washington, D.C.

Akerlof, A.G. (1970), 'The market for "lemons": Quality uncertainty and the market mechanism', *Quarterly Journal of Economics* 84: 488–500.

Alamgir, D.A.H. (1999), *Micro-financial services in Bangladesh: Review of innovations and trends*, Credit and Development Forum, Dhaka.

Awano, Haruko (1996), 'Situations, savings and borrowing behaviour of SEWA Bank members and non-members', unpublished manuscript, SEWA Bank, Ahmedabad.

BASIX (1999a), *Case studies on select micro-finance institutions in India* (study produced for the International Fund for Agriculture Development), BASIX, Hyderabad.

_____ (1999b), *Report on preliminary impact assessment* (produced by Catalyst Management Services, Bangalore), BASIX, Hyderabad.

_____ (1999c), *Women's savings and credit movement in Andhra Pradesh and a proposal for a new institution (APMAT) to facilitate its growth* (study sponsored by DfID [UK] India Office with support from the Commissionerate of Rural Development, Government of Andhra Pradesh), BASIX, Hyderabad.

Bennett, L., M. Goldberg and **P. Hunte** (1996), 'Ownership and sustainability: Lessons on group-based financial services from South Asia', *Journal of International Development* 8(2): 271–88.

Bhatt, Ela (1996), 'Beyond micro-credit: Structures that increase the economic power of the poor', SEWA Academy, Ahmedabad.

Blair, H. (2000), 'Civil Society, empowerment, democratic pluralism, and poverty reduction: Delivering the goods at national and local levels' in Lewis and Wallace (eds), 109–19.

Bouman, F.J.A. (1995), 'Rotating and accumulating savings and credit associations: A development perspective', *World Development* 23(3): 371–84.

CDF (Cooperative Development Foundation) (1993), 'Women's thrift co-operatives and external funding', unpublished paper (August), CDF, Hyderabad.

CDF (Cooperative Development Foundation) (1994), 'Alternative rural finance', paper presented to the Asian Development Forum (February), CDF, Hyderabad.

———— (1996), 'Autonomy: Making cooperative democracy meaningful', unpublished paper (May), CDF, Hyderabad.

———— (1999a), *Member participation in new generation thrift cooperatives around Warangal Town in Andhra Pradesh, 1997*, CDF, Hyderabad.

———— (1999b), *New generation thrift cooperatives in CDF's field work area in Andhra Pradesh: Performance report, 1999*, CDF, Hyderabad.

———— (2000), *25 years of learning, 1975–2000*, CDF, Hyderabad.

———— (2001), *Newsletter from the Cooperative Development Foundation* 3(8) (August), CDF, Hyderabad.

CDRA (Community Development Resource Association) (1996), *Shadows: The development sector—Face to face with itself, Annual report 1995–96*, CDRA, Woodstock, South Africa, available at *www.cdra.org.za.*

———— (2000), *The high road: Practice at the centre, Annual report 1999–2000*, CDRA, Woodstock, South Africa, available at *www.cdra.org.za.*

CGAP (1997a), 'The challenge of growth for micro-finance institutions: The BancoSol experience', *Focus* 6 (March), available at *www.cgap.org.*

———— (1997b), 'Effective governance for micro-finance institutions', *Focus* 7 (March), available at *www.cgap.org.*

———— (1998), 'Cost allocation for multi-service micro-finance institutions', Occasional paper no. 2, available at *www.cgap.org.*

Chen, M.A. and **D. Snodgrass** (1999), *An assessment of impact of SEWA Bank in India: Baseline findings*, AIMS Project Report, Management Systems International, Washington, D.C., available at *www.mip.org/componen/aims/pubs/english/impact3.htm.*

Cheney, G. (1999), *Values at work: Employee participation meets market pressure at Mondragon*, Cornell University Press, Ithaca, NY.

Clar de Jesus, R.B. (1997), *Assessment of six linkage banking projects in Asia: Synthesis report (draft)*, Asia Pacific Rural Credit Association and GTZ, Frankfurt.

Christen, R.P. (1999), 'Bulletin highlights', *Microbanking Bulletin* 4 (February): 41–46.

Credit and Development Forum (1998), *CDF Statistics: Micro-finance statistics of NGOs and other MFIs*, Credit and Development Forum, Dhaka.

Das, B. (2001), *Role and impact of micro-finance on the poor*, FWWB, Ahmedabad.

Datta, Samar and **M.S. Sriram** (2000), 'Flow of credit to small and marginal farmers in India: Proposal for the Ministry of Agriculture, Government of India', mimeo, Indian Institute of Management, Ahmedabad.

Datta, Sankar and **Gitali Thakur** (2001), 'Livelihood initiatives by BASIX', BASIX, Hyderabad (a version of this paper appears as a case study in Datta et al., 2002).

Datta, Sankar, Thomas Fisher, K. Mamata Krishna, with **Gitali Thakur** (2001), *A resource book for livelihood promotion*, BASIX, Hyderabad and the New Economics Foundation, London.

Dichter, Thomas W. (2001), *Organisation learning and evolution process: Organisational review*, BASIX, Hyderabad.

Dichter, Thomas W. and **Vijay Mahajan** (1990), 'A contingency approach to small business and micro-enterprise development', *Small Enterprise Development* 1(1): 4–16.

Eade, D. (1997), *Capacity-building: An approach to people-centred development*, Oxfam, Oxford.

Emery, F.E. and **E.L. Trist** (1965), extract from 'The causal texture of organisational environments' in Lynton and Pareek (eds) (1992: 150–55).

Farrington, T. (1999), 'Efficiency in micro-finance institutions,' *Microbanking Bulletin* 4 (February): 18–24.

Fernandez, Aloysius P. (1998), *The MYRADA experience: Alternative management systems for savings and credit of the rural poor*, 2nd edition, MYRADA, Bangalore.

_____ (2001), *Putting institutions first—even in micro-finance*, MYRADA, Bangalore.

Fisher, Thomas, Malcolm Bush and **Christophe Guene** (2001), Regulating micro-finance: A global perspective, New Economics Foundation, London.

Fisher, Thomas, Vijay Mahajan, with **Ashok Singha** (1997), *The forgotten sector: Non-farm employment and enterprises in rural India*, Intermediate Technology Publications, London and Oxford & IBH, New Delhi (available in India from BASIX, Hyderabad).

Fowler, Alan, Liz Goold and **Rick James** (1995), *Participatory self-assessment of NGO capacity*, Occasional Paper Series no. 10, INTRAC, Oxford.

Fugelsang, A. and **D. Chandler** (1986), *Participation as process: What we can learn from the Grameen Bank*, NORAD, Oslo.

FWWB (Friends of Women's World Banking) (2001), *Annual report, 2000–2001*, Ahmedabad.

Goetz, A. and **R. Sen Gupta** (1996), 'Who takes the credit? Gender, power and control over loan use in rural credit programmes in Bangladesh', *World Development* 24(1): 45–63.

Grameen Bank (1999), *Annual report 1998*, Dhaka.

Grameen Trust (2000), *Annual report 1999*, Dhaka.

Harding, Dave (1997), 'Working with the challenge of change and complexity: "Adaptive" management approaches', unpublished paper, Oxford.

Harding, Dave and **Jenny Chapman** (2000), 'Capacity-building: A deep challenge needs a more effective response', unpublished paper, Oxford and London.

Harper, A. (1998), 'Group-based management of savings and credit: The case of AKRSP, Pakistan', *Small Enterprise Development* 9(2): 29–41.

_____ (2000), 'Micro-finance peer-lending groups: Empowering the poor or perpetuating inequality?', unpublished M.Sc. thesis, School of Oriental and African Studies (SOAS), University of London.

Harper, Malcolm (1996), *Empowerment through enterprise*, Oxford & IBH, New Delhi and Intermediate Technology Publications, London.

Harper, Malcolm (1998), *Profit for the poor: Cases in micro-finance,* Oxford & IBH, New Delhi and Intermediate Technology Publications, London.
_____ (2000), *Co-operative success: What makes group enterprise succeed?* Oxford & IBH, New Delhi and Intermediate Technology Publications, London.

Harper, Malcolm, E. Esipisu, A.K. Mohanty and **D.S.K. Rao** (1998), *The new middlewomen: Profitable banking through self-help groups,* Oxford & IBH, New Delhi and Intermediate Technology Publications, London.

Hishigsuren, G. (2000), *Holistic approach to development: Practitioner-led impact assessment of ASA (Activist for Social Alternatives),* ASA, Tiruchirappalli, India.

Hoff, K. and **E.J. Stiglitz** (1990), 'Credit markets: Puzzles and policy perspectives', *World Bank Economic Review* 4(3): 235–50.

Holcombe, S. (1998), *Managing to empower: The Grameen Bank's experience of poverty alleviation,* University Press Limited, Dhaka and Zed Books, London.

Hulme, D. (1999), *Impact assessment methodologies for micro-finance: Theory, experience and better practice,* IDPM Working Paper, University of Manchester.
_____ (2000), 'Is micro-debt good for poor people?' *Small Enterprise Development* 11(1): 26–28.

Hulme, D. and **R. Montgomery** (1994), 'Cooperatives, credit and the poor: Private interest, public choice and collective action in Sri Lanka', *Marga* 13(3): 35–55.

Hulme, D., R. Montgomery and **D. Bhattacharya** (1994), *Mutual finance and the poor: A study of the Federation of Thrift and Credit Cooperatives in Sri Lanka (SANASA),* IDPM Working Paper no.11, University of Manchester.

Hulme, D. and **P. Mosley** (1996), *Finance against poverty,* vol. 1, Routledge, London.

Jain, S.P. (1996), 'Managing credit for the rural poor: Lessons from the Grameen Bank', *World Development* 24(1): 79–89.

Johnson, S. (1998), 'Micro-finance North and South: Contrasting current debates', *Journal of International Development* 10(6): 799–810.

Johnson, S. and **B. Rogaly** (1997), *Micro-finance and poverty reduction,* Oxfam, Oxford.

Karmakar, K.G. (1999), *Rural credit and self-help groups: Micro-finance needs and concepts in India,* Sage Publications, New Delhi.

Korten, D.C. (1980), 'Community organisation and rural development: A learning process approach,' *Public Administration Review* 40(5): 480–511.
_____ (1990), *People versus government: Restoring cooperative democracy through voluntary action in Andhra Pradesh, India,* CDF, Hyderabad.

Ledgerwood, J. (1999), *Micro-finance handbook: An institutional and financial perspective,* The Sustainable Banking with the Poor Project, World Bank, Washington, D.C.

Lewis, D. and **T. Wallace** (eds) (2000), *New roles and relevance: Development NGOs and the challenge of change,* Kumarian Press, West Hartford, USA.

Lynton, Rolf (1998), *Social science in actual practice: Themes on my blue guitar*, Sage Publications, New Delhi.

Lynton, Rolf and **Udai Pareek** (eds) (1992), *Facilitating development: Readings for trainers, consultants and policy-makers*, Sage Publications, New Delhi.

Mahajan, Vijay (1997), 'Is micro-credit the answer to poverty eradication?' *AWID Journal*, vol. 2(1): 8–9.

_____ (2000), 'Building a sustainable rural financial system', pp. 161–87 in P. Reddy and K. Singh (eds), *Designing and managing organisations for rural development in the new millennium*, Oxford & IBH, New Delhi.

_____ (nd), *Issues in the sustainability of micro-finance institutions: A practitioner's viewpoint*, BASIX, Hyderabad.

Mahajan, Vijay and **G. Nagasri** (1999), 'Building sustainable microfinance institutions in India', paper presented to Seminar on New Development Finance, Frankfurt, Germany (September 1999), BASIX, Hyderabad.

Mahajan, Vijay and **Bharti Ramola** (1996), 'Financial services for the rural poor and women in India: Access and sustainability', *Journal of International Development* 8(2): 211–24.

Marr, A. (1999), 'The poor and their money: What have we learned?' *ODI Poverty Briefing* 4, Overseas Development Institute, London, available at *www.odi.org.uk/briefing/pov4.html*.

Matin, I. (1997a), *Grameen and Shakti groups: Unpacking joint liability credit contracts*, PRPA working paper series 6, Grameen Trust, Dhaka.

_____ (1997b), 'The negotiation of joint liability; notes from Madhupur', in G.D. Wood and I. Sharif (eds), *Who needs credit? Poverty and finance in Bangladesh*, University Press Limited, Dhaka and Zed Books, London.

Mayoux, L. (1998), *Women's empowerment and micro-finance programmes: Approaches, evidence and ways forward*, Development Policy and Practice Working Paper 41, Open University, Milton Keynes, UK.

McClelland, David and **David Winter** (1969), *Motivating economic achievement*, Free Press, New York.

M-CRIL (2001), *The M-CRIL report, 2000*, Micro-credit Ratings and Guarantees International Limited, New Delhi.

Miller, T. and **N. Andrews** (1998), *Velcro arms, teflon heart: Enhancing livelihoods through community development finance*, Ford Foundation paper written for the Foundation's Affinity Group on Development Finance (December), New York.

Mintzberg, H. (1996), 'Managing government, governing management', *Harvard Business Review*, May–June, pp. 75–83.

Murthy, Sharmila (1999), *Assessing the impact of SEWA Bank's rural savings and credit program in Gujarat, India*, 2nd draft (3 September), unpublished manuscript, SEWA Bank, Ahmedabad.

MYRADA (2000), *The MYRADA experience: A manual for capacity-building of self-help groups*, MYRADA, Bangalore.

NABARD (1998), *SHG-bank linkage programme: Status as on 31 March 1998*, NABARD, Mumbai.

———— (1999a), *SHG-bank linkage programme: Status as on 31 March 1999*, NABARD, Mumbai.

———— (1999b), *Task-force on supportive policy and regulatory framework for micro-finance: Report*, NABARD, Mumbai.

———— (2000), *NABARD and micro-finance*, NABARD, Mumbai.

Narender, K. (1999), 'Building community financial institutions—"Kalanjiam Way"—for generations' (paper presented at the third annual Seminar on New Development Finance at Frankfurt, Germany), the DHAN Foundation, Madurai.

Narendranath, D. (2001), 'Group dynamics: Clearing the concepts, motivations and methods of our self-help group programme to better assess its impact', *Newsreach*, the in-house journal of PRADAN, pp. 1–5 (July), New Delhi.

Noponen, Helzi (2001), 'The Internal Learning System for participatory assessment of micro-finance', *Small Enterprise Development* 12(4): 45–53.

Noponen, Helzi and **P. Kantor** (1996), 'Crises, setbacks and chronic problems: The determinants of economic stress events among poor households in India', based on research conducted at SEWA Academy, Ahmedabad.

North, Douglass (1981), *Structure and change in economic history*, Norton, New York.

———— (1990), *Institutions, institutional change and economic performance*, Cambridge University Press, Cambridge.

Oberdorf, C. (ed.) (1999), *Micro-finance: Conversations with the experts*, A Microenterprise Policy Institute publication, ACCION International, Boston and Calmeadow, Toronto.

ODI (Overseas Development Institute) (2001), 'Economic theory, freedom and human rights: The work of Amartya Sen', *ODI Briefing Paper* (November), available at *www.odi.org.uk.*

Pfieffer J.W. and **J. Jones** (eds) (1976), *The 1976 annual handbook for group facilitators*, University Associates, San Diego.

Prathama Bank (2000), 'SHGs and Prathama Bank', unpublished mimeo, Moradabad, India.

Puhazhend, V. and **K.J.S. Satyasai** (2000), *Micro-finance and rural people: An impact evaluation*, NABARD, Mumbai.

Ray, N. and **D.P. Vasundhara** (1996), '"Like my mother's house": Women's thrift and credit cooperatives in South India', in M. Carr, M. Chen and R. Jhabvala (eds), *Speaking out: Women's economic empowerment in South Asia*, Intermediate Technology Publications, London.

Reserve Bank of India (2000), 'Circular RPCD NO.PL.BC. 62/04.09.01/ 99–2000', Mumbai, February 2000.

Rogaly, Ben, Thomas Fisher and **Ed Mayo** (1999), *Poverty, social exclusion and micro-finance in Britain*, Oxfam, Oxford and New Economics Foundation, London.

378 Beyond micro-credit

Rose, K. (1992), *Where women are leaders: The SEWA movement in India.* Vistaar Publications, New Delhi.

Rutherford, Stuart (2000), *The poor and their money,* Oxford University Press, New Delhi.

Rutherford, Stuart and **S.S. Arora** (1997), *City savers: How the poor, DfID and its partners are promoting financial services in urban India,* UPO, DfID, New Delhi.

Sa-Dhan (2001), *Micro-finance regulation in India,* Sa-Dhan, New Delhi.

Schein, E. (1999), *Process consultation revisited: Building the helping relationship,* Addison-Wesley, New York.

Schon, Donald (1983), *The reflective practitioner: How professionals think in action,* BasicBooks (HarperCollins), USA.

SEARCH (1999), *Micro-credit sans empowerment: Quickfix approaches to poverty alleviation,* SEARCH Bulletin XIV.1 (January–March), Bangalore.

SEWA (1997), *25 years of SEWA movement, 1972–1997,* SEWA, Ahmedabad.

Shah, Tushaar (1995), *Making farmers' cooperatives work: Design, governance and management,* Sage Publications, New Delhi.

SHARE Microfin Limited (2000), *Annual report for 1999–2000* and accompanying brochure, Hyderabad.

Simanowitz, A. (2001), Background paper for virtual meeting on impact assessment methodologies for ImpAct (Improving Impact of Microfinance on Poverty), an action-research programme of the Institute of Development Studies, University of Sussex, UK.

Sinha, Sanjay (1999), 'Sweat, toil and tears: Capacity-building for microfinance in India', presentation at Seminar on New Development Finance, Frankfurt (September); available at *edarural@giasdl01.vsnl.net.in.*

Social Enterprise London (2001), *Introducing social enterprise,* London, available at *www.sel.org.uk.*

Srinivas, S. (1997), 'Providing health insurance and social security for over 15,000 poor women workers: a profile of the SEWA health insurance scheme and the women who use it', incomplete and unpublished manuscript (October), SEWA Bank, Ahmedabad.

Titus, Mathew (1995), 'Study of urban savings and credit', Sharan, New Delhi.

Trist, Eric (1983), extract from 'Referrant organisations and the development of inter-organisational domains' in Lynton and Pareek (eds) (1992: 314–16).

Tuckman, B. (1965), 'Development sequence in small groups', *Psychological Bulletin* 63: 384–89.

USAID (1987), *A field manual for subsector practitioners,* GEMINI Project, Washington, D.C.

Versluysen, E. (1999), *Defying the odds: Banking for the poor,* Kumarian Press, West Hartford, USA.

Wahid, A.N.M. (1995), *The Grameen Bank: Poverty relief in Bangladesh,* Westview Press, Boulder, USA.

World Bank (1987), *World Development Report 1987: Barriers to adjustment and growth in the world economy: Industrialisation and foreign trade,* World Bank, Washington, D.C.

World Bank (2000), *World Development Report 1999–2000. Entering the 21st century*, World Bank, Washington, D.C.

Wright G. and **L. Mutesasira** (2001), 'The relative risks to the savings of poor people' *Small Enterprise Development* 12(3): 33–45.

Wright, G.A.N. (2000), *Micro-finance systems*, The University Press Limited, Dhaka.

Yunus, Muhammad with **Alan Jolis** (1998), *Banker to the poor: The autobiography of Muhammad Yunus, founder of the Grameen Bank*, Aurum Press, London.

Zadek, Simon (2001), *The civil corporation*, Earthscan and the New Economics Foundation, London.

Index

Aanganwadi scheme, 246, 249
accident insurance, 67
accountability, 29, 151
achievement motivation, 244–45
Activists for Social Alternatives
    (ASA), 188, 194, 286–89,
    292, 295, 296
'affinity groups', 135n. 1
Agricultural Credit Department,
    34
Agricultural Refinance and
    Development Corporation, 34
Akerlof, George, 202
All India Debt and Investment
    Survey, 34, 35
All India Rural Credit Survey, 34
Andhra Pradesh Dairy Develop-
    ment Cooperative Federation
    (APDDCF), 88, 90
Andhra Pradesh Mahila Ab-
    hivruddhi Society
    (APMAS), 36, 145, 148, 310
Andhra Pradesh State-level
    Employment Generation
    Mission, 146
Andrews, N., 114
apex bank, 287
Ashrai, 189
ASMITA, 70
asset creation, 71, 74
asset insurance, 42, 60
Association of Community
    Development Finance
    Institutions, 150
Association for Sarva Seva
    Farms (ASSEFA), 146
Association for Social Advance-
    ment (ASA), 191, 345, 353

Bank for Agriculture and Agricul-
    tural Cooperatives (BAAC), 97
Bank Rakyat Indonesia (BRI),
    97, 169, 319
BASIX: clientele of, 82–86;
    commitment of, 142–43; and
    Customer Satisfaction Audits,
    85–86, 295; and Customer
    Service Agents (CSAs), 80,
    81, 85, 100, 101, 345, 346;
    and direct loans, 84–85;
    Dryland Agriculture Produc-
    tivity Enhancement
    Programme of, 88; and
    emphasis on non-farm sector,
    96–97, 100; and employment
    generation through loans, 85;
    as a for-profit MFO, 43, 331,
    357; Ford Foundation, 361,
    362, 363, 366, 367 and
    indirect loans, 84–85; as
    influencing other finance
    providers, 158; as an
    innovative organisation, 67,
    139–49, 327; Inter-Borrower
    Expertise Exchange
    Programme of, 86, 88; and
    livelihood promotion, 28–29;
    and managing risks, 96;
    Market Linkage Programme
    of, 88–89; and micro-finance
    agents, 260; mission of, 80,
    82, 84, 95; as a NBFC, 43,
    44, 287, 321; outstanding
    loans of, 81, 85; Risk
    Mitigation Programme of, 89;
    Rural Infrastructure Revival
    Programme of, 88; and

Sa-Dhan, 151, 164; and
SHGs, 187–88, 262, 287;
setting up of, 79–80; and
women borrowers, 85
Bhartiya Agro-Industries
Foundation, 302
Bhartiya Samruddhi Finance
Ltd, 102n. 2
Bhartiya Samruddhi Invest-
ments and Consulting
Services Ltd (BASICS Ltd),
102n. 2
Bhatt, Ela, 23
bishis, 41, 44
Blair, Harry, 106
Brahm Prakash Committee, 35
Buro Tangail, 191

Campaign for Recognition of
Unorganised-Sector Workers,
156
capacity-building, 51, 52, 71, 91,
111, 115, 125, 131, 134, 150,
151, 152, 249, 259, 260, 267,
287, 310, 314, 316, 318, 323,
325, 327, 336–38, 357–59;
funds, 311; organisations,
148, 195, 336
Cashpor, 178
cattle insurance, 89. See also
livestock insurance
Central Banking Enquiry
Committee, 33
Chandler, D., 170
Chen, M.A., 60
Cheney, G., 340
chit-funds, 41, 44, 112, 197,
198n. 1
Clean Ahmedabad Campaign,
155–56
cluster meetings, 116, 117,
245. See also federations
collective action, 139
collective power, 165
collegiate linkages, 144, 145, 150
commercial banks, 43, 44, 52,
81, 98, 144, 160, 173, 174,
264–68, 275, 340; and
agricultural credit targets,

40; and default rates, 39;
and share of rural credit, 40
Committee on Cooperative
Credit, 34
community development finance
institutions, 300, 323, 341
Community Development
Resource Association (CDRA),
331, 344, 348
Community-based Group
Promoters (CBGPs), 258–60,
261
consensus, 220, 255
cooperative banks, 36, 38, 43,
44, 45, 52, 80, 173, 287,
306; urban, 43, 320, 321
Cooperative Development
Foundation (CDF), 24, 29,
30, 56, 66, 73, 95, 106,
118–23, 124, 131, 139, 141,
156, 287–90, 326, 332, 335,
345, 355, 361, 363, 364,
367; and cooperative law,
158–64; and democratic
governance, 161; and
membership, 125–28
cooperative law, 156, 158–64, 316
Cooperative Planning Committee, 34
cooperative values, 220
cooperatives, autonomy of, 122;
characteristics of good, 121;
governance of, 123–24;
ownership of, 123–24; for
rural women, 120
Cordaid, 103n. 4
credit unions, 334–35, 354, 355
credit usage, 301, 302, 303
crop insurance, 42, 89, 301
crop loans, 97, 273

Darling, Malcolm, 34
Death Relief Assurance Scheme,
66
decentralisation, 177, 329
decision-making, 241; processes, 131, 220, 221, 224,
233n. 3, 273

development banks, 264, 275
Development of Human Action
(DHAN) Foundation, 106, 110,
114, 115, 116–18, 150, 151,
158, 194
Development of Women and
Children in Rural Areas
(DWCRA), 35, 44
Development Organisation for
Women (DOW), 70
Dichter, Tom, 75, 76, 77–78,
92, 93, 94, 96, 98–99, 141,
142, 327
diffuse linkages, 144–45

economic liberalisation, 35, 37,
149
EDA Rural Systems Private
Limited, 265, 296
enabling linkages, 143–44
enterprise promotion, 27, 142,
300. See also micro-
enterprises: promotion of;
small enterprise: lending to
extension motivation, 245
External Commercial Borrowings (ECB) scheme, 318
External Developmental
Borrowings (EDB) scheme,
310

Farmers' Service Cooperative, 34
federations, 116–18, 205, 206–
31, 237, 335, 336
Fernandez, Al, 106, 109, 115,
177, 194, 340
Financial Accounting and
Management Information
System (FAMIS), 81. See also
MIS
Food Security Campaign, 155
Ford Foundation, 103n. 4, 140,
141, 142, 296, 320, 337,
347, 361–63, 365–66, 369
Foreign Contribution Regulation
Act, 306
Foundation for Democratic
Reforms, 162

Foundation for Micro-Credit, 145
Friends of Women's World
Banking (FWWB), India, 45,
67, 70, 151, 157, 264, 287–
90, 291
Fugelsang, A., 170
functional linkages, 144

Gandhi, M.K., 24
General Insurance Corporation
(GIC), 42, 43
Global Trust Bank (GTB), 44,
103n. 4, 144
globalisation, 94
gram sabha, 114, 129, 155, 251,
252. See also panchayats
gram panchayats, 194
gram sevak, 251
Grameen Bank, 65, 106, 107,
135–36n. 7, 143, 169, 172,
176, 178, 182, 222, 267, 309,
350, 352–53; style groups, 30,
43, 66, 113, 132, 185, 188,
329, 340. See also MFOs,
Grameen system
Grameen system, 169, 172–73,
176–96, activities of, 170–71;
as homogeneous, 178; and
loans for productive purposes,
191; membership of, 170; as
older than SHG system, 187;
as requiring more staff per client, 182, 193; as rigidly structured, 173, 177, 181–82, 193,
197; as suitable for densely
populated areas, 177; and voluntary savings, 191
Grameen Trust, 143

'hand-holders', 55, 64, 345, 349
Harding, Dave, 357–58
Hazari Committee, 34
health insurance, 59, 60
Heilbronner, Robert, 166n. 1
Hivos-Triodos Fund, 103n. 4
Holcombe, S., 170
Home-based Workers Campaign,
155

Housing and Urban Development Corporation (HUDCO), 62, 307
Housing Development Finance Corporation (HDFC), 62, 103n. 4
housing finance. See housing loans
housing loans, 61–62, 68–69, 110
Hulme, D., 74, 222

ICICI, 141; Bank, 44, 103n. 4
Improving Impact of Microfinance on Poverty, 296
income generation, loans for, 110, 291
Income Tax Act, 306
Indian Association of Community Development Financial Institutions, 145
Indian Grameen Services (IGS), 86, 87, 88, 89, 90–91, 92, 97, 98, 102n. 2
Institute of Development Studies (IDS), 296
institutions, 30, 203; meaning of, 138
Integrated Rural Development Programme (IRDP), 35, 37, 39, 42, 185, 301
interest rate ceilings, 175, 305–6, 308
International Development Enterprises, 89
International Finance Corporation (IFC), 81, 103n. 4, 140
International Fund for Agricultural Development (IFAD), 142
International Labour Organisation (ILO), 153, 155
Islami Bank of Bangladesh, 173

Jain, L.C., 159
Jain, S.P., 222
Jamuna Gramina Bank, 179
joint liability groups, 83

Kalanjiam Community Banking Programme, 110
Khusro Committee, 35
Kreditanstalt für Wiederaufbau (KfW), 62
Kurien, Dr V., 159

Life Insurance Corporation (LIC), 43, 59, 210
life insurance, 67
Livelihood Initiatives in Northern Karnataka (LINK), 91
livestock insurance, 42, 67, 301. See also cattle insurance
loans: consumption, 82, 149, 191, 275, 276, 291, 292; emergency, 63–64, 170, 276; refinancing, 175, 183, 287; waivers of, 35, 37, 39, 78; for working capital, 83, 149
Local Area Banks (LABs), 36, 37, 98, 102n. 2, 141, 144, 145, 148, 305, 321
Lynton, Rolf, 153, 162, 166n. 2

Maclagan Committee, 33
Madhya Pradesh Livelihood Enhancement Action Platform, 91
Mahajan, Vijay, 74–75, 77, 96, 303, 305
'Mahajan Mukti' loan, 64
management information systems (MIS), 78, 281–82, 315, 359
Marr, Ana, 64
Mayoux, Linda, 129, 130
men's cooperatives, 127–28
Micro-Credit Ratings International Limited (M-CRIL), 264, 265–83, 299n. 1; Report, 180–81
micro-credit: and costs due to illiteracy, 111, 219; and empowerment, 110–11, 115, 117–18, 128–33, 134, 192–95, 252,

261, 263, 283, 284, 292–93, 297, 326, 329, 334, 354, 355; and impact, 19, 22, 37–38, 71, 297–98, 330, 334, 337, 347, 348, 354; for income generating programmes, 238; and outreach, 19, 21, 22, 58, 74, 79, 89, 94, 187–92, 269–70, 283, 286, 287, 289, 295, 297, 298, 300, 302; and poverty eradiction, 75, 263, 267; and poverty reduction, 286, 289, 291, 298; and the promotion of livelihoods, 61, 71, 74–79, 80, 82, 84, 85, 90–91, 92, 94–102, 235, 262, 263, 276, 326, 327, 344, 346; and risk reduction, 26–27; and sustainability, 19, 20, 21, 23, 56, 66, 68, 79, 94, 95, 231, 263, 280–83, 294, 297, 305, 317, 337, 340, 342. See also micro-finance

micro-enterprises, 84, 291; and policy, 305, 316, 324; promotion of, 75; as subsistence enterprises, 76; as a supplement to wage employment, 77

micro-finance, 68, 121; aim of, 187, 190, 196; bank, 20; and defaults, 68; as a donor-driven phenomenon, 179, 180; as not reaching the poorest, 187, 189; and risk-management, 273; and women's empowerment, 128–33. See also micro-credit

micro-finance agents, 260

micro-finance organisations (MFOs), 23, 36; appraisal, 264–65; commercial, 43, 307, 321; as development/social enterprises, 339, 340, 343; as evolving from NGOs, 282; governance of, 29, 147, 353–57; Grameen Bank type, 267–73 passim, 277, 279–80, 287, 320; and Grameen groups,

176, 186, 190; and housing loans, 68, 69; impact of, 283–93; Indian, 24, 25; individual banking programme (IBP) type of, 267, 269, 270, 271, 273, 276–77, 279–80; as influencing local markets, 333; and institutions, 30; mutual-benefit, 43, 306–7, 320, 321, 324n. 2; non-profit, 43, 306, 320; and operational self-sufficiency (OSS), 279–80; ownership of, 147, 353–57; regulation of, 305–9; risk-analysis of, 264–65; and SHGs, 115, 171–72, 173, 174, 267, 269, 270, 271, 272, 279, 320; specialised, 37, 38; sustainability of, 180, 186; using SHG method, 175

micro-financial services: and collective ownership, 28, 29; and the reduction of poverty, 21–22, 26–28

micro-insurance, 42, 49

micro-loans, 52, 75

micro-savings, 49

Miller, T., 114

moneylenders, 24, 44, 58, 64, 84, 157, 158, 191, 208–9, 289, 291, 333

Mosley, P., 74

Mulkanoor cooperative, 67–68, 119, 122, 158, 162, 330

mutually-aided cooperative societies (MACS), 36, 37, 38, 41, 43, 44, 45, 146, 148, 160, 165, 306–7, 321, 335; Act, 36, 45, 159, 321, 335

Mysore Resettlement and Development Agency (MYRADA), 70, 105, 106, 114, 268, 286, 287–90, 294; and the building of institutions, 109; and capacity-building, 115, 125; and a community development approach, 130; and empowerment, 292, 327, 340; as

promoting SHGs, 108, 111,
115, 116, 123, 129, 151,
177, 189, 194, 287; and the
rotation of leadership, 261;
and targeting of the poor for
membership of SHGs, 124,
189, 191, 293; and the
training of bankers, 150

Nagasri, G., 303, 305
Narasimham Committee, 35
Narendranath, D., 109, 110–
11, 243
Nariman Committee, 34
National Bank for Agriculture
and Rural Development
(NABARD), 141, 145, 286–
90, 307, 317; funds from,
43, 147; and refinancing,
144, 183; as encouraging
bank lending to SHGs, 35,
37, 38, 108, 148, 174–75,
176, 179–80, 183, 199,
268, 275, 303, 335; SHGs
promoted by, 44
National Centre for Labour
(NCL), 156
National Commission on
Agriculture, 34
National Dairy Development
Board, 302
National Small Savings
Organisation, 43
Nehru Foundation for Development, 141
New Economics Foundation
(NEF), 25, 74, 361–69
nidhis, 307, 324n. 2
non-governmental organisations
(NGOs), 35, 65, 78, 87, 88,
98; and civil society objective, 267, 268; as financial
intermediaries, 174; as a
flexible organisational form,
331; ideology, 31, 220; and
training of promoters, 258,
260; values, 332
North, Douglass, 138, 202, 211

on-lending, 84, 86, 90, 108,
116, 144, 171, 172, 174,
180, 252, 253, 267, 274,
307
organisations, 30, 203–4, 223–24;
and practice, 343–50, 359

Pakistan Poverty Alleviation
Fund, 264
Palli Karma Sahayak Foundation
(PKSF), 180, 264
panchayats, 155; and SHGs, 110,
112, 132, 194, 235, 262, 292.
See also gram sabha
participatory wealth-ranking,
293, 297
peer lending, 109–10, 115, 235
Peerless, 41, 43, 44
personal lending, 208–9
Planning Commission, 146, 159
poverty alleviation programmes,
178, 185, 193
poverty: measures of, 293;
understanding of, 328
Prathama Regional Rural Bank
(RRB), 178–79
Price Waterhouse Coopers, 141
Professional Assistance for
Development Action
(PRADAN), 95, 105, 106,
109, 111, 114, 116, 141,
142, 150, 151, 189, 235–62,
268, 361, 362, 363, 364,
366, 367
Proshika, 172

R.V. Gupta Committee, 36
Rajiv Gandhi Mission on Livelihoods Security, 146
Rashtriya Gramin Vikas Nidhi
(RGVN), 151
Rashtriya Mahila Kosh (RMK),
35, 44, 45, 147
Regional Rural Banks (RRBs),
34, 36–37, 38, 41, 43, 44,
80, 116, 146, 173, 306, 310
repayment culture, transformation of, 304

repayment, 229, 289; ensuring, 203; rates, 39, 80, 96, 147, 175, 335, 351
reputation capital, 203
Reserve Bank of India (RBI), 34, 36, 43, 141, 144, 145, 147, 176, 233n. 2, 270, 307, 317, 318; Act, 306, 308
residuary non-banking companies (RNBCs), 43
Rhyne, Elizabeth, 335
risk-taking, 115, 241, 256
Rochdale cooperatives, 360n. 3
Rogaly, B., 129
rotating savings and credit associations (ROSCAs), 100, 171, 184, 195, 197, 198n. 1, 207–8, 212, 218, 219
Royal Commission on Agriculture, 33
Rural Banking Enquiry Committee, 34
rural capitalisation, 157
rural employment opportunities, 157
Rutherford, S., 49–50, 56, 65, 135n. 3, 312, 345, 351–52

Sa-Dhan, 29, 36, 145, 150, 164, 300, 322
SafeSave, 65, 353
Sahara, 41, 43, 44
SANASA, 222
Sanchayani, 41, 43, 44
Sanghamitra, 44, 70, 151
savings and credit cooperatives, 30, 120, 122, 126, 159, 161, 162, 165, 330, 332, 334, 335, 354
savings, emphasis on, 52–57, 58, 64, 68, 69, 73
Schein, E., 358
Schon, Donald, 350, 352, 357
Self-employed Women's Association (SEWA), 29, 51, 130, 139, 141, 152, 289, 332; movement, 51–52, 57, 61, 130, 154, 156, 264

Self-employed Women's Association (SEWA) Bank, 271, 286–90, 291, 292–93, 294, 345, 349, 352; and children's education, 70; as a cooperative bank, 43, 267, 287, 320; credit-deposit ratio of, 56; differences between urban and rural operations, 54–55, 60; and emergency loans, 58, 63, 71; and extension services, 55; and Ford Foundation project, 361, 362, 363, 365, 366, 367 founding of, 23; and insurance, 57–61; and livelihood promotion, 95; and loan applications, 56; as the oldest Indian MFO, 24; and outstanding loans, 61; and Sa-Dhan, 151, 156–57; and sustainability, 56; trade union roots of, 51, 65
self-employment, 80, 330; schemes, 37
self-esteem, 53, 252
self-help groups (SHGs), 23, 36, 41, 43, 44, 104, 105, 106, 107, 169; advantages of, 209; autonomy of, 115, 239, 261, 262, 336, 339; average membership of, 173, 175–76; and BASIX, 83, 84, 85, 87, 88, 100. See also BASIX; churning in membership of, 242; costs of, 199–233; costs arising from lack of information, 211–12, 226; and the empowerment of women, 235–36; evolution of, 238–42; formation of, 225, 226, 239, 240, 241, 245, 248, 249–50; and FWWB, 70; and the importance of ideology, 222; and the importance of information gathering, 227–31; initial development costs of, 183; and linkage programme of NABARD, 35, 37, 38, 42. See also NABARD; and linkages with banks,

173, 174, 267–68, 272, 275, 287, 303, 309, 318–19, 321, 334; maintenance processes in, 243; membership of, 124–28, 199, 234; as a micro-bank, 171; model, 107–8, 118, 199, 269, 329; movement, 195, 197, 199, 234–62, 309, 321, 334, 336–37, 352, 355; multiple membership in, 224, 225; and MYRADA, 108. *See also* MYRADA; ownership of, 108–9, 114, 123–24, 131, 193, 218, 336, 355; and PRADAN, 95; as promoted by banks, 183, 184; promoted by NGOs, 44, 111–18, 123, 129, 149, 171, 173, 174, 175, 182, 183, 189, 194, 205, 212, 225, 236, 241, 261–62, 268, 309, 310, 321, 332, 335; and proxy membership, 224, 225; as not reaching the poorest, 189, 190, 192; re-engineering of, 242; responsibilities of, 108–9, 114, 218, 226–27, 242, 250, 254–55, 257; role of, 109–10; and screening process for membership, 215–16, 225, 228; staff productivity of, 272; and supported by SEWA Bank, 53, 54; system, 108; 171–72, 173–76, 177–96; task processes in, 243; urban, 307; and women leaders, 133, 236, 250–57, 261, 262

self-help groups (SHGs) system: disadvantages of, 193, 196–98, 335; as flexible, 178, 181–82, 190, 191, 192, 193, 196, 197, 226; and initiative, 190

self-insurance, 50, 57

self-reliance, 51, 129, 154, 165

Self-Reliant Cooperatives Bill, 160

Sen, Amartya, 327–28

Shah, T., 355

Sharan, 200, 204–31; and the Gautam Nagar Federation, 227–31; and Mongolpuri Q Block Federation, 206, 219–23, 224; and Mongolpuri Y Block Federation, 224–27, 230; and Sultanpuri Federation, 206, 214–16, 224; and the Tamil Federation, 206, 216–19

Shorebank Corporation, 98, 103n. 4, 342

Small enterprise: lending to, 75, 83, 84, 95–96, 97, 98, 101, 140, 148, 149, 319, 346; and employment, 29, 77, 80, 158, 305, 330

Small Enterprise Foundation, 295

Small Industries Development Bank of India (SIDBI), 36, 37, 103n. 4, 145, 175, 303, 307; Foundation for Micro-Credit (SFMC), 175, 176, 296

Snodgrass, D., 60

social capital, 104, 105, 326

social entrepreneurs, 244, 245; challenges for, 248–50; financial rewards of, 252–54; qualities of, 254–57; risks taken by, 254; social rewards of, 250–52; training of, 257

'social intermediation', 104–6, 133, 326

Society for Helping, Awakening Rural Poor through Education (SHARE) Micro-Financial Limited, 43, 44, 55, 66, 69, 151, 176, 178, 183, 184, 187–88, 191, 287–90, 291–92, 293–94, 321

solidarity groups, 169

Sonali Bank, 264

Soubhagya Seeds Pvt Ltd, 89

Stiglitz, Joseph, 202

Subsidy Dependence Index (SDI), 279–80

Swarna Jayanti Swarozgar Yojana (SJSY), 37, 42, 185

'Swayambhoo' cooperatives, 44

Swiss Agency for Development
and Cooperation (SDC),
103n. 4, 141

Telugu Desam Party, 132
thrift cooperatives, 120
transaction costs, 203, 222
transparency, 151, 225
Triodos Bank, 356
Trist, E., 152
trust, 104, 105, 115, 126, 217,
241, 255, 256, 257, 259, 326

United India Insurance Co., 67
UNDP: South Asia Poverty
Alleviation Programme of, 89

Vendors Campaign, 155

wage employment, 27, 77, 80, 330
Wahid, A.N.M., 170
water-user associations, 95,
105, 236
women's cooperatives, 126, 127
Women's World Banking (WWB),
157
Working Women's Forum, 130
World Bank, 81, 140, 141, 147,
293

Yunus, Prof. Muhammad, 172,
348, 350, 353, 354

About the authors and contributors

Thomas Fisher was the Programme Director for Local Economic Renewal at the New Economics Foundation (NEF), London. He has worked in India over 12 years, on rural non-farm employment, with the Tibetan refugee community, and leading the NEF project with four micro-finance organisations in India which gave rise to this book. He has published on the rural non-farm sector in India, on micro-finance in the UK, Europe and internationally on institutional development and on the United Nations.

M.S. Sriram is a Faculty Member at the Centre for Management in Agriculture at the Indian Institute of Management, Ahmedabad. In the past, Sriram has worked with the Cooperative Development Foundation and BASIX, and was an Associate Professor at the Institute for Rural Management (IRMA), Anand.

Malcolm Harper is Emeritus Professor at Cranfield University, UK, the author of numerous books and articles on micro-enterprise and micro-finance, and the editor of the journal *Small Enterprise Development*. He has been working in India for many years.

Ajit Kanitkar works for the Swiss Agency for Development and Cooperation (SDC) at New Delhi. Formerly he was a Faculty Member at IRMA, Anand and the Entrepreneurship Development Institute in Ahmedabad, and later an independent development consultant. He has long been associated in a voluntary capacity with Jnana Prabodhini, a non-governmental organisation (NGO) in Pune.

Frances and **Sanjay Sinha** are economic development consultants who have been engaged in research, policy studies, monitoring, evaluation and capacity-building activities relevant to the livelihoods of poor people in India and other countries of

South Asia for nearly 25 years. Their companies (EDA Rural Systems and M-CRIL) are leading organisations in this field in the region. Both organisations are now increasingly working in South-East Asia as well as South Asia.

Mathew Titus is the Executive Director of Sa-Dhan, the Association of Community Development Finance Institutions in India. Previously he worked for 12 years for Sharan, an NGO working in the slums of Delhi on health, education and micro-finance. For his last five years at Sharan, Titus was the Secretary and Executive Director. He completed a thesis on micro-finance in Delhi slums at the University of Bath in the UK.